Homilies

—from the—

HEART

Stories to Live, Love, and Serve One Another

FATHER GEORGE RINK

The Jerusalem Bible. Readers Edition. General Editor Alexander Jones, L.S.S. S.T.L. I.C.S. Published by DoubleDay a division of Random House, Inc. 1540 Broadway, New York, New York 10036. The Popular Edition of the Jerusalem Bible, upon which the Reader's Edition is based, was first published in Great Britain in 1974 by Darton, Longman and Todd Ltd. Nihil Obstat: Lionel Swain S.T.L., L.S.S. Imprimature + John Cardinal Heenan. Wesminster: 4 July 1966. Library of Congress Catalog Card Number 74-153643. ISBN: 0-385-49918-3. Copyright 1966, 1967 and 1968 by Darton, Longman & Todd Ltd and Doubleday, a division of Random House, Inc.

ISBN: 978-1-4834-3766-8 (sc)
ISBN: 978-1-4834-3765-1 (e)

Lulu Publishing Services rev. date: 10/16/2015

Dedication

I met Father George Rink in Orting, Washington at St. Cosmos and Damian Catholic Church. Each Sunday I would listen to his homilies and the stories he told as they related to the sacred scripture reading. His stories always touched my heart. The stories all contained practical tips, advice and suggestions in becoming a better person. I was able to put a lot of his advice and encouragement into practice. He knew life was tough and that we would have problems in this life but his words of love and encouragement always made me feel God's love and mercy. He knew we were all sinners and unworthy but he always reminded us how much God loves us and how he died for our sins on the cross so we could have eternal life with him. The stories were easy to remember and oftentimes I found myself retelling the stories to friends and family members who were in need of comforting words. I found sharing these stories was also an easy way to tell others about our loving and merciful God.

One day, during confession, I asked Father George if I could publish his homilies. At first he did not take me seriously but I persisted and he finally agreed to have his homilies published. Typing the handwritten homilies took over two years to critique and complete. His stories were from his experience in his life of 80 plus years, serving as a Catholic priest and helping people along life's difficult and joyous journey. His homilies were uplifting and always with a message of love and the importance of loving and serving others.

I want to end this dedication to Father George with a heartfelt thank you to Father George for all he has done for the Catholic faith and the people's lives he has touched throughout his ministry. The blessings and graces you will receive, after reading these true life stories, I hope, will encourage and inspire you to pass them along to others who may need an uplifting story or a friend who will tell them how much they are loved by our Lord, who is a merciful and loving God and whose image resides in each one of us. The life we have been given should be a life of giving and serving others here on earth, which is, according to Father George "heaven on earth."

Contents

YEAR A

YEAR C

YEAR

A

First Sunday of Advent "A"
Matthew 24-37-44

Being a mom to Brendan (7 years old) and Maggie (4) was the most important thing in the world to Karen. The best time of the day was when she, and the kids, would read stories, and sing together!

Four years ago, Karen was diagnosed with breast cancer, and earlier this year, she learned that the final treatment was not working! So, with the help of the nonprofit group called "Life Chronicles," Karen and her husband, Jeff, gathered Brendan and Maggie together in their living room to make a video. Karen told her giggling children it was just a fun thing for them to do! The kids knew their mom was sick, but didn't understand that she soon would be gone!

Over the next 90 minutes, they read stories together, including Maggie's favorite, Dr. Seuss! Karen sang the kid's their favorite songs "Que Sera Sera!" Mom and dad and the kids reminisced about family events and vacations. Karen and Jeff told the kids how much they loved them and loved each other. After the kids left and went to bed, Jeff recounted how they met and fell in love. Off camera, Karen told Jeff: "I want our kids to see me when I'm gone, to see us together as a family, and to remember how happy we were! I want something more than just pictures for them to remember me!"

"Life Chronicles" was organized in 1998 to help record interviews with the terminally ill for their families! "It's not talking about death," Karen explained, "but it's about celebrating our life together as a family! It makes me sad they won't have a mom someday, but this is a why I can be with them after I'm gone!"

As Karen survived each year (despite the initial prognosis), she became more aware of each rich moment, as she watched her children grow.

Karen died last September 5ᵗʰ! She was 38 years old! She is survived by her husband and two children and many happy memories. I tell this story because; Today is the first Sunday of Advent! The Advent Season is a "wake-up call" for us to "watch out for" and "pay attention" to the signs of God's unmistakable presence in our lives! As Karen and her family came to understand – this lifetime on earth which is so often taken for granted, is precious and limited; a gift that God gives us that we might discover God in the love of others and that we might realize the goodness of this world in anticipation of the next! These days before Christmas call us to embrace God's Presence in all that is good, and beautiful; in all that is "life-giving" and "nurturing!"

In today's gospel, Jesus reminds us that the most important moments in life can come upon us suddenly; almost without notice – just like the end of life can come without warning! Jesus gives the example of the destroying flood that killed man during the time of Noah…and tells the parable of the two men in the field; and the two women grinding meal – one will suddenly be taken by death, and one of them will be left!

The appropriate response to the gospel is not fear – anxiety – but an urgency not to waste the precious gift of time! Jesus is telling us to "seize the moment" and to do good while here and to live courageously; to give to others generously; to forgive readily; to make peace not war (as Isaiah advises in today's first reading) by "beating our swords of war into plowshares; and our spears into pruning hooks!" At the end of time, these are the moments that will last!

When Robert Shaw was director of the Atlanta Symphony and Chorus, a reporter asked him how he was able to have such passion and energy in conducting his music, especially since he had conducted those same great compositions hundreds of times during his career! Shaw told the reporter any time he was getting ready to walk onto the stage he would try to remember I that someone in the audience would hear these great pieces of music for the very first time; and someone would hear the same music for the very last time so he tried to conduct the music for both of them.

Perhaps, during this Advent Season, we can conduct our lives the same way! Advent is the time we have to "wake-up," to "watch" and to "pay attention" to the many signs of God's unmistakable presence in our lives!

Second Sunday of Advent "A" Matthew 3:1-12

We're in the Second Sunday of Advent, and today's message is: "Repent and Sin no more!" That phrase "Repent and Sin no more" reminds me of my favorite advent story:

A house painter was widely suspected of cheating his customers by "watering down" his paint.

In spite of his reputation, he managed to get a job painting a church steeple.

True to form, he began painting the church steeple with "watered-down paint!" But, as he was just about finished with the job – a sudden heavy rainstorm washed away his work! Then the clouds parted and a voice from the heavens said to him; "REPAINT AND **THIN** NO MORE."

John the Baptist's message to us on this second Sunday of Advent is the same; "Reform your lives! The reign of God is at hand."

John the Baptist didn't "water down his message." He was a no nonsense type of preacher, who called a spade a spade. When the religious professionals of his day (the Pharisees and Sadducees) came out to be baptized by him, he insulted them and called them names. He called them a brood of vipers, and told them to try and give some evidence you mean to reform!

These were respectable, church going folk (people like you and me), but John wanted them to understand that his message of conversion was for them; as well as for people they considered to be sinners! There was a sense of urgency in John's voice. There wasn't much time left! The Messiah was coming soon and they needed to be ready. "Even now the ax is laid at the root of the tree" he warned them!

When I was Assistant Pastor of St. Joseph's Parish, in Vancouver, WA, the Pastor, Father Tom Pitsch, decided the ivy he planted some 12 years before, around the Church, should be taken down. The ivy had gotten out of hand. It attached itself to the Church's wall, and permanently forced open some of the windows near the roof. Birds made their nests in it, and often came through the open windows to fly around inside, and perch on the rafters – much to the consternation of those attending mass. (That's why people would often say that Father Tom's and my homilies were "for the birds.")

To my surprise, the ivy came down quite easily, dragging with it much of the paint from the wall as well! But the roof section was something else. We hacked, chopped, pulled and dug it out as best we could. We soon came to realize we could never get all the roots out. Over the years, we had to keep cutting back those roots, so they would not return, and take over the Church building once again. John the Baptist returns every year during Advent, telling us to clear away the "overgrown clutter" that overtakes our lives – preventing us from being the people Jesus calls us to be!

Clearing out our lives is not a onetime thing, but is something we must do constantly to prepare for Christ's coming. Conversion is a lifelong process. John's call is for us to cut back that which is ensnaring us, to straighten that which is crooked, to smooth out that which is rough – "To prepare the way of the Lord."

John's message was simple and to the point! Reform our lives because the reign of God is at hand. It was a call to real conversion; to change the direction of our lives; to experience a change of heart; demanding a radical transformation!

In the early days of American history, punishment for public crimes was often, cruel and unusual! An example: A man was caught stealing sheep. The authorities ordered the letters "ST" which stood for "sheep thief" to be branded on his forehead! The man spent the rest of his life trying to live down those words. He succeeded beautifully. He experienced a real conversion during his lifetime. He was generous. He became honest; hardworking and truthful. He was generous with his time to his neighbors, a good citizen, and an active member of his church community!

When he reached old age, the letters "ST" could still be seen on his forehead! When children asked their parents what the letters stood for, they answered with reverence, "ST" stands for the word "saint" because he was such a good and holy man"

Advent is that time for us once again to begin the transformation; a process from being sinners to becoming saints! It's a time for us not to "water down" our commitment to living the Gospel values. It's the season that invites us to take to heart the words of John the Baptist in today's Gospel: "Reform your lives. The Kingdom of God is at hand!"

Third Sunday of Advent "A" Matthew 11:2-11

Father Daniel Berrigan is a Jesuit priest, who powerfully spoke out against the social injustices and the Vietnam War in the 1960's. It was not uncommon for him to end up in jail, once in awhile, for his civil disobedience.

But times have changed! Recently, when he was invited to speak at a university on "The Presence of God in Today's World, he toned down his rhetoric! Speaking without his characteristic fire, he quietly told his listeners how he works in a hospice for the terminally ill. How, each week, he spends time quietly sitting at the bedside of a young boy, who is totally incapacitated.

The boy can't speak, hear, move or respond in any apparent way to those around him. He just lies there, totally helpless, and dependent on others for his very survival! Father Berrigan says that as he sits there, seeing the powerlessness of this young boy, he experiences the Presence of God – a God who has chosen to be born as a helpless infant in a stable – totally dependent on us for his survival in our world today! He thinks about the words this child would someday say; "What you do to the least of my brothers and sister, you do to me." And to think that some people would look upon this powerless boy as a burden to society; to his family; and to himself – and would choose to put closure to his life!

On this third Sunday of Advent, as we prepare to celebrate Jesus' Presence in the world this Christmas – we, too, may be surprised at the ways Jesus chooses to make His Presence known to us!

When John sent messengers from prison to ask Jesus if he you was the one who is to come, or are we to wait for another? Jesus spoke NOT of power or strength – but of healing compassion! He pointed to His miracles and pointed out that the blind see, the lame walk, the lepers are cleansed, the deaf hear, and the dead are raised.

For some people, Jesus' presence among the helpless and the dependent was a "stumbling block." They were expecting a Messiah who would sit in judgment of those who had sinned; and reward the "righteous" with wealth and power! In fact these people looked down on the poor and disabled as God's condemnation and punishment for their sins.

But Jesus says to them and to us that the one who is blessed is the one who takes no offense at Me. Jesus' way is the way of respect, compassion and openness to the need we have for one another. He is challenging John the Baptist and us – to have faith in HIS way of relating to one another – not by domination or power or conquest; but by our loving acceptance and compassionate Presence.

So, like Father Berrigan, let's take time to sit quietly in the presence of God we find in OUR world. Perhaps, God will be revealed to us in the needs of the poor, in the demands of the helpless, or in the persistence of those who depend on us for their very survival! And, let today's liturgy disturb us a little bit, and encourage us NOT to lose faith – but to recognize and rejoice in the many, mysterious ways God's Presence is revealed among us!

Fourth Sunday of Advent "A"
Matthew 1:18-24

On this fourth Sunday of Advent – just one day before Christmas Eve – I think it's appropriate to look back and remember Christmas '41. Not Christmas 1941, but Christmas in the year '41 A.D. – almost 2000 years ago!

Mary would have been a woman in her mid 50's. I'm sure she must have celebrated the birthday of her only son – even thou He was not with her in person, having died eight years earlier. Mary celebrated His birthday, but it was not called "Christmas" in '41 A.D., even though that's what it's called today. Like Mary, we also celebrate His birthday, without Jesus being "physically" present with us.

It must have been a lonely day for Mary. She missed her son so terribly - and those good, and some bad, memories of his short life. She must have also missed Joseph, her husband, who died some years before her son's tragic death on the cross.

And no matter how many of her relatives may have been living near her in the little village of Nazareth – her son's birthday was probably lonelier for her, than most other days.

For some people today, Christmas is often lonelier than some other days – people who have lost their husband or wife; people who are divorced; people who are ill; or living in a nursing home; people who don't have any family close by; or people who have lost a son or daughter in the war.

Yes, Christmas can be a sad, lonely day for some! Thinking about Christmas '41 A.D., let's go back to Mary. She must have thought about what the angel told Joseph about not being afraid to take Mary as your wife and into your home. For it is by the Holy Spirit that this child is conceived in her. She will bear a son; and you are to name Him Jesus because He will save his people from their sins.

And in today's gospel, Matthew goes on to explain it this way. All this took place to fulfill what the Lord God said through the prophet that we should wait and watch because a virgin shall conceive and bear a son; and will be named Emmanuel, a name which means God is with us. And, Mary believed in those words – and now, years later, when she was older, and alone – she still believed!

Christmas 2010 Luke 2:1-20

It was Christmas Eve at New York's famed Riverside Church! The Christmas pageant was on; and had come to the scene where the innkeeper was to say that there was no room at the inn for Joseph, and Mary, who was pregnant, and about to give birth to Jesus!

The part of the innkeeper seemed perfect for Tim, who was a faithful, long time member of the congregation, who had Downs Syndrome! There was only one line to memorize and he had practiced it time and time again with his parents; and with the pageant director! He seemed to have mastered it.

So there was Tim, standing at the altar; wearing his bathrobe over his clothes; - as Joseph and Mary slowly made their way down the main aisle. They approached; said their lines, and waited for the innkeeper's reply!

"There's no room at the inn," Tim boomed out. He nailed it! Just as he had rehearsed it so many times before! But then, when Mary and Joseph turned away, disappointed, to look for a place to stay – Tim suddenly yelled out at them; "Wait," he shouted! Mary and Joseph turned around startled! "Wait," he said again. "You can stay at MY HOUSE." At that point, thinking quickly, the pastor rushed to the pulpit, and shouted "AMEN." And, the congregation repeated "AMEN." Both the pageant and the pastor's planned sermon came to an abrupt, and unexpected, ending! The Christmas Eve service ended, then and there, with everyone singing Joy to the World!

Tim's spontaneous "twist" to the Christmas Pageant points out to us the true meaning; and the true miracle of Christmas! In the Child of Bethlehem – God makes a dwelling place, (here and Now) in our own homes. And, in our hearts! In the gospel accounts of Jesus' birth – Mary and Joseph are challenged by God to accept this Child under the most difficult circumstances! But, (responding out of a deep sense of faith and love) they both said "yes" to God's Plan! Likewise, God challenges our own hearts this

Christmas Season (and on this feast of the Holy Family) to prepare Him a Room; to make a place for the Child of Bethlehem in our lives and to allow Christ to transform our hearts and homes with his peace and reconciliation.

And so, on this Christmas Day (and on this feast of the Holy Family, let Time's "heart- felt" invitation be <u>our invitation </u>to Jesus (and to the Holy Family). You can stay in MY house! Take Jesus home with you tonight (today)! Merry Christmas to you and your family.

Holy Family "A" Matthew 2:13-15, 19-23

Posada is a Spanish word meaning "shelter." It's also the name of a Christmas-time tradition among people who live in the border towns between Mexico and the USA. In this game, the neighbors play the roles of Mary and Joseph on their way to Bethlehem. The neighbors go door to door asking for shelter; and each time, they ask; they are turned away.

The "Posada" game not only recalls the experience of the Holy Family seeking safety in Bethlehem; but also recalls their dangerous journey into Egypt, as they fled for their lives from King Herod.

"Posada" also draws attention to the plight of modern day migrants from Mexico; trying to enter the U.S. Many have crossed a dangerous desert in scorching temperatures seeking jobs; security; and a better life. And, many have died in the process. Migration today puts families under great pressure; and families can be torn apart for years to come! Recently, a Presbyterian minister in a border town watched as a young family – water jug in hand – began their dangerous trip across the Arizona desert.

"The young family; a man, a woman, and their baby were Mexican immigrants, desperate to flee their country; and give their child a better life," he recalled. He went on to say, "Like Mary, Joseph and Jesus on their way to Egypt, they set out on their journey poor and desperate."

Now, don't get me wrong! I'm not choosing sides in the debate for or against illegal immigration; nor am I attempting to solve their very complex problem facing our country. <u>I'll leave that up to the politicians" But, what I want to do is put the immigration question in the context of the gospel story of the Holy Family's experience. And perhaps, offer a new perspective – a new way of looking at this very volatile question!</u>

In today's gospel, Matthew describes how Joseph was told by an angel to take Mary and the baby Jesus, and to flee into Egypt immediately, that very night, because King Herod wanted to kill their newborn child. <u>There was only time to pack a little food; some clothing ; and Joseph's carpenter tools. Everything else had to be left behind! The Holy Family had to avoid the well-traveled roads out of fear of being recognized. So, they picked their way through the hidden valleys; and across uncharted plateaus on the rugged hills of Sinai – enduring the scorching heat of the sun by days, and the bitter cold of the desert nights – all the time fearing for their infant's safety.</u>

Along the way, they heard the rumors of the slaughter of the Holy Innocents – how Herod had ordered the murder of all the male infants two years old and younger in and around Bethlehem, so he could destroy the newborn King.

The U.S. Bishops recently came out with a statement encouraging Congress to change and update the current immigration laws; to make them more "FAMILY FRIENDLY" by protecting the family unit from being separated and destroyed; and to streamline the complicated and lengthy process of applying for citizenship in our country!

<u>During this Christmas Season, we celebrate the incarnation, which can be described as a "Divine Border Crossing" in which God became human in order to dwell among us. Jesus crossed many "borders" during his ministry.</u> He ate and drank with sinners; he preached to and healed pagans; he spoke to women and children; he talked to and forgave his enemies; he welcomed the poor, as well as, the wealthy, to the Kingdom of God. He tore down the walls of hatred and fear between peoples like Samaritans and Jews!

His own life began when no one would make room for him and his family. The rest of his life was spent "making room" for outsiders to be included in the fullness of God's love. Likewise, we are called to follow his generous outreach to others.

On this Feast of the Holy family, let us pray that our nation maybe a safe haven to those, who like Mary, Joseph and Jesus, flee from modern day Herods! May we nurture holiness within our own families! May the gift of Emmanuel, "God within us," be with all the families of the world!" Amen!

Epiphany "A" Matthew 2:1-12

In the Gospel according to "Charlie Brown," Charlie and Lucy are gazing into the starry night sky. Charlie muses that out of all those stars – one star must be his.

He tells Lucy that just as he is alone among millions of people here on earth – HIS tiny star, out there among millions of other stars, is also alone!

Charlie asks: "Does that make sense, Lucy? Do you think it means anything?"

Lucy replies: "Certainly! It means you're cracking up, Charlie Brown!"

Perhaps the Magi, following the star, had some second thoughts about continuing their search for the King to be born! They might have asked themselves: "Does this really mean anything? Does this make any sense?" But, still they persevered until they found Jesus, the newborn King!

Today's gospel invites us to continue the journey of faith to discover Jesus in our life! Every journey is different for each person! And the path each person takes to Jesus is also different!

Sometimes, we think the journey ends at certain high points of our life… like when we make a good retreat or kick a bad habit! Or, when we graduate from a Catholic grade school, high school, or college or when we receive the sacrament of confirmation or when we leave home! Or when we come back to church or when we go through the RCIA Program, and are baptized! But these events are simply different phases of our spiritual journey! The real journey of faith, leading us to the Lord, MUST continue our entire lives! The journey ends only when we die!

Sometimes, we become fearful along the way! We think we should "have it all together" as far as faith, and religion go…but now (perhaps), there are doubts! We are confused and seem lost. We wonder why God allows bad things to happen to good people. So, we ask: "Is this journey of faith supposed to be THIS hard?"

That's why we have to remember that our relationship with Jesus has to be a constant, unending Journey! There will be ups and downs, moments of great joy, moments of sadness, moments of doubts, and fear, and moments of pain and uncertainty! But a relationship with Jesus is so rich; and so full that it requires a lifetime to discover, and to appreciate!

The Magi did not have a smooth trip either. Travel was difficult and dangerous. Roads were bad. There were no signposts to guide them along the way. Inns were awful places to stay in. There were always thieves (especially outside of towns) where there was no police protection! The Magi occasionally got lost; and like most men, they probably too proud to ask for directions! (Times haven't changed).

But, the Magi had resources to fall back on! They had each other… their little community! They had the star to guide them! And when they got to Jerusalem, they had the scribes and chief priests to help them locate Bethlehem as the place where they should go!

The journey we all take to the Lord is also a long and difficult one! The Church is our main resource-the people of faith in our parish community! And the sacraments are there to help us journey to the Lord! For example: The Eucharist (the Body and Blood of Christ under the form of bread and wine) is OUR star! It's where we find the "Bread of Life," traditionally called "the food for the journey." When we stumble and fall or lose our way, we have the Sacrament of Reconciliation, where our sins are forgiven; and we're given a second chance.

And the grace to change our lives (and when a serious illness comes, there's the Sacrament of the Sick, that prepares us to accept the cup of suffering, in preparation for the end of our journey! But, most of all, we have each other! We are meant to be a parish community that helps us to be there for one another!

The Magi ended their journey when they found Jesus the Lord, who is: the Promised Messiah; the Prince of Peace; the Son of God: "Emmanuel;" the God who lives among us! The most important purpose of the Church is to help us do the same! We don't live to find the Church! NO! The Church lives to help us find the Lord!

Christ's Baptism "A" Matthew 3:13-17

On the first Christmas of his Pontificate, in 1958, Pope John XXIII visited "Regina Caeli," a large prison just outside of Rome! The new Pope quickly won over the hearts of his prisoner audience!

He told them he had come as their brother; and that a couple of his own relatives had done some time in prison! "I want my heart to be close to yours," (he told them), "and I want to see the world through your eyes!"

Today, these words of John XXIII are inscribed on a plaque in that prison's chapel.

It wasn't only what the Pope said; but the very fact that he had come among them "as one of them," that touched the hearts of many of the prisoners; and brought tear of joy to their eyes!

Today we celebrate the fact that Jesus (God's own son), has come into our world "as one of us;" and has associated himself with us sinners; by being baptized at the hands of John the Baptist- who was a mere human being.

How remarkable that Jesus should have joined this crowd of sinners on the banks of the Jordan, waiting to be baptized! Jesus (the totally sinless one), has no need of repentance! But "takes on" the guilt of all sinful humanity as Jesus emerges from the Jordan, his body still glistening with water, the heavens suddenly open up! The Holy Spirit descends on Him and the Father's voice is heard: "This is my Son, my Beloved; my favor rests on him."

One of the prisoners, a murderer, knelt before Pope John and asked, "Holy Father, can there be any forgiveness for the likes of me?"

Pope John's eloquent response was to raise the man to his feet; and put his arms around him (like the father in the story Jesus told about the prodigal son), embracing, and forgiving his wayward boy.

And much like the action of Pope John; Jesus' baptism carries a powerful message for us! His baptism is a revelation of who Jesus is (God's beloved

Son). But also, who Jesus is for us! He is our compassionate Savior; our dearest friend; and our loving brother! The feast of the baptism of Jesus is a good time to look at our own baptism! The commission given to Jesus "You are my beloved, with whom I am well pleased" is also given to each one of us in our baptism!

Just imagine what our parish would be like if every member took their baptismal commission seriously! What would happen in families, in the neighborhood, in schools, and in workplaces? What be relieve? What suffering made meaningful?

There is more to our baptism that just an external ceremony or ritual of washing. YES! Baptism is the revelation of our true identity as Children of God! We are baptized into the life of God, the Father; God the Son and God the Holy Spirit! This makes a world of difference. It tells us how great our dignity and vocation are! So, today we can ask ourselves: Are we living up to our dignity and our vocation as baptized Christians?

Let me give you an example of someone who did. A few years ago, a remarkable movie was made called "Entertaining Angels." It's the story of Dorothy Day's spiritual journey as the foundress of the "Catholic Worker Movement" in the United States. She is now being considered for canonization; and is often referred to as the "American Mother Teresa" for her work with the poor.

In the movie, she is shown as a young woman fighting for social justice; but her freewheeling life-style resulted in her having an abortion; and later on, becoming a single parent!

Gradually, she is drawn to the social mission of the Catholic Church! She takes instructions in the Catholic Church, is baptized, along with her child!

In one of the film's most moving scenes, she is alone, praying in front of a statue of Jesus! She is asking the Lord about the gospel's call to see Christ in those most rejected by society.

"Let me tell you something" she tells Jesus in prayer." "They smell, they have lice and tuberculosis. Am I to find YOU in THEM?" she asks. And the answer she hears in your heart is a definite "YES! That's where you'll find ME." Dorothy Day went on to serve the poor; and to fight injustice; until her death in 1980, at the age of 83!

More than 100 "Catholic Worker Soup Kitchens and Shelters" continue her work today! There is a very active one locally; run by Father Bill Bichsel,S.J., in the Hill Top area of Tacoma, Washington!

Our baptismal call is to carry on the work begun by Jesus; by serving the needs of others! John the 23rd, and Dorothy Day did, because they believed that "the Spirit of God, descending like a dove," came not only on Jesus at his baptism – but upon THEM as well. Have you heard the same call??? If so, what IS your response?

Ash Wednesday "A" Matthew 6:1-6, 16-18; Joel 2:12-18; 2 Corinthians 5:20-6:2

There is no penitential rite at the Ash Wednesday mass; no public confession of our sorrow for sins. Instead of merely calling to mind our sins, we receive a very public reminder of our sinfulness! The ashes on our foreheads tell everyone we meet: "I'm mortal; and I am a sinner, in need of God's forgiveness and redemption!"

The ashes given us this day are a kind of a liturgical "slap in the face" to wake us up; and bring us to our senses! We are signed with the cross as our first step towards Easter joy! The ashes are signs of both death and life. They are signs of our dying to sin; and our rising to new life with Christ at Easter!

The Church gives us a choice of two formulas for giving the ashes; one rooted in Genesis; and one in Mark's gospel! The one from Genesis is to remember that you came from dust and you shall return to dust which reminds us of our mortality; and our total dependence on God for our very life! The other formula from Mark calls us to action. He wants us to turn away from sin and be faithful to the gospel!

In our first reading from Joel, we are told to "rend our hearts; and not our garments, but returning to the Lord our God." And Paul tells us in the second reading; "to be reconciled to God." So, the focus during Lent is not just on our sinfulness; but on our reconciliation with God and with our neighbor! Paul goes on to say that through his passion, death and resurrection, Christ was "made sin" for us; that we might become the very righteousness of God in Christ!

The ashes on our foreheads are not a gloomy symbol or sign. Rather, they express our belief that through death we find life! And, dying to the old ways of sin brings the peace we have always wanted.

Have you every wondered what happens to the palm branches left over from last year's Holy Week? They have been burned and the resulting ashes are what we receive on Ash Wednesday. This custom was begun by Pope Urban II in the year 1091.

So, you might say that long before recycling became so popular today, the Church has been doing it for Centuries! By recycling the old palms, the very symbol of Christ's glory on Palm Sunday has now become the symbol of our sin on Ash Wednesday. Think of it in another way. *On Ash Wednesday, you're not just another dirty face!* **No you've tossed yourself into the recycling bin of Lent, to be completely transformed with the Risen Christ, this coming Easter!**

First Sunday of Lent "A" Matthew 4:1-11

Mark Twain once said that if Adam was only human it would explain everything. He went on to say that maybe Adam didn't want the fruit for the fruit's sake – He wanted it because it was forbidden! If the serpent was forbidden; he would have eaten the serpent!"

The Genesis story is our own personal stories and what happens in our lives. It's the story of the world. It has a plot, characters, conflict, decisions, and a resolution. It's a drama about life, temptation, decision, and turning away from God (sin).

Adam and Eve had everything! But being human, they had limits. They were not God. It was their "humanness" that made them susceptible to the serpent's lies. Ah, just think, to have no limits in life. To be God! To know it ALL! To be self sufficient and self-made. Wouldn't that be wonderful! And that's the lie they fell for.

The price for us was Original Sin! We are born with a tendency to sin. Adam and Eve's falling for a lie was like Pandora's Box opening – and out flew all the sins of the world!

The writer of Genesis doesn't tell us the exact nature of their sin. The point of the story is that sin was introduced by humans, and from it came a flawed humanity, alienated from God.

Reading the Genesis story reminds me of other stories I grew up with, stories that demanded a lot of questions. For example, take the story of Little Red Riding Hood. How do we know her "riding hood" was actually red?" Maybe, it was more of a rose, or scarlet, or a maroon color. And another thing, why was she called "Little Red Riding Hood" when the story says she walked to her grandmother's house? And, if she walked, wouldn't she be wearing a "walking hood" instead of a "riding hood?" And everyone knows that wolves don't talk – they howl! Their mouths aren't shaped right and their tongues are too big, for one thing.

We tend to approach the Genesis story in the same way, with a lot of questions. We wonder if the serpent really talked; or just what kind of a fruit tree was involved – was it really an apple tree? Or, could it have been a prune or peach tree? And, why did God make a single tree so off-limits? We have to remember that Genesis is a story; it's not intended to be taken literally. It's a story about how sin; and evil; and death came into the world. We take the story literally. So, what are the real points of this Story?

First of all, the story shows that temptation and sin often looks good; it seems like a lot of fun. It shouldn't but it does. For example, if we had it all together, as human beings, we would react to temptation the same way we would react to a bowl of steaming hot fresh worms. We would be repulsed!

But, instead, we often react by saying; "Hey, that looks pretty tasty!" Our judgment is often flawed because of Original Sin.

A second point of the story is this; Giving into a temptation means believing in a lie – actually a set of lies. Think about the serpent's lies to Adam and Eve.

"That forbidden tree thing God told you about? It's a stupid rule! God is so into power – God wants to control you; and call all the shots." And, there won't be any bad consequences if you do this. In fact, it'll be all good…. You'll know what God knows and be equal to God. You'll be **making a break for** freedom – and you'll show you can decide what's right or wrong for yourselves." I suppose.

Today, the serpent would probably say something like this to us: "That rule is left over from a long time ago, probably the 40's or 50's. No one pays attention to that anymore. It's not your fault **that God** doesn't keep up with the time; or know what's going on in the 21ˢᵗ century." Relax – enjoy life, and yes, Satan is still trying to tell us lies; and half truths today. We don't always buy the lies completely – but just enough to buy What Makes us and Tempts Us?

It might go something like this when we rationalize it to ourselves; "Well, usually this would be wrong, at least for some people, but it's not all that wrong for me now in this circumstance; and besides, I really don't have that much choice."

Today is the first Sunday of Lent. Perhaps, one of the best things we could "give up" during Lent is buying any more of those LIES!

After mouthing its message, the serpent disappears from the story – its evil work is done; but humankind will forever live with the consequences of mistrusting God.

But, even though humankind chose to listen to a voice other than God's – God does not disappear from the story. On the contrary, God will always come seeking out the sinner – offering forgiveness, rehabilitation, and ultimately, redemption in the person and through the mission of Jesus.

Lent is the time to look for and listen to Jesus, who overcame his temptations by saying; "Be off, Satan".It is written; "You must worship the Lord your God and serve him alone."(Matthew 4:9-10) Then the devil left him – and behold, angels came and ministered to Him!

Second Sunday of Lent "A" Matthew 17:1-9

It was Wednesday, April 3, 1968, the day before Dr. Martin Luther King, Jr. was assassinated. He was at the Masonic Temple in Memphis, Tennessee, preaching his last sermon. It was then that the great civil rights leader preached words about going to the mountaintop. These now famous words have since echoed down these years! Looking back, it seems Dr King was bravely facing his own death.

He told them that day that we had some difficult days ahead. But it doesn't matter to him now, because he had been to the mountaintop. He went on to say: that he just wanted to do God's will; and God's will allowed him to go up to the mountain; and he had looked over. He had seen the Promised Land. At the end of his speech, Dr. King declared that he did not fear any man because he had seen the glory of the coming of the Lord.

In today's gospel, Jesus takes Peter, James, and John up to the mountaintop, where they see Him transfigured before their eyes. The vision, and the assuring voice of God the Father, enabled THEM to see the Promised Land, and witness, firsthand, the glory of the Lord.

All of us either have had, or will have, our own mountaintop-experience of God…..a time when we have seen God up-close and personal, and felt God's Presence. Perhaps it happened on a certain retreat when you were touched by the revelation of God's love and wisdom.

It may have happened for a parent while holding in their arms, their newborn son or daughter, for the first time. Or Perhaps, in the rush of the emotions of falling in love for the first time; or in the ecstatic experience of skiing down a mountainside on a cold, crispy day, with the snow all aglow in the bright sunlight.

For me, it was my ordination day, May 18, 1957, and the next day, when I said Mass for the first time in my home parish, St Patrick's, Tacoma,

Washington. Those two days seemed to be suspended in a moment of glory!! God was so real; and so powerfully present. And, I wished that feeling would never end!

But, notice Peter didn't want the experience to end either. He asked if they could make three tents and live here on the top of the mountain for awhile but Jesus said no. This glorious moment; this spiritual high, has to end. Jesus gave them a glimpse of what his life would be like after his resurrection on that first Easter. But, in order to arrive there, they had to go back down the mountain where real life is lived. The Transfiguration was a spiritual peak – but Jesus had to pass through pain and suffering to get there! And so do we!!

We human beings need these beautiful vistas; these moments of sheer joy; these mountaintop experiences, in our lives. But, Jesus takes us one step further! Our salvation lies in finding God in the everyday circumstances of life – the smells, the grubbiness; the pain; the setbacks, the rejections….along with the joys; and exciting passions; and the fun of life.

I suppose it's only human to try to escape from the chaos that co-exists with our faith; to opt out; to try to find God <u>only</u> in the consolations, and the good times of life. But, it's often through our pain and struggle that we encounter the reality of life that makes us strong.

In a sense, we're like rocks in a polishing tumbler. Occasionally, the rocks get tossed high up in the air for a couple of seconds until gravity brings them back down; where they spend most of the time bumping up against other rocks. In fact, that's precisely what polishes them and makes them smooth and beautiful stones!

Let's remember that image, during this Lent, when we bump up against life. That's how we get spiritually polished.

That's how we get those rough edges smoothed down That's what gives us so much value in the eyes of God; and in the eyes of each other!

But let's also remember those times of free-floating-high-soaring through the air. Because, that's one of the ways God gives us a special foretaste of Heaven. And, then, we can imagine God saying, with good reason: <u>"If you think you're on a spiritual high, you just wait! You haven't seen anything yet!"</u>

Third Sunday of Lent "A" John 4:5-42

The Samaritan woman comes to the well simply to draw some water – a very ordinary thing to do; an everyday task!

But in that ordinary, everyday task; she has a personal encounter with Jesus – and she is profoundly touched by this "casual" meeting! Her life will never be the same again because her life is transformed and changed forever!

She had come to the well to draw "ordinary water." But Jesus gave her something much more precious; the taste of "living water:" the promise that would give her "inner peace; and happiness" that she so desperately longed for!

Our gospel writer, John, notes that: "it was "noon" when she came to draw water at the well; and that she was "alone!" Why did he mention these two details?

No one came to draw water in the heat of the day! They either came earlier in the morning, or later on, in the day, when it would be cooler! But, she came at "noon" because she knew she would be alone! That's what she wanted! She wanted to avoid the other town's people; because they kept asking her questions about her life! She was going through a series of unhappy experiences in her life; she would rather NOT talk about; or have to explain them to others! She was working on her sixth marriage!

Jesus begins the conversation with a simple request asking for a drink of water...." A very ordinary request! Then, Jesus goes beyond the "ordinary" into the "mysterious" – into the realm of faith! He touches on a deeper response in her heart! She is now spiritually moved; and opened to God's grace.

Jesus comes into her life at its weakest point; where there is pain; and suffering! He does so in order to bring her freedom; and a new beginning! "Go, call your husband, and come back here," Jesus says to her. Perhaps that was a cruel and harsh request! After all, that was the source of shame for her….the very reason the other people judged her so harshly; and rejected her!" I have no husband," she told Jesus. And, Jesus replied; "You are right in saying you have no husband. The fact is, you have had five, and the man you are now living with is not your husband. What you say is true!" (John 4:16-20)

The woman immediately tries to change the subject to a safer topic, by asking Jesus where we were to worship but Jesus won't let her change the topic. She must face the unpleasant issues of her life – to recognize what it is that brings her such unhappiness, pain, frustration, and separation!

It's the same question we must ask ourselves; "What's at the center of my life that needs to be changed?" Once we can name those issues; and identify them (then, and only then), can Jesus call us to conversion; and the beginning of a new life!

The Samaritan woman finally surrenders herself in faith to Jesus, who reveals Himself as the Messiah! She believes in Him and she is changed! She then goes back into town (to tell the very people she has been avoiding" all about Jesus; that she is a prophet sent by God! And they all believe in him because of her testimony! She thus became the first evangelist of the gospel!

All of us are the woman at the well! During this Lenten Season, Jesus meets us at the baptismal font and looks into the depth of my soul! He sees whatever it is that brings me alienation; pain; sadness; or suffering! And, he offers me "living" water, which will bring me new life! A new beginning! Forgiveness and Freedom!

But, like the woman at the well, we avoid eye contact with Jesus; and we try to change the subject because we are embarrassed; and afraid to change our lives! We know what Jesus wants! He only wants me and my love! He wants to change my life! But then, suddenly, Jesus is gone! I'm alone now; looking into the still waters of the baptismal font! I see the dim reflection of my own face staring back at me from the mirrored water – and I make a wish: "Lord, my wish is that I (more and more) become aware of your love for me; your forgiveness and your Presence in my life! I want to share that good news with others, as your Apostle! And help me during this Lenten Season, to continue the long process of my own conversion!"

Fourth Sunday of Lent "A" John 9:1-41

I read a poem the other day that impressed me! It goes like this:

"You are writing your own gospel; a chapter each day…. By the deeds that you do, and by the words that you say….and people read what you write; whether faithless, or true! Oh, by the way – what _is_ the gospel, according to you?"

That poem for me, seems to capture the spirit of today's readings and gospel! Here is a man born blind! He had grown up having never seen the light of day! Then, Jesus came along; and opened his eyes; and gave him sight! It should have been an occasion of great joy for all – but, instead; it turned into a very nasty, theological debate!

The enemies of Jesus were so offended by the miracle that they tried to disprove it! When that didn't work; they tried to explain it away! They questioned the man's parents; then they questioned the town's people! Then, they questioned the man himself; and tried to confuse the man until the man was unable to answer their religious questions. But, his response was classic, and refreshingly honest! He simply said: "I don't know how this happened! I can't answer all your questions about Jesus….who He is; or how He was able to do what He did! All I know is that I was blind, and now I see!" These seven little words compose the shortest and most eloquent sermons ever preached! It was the blind man's first sermon! "I was blind and now I see" is the simple gospel we can preach each day! Because, like the man born blind, we once were spiritually blind! Then, we met Jesus along the way! We experienced a real conversion. We were baptized, and Jesus took away our "spiritual blindness" so we could see everything with the eyes of faith! This is the gospel of hope we are trying to write every day for others to read! All of us can preach this simple gospel!

Yes, we are the "blind" man in today's gospel. Like him we also have to deal with the mystery; and doubts of our faith!

There may be some difficult questions which we feel are beyond our ability to answer or to explain, or even to fully understand! Our belief in Jesus, and in his teachings, may seem complex at times; clothed in mystery! But, when we read the gospels, we find a Jesus who has the ability of teaching us profound religious truths, in simple, and understandable ways!

For example, one day a man wanted to know: "Who is my neighbor?" Jesus didn't get involved in a deep theological discussion! He just told a story about a Jewish man traveling from Jerusalem to Jericho. Along the way, he was robbed and beaten. A Samaritan (and in Jesus's day), Samaritans and Jews hated each other)....a Samaritan saw the man; stopped, and took care of him by taking him to an inn, and gave him money! And, Jesus said explained that this is what it means to be a neighbor!"

Or when Jesus wanted to explain "greatness" to his disciples, He didn't talk about kings, or great thinkers or military heroes. NO. He just calls a little boy and placed him in the middle of the group. Then, He explained to them that if they could be as humble as this little child then they could be great in the Kingdom of Heaven. Jesus had the ability to explain profound religious truths in simple, practical ways that people could understand!

I can't unlock all the complexities or explain all the mysteries of faith! All I can do is allow Jesus' simple truth to find expression in my own life! I can't answer the age-old questions of evil or why God allows suffering! I can't even prove that God exists to an atheist or to an unbeliever! Nor can I solve the worldwide problems of poverty, bigotry, prejudice and hatred! But, I can do something about these evils, with my own life! I can be honest and truthful. I can be generous. I can be kind and I can be gentle and forgiving and humble! I can even live the gospels.

This is how we write our own gospel every day! And it's amazing, how many people actually read what we write! This is a simple gospel that all of us can preach!

Fifth Sunday of Lent "A" John 11:1-45

A little boy was afraid of the dark! One night, his mother told him to go out to the back porch and bring her the broom. The little boy told his mother: "I don't want to go out there! It's too dark and I'm afraid of the dark!"

His mother smiled and said; "You don't have to be afraid of the dark – Jesus is out there! He'll look after you and protect you!"

The little boy looked at his mother quizzically and asked; "Are you _sure_ he's out there?" "Yes, I am sure" she answered. "Jesus is everywhere you know and he's always ready to help you when you need him" she assured him!

The little boy thought a minute, and then, went to the back door, and cracked it open a little bit and said: "Jesus….if you're out there –would you _please_ hand me the broom?"

In just two more weeks, we will recall the death of Jesus! But today, we are confronted with the death of Lazarus (a close friend of Jesus). We are asked to reflect on something difficult – on death; our own death; or the death of a loved one! We are asked to ponder the little boy's question; "Jesus, are you out there in the dark? Really? The best answer to that question is found in another story about a little boy whose parents had died!

He was taken in by an aunt, who raised him as her own child! Years later (after he had grown up and moved far away to another country), he received a letter from her! She was terminally ill, and from the tone of her letter, he knew she was afraid of facing death! So he immediately wrote her a beautiful letter in which he told her; "It is now 35 years since I (as a six year old little boy) was left alone in the world! You sent me word that you would give me a home, and be a mother to me! I've never forgotten the day when I made the _long_ journey of 10 miles to your house!

I can still remember my disappointment when, instead of coming for me yourself; you sent your servant (James) to pick me up! I remember my tears and my anxiety as (perched high on your horse, and holding tightly to James) I rode off to my new home!

Night fell before we finished our journey and it grew dark. I became even more afraid! "Do you think she'll go to bed before I get there?" I asked James. "Oh, no" James said. "She'll surely stay up for you! When we get out of these woods, you'll see the light shining in her window!"

Presently, we rode into a clearing, and there was your light! I remember that you were waiting for me at the door; that you gently lifted me, a tired, frightened, little boy, down from the horse, and that you put your arms tightly around me! You had a warm fire burning on the hearth; and a hot supper waiting on the stove! Then, after supper, you took me to my new room! You heard me say my prayers, and then, you sat with me until I fell asleep!

"You may be wondering" he wrote, "why I'm writing about all these past memories! It's because, it sounds like God may soon be sending for you – to take you to your new home in heaven! I'm trying to tell you that you needn't be afraid of the dark, mysterious journey that lies ahead! God can be trusted to do as much for you as you did for me so many years ago! At the end of the road, I know you'll find love; and a warm welcome waiting….like I did back then!! Be safe in God's warm care and embrace. I also know that someday, I'll make the same journey myself, and I'll find you at the end of the road waiting for me, once again!"

What a beautiful description of death and dying! Did you notice the symbols found in this story? James, the servant, is the symbol of death we will have to meet someday! The "light" at the end of our journey is Jesus, the "light of the world! The house is the many rooms in the Father's house, that Jesus promised to prepare for all of us! The "hot supper" is the heavenly banquet! And, GOD is the "loving aunt."

It's a story of a joyful home coming! It's the gospel story full of hope and the promise of a new life after death!

Remember the little boy's question: "Jesus, are you really out there in the dark?" It must have been the very same question Martha, Mary and Lazarus also asked! And, the "Good News" is that Jesus was there to raise up Lazarus from the dead – and the same Jesus will also be there for you, and for me, to raise us up to eternal life!!

Palm Sunday Matthew 21:1-11

The unique symbol of our Catholic faith is the crucifix – not the empty cross or even the cross with the risen Christ on it – but the cross with the tortured, humiliated figure of Jesus, whom we believe is God – made- man! This is a God who suffers and yet is glorified.

In the Passion narrative today, we hear how Jesus suffered. He is betrayed by a friend, abandoned by the disciples, slapped, denied, spit on, mocked, struck, scourged, and stripped of his garments. We are horrified as he is nailed to the cross and left there to die with unthinkable pain. Yet, despite all this pain and suffering, Jesus did not lash out, call for vengeance, or curse his killers. He prayed for them, and forgave them "because they did not know what they were doing." He did as he lived, ushering in the Kingdom of God that is like no other. He gave his life that justice and peace might come and He did it by stopping the circle of violence.

Jesus once explained that even though you have heard the Commandment to love your neighbor but hate your enemies, my command to you is to love your enemies and pray for those who persecute you.

Hating our enemies is really hard work and it's very painful. It hurts us all and destroys our lives.. It keeps the Kingdom of God out of our reach. It keeps us stuck in a cycle of violence begetting more and more violence. It causes suffering, indignity, injustice and even death.

But is it by letting the violence stop here or by loving our enemies? Jesus couldn't really have meant that, could he?

The bishop of Notre Dame Cathedral in Paris, many years ago, was a great preacher and evangelizer. He tried to reach out to unbelievers, scoffers and cynics. He liked to tell the story about a young man who would stand outside the Cathedral and shout hateful things at the people entering to worship. He would call them fools and all kinds of names. The people tried to ignore him but it was difficult.

One day, the parish priest confronted the young man. The young man ranted and raved against everything the priest tried to say. Finally, he said to the young scoffer: "Look, let's get this over with once and for all. I'm going to dare you to do something…..and I bet you can't do it." And, of course, the young man shot back: "I can do anything you propose."

"Fine," said the priest. "All I ask you to do is to come into the sanctuary with me. I want you to look into the face of the figure of Jesus on the cross and I want you to scream as loudly as you can: "Christ died on the cross for me and I don't care one bit."

So, the young man went into the sanctuary, and screamed as loud as he could, looking at the face of Jesus on the cross –"Christ died on the cross for me, and I don't care one bit." The priest said: "Very good. Now do it again." And, again, the young man screamed with a little more hesitancy – "Christ died on the cross for me and I don't care one bit."

"You're almost done now," said the priest. "Now, say it one more time."

The young man looked up at the crucifix, raised his fist in defiance- but the words just wouldn't come! He just could not look at the face of Christ and say that anymore.

The rest of the story came when, after telling the story, the bishop said: "I was that young man…..that defiant young man was me! I thought I didn't need God; but I found out that I did."

This coming week is called "Holy Week" – a chance for us to relive the holy events of Jesus' suffering, death, and resurrection. On Holy Thursday, we hear Jesus say over bread and wine the words of consecration, this is my body and this is my blood. We watch Him wash the disciples' feet and hear Him tell us to do the same for one another in loving service.

On Good Friday, we look into His face as He is dying on the cross and hear Him ask his Father to forgive them for they don't know what they are doing. To the good thief he tells that today he will be with Jesus in Paradise. And to his Father he asks why he had been abandoned. On Holy Saturday, we celebrate his resurrection, his victory over sin, suffering and death. He invites us to his empty tomb, to believe in him, as our resurrection and life. Yes, during these High Holy Day of our faith, we are invited to experience a conversion (as the young man was converted) by looking in the face of Jesus on the crucifix.

Holy Thursday 2008 John 13:1-15

On entering the Holocaust Memorial Museum in Washington D.C., visitors pass by a sign that reads: "Think about what you saw." The sign is a call to action! It calls visitors to remember the past, and let it shape the future.

In the way, the Holocaust Museum remains a "living memorial" – a means to preserve the memory of the victims,

While calling the present and the future generations into action!

Tonight we gather as Christians, to share in the Supper of the Lord – a "living memorial" that Jesus commanded we celebrate in remembrance of him. In the second reading from Corinthians, Paul tells us: "Every time you eat this bread and drink this cup, you proclaim the death of the Lord until He comes."

But, this remembrance of Jesus's death must be a remembrance that also calls us into action – to the service of our brothers and sisters, and to help all who are in need. To drive home this point, John, in tonight's gospel, tells us something really amazing about the Last Supper. In describing the Last Supper (the "changing" of the bread and wine into his Body and Blood, his real presence) – is only alluded to. Instead, John gives us a sign that, in reality, says: "Think about what you saw!" And what do we see at the Last Supper? We see Jesus taking the place of a humble servant, by washing the feet of his disciples! We see Jesus "fully aware" of what will happen in the hours ahead, "fully aware that his hour of suffering and death was near; and fully aware that his body would be broken, and his blood would be shed in a living sacrifice on the cross. Yes, Jesus will freely lay down his life for the sins of the world!

Tonight, Jesus gives us that humble sign - the humble washing of his disciples' feet, as a model for us to follow, so that as he has done for his disciples, we should do for others.

That's why, on Holy Thursday, we ritually re-enact the washing of feet; and we "think about what we saw." It's a time to think about who we are - a people who are willing to lay down our lives in humble service to others! It's also a time to think about what we receive in the Eucharist – the Real Presence of Jesus under the form of bread and wine that is consecrated!"

Tonight, we remember that we are sent forth from each and every mass – "to love and serve the Lord." And that we are nourished in word and sacrament to love in great and small l ways.

So what does love look like? Saint Augustine once answered that question this way by telling us that love has hands to help others! It has the feet to hasten to the poor and needy. It has eyes to see misery and want. Love has the ears to hear the pleas and sorrows of people…..That's what love looks like!

During this Holy Week; (1)let's think about what love looks like, (2) let's think about what we saw, (3) think about who we are and (4) and think about the amazing gift we receive in the Eucharist!

Good Friday 1996 John 18: 1-19:42

The one word that best describes Good Friday for me is "abandonment." Jesus felt "abandoned" as he hung on the cross – suspended between Heaven and Earth; i.e., TOTAL failure, rejected by most of his friends, ridiculed, betrayed, a laughing stock for all, feeling worthless and of no account, with no one to defend him…all alone and powerless.

Perhaps his abandonment was the most difficult cross to carry during his Passion. I know it is for most of us.

One of my closest friends was abandoned by her husband. He deserted her after 10 years of marriage. She was seven months pregnant with their first child, and the last thing he said to her was: "I don't want to be a father." The little girl is now 3 years old, and my friend is raising her alone, with the support of her family and her Church Community.

Abandonment is one of the cruelest of all human experiences. It hurts us so much because the assault comes, usually, not from the enemy but from one whose love and fidelity we have every right to expect.

We read with horror the stories of infants found in garbage cans, children living in abandoned buildings, the elderly deserted in nursing homes, never visited by their children or relatives. Acceptance and belonging are two essential needs of the human heart.

My friend, whose husband walked out on her, wrestles with the task of forgiveness everyday working hard not to define her life by the self-doubt and despair that abandonment brings.

On Good Friday, we descend into the darkest abandonment of salvation history; the betrayal and death of the Lord of the Universe. One of his closest followers delivers Him over to his enemies for a few pieces of silver. One of his dearest friends denies, three times, that he even knows him. The rest of his friends scatter, like sheep, when danger befalls him. The religious leaders of his own People denounce him to the occupying government, who condemn him and put him to death. God the Father, in whose name he had traveled this long road, has even fallen silent. Jesus' abandonment is made even more unbearable when we remember the cheering crowds who had so recently claimed to follow him as their King! Can any of us not shudder when the cries of "Hosanna! To the Son of David" turn into the cries of hatred, "Crucify Him. Crucify Him!"

"My God, My God, why have you abandoned me?" is one of the most piercing cries in all of history. The Son of God seems forsaken by the very one he has called "Abba" – Father; dad or daddy; and Jesus calls out in anguish from the ancient prayer of the Chosen People, Psalm 22. Whatever its original intention, Psalm 22 has become immortalized as the prayer of the Crucified One. All four Gospels draw on images from this Psalm in their portrayals of the Passion of Jesus.

But Psalm 22 is more than a cry of despair. It is an affirmation of confidence in the God who eventually delivers the abandoned One from all harm. For Jesus to use these words on the cross IS a cry of anguish; but it is also one last act of faith in a God who loves Him, and will give Him the ultimate victory.

<u>Some years ago, when I was going through a mild period of depression or despondency, a priest friend asked me:</u> *<u>"What's the bottom line? What do you believe in when you doubt everything else?"</u>*

The question surprised me, but I knew the answer instinctively. "I believe in the love and mercy of GOD, to the depths of my soul, I count on that." I replied.

That kind of Act of Faith is what Psalm 22 is all about. When we fall beyond the answers of theology, and the catechism, what we really hold true in our hearts will sustain us. I know that belief was the beginning of my healing." I told myself; "Just do your best in the circumstances; and let God do the rest. I can't do it all!" And so, *<u>my prayer for tonight is this:</u>* "God of the forsaken-you know where your people are dying, where they suffer, where the lonely, the hungry and the desperate are. Be with your people and save them from destruction. <u>On this Good Friday, make us mindful of the forsaken in our prayers, in our works of charity, and in our politics. Amen."</u>

Holy Saturday 2008 Matthew 28:1-10

The main symbols of the Easter Vigil are darkness and light-representing death and life/sin and grace. The ceremony begins in total darkness-and the light which "overcomes" this darkness of death and sin, is the "new" fire, which is blessed, and used to light the "paschal candle"-the symbol of the Risen Christ. From this one candle, the people's candles are lit. Through our baptism "in" Christ, we are called to bring the light of Christ to our darkened world.

The readings tonight trace the history of our salvation-beginning with the story of creation in Genesis! The story of the Exodus, describing the Chosen People's freedom-walk from their slavery in Egypt, and ending with Saint Paul, telling us what our baptism "into" Christ means that: "just as Christ was raised from the dead by the glory of the Father, we, too, might have a new life." And finally, Matthew describes the First Easter, when Christ rose from the dead."

It's interesting-our salvation history began in a garden-The Garden of Eden-when Adam and Eve (our first parents) sinned, and were cast out of the garden. Along the way, there was another garden, the Garden of "Gethsemane" into which Jesus and his disciples entered. Judas, His betrayer, also knew the place."

And it all ends in another garden. Saint John tells us that Jesus was buried near the place of his crucifixion and that the tomb was "in a garden." But this garden is not just the garden of his burial. It is also the garden of his Resurrection-the beginning of the glorious birth of all creation into its final destiny and fulfillment!

In a sense, "going into the garden," describes our own personal journey of faith; our own personal history of salvation. We are born; we live; we sin; we meet Christ in baptism, and we die. We may have our own gardens of Gethsemane along the way, where we suffer and are tempted. But, we manage, with the help of God's grace, and the help of family and friends.

Saint Paul tells us what the Good News of Easter really is, that our old self was crucified with Christ, so that the sinful body might be destroyed, and we might be slaves to sin no longer.

Happy Easter to you and your family!!

Easter "A" John 20: 1-9

When it comes to the celebration of Easter, we're often like people who've skipped the last chapter of a thriller. We already know what's going to happen, and how it's going to end. So, much of the suspense and much of the wonder of Easter is lost for us!

This is how one Theologian explains Easter, when the events of Good Friday and Holy Saturday are skipped over: "on the day after his death, Jesus was NOT considered a hero, a savior, or a redeemer! NO, far from it! Jesus was dead and gone, put to death as a common criminal-a rebel, a blasphemer, a total failure! He simply died, and his cause died with him."

Isn't that exactly how it must have seemed to Jesus' disciples and friends? Their Master, whom they loved so much, and on whom they'd pinned all their hopes and dreams, was gone. He was no more; and all that he taught and stood for, was buried with him." No wonder Mary Magdalene, approaching Jesus' tomb early on the first day of the week, while it was still dark"-gazes wide-eyed with disbelief at the large stone that had been rolled away from the entrance. But something even more incredible awaits her-peering inside, she discovers that the tomb is empty! What has happened? Did someone steal the Body? She rushes off to tell Peter and John, and the three run back to the empty tomb. The evidence is right there before them-the burial clothes on the ground, and the head cloth laying by itself, apart-but no sign of the body! Today's gospel tells us "until this very moment they had failed to understand the scriptures that Jesus had to rise form the dead." That Jesus would actually rise from the dead was the last thought on their minds. Resurrection from the dead was not something they even expected!

Then, slowly, almost against their better judgment, they begin to suspect the fantastic truth that Jesus truly is risen, and He lives! Today's gospel records John's conversion in four simple words; "He saw and believed!"

Jesus' Resurrection is not a case of "grave" robbery. It's something far more extraordinary! Jesus' resurrection is a case of "death" robbery! Death is now robbed of its prey, death is robbed of its power! Now we can say; Death, where is your victory? Death, where is your sting?" Yes, Jesus is risen! Life has replaced death! Life and hope now can come surging into the hearts of his disciples, into the whole world, and yes, into our own lives!

The world today needs the life, and the hope that only Easter joy can give! We live in a world that is often dark-aworld of scandals; of children dying of hunger, of men and women, and children, dying of aids, of personal tragedies, of a Church sometimes doesn't live up to our expectations, a world filled with hatred, violence, wars, and ethnic cleansing. And yet, the message of the Easter Day is one of hope; that we can still trust our God, who raised Jesus from the grave!

During the dark days of World War II, amid the horrors of the Nazi regime, comes the story of Private Joseph Schultz, a young, loyal German Soldier. One day, while Schultz was on duty, his sergeant ordered him to join seven others to go on a "routine" patrol. As they made their way over a hill, they came upon eight Yugoslavians-five men, and three women civilians. Only after they came to within 50 feet of them, did the soldiers realize what their mission was!

The sergeant barked out his orders; and the eight soldiers lined up. "Ready," he shouted; and they raised their rifles. "Aim," he said, and they focused their sights. Suddenly on, the silence that hung heavy in the air, they heard the thud of a rifle butt hitting the ground. As the sergeant and seven soldiers turned to look, they saw Private Schultz walking toward the Yugoslavians, ignoring the order to come back, Schultz line himself with the five men and three women. After a moment of stunned silence, the sergeant yelled "fire"-and Private Schultz died; mingling his blood with the blood of those innocent people.

Later on, an excerpt from Saint Paul's letter to the Corinthians was found on his body. It talked about love not rejoicing over wrong doing but rejoicing with the truth. Love bears all things, believes all things, hopes all things, and endures all things. Love never fails!

I tell this story on this glorious day of Easter, because it reminds me of what Jesus did for us! Though innocent, he shed his blood, that we might live-and, *all this* he did out of love-a love that makes right that which is wrong; a love that bears all things, hopes all things, and a love that never fails!

Though Divine, Jesus came among us and took upon himself all the burdens, and sorrows and sins, of our human condition. He held us by the hand! He mingled his humanity with ours! Easter is the story with a happy ending! It's also a happy-ending story for us. Saint Paul, in the second reading, tells us that we have been raised up in company with Christ, and that we have died (to sin). Our lives are now hidden with Christ in God and when Christ our life appears and then we shall appear with him in glory.

Happy Easter!!!

2nd Sunday of Easter "A"

<u>WE ARE COMPLICATED PEOPLE</u>:

All of us are a mixture of fear; and doubt; of pessimism; and trust; of belief; and unbelief! And that's a difficult place to be in; because our human condition has such a yearning for certainty! For examples; we want to know for sure whether there is a God or not, and that God loves us unconditionally, and we want to know for sure that we'll go to heaven, or not!

In our personal lives, we would like to know, without a shadow of a doubt, that our spouse really loves us; and will always love us not matter what! That we really matter to somebody in this world! That no matter what happens; there's always somebody who loves us unconditionally! But, the fact is, we don't always have that certainty. And so we are like Thomas in today's gospel. He wanted to know for sure that Jesus really did rise from the dead! He refused to believe it, until he "saw" the Risen Christ himself!

Our scripture today has something to say about our doubts, and our uncertainties! But, as usual, the gospel doesn't give us a direct answer, it leaves room for faith! But, this gospel does have some hints about dealing with the uncertainty and doubts in our lives. Notice, the gospel mentions that Thomas was "absent" from the group when Jesus first appeared to them. We can certainly understand that there could have been good reasons why he was absent! After all, his little group of disciples had just broken up, and their leader, Jesus, was put to death on the cross! Everything that he believed in, everything that he had given himself to, has just collapsed! I'm sure he was very depressed and disillusioned. He just wanted to be alone, like many of us when we find ourselves in tragedy or in hard times.

Even though the gospel sympathizes with that, it mentions that Thomas was "absent" from the group. And not being part of the group, part of the church fellowship. Thomas "missed out" seeing the Risen Christ! And here's a little hint that can help us. Sometimes people will say, "I don't have to go to church." I can worship God alone, and in my own way. The story is told of an old Irish pastor visiting the home of a parishioner, who had not attended mass in a long time. It was a cold winter's day and there was a warm fire going in the fireplace. As the pastor was leaving he walked over to the fireplace and took out a glowing piece of coal and put it on the stone hearth. As both of them watched, in a very short time, the coal went out! For the coal to maintain it's warmth it needed the other coals! The pastor didn't have to say a word he made his point. The very next week the "absent" parishioner was at mass with his community! All of us have our doubts and fears but to help us cope with them we need each other in community. After all, it was only in the presence of the other disciples that Thomas found the Risen Christ!

Our biggest doubts about God or our faith usually come at tragic times when we're discouraged or angry with God. Look God, we say, I go to mass every Sunday. I keep the commandments and say my prayers. How could you let my daughter die or how could you let my spouse walk out on me? How could you let me get sick? After all I've done for you, God, now you do this to me?

But what the Gospel is saying is that having such doubts is understandable because, like Thomas, we also experience the "absent" Christ! There's nothing wrong with that and there's nothing to be ashamed of. After all that's a reality in all friendships. Even the most fervent friendship has its weak moments. And there's hardly a believer, here today, who hasn't at one time known that "absent" Christ. Even the great saints, like St. John of the Cross, Saint Theresa, or Mother Theresa experienced the dark of the soul. But the Gospel tells us that, like Thomas, we must remain in or return to our faith community, where we can cry out in faith like Thomas, "My Lord and My God!"

Every Christian is at a different place in their life's journey. There are some who are up front leading in the parade, who have never flinched and never wavered from the time they were born, until the time they die. Then there are those "at the back" of the parade, bringing up the rear, not quite sure they should even be in the parade to begin with! And, I guess, most of us are somewhere in the middle, we seem to waver between moving "up front" and lagging behind! But no matter where we are in the parade, the important thing is simply to be there "on the journey"! That's the sign of vitality that's the sign I have not "absented" myself from my faith community. This Gospel teaches me that I need the witness and discernment of others to encourage me. I can't survive in my Catholic faith, in my religion, or in my church, without the support of others and my fellow parishioners. So, today's Gospel is about us. Because we have met Thomas "the doubter" and he is us! And, Like Thomas, we also have met the Risen Christ in our fellow travelers!

3rd Sunday of Easter "A" Luke 24:13-35

<u>The Story of Emmaus is Our Story As Well</u>

It's the universal story of our search for the Risen Christ, as we walk the road of pain, or sadness, amid the disappointments of life.

In a sense, we are Cleophas and his companion, as they sadly travel the road from Jerusalem to their home town, on that first Easter day. We were hoping that Jesus would be the one to redeem Israel, they were saying to one another.

These two disciples had heard the rumor that Jesus had risen from the dead, but they had not, as yet, seen any evidence that he was alive! They didn't know what to think, or believe. What they did know was that they had seen Jesus die a horrible death on Friday and with his death, died their hopes of Jesus being the Messiah!

We were hoping that Jesus would be the one to redeem Israel, was what the two sadly shared with the stranger now walking with them. What made Jesus crucifixion so distressing to them was not that he had died, though that was painful enough, what made his death so heartbreaking was that, if Jesus was the one to redeem Israel as the Messiah, he should have defeated the Roman authorities! A crucified Messiah was a failed Messiah for them.

When Cleophas, and his companion expressed their sadness and disappointment to Jesus, by saying "we were hoping" that's where we're drawn into this story! When we find ourselves going through some difficult times, this gospel story can give us hope, comfort, and understanding.

How often have we said to Jesus, "I was hoping for a better outcome to my life". I had certain hopes and dreams about my life, about my marriage, about

46

my children, about my relationships, about my job, or about my church! But sadly enough, much of my life hasn't turned out the way I expected!

This gospel story is a reminder that whenever we travel the road of disappointments, the Risen Christ is always there, waling along with us, listening and ready to give us courage, and a sense of hope!

The trouble is, like Cleophas and his companion we don't recognize God's divine presence. We are walking with Jesus, but we don't even know it!

But then, there comes a turning-point, a revelation, and "aha" moment when we recognize God's presence in what is going on in our lives! We finally realize God has not abandoned us, that we are not left alone! Christ is there, walking with us on our journey!

And usually, such a revelation, or discovery, is made in hindsight…like the two disciples, who finally recognized Jesus in the breaking of bread and in his explaining the scriptures to them. Were not our hearts burning within us while he spoke to us "on the way" and opened the scriptures to us, they recalled later on!

Put in other words, they were saying in effect, "now that we think about it, when we were walking along that road, being so bitterly disappointed, and sad, wasn't there something we couldn't quite put our finger on? Wasn't there a grace from God there? And often this is the way with us. Just think of the times in your life when things were difficult and trying. And think of years later, looking back and saying, "I wouldn't want to go through that again! But now I can see that there was a grace there! I probably would not be in church today, if it were not for this, or that!

It was a terrible time in my life, but still, there was a Divine Presence! God had something in mind for me! At the time I didn't understand it, or even recognize it, but in hindsight, I am what I am today, by the grace of God! God was there! I can see that now!

Now, we can see why the Emmaus story is also our story! It's a story, saved by the church, to remind us and encourage us that we do not walk alone! That it's O.K. to be disappointed, it's O.K. to complain, and it's O.K. to talk about our hopes, and dreams that have been dashed!

But the story also promises us God's caring presence along the way, and promises us the revelation of God's love, that often comes in hindsight! It also promises us that, like the two disciples, our eyes will also be opened to recognize the Risen Jesus, "in the breaking of Bread of the Eucharist" and in the living words of scripture we hear proclaimed at Mass!

4th Sunday of Easter "A"

Also: Mother's Day

In Jesus' time, a sheep pen consisted of a circular stone wall about four or five feet high with a narrow opening in it. Often the sheep were herded into the pen at night; the shepherd would lay down across the narrow entrance in order to protect the sheep. That way, no sheep could leave the pen and no wild animal could enter; no thief could steal them without going through him. The shepherd was the gate.

Two things stand out in this description:

The first thing is the closeness that develops between the shepherd and his sheep. Most flocks of sheep were kept for their wool. This meant that shepherd was with his flock 365 days a year and often 24 hours a day…over a number of years! The shepherd got to know his sheep so well that (1) he knew which one had tender hoofs; (2) which one got sick from eating certain things; and (3) which one was prone to straying away.

The second thing that stands out is the deep dedication of the shepherd to his sheep. It meant even risking his life for them. Being a shepherd was not just a job – it was a vocation, a special calling. It is with this background that Jesus could say that He was the sheep gate and that whoever wanted to enter through him would be safe.

Life a Good Shepherd, Jesus is always with us – 365 days a year, 24 hours a day! And like a good Shepherd, Jesus knows each one of us by name in a deeply personal way. He knows, for example, (1) which one of us has a weak faith; (2) which one of us is apt to become discouraged and (3) which one of us is prone to stray from the flock. But Jesus NEVER deserts us! He is always there to help us! And, should we stray from the flock, Jesus will leave the 99 sheep and go in search of us.

Today's gospel reading is especially appropriate for Mother's day. Like the shepherd and like Jesus, a mother has a very close and deep relationship to her flock, her family. The recollection of my own mother is that SHE was always there; staying up all night with us when we were sick or had a fever; the smell of home-made bread and coffee cake when I got home from school. All the kids in the neighborhood came over Saturday morning because that's when Mom made her home-made donuts! She loved all sports, especially baseball. She heard every Tacoma Tiger game on the radio, and often during the summer, she walked with us to the old Athletic Field to watch the tigers play in person.

I remember he insisting we always do our homework and helping us with it, even though her formal education stopped in the fifth grade.

I'll always remember her supporting me in my vocation to the priesthood, allowing me to make the decision to go and remain in the seminary without pressure from her.

For twelve years I sent my laundry home every week in the mail… and it always returned with some home-made cookies or sweets.

It's hard to imagine the countless hours that Mom spent shopping, cooking, washing, cleaning and sewing for us kids. No wonder she had no time for herself.

Today we honor mothers – my prayer is that all family members draw closer together and Lord, please give them a deeper appreciation of each other, especially their mother!

5th Sunday of Easter "A" John 14:1-12

Women in the Sumner Parish:

There's a group of women who meet on a regular basis in our Mission parish in Orting, Washington. They are part of a ministry that has touched many lives in churches across the country!

Their ministry is they knit, and crochet "Prayer Shawls"! The shawls then are given as a gift to parishioners or to people in the local community who are coping with some kind of crisis! It could be a death in the family, a serious illness, or a financial lost, whatever the crisis, they are sent a "hug" from the parish in the form of a shawl and a prayer!

Those who receive the shawls say they feel loved, cared for, and most of all, they feel surrounded by God's presence and compassion! They are deeply moved to know that someone has cared enough to pray for them in their time of need and has taken the time to make them such a warm and comforting gift!

A young girl battling cancer told the knitters, in her parish, that when she felt bad, or depressed, she wrapped herself tightly in the shawl and it made her feel better! Another woman refused to take her shawl off during the final days of her life, because she considered it her "shawl of love"! Others who have received a prayer shawl, in the final days of their life, have requested to be buried with the shawl around their shoulders!

But the knitters involved with this ministry believe they themselves receive as much from "making" the shawls, as do those who "receive" them! Their simple knitting and their prayers become offerings and symbols of God's compassion for others! So, God is as present to them, as much as God is present to those who receive their gift!

I mentioned the "prayer shawl" ministry to your because in today's gospel, Jesus tells his disciples that the simplest work of compassion, done in the spirit of God's love, carries on the work begun by Christ himself. And that the most hidden and unseen acts of kindness, will, someday, be proclaimed as "great" in the kingdom of his Father!

Today's gospel takes place at the last supper, the night before Jesus was to die! He is giving his disciples some last minute instructions! He tells them to continue the work he has begun. And what is that work? He explains to them to do what he does which is the work of servanthood that places the hurts and pains of others before our own. The work of charity that doesn't count the cost, the work of love that transcends our own wants; and needs!

In his example of humble, selfless love, Jesus tells his disciples that he is the way, the truth, and the life, and that is what will lead them to his Father! And by embracing this spirit of humble servanthood, we make our way to the Father through Jesus!

Jesus is telling his disciples that God is present among them in every hidden "work" of kindness, charity, and selflessness! Yes, even the simple knitting of a shawl, becomes a "sacred" act, a participation, and a sharing in the "holy" work Jesus himself began!

This "holy" work of Jesus continues today in the lives of many people, whether they realize it or not. For example, in the countless acts of being a good parent, in the everyday feeding, the clothing, the driving, and picking up, the paying tuition, etc., etc. These are "holy" acts that take on a "spiritual" character when they are the work of transforming a child into a responsible adult!

For parents, whether they realize it, or not, the "spiritual" or the "holy" is not something ethereal, or remote, nor is it something "abstract" confined only to saying pious prayers in church! No, the "spiritual or the "holy" is painfully "real" to them. Something directly connected to the most ordinary and mundane of human activities in family life! It's often been said of married couples that "our home truly is a little church" where love, patience, forgiveness, and reconciliation take place. That's why parenthood is one of the holiest vocations!

In today's gospel Jesus is telling all of us, whether single, married, or divorced, "Do the Works that I Do"! So may our prayer today be: "Lord Jesus, open our hearts that every act of comfort we offer, every quiet moment of consolation we extend, that everything we do be part of the sacred work that the Father entrusted to you and that you now, entrust to us. Amen.

6th Sunday of Easter "A" John 14:15-21

<u>My Fair Lady:</u>

One of my all time favorite musicals is: My Fair Lady! One of the songs Eliza Doolittle sings is called, "if you're in love – show me"!

The words of this song remind me of today's gospel when Jesus tells his disciples that if they love him they will keep his commandments.

The song goes like this:

"Don't talk of stars burning above. If you're in love…show me! Haven't your lips longed for my touch? Don't say how much…show me! Don't talk of love lasting through time, Make me no undying vow…show me now!

Eliza sang those words, right after she sang, "words, words, words, I'm just sick of words"! When she sang the song, I'm sure Eliza wasn't thinking of today's gospel, but the title of the song sure fits. "If you're in love…show me"! In essence that's what Jesus was saying to his disciples in the gospel, the one who obeys my commandments, is the one who loves me!

But, what does it mean to love Jesus? That's the question each of us has to answer ourselves.

You probably have seen the bumper sticker that says "honk, if you love Jesus"! But that doesn't say much about our love for the Lord! That's too easy! In fact, just saying the words, "I love you Jesus" is also too easy to say!

Jesus was always linking action to love and if the action wasn't there he cared little for the words! Remember on one occasion Jesus warned "those who say Lord, Lord will not enter the Kingdom, but only those who do my Father's will, will enter"! And in today's gospel, Jesus seems to be saying, "If you love me…then show me"! He also seems to be saying, "words, words, words, I'm sick of words"!

So it means very little for us merely to "talk" about our love for the Lord, unless we show it by our actions! But what can you or I do that will tell Jesus of our love for him? We know all kind of ways to show our love for one another, bringing flowers, or gifts, spending quality time together, helping with the household chores. But since Jesus is no longer "physically" present among us, what can we possibly do that will tell Jesus of our love for him?

If we lived at the time of Jesus and had been the innkeeper in Bethlehem, we could have made room for him to be born in a more suitable or decent place! Or if we had been a wealthy landowner in Jerusalem, we could have given the upper room "free of charge" to celebrate the Passover dinner with his friends. Or, if we had been Simon of Cyrene, we could have helped Jesus carry his cross to show him our love.

But today, we live in another day and in another time! Jesus is no longer with us in his bodily form! But he is Risen and now lives among us in the people we meet and deal with everyday! There is only one way we can show our love for the Lord and that is by loving one another!

At the Last Supper Jesus told his disciples, and us, how to love him. He gives them a new commandment and that is to love one another as he has loved them.

So the real test of our love for our Lord is not what we "feel" or what we "say" but in what we do! Love is an action, a "Christ like" way of living our lives at home, at school, at work, at play, at church, wherever we happen to be!

And we can "talk" all about our love for the poor! We can shed tears of compassion for the plight of the homeless! But unless we are willing to invest sometime, talent, or treasure to help better their lives, our "words" and "tears" mean very little, or nothing!

I'm sure Jesus would agree with Eliza Doolittle when she sang about being sick of words. Then I'm sure he would add, "If you're really in love with me, then show me! Show me by loving one another as I love you!

7th Sunday of Easter "A" John 17:1-11

The Agony in the Garden:

A Catholic high school teacher found she had a serious form of breast cancer. After breaking the news the doctor wanted to waste no time; insisting she go straight to surgery the next day, and then begin very aggressive chemo and radiation therapies.

The women understood the urgency; but wanted a delay. She wanted to make a quick retreat – two or three days; and then be anointed at a Mass, inviting her fellow faculty members to attend.

The principal, a priest, told her he thought the idea of making a retreat before surgery was a very noble but he advised her to go straight to surgery.

But the teacher was adamant about making a retreat. She talked about the Passion of Jesus, telling her Priest-Principal how she was always impressed that Jesus had prayed before he started his Passion. She knew she was about to start a whole lot of suffering herself; and she too wanted to begin in prayer – dedicating her suffering to God the Father, as Jesus did.

At the anointing Mass, every faculty member who could possibly be present attended; and there was hardly a dry eye! This is almost exactly what we see in today's Gospel. John presents Jesus to us at the Last Supper. Jesus' dialogue with his disciples is very long. But as the high school teacher said, the last thing Jesus did before leaving the Upper Room to face the agony in the garden, was to Pray. Jesus was offering his suffering to His Father.

The beginning of the high school teacher's journey of suffering with cancer became for her a way to share in the sufferings of Christ.

How many of us make this profound connection when we face our own hardships? Do we identify with Christ when we make the hard choices of life? Do we take our pains and disappointments of life and use them to try to understand what Jesus went through for us?

The reading from Acts tells us how to do this. Jesus had ascended to Heaven. He promised to send them the Holy Spirit. The disciples returned to Jerusalem and waited in prayer for ten days until Pentecost. Acts leaves us with a list of the remaining eleven Apostles; and with them were also some women; and among them Mary, the Mother of Jesus.

This group of people from many different areas; of different ages; and many different walks of life; and in fear must have been divided among themselves as to what to do. We can imagine them arguing. They must have struggled to encourage each other, to keep from quitting, and returning home. And during that time they learned to pray, like they never had to pray before! They learned to depend on God and each other, like never before, and they learned to use their new found faith. In the absence of the physical presence of Jesus; they allowed their faith in His Word to grow. Acts makes a point of telling us that despite their differences, they "devoted themselves with one accord to prayer."

Within a school faculty, there are many differences, professionally if not personally. But a faculty did gather in prayer for one of its own. The Apostles, and the women gathered and their prayer made them of one accord. This is exactly the prayer of Jesus to the Father in today's gospel that we will, through prayer, come to an intimacy with the Father and therefore be held together by the Father. This is the whole point of prayer. Jesus found strength and purpose for His suffering. The Apostles and the women found unity. The first letter of Peter says prayer can turn over suffering into a way of glorifying God.

Prayer is the way of intimacy. It can be the most intimate thing in our lives. And Prayer is something we can share with others. This is what Jesus' prayer for us is – that we become intimate with God; and this always feels secure. If we know that our lives are safe and secure in the hands of God, we are not anxious or afraid when we are threatened. If our lives belong to God, we are not frustrated when our plans do not turn out as intended. If time belongs to God we are not angered by the rearrangement of time due to changing circumstances. The interruption to our work may be the main work to do for God that day. Our "to do list" may not match God's list of things to be done.

The Apostles, and the women, waited and prayed in the upper room. After going beyond their fear and anxiety, they became the men and women Jesus always knew they could be. They became Church, just wait; and pray. It can happen to us too.

Ascension Sunday "A" Acts 1:1-11; Matthew 28:16-20

<u>The Goodbye Places:</u>

We have all experienced it! Whether at home; at school; at airports; or train stations! We have experienced those "goodbye" places that are so often awkward; sad; and painful! Yes; saying "goodbye" is often hard to do! There are the handshakes; hugs; the kiss of tears; the prayerful embrace – and you let go! There's a final wave of a "goodbye" from a distance – and then they are gone!

Today, the friends of Jesus stand in that place of saying "goodbye" to their good friend Jesus and letting him go! Jesus has completed his work and life with them; and now says his own "farewell" to them! He lets them know that painful; empty; feeling of separation – but promises them that the Holy spirit will soon come and take his place among them to teach; and guide them! Then he sends them out into the world with the promise that he will always be with them – "Yes" to the end of time!

What a wonderful way for Jesus to say "goodbye" to his disciples! His final words to them are full of life; and promise! He tells them –"yes", I believe in you; Yes, I entrust everything to you – my words; my church; my very life; and the precious gift of the Holy Spirit. And "yes", I will be with you always he assures them to the end of time! And then he tells his disciples a paradox that all this will happen "only" when they finally are willing to let him go, only then, can they receive the Holy spirit as his final gift to them!

In our Ascension celebration and prayer today, we can remember those people today, who, (like the friends of Jesus), are standing in their "goodbye" places of sadness and tears, for examples: those who keep vigil, day and night, at the bedside of a loved one, struggling to "let them go!"

We can also pray today for those who are facing some big decisions or changes in their lives – like those who have to move to another city; those who are going to a new job, or who are losing their job; those who are facing retirement; or those who are facing the decision to go to a nursing home; or to assisted living and those who are suffering through a difficult divorce!

These are some of the "goodbye" places people find themselves in today – but (like the disciples), Jesus promises to send them and us the Holy spirit to guide us; and "to be with us always!"

Ascension Day, then, is the feast of all those who are learning to "let go" so they can complete the past without the need to "cling" to it in fear; in bitterness; or in anger and who are willing to "let go" of those past sins and failures in order to accept God's unconditional love; and forgiveness!

Besides being the fest of "letting go", Ascension is also the feast of "waiting", waiting patiently in the upper room with Mary and the disciples. Waiting for the Holy Spirit to come on Pentecost!

Ascension is also the time to pray for those who are "waiting", those waiting in the maternity wards; for those "doing" time waiting in prison cells; to pray for those who find themselves waiting in overcrowded emergency rooms; those waiting for their loved ones to return home safely from the battlefields of war!

It's a time to pray for those waiting for their chemotherapy treatments to end; to pray for students waiting for the results of their school test scores; to pray for those who are waiting for their grief to ease!

Yes, Ascension is the feast of saying "goodbye" to Jesus – and waiting for the Holy Spirit to arrive on Pentecost! It's the feast of, "letting go" and "holding on" – of waiting to hear Jesus send "us" out to the world as his disciples, and of being told the Good News: "I am with you always – until the end of time!"

Pentecost Sunday "A"
Acts 2:1-11; John 20:19-23

<u>**Finishing Touches:**</u>

Like most artists of his time, the Flemish painter Rubens had a group of student artists working with him. They watched very closely, and tried to imitate him.

Rubens would sometimes pause for a moment; gazing at the rather hesitant creation of one of his would be artists, then, seizing the brush from the hand of the student, he would add the finishing touches. It was those touches which brought the painting to life.

After reflecting on this practice of Rubens; a scripture scholar recently wrote this, "Until the day of Pentecost the disciples, (our Lord's students), had been unsuccessfully trying to copy their Master – but on the day of Pentecost – the Holy Spirit finished their painting!"

I think it's a great way to explain the tremendous effects of that first Pentecost! It explains why Pentecost is spoken of as the Church's birthday – the day the church was born; and sprang into life! It explains the day when the church was made ready for the mission of taking the Good News to the ends of the earth.

On that first Pentecost, the mighty wind, which shook the house where the disciples had gathered, soon grew still. The flames of fire which hovered over their heads, soon disappeared. But the Holy spirit, whose coming had been announced by wind, and fire, had come to stay – had come to be with the church until the end of time – to be its very soul; it's very life principle. The Holy Spirit would never grow cold; or never grow old!

In the second reading, St. Paul explains what the Holy Spirit has given to the church. He says that it is not even possible "to acknowledge that Jesus is Lord," without the assistance of the Holy Spirit. It is only through the Spirit that enables us to accept the truth at the very heart of Christianity; that Christ has died. Christ has risen; and Christ will come again. Yes, Jesus is Lord; and he lives with us in the church until the end of time!

Paul goes on to explain that the Spirit blesses the church with a variety of gifts. These spiritual gifts are special graces given by God for the common good of the church. Such gifts are given to all the baptized, to the laity; as well as to the clergy; and religious.

Some gifts are more dramatic than others; such as those of healing; or of speaking in tongues; or interpreting tongues. But many gifts are less dramatic –such as those of teaching; of helping others in need; or of administration. Indeed; every gift we have is something we can put to the service of all.

Paul insists that the Holy Spirit, who is responsible for the rich diversity of gifts in the church, is also responsible for the gift of unity. He tells us that there are many gifts but always the same source; the Holy Spirit!

There are all sorts of services to be done "he says, but always to the same Lord Jesus." And these gifts are in all sorts of different ways; and in all sorts of different people; but always it is the same God who is working in all. "Just as a human body is made up of many parts, and yet remains a single unit, says Paul," so the church is one though made up of many different members, each with their own unique gifts."

An early Christian writer, speaking of the effects of Holy Communion, noted that "whoever eats the bread of the Eucharist with faith; eats at the same time, the fire of the Holy Spirit."

On the Pentecost Sunday we might look at our own parish community; and ask to what extent the "fire" of the Holy Spirit" is in evidence here. Is our parish alive? Are people giving their time; talents; their energies to the building up of community? Are we open to new ways of doing things or are we firmly rooted in the past?

Are we self centered as a parish or does we look beyond our parish boundaries? Is our unity shown in genuine friendliness to one another; in readiness to listen to, and to serve one another? Does our Parish Community live in harmony; or is it riven by divisions?

Asking such questions can be valuable! But only if we are willing to ask a deeper question: "if things are not as they should be; what can I do to improve the situation? If enough of us were ready to adopt that attitude – who knows what might happen?

The Holy Spirit might put the finishing touches to our small efforts, thus bringing about a miniature painting of Pentecost in our midst, and so renewing the face of the earth right here in Orting, Washington!

Trinity Sunday "A" John 3:16-18

<u>Feast of the Blessed Trinity:</u>

I recently attended the 50 anniversary Mass for Father Jim Boyle! Father Jim spent the last 37 years of his priesthood, ministering to the "little people," (as he calls them) – the mentally handicapped people living at the Rainer School at Buckley.

In his homily he talked about what the "little people," (or mentally handicapped) taught him about God; and taught him about himself over the years! Working among them turned out to be life-changing experience for him! He found a deep "spirituality" in the rich relationships he formed with them – relationships not built on being powerful; or strong; or verbal; but built on compassion; on mutual affection; and on care!

He found that the people he worked with were "poor" and "little" in the sense of the beatitudes "blessed are the "poor" in spirit," for theirs is the Kingdom of God."

What Father Jim found out about himself is that he was hiding behind his own needs and fears; he didn't want to be "poor," or "needy," he didn't want to be dependent on others; no, he wanted to be in complete control of his own life; and to know all the answers!

Father Jim also found out what it means to be "compassionate!" Being "compassionate" is not just "sympathizing" with others from a distance. No, it's much more than that! Being "compassionate" means entering into the suffering of others; to "suffer-with" them; so that their goodness and their beauty beings to be revealed! Once Father Jim could do that; then he could "identify" with them; and become more, and more like them!

But, what does all this have to do with today's feast of the Blessed Trinity? I mention it because we "normal" people seem to have the need to know; and understand the deepest mysteries of life – including even the deepest mysteries about God; and our faith.

But for the "little" people," everything in their life is simply a mystery; including everything about God! They can't explain it; or understand it; they just accept it! They accept that there is a God. That God loves them; and they will live with God forever someday in heaven! And that's all they need to know about God! Father Jim's comment in his homily was; "I wish I could have that type of faith in God!"

There are many metaphors that can help us better understand the mystery of the Blessed Trinity! Let me share with you one metaphor that has helped me! It came to me at a wedding reception party I once attended!

During the reception, the whole family is on the dance floor! The groom's brother, (who served as best man at the wedding), dancing with his mom! The new bride is dancing with her dad! Soon the four of them are dancing together; holding hands; clapping; laughing; and crying! Before long the new husband joins his wife in the dance! It's a moment of complete joy; and love for both families! It's the picture of God; the picture of what the Blessed Trinity is!

God the Father; God the Son; and God the Holy Spirit are like three Dancers; holding hands; dancing together in perfect love; in perfect freedom; and in perfect harmony! They are completely one God – and yet they are three distinct persons! They form a Divine Community!

And today, on Trinity Sunday, they invite each one of us to join-in the joyful dance with our loving God! Now, that's an invitation that all of us can understand!

Corpus Christi Sunday "A" The Body and Blood of Our Lord – John 6:51-58

The Real Presence of Jesus in the Eucharist:

Today we face another "mystery" of our faith, as we did last Sunday on the Feast of the Blessed Trinity!

Today's feast celebrates the "real" presence of Jesus in the Eucharist; his living presence among us under the "appearance" of ordinary bread and wine!

But how is it possible that, (nearly 2000 years after his death; and resurrection), Jesus is still with us in this way? For example, how do we know, for sure, that it really is him – his body; blood; soul; and divinity? Or, are the bread, and wine just mere "symbols" that "remind" us of Christ's presence today?

No! The Catholic Church has always taught that the bread and wine, (after the words of consecration at Mass), actually become the body and blood of Christ under the form of bread and wine!

That's the "mystery" surrounding the Catholic teaching about the Eucharist! But, how can this be? Let me try to explain it this way!

When Jesus rose from the dead that first Easter morning, he was the same Jesus as before his death; but now he was different because now he had a "Risen Body!" He could still talk; eat; walk; teach; and work miracles!

But now with a Risen Body, he could appear through locked doors to his disciples; the wounds of crucifixion were still visible on his new Risen body and he knew the disciples by name! and now he would hand his mission over to them; and then he would ascend back to his Father; and he would give them the gift of his Holy Spirit to teach; and guide them!

The church teaches that it is this "Risen" Christ, (no longer constrained by the ordinary laws of nature), who is now present in the Eucharist – to nourish; and save us! That's why sometimes at mass, I'll hold up the consecrated bread and wine and say; "this is Jesus the Risen Christ present among us; happy are we who are called to receive the sacrament of his love!"

If we don't immediately recognize the Risen Lord in the Eucharist; we are in good company! Mary Magdalene thought the Risen Jesus was the gardener, when he appeared to her that first Easter morning; the disciples thought he was a ghost; until he ate the grilled fish with them on the shore; and the two travelers on the road to Emmaus thought he was just a "well-informed" stranger, who explained the scripture to them!

I think it is here, in this last story, that can help us better recognize the Risen Christ, now present in the Eucharistic bread and wine! We also study the scriptures about this life; death; and resurrection; we ponder the Last Supper, when he explained that this was His body; this was his blood over the bread and wine – thus changing them into his "real" presence sacramentally! We believe in the literal translation! And we have just heard the words of Jesus in today's gospel saying that He was the living bread come down from heaven and that whoever eats this bread will live forever. Whoever eats of His flesh and drinks of His blood would have eternal life; and He would raise them up on the last day!

So putting all this together; every time we celebrate mass in his memory, we can recognize Jesus in the "breaking of bread;" and in the pouring out of the wine! Our faith helps us to "see" what our eyes alone, cannot see! That's the "mystery" of today's feast!

In the third century, St. John Chrysostom asked the question: "What is the Eucharistic bread, actually?" (He answered): "it is the Body of Christ!" and what do those who receive it become, (he asked)? They "become" the body of Christ, he answered!

The gift of the Eucharist comes with one important "string" attached – it must be shared! In sharing the body of Christ, we "become" the body of Christ!

In this sacramental encounter with the Risen Lord; we are called to "become" what we have received; to "become" Eucharist for one another, as Christ "became" Eucharist for us!

As we ponder this great mystery today, we can realize how "life – transforming" it can be for our family; our parish; our community; and indeed, for our world! Today, on this feast; (and every time we gather around the Altar in his name) – we remember; we celebrate; and we share our wonderful gift of the Eucharist!

2nd Sunday "A" After Epiphany – John 1:29-34

Don't Call Me; I'll Call You!:

I'm sure you have heard the expression: "don't call me; I'll call you!" When that's said, it's usually another way of saying; "If I want to talk to you; it will be on my own terms; and on my own schedule! It's a way of taking control of a relationship with another!

Sometimes, (without even realizing it), we might be saying that very same thing to God: "Don't call me; I'll call you; when and if I need you! Oh, we know that God is important to us; and God loves us; but we still like to think that we are in control of our relationship with God! Fortunately for us; God doesn't think that way or work that way! But when God does call us to do something important; God expects us to respond; and God doesn't want to be "put on hold!"

Today's readings are about God's call to Isaiah; to Paul; to Jesus; and to us! In the 2nd reading Paul heard God's call to be an apostle of Jesus! At first, he didn't understand what that really meant, but he slowly came to realize that his role was to announce the Good News of God's salvation to the Gentiles; as well as to the Jews! And as a result of Paul's response to God's call; and saying "yes" to God; we are here today as Christians!

In our first reading Isaiah heard a similar call from God! He realized he was formed as God's servant and prophet, in his mother's womb; - even before he was born! From all eternity; God called Isaiah to bring God's salvation to the entire world; not just to the twelve tribes of Israel! That was God's divine plan for Isaiah! But God, likewise, has a plan for each one of us; even before we are born! And God's plan for us is that we get to heaven! And in the process, that we bring others along with us!

In his baptism, Jesus also heard God's call; especially when the Holy Spirit came upon him; "hovering" over him like a dove! And God the Father declared that Jesus was His beloved Son, and He was very pleased with him! The Spirit of God's peace; the Spirit of God's love; and compassion will be the constant presence dwelling within him.

And in our own baptism, we embrace that same Holy Spirit that now "hovers" over us; "making us beloved sons and daughters" of God's family; and guiding us in our journey to our heavenly home!

Also through our own baptism; God is calling us to the same ministry of Jesus! The anointing we receive with the holy chrism at our baptism, and the prayer said over us remind us of whom we are as baptized! "As Christ was anointed Priest; Prophet; and King, so may you always live as members of Christ's body (the church); sharing everlasting life"!

Yes, our baptism calls us to be like Christ in the world! To be like Christ, the Priest, to be holy! And to offer prayer; and sacrifice for ourselves; and for others in need. To be like Christ, the Prophet, to speak God's word of love, and mercy to a world desperate to hear it! To be "good news" and not "bad news" to all those we meet! To be like Christ, the King, to live our lives as members of God's royal family! Free from sin; and alive in God's grace! That's what God is calling us to be like through our baptismal promises!

But, why are we tempted to "postpone" or "put off" answering God's baptismal call? I think it's because we feel we don't have the proper gifts needed to answer that call! We think it's because we feel that God couldn't possibly want; or even; need us (me) to do anything that spiritual; or that good in the world! We feel we're not properly equipped with the necessary holiness; or training for the job!

Of course, many, (if not all the prophets, including Isaiah and Paul), felt exactly the same way!

But we know in the end, that God doesn't call "the equipped!" No, God "equips" those whom God calls, with the power of the Holy Spirit; and with God's amazing grace!

As we approach the Lord's table today for Holy communion; (with Isaiah; Paul; and Jesus); let our prayer be; "Lord God, I come to do your will!" and, as we receive the Body and Blood of Christ, let's ask him for the grace; and the strength needed to answer God's call – and to stop putting God "on hold" when God calls us!

3rd Sunday "A" After Epiphany – Matthew 4:12-23

Just Follow Me:

Have you ever been in a strange city, lost, and asked someone for help in finding directions? If so, you know that the most welcome words you can hear at the moment are, "just follow me." It happened to me during a sick call on Herron Island.

I had the phone but my cell phone didn't work on the island and I forgot to bring the address with me. As I was slowly driving along, looking for names on the mail boxes, a woman stopped her care and asked if I were lost. "Yes," I said, "would you happen to know where the Crowleys live?" "Why, yes, she replied, in fact, I was just there visiting them. They live about four blocks from here. Just follow me, and I'll take you there!"

Jesus does something like that for us. But he takes it one step further. Not only does he lead the way, he also provides the destination. His invitation, to follow him, is that we join him now on this journey, and follow him to the place where he is going to heaven.

There is something appealing about a leader who is going someplace! When a person comes along with a purpose, and a plan, things begin to happen. Jesus is such a leader!

He had a purpose and a plan that nothing could prevent him from doing, not even a cross. He knew where he was going, and he invites all of us to share that same sense of direction, by sharing in his ministry of love and service.

Jesus will never allow his followers to live in the past! His face is always turned to the future, and he calls us to follow him toward tomorrow. With him the important thing is not where we have been, but where we're going, not if we have fallen – but, if we get up! The failures of the past are not important – what is important are the possibilities of the future! Jesus was always pointing people toward a better tomorrow! When he says to follow him it is always an invitation to walk with him into a future filled with hope.

In our following Jesus, we must not make the mistakes of dividing life into the "sacred," and the "secular." All of life is "sacred" when it is touched by the presence, and power of Christ! A deeply spiritual purpose for living can be found everywhere, on the farm, or in the factory, or in the office, just as surely as it can be found in the Church.

You don't have to quit your job the follow Christ. You don't have to move to another house or another town to follow Christ. You can follow Christ right where you are! It has nothing to do with how you make your living, it has everything to do with how, and why you are living!

I recently heard of a woman who has a little plaque hanging above her kitchen sink where she cooks the family meals; and washes the dishes. The plaque reads, "Divine Services are Conducted Here, Three Times a Day." That woman has caught the vision of a higher purpose. She isn't just a housewife doing chores, she is a homemaker. She's in business with Jesus. She is living her sacrament of marriage. She is making what is "secular" in her life, into something that is "sacred!" She is choosing "to bloom" where she is planted.

That same idea can be applied to our lives whether it be at home, at school, at work, or at play! Our plaque can read: "Divine Services Conducted Here Daily!" All of life can be touched with a sense of the sacred. We are not just catching fish, building cars, sweeping floors, or selling clothes. Whatever we're doing, we're in business with God, and we're following Christ!

Christian living is something basically simple! First and foremost it's a matter of following Christ. When the early Christians set out to change the world, they had no detailed programs or plans. All they had was a profound faith in Christ, and a burning desire to follow Him! They were his followers walking with Him, trying to think as he thought, and live as he lived, that's what changed the world!

You and I can do the same today! In every generation, Jesus' call is the same, "Follow Me." If we are doing that our lives are counting for something good, we have found a higher purpose in living! Jesus gave Peter, Andrew, James, and John something better to live for, than just themselves. They were still fishermen, but now they had a higher purpose. A more important job, they were now "fishers of people." Jesus wants to do the same for anyone of us, who has the courage to follow Him.

4th Sunday "A" After Epiphany –
Matthew 5:1-12

<u>Beatitudes:</u>

We have heard and read about the eight Beatitudes all of our lives! They are very familiar – perhaps too familiar! They challenge us because they totally oppose what the world promises will bring us happiness, success, and fame!

Let's face it, if the Beatitudes were written today to reflect the values of 21 century America, they might read something like this:

1. Blessed are the powerful, for they shall control others!
2. Blessed are the movers and shakers for they shall make things happen!
3. Blessed are the strong, the young, and the beautiful, they shall be greatly admired!
4. Blessed are those of white Anglo-Saxon decent, for they shall inherit the earth!
5. Blesses are the winners for they shall be lauded and applauded!
6. Blessed are the affluent, for they shall have all they need or want!
7. Blessed are Americans for they shall live in God's beloved country!
8. Blessed are those in authority for they shall possess all power and truth!

These are the beatitudes that reflect the values of our culture! Now we all know there is nothing wrong with being powerful, or movers, and shakers, or winners, or Americans, after all, most of us have been encouraged since childhood to value these values as part of the American dream! And if we don't reach them ourselves, we can at least, admire them in others!

It seems that the powerful, the beautiful, the wealthy, and the well known, control the world! They are the ones who grab the headlines! They are the ones interviewed by Larry King on CNN. They are the ones often elected to political office, and they are the ones who get things done in the World!

But the Bible tells a different story of how things get done in the world! According to the Bible it is often the "little" people, the "powerless" people, the "ordinary" people whom God uses to get things done! Jesus describes the character of these "ordinary" heroes as the poor in spirit, those who mourn, the meek, the pure in heart, the peacemakers, and the persecuted! Not a mention is made of the need for wealth, fame, power, or beauty!

Can such a group of "nobodies" really be an influence in the world? What is God doing collecting such a "rag-tag" army? I think Jesus is saying, "God is not limited by the rich and the famous, or by the "who's Who – types! In the Old Testament God led the chosen people out of Egypt through a man who stuttered – Moses! God defeated the giant Goliath by using a young shepherd boy, David, who slew the giant with a child's sling shot! And God created the nation of Israel from a group of run-away-slaves! In the New Testament Jesus chose the Apostles from a most unlikely group – uneducated fishermen, a despised tax-collector, a loser who committed suicide and all of them abandoned him! And on one occasion Jesus fed five thousand people with a few pieces of bread, and some fish, a little boy was willing to give!

In the 2nd reading today, Paul reminded the Corinthian Church that most of them were not from wealthy families! Not many of them were well-educated. Not many of them were powerful in the community. Yet Paul wanted them to know that God "chose" them on purpose to reveal God to the world! God wants everyone to know they are somebody important to God, and to God's Kingdom!

As Paul said "God chose the weak to confound the strong, and God chose the foolish to confound the wise!" Even the preaching of the Gospel is foolishness to the world, Paul says. But God knows that a trusting people armed with God's Word, can change the world! The poor, the meek, the powerless, realize they don't have the power, or the strength to change the world themselves! They know that power belongs to God alone, and to God's grace!

For Example: Joseph Stalin once mocked the church by asking if the Pope had any military divisions. Compared to the Military might and cruel power of Stalin, the church looked very weak indeed! But today, the

Church is thriving in Russia, the Berlin Wall has crumbled and where is Joseph Stalin? Or where is Communism today? Yes! God moves through the "powerless" to confound the "powerful"!

Many of the Beatitudes do, indeed, seem foolish, impractical and even dangerous! They are certainly counter-cultural! What does it mean to be meek, to be merciful, to be peacemakers? What are we expected to do? There are no easy answers to these questions. It would be easier to pretend the challenge isn't there! Perhaps there should be another beatitude added (something like this) – Blessed are those who struggle with these issues, who suffer criticism for acting on behalf of the Gospel. And the reward for keeping his beatitudes, Jesus says is this, the Kingdom of God will come alive in your heart, you will be comforted, you will inherit, you will be filled, you will be shown mercy, and you will be called children of God! Now, that's something worth working for!

5th Sunday "A" After Epiphany – Matthew 5:13-16; Matthew 5:13-20

<u>Taste The Salt of God's Word and Savor it!</u>

Have you ever been called computer illiterate? I have been told that! When I tell people I don't have a computer they are shocked! Then you don't have access to the internet? You don't have Google, and you don't have e-mail, they respond!

No, I answer, I don't have any of those modern-day wonders! Actually, I prefer not spending my life looking at screens, and constantly updating to a newer, sharper, and faster computer! Rather I prefer using paper and a pen when writing a homily. They always work, even when there's a power shortage! Yes, I have to admit that "computer" technology has passed me by!

But there's another field of knowledge, (far more important), in which we may find ourselves "by-passed"! And that's the field of "religious" knowledge! The knowledge of the scriptures, of theology, of Church teachings, the knowledge of morality, and ethics, which may have passed us by!

If we still have a "grade school" knowledge of our faith, we may not be able to answer basic questions about religion today!

Without the proper knowledge, it's difficult even to answer the doubts, and questions of our children! Religious understanding is something that has to grow and develop and mature, if it is to be practical, and useful in our daily lives!

In today's Gospel, Jesus tells us that our faith in God must be "practical" and touch our lives and the lives of others! The lifestyle of a true believer, Jesus says must be like salt, and like light! What does that mean in a "practical" way?

In Jesus' day, salt was one of the world's most valuable commodities! Wars were actually fought over salt and the rights to mine it in salt rich lands. In the days before freezers, and refrigerators, salt was used as a preservative. It could keep meat from spoiling for months! Salt was also used as a form of money! Workers were often paid with salt, which could be exchanged for other things of value! The popular saying, "he's not worth his salt" comes from that ancient time!

The other image of faith Jesus uses in today's gospel is light! Light always banishes the dark, (which in our own minds), represents everything that is evil, and fearful – even death itself! Light reminds us of the sun which is life giving, warm, bright, cheerful, and it dispels the darkness of sine and evil!

In the gospel Jesus "commissions" us, and sends us out into the world to be "the salt" of the earth," and to be "torchbearers of light"! We can do it, even though our lives may seem to be small, and insignificant!

Remember, just a small amount of salt, or a tiny little light can produce wonderful results! Many recipes call for just a "pinch" of salt! Just one, small, caring, loving, act of kindness can enrich the lives of dozens of people! We can do that!

Even a small amount of light can "light up" an entire room! So can a smile do the same thing, or a phone call, a word of comfort, or encouragement, or a visit to someone who is ill or alone! We can do that!

So, if our faith seems to have lost some of its zest it once had – could it be that we aren't adding to it the "distinctive "flavor of a "pinch" of salt! And if we are longing for more light in our own lives – could it be that we will actually find it, by sharing the light of God's love with those living in the darkness of sadness, or depression?

Today, at this Eucharist, we are invited to "taste" the salt of God's word; and to savor it! Ant to open our eyes to see the light of God's love, and God's plan for us! Once we have tasted and seen the goodness of the Lord – we shall be renewed in our own ministry of being salt and light for others!

Jesus ends today's gospel by saying that if your light shines before others people may see your good deeds, and glorify your heavenly Father!

6th Sunday "A" After Epiphany – Matthew 5:17-37

A Rabbi Talks with Jesus:

In his recent book entitled "Jesus of Nazareth" Pope Benedict XVI tells the story of a Jewish scholar, deeply respectful of Christianity, and of Jesus! This Jewish scholar also recently wrote a book (a novel entitled "A Rabbi Talks with Jesus"! The book pictures the Rabbi in Jesus' company – listening to him, watching him, asking him questions, and enjoying him in conversation!

The story begins on the day Jesus preached his famous Sermon on the Mount! The Rabbi is part of the vast crowd! He would have heard the same words spoken by Jesus, as we have just heard in today's gospel!

How did the story turn out? What happened to the Rabbi? The Rabbi was both attracted to Jesus, and troubled by him! Attracted by the purity and loftiness of Jesus teachings! But also bothered by Jesus claiming equality with God – a claim that was considered blasphemy to any pious Jew! So, finally the Rabbi walks away from Jesus, but rather sadly! Still full of admiration for Jesus, but unable to accept Jesus' claim to be divine! But in the final chapter the Rabbi writes, "I now realize, only God can demand of me, what Jesus is asking!

How right the Rabbi was! In today's gospel, Matthew portrays Jesus as the new; and the greater Moses! It was on a mountain (Mt Sinai) Moses delivered the Law of God (the Ten Commandments)! And now Jesus delivers the new and improved Law of God, in his Sermon on the Mount!

When Jesus said to the crowd about what was said to our ancestor his audience knew, at once, he was referring to Moses, and to the Ten Commandments he had received from God! And when Jesus said, "But, I say to you" they realized Jesus was claiming to be greater than Moses! In fact, he is putting himself on a par with God. He is speaking with God's Power, and authority! He is daring to expand, and adjust God's Law! But it's just an adjustment (or tweaking) of God's Law – not a revoking of God's Law! Jesus explains he has come, "not to abolish the Law," but to complete the Law! To point out the more demanding things involved in keeping God's Ten Commandments!

For Example: According to God's Law, murder is wrong! "Yes", Jesus says, but he also says so is anger, hatred, revenge, prejudice, un-forgiveness, anything that harms another; and which can easily flare-up into violence! In fact, Jesus says it is better not to come to temple-worship, if you harbor hatred for a brother, or sister! Go first to be reconciled then come to the altar to worship God!

And according to God's Law, adultery is wrong! "Yes" Jesus says, but so also is looking lustfully at another human being, (with the full intention of committing adultery)! That's a sin, a violation of a person's dignity! While the Scribes and Pharisees were obsessed with the keeping of the "letter" of the law, only Jesus taught the more important task of embracing the "Spirit" of the law- the underlying attitude of love, and humility that gives all just laws their true life, and their true meaning!

Keeping the Law of God hangs on the double commandment of love of God, and love of neighbor! It is in rising to this twofold love that we prove our love for Christ! In John's gospel Jesus tells his friends that if they love him, they need to keep his commandments. True love is difficult and demanding! It is true (as the Rabbi realized) that only God can make the demands that Jesus makes of us! But it is also true that Jesus not only makes demands of us, Jesus also gives us the grace to live out those demands in our daily lives!

Jesus knows that even good disciples, (people like us), will (at times), get angry and upset. That we will suffer broken relationships, and we will be unfaithful, or selfish! But when we fail, we need to make the situation right! We need to follow Jesus' advice and become reconciled!

Just think, (if we, as individuals) could do that, and if nations of the world would try to become reconciled, after disagreements, instead of going to war – what would our families be like? And, what would our world be like?

So, today, Jesus is warning us that breaking the "big" laws of the Ten Commandments, always begins with breaking God's "little" laws! Jesus is calling us to a higher standard of morality, by encouraging us to "prune" away all sin from our lives, even the "little" sins!

7ᵗʰ Sunday "A" Matthew 5:38-48

<u>To Forgive is to Forget:</u>

The Dalai Lama is a hero to many people around the world, especially, as a man of peace and reconciliation! But, who is his hero? To whom does he look up to for inspirations, as an example of a holy life? That very question was once asked of him! His answer may surprise you, as much as it did me!

"My hero, and my friend, he answered, is an Irishman, who was blinded by a rubber bullet fired at him during the troubled times in Northern Ireland!" Richard Moore was only ten years old, and on his way home from school that day in Derry, in 1972, when he was shot at point blank range in the face! "All I remember, he recalls, is that everything went dark, that I was blinded and that my life was changed forever!" Richard Moore has been on an extraordinary journey ever since that day and he has inspired many people along the way, including the Dalai Lama! While in his twenties, Moore began a worldwide charity called "the children in crossfire" to support children caught up in violence and poverty! He not only forgave the soldier who fired that rubber bullet, he has even befriended him! And now in his late forties, he continues giving talks to young people about the importance of putting aside grudges and trying to forgive their enemies!

In today's gospel Jesus calls us to reject the belief that aggression, violence and retaliation, are the ways ot solve problems! Richard Moore may be blind, but as he says, "my physical sight has been taken away, but not my vision for a better and more peaceful world!"

Efforts to build bridges with people we don't like; or who have harmed us might bring us surprising results! If not, then we can be consoled with the thought that, at least, we are trying to do what Jesus is asking of us! We are told to turn the other cheek, to love in the face of hatred, and to love everyone even our enemies! Even the great humorist, Oscar Wilde, enjoyed saying "always forgive your enemies, nothing annoys them more."

But Jesus gives us a better reason for forgiving others! Be perfect as your Heavenly Father is perfect, he is telling us. Forgive one another, as your heavenly Father always forgives you!

8th Sunday "A" Matthew 6:24-34

<u>The Lasting Treasure of God:</u>

Imagine spending many hours creating a beautiful work of art and then destroying it, as a prayer offered to God! That is what happens when a ritual ceremony called "Mandela" is performed at many of the Buddhist monasteries in Tibet to introduce students to the principles of Buddhism.

Over a nine day period, with prayers and chanting, the monks create a beautiful sand painting, about seven feet in diameter, composed of colored sand, chalk, spices, and wheat! The finished "Mandela" contains the many symbols of the sacred principles of Buddhism!

Once completed, the monks then pray that the Divine presence of God will descend from heaven and temporarily enter and live within the "Mandela"! Only then are the students invited in to see it and to study the meaning of the various symbols of Buddhism, and through their experience to be "reborn" in faith. Then after thanking God for God's presence in their work of art, the monks pray that God now leave the "Mandela" then it is dismantled and its contents are poured into special urns! The monks solemnly take the urns in procession to a nearby lake, or river, and prayerfully pour the sand into the waters and like the passing away of all created things, the sands of the "Mandela" are washed away, washing away the memories of those who created it, and those who discovered God in it!

This Buddhist ceremony reminds me of what Jesus is trying to tell us in today's gospel! I think he is trying to tell us that everything we possess, everything we create, and everything we use in this life, is like the Buddhist monks painting made of sand! Someday, sooner rather than later, it will all be washed away!

Today's gospel calls us to "let go" of those material things that fill our lives, and instead, seek to possess the spiritual, and the lasting treasures of God, the love of family and friends, the sense of meaning that comes from living the truths of our faith, the principles of justice, and mercy, and the joy of helping others realize their hopes and dreams for themselves, and for their loved ones!

In the gospel, Jesus is not condemning our work, or our possessions, but he is merely putting them in "perspective"! Material wealth, our money, investments, savings accounts, 401K's, property, etc, are all necessary, and good things to have, but they are "tools" given to us to cooperate with God's plan in the work of completing creation by helping God create a just, and peaceful world!

So, Jesus is saying to us it's not a sin to possess and to enjoy material things. The only danger of sin comes when material things take over our lives, and "possess" us instead of us possessing them! When that happens, material things become "barriers" between our lives, and the life of God. They can become "false" idols, or "false" gods to be adored!

That's why Jesus is warning us that we cannot serve two masters. We cannot serve God, and money, or material things, at the same time! He is telling us that either you will love the one, and hate the other, or be devoted to one, and despise the other. You cannot serve God and money!

In the parable, Jesus gives today, he tells us that the God he knows as his Heavenly Father, is the God who provides food for the birds of the air, the God who clothes the simple flowers in the field with elegant beauty, and is the same God who holds our tomorrows in the palm of his hand, because God loves each and every one of us!

Jesus tells us that our first priority must be to know, and trust this God, and in that profound trust we will find our true purpose in life, our security, and the confidence to face whatever the future may hold! If you seek the Kingdom of God, then all these things will be given you. Don't worry about tomorrow because it will take care of itself."

Such trust doesn't mean we don't have to work or we don't have to care about the basic needs of life but it does mean we are not alone in this world. God is always with us, watching over us, and caring for us! It means our true value is not measured by our portfolio, our state in life, or who we know, but by our relationship with God, and our relationship with one another in trust and in love!

9th Sunday "A" Matthew 7:21-27

What True Christian Living Means:

Today we hear the final words of his Sermon on the Mount. Jesus is describing what true Christian living means. He ends his sermon with a plea to avoid any form of "hypocrisy" in the practice of our faith! Mere words, like, "Lord, Lord," will not be enough for salvation! Even preaching the gospel, or performing miracles in his name will not be enough for salvation! Giving "lip service" to God is not enough!

But what is required is actually doing the will of our Heavenly Father, to the best of our ability! The word "hypocrite" has an interesting meaning, it comes from the Greek word for an actor, and actor playing a role on stage, pretending to be someone, he or she, is not! It's alright to act that way on the stage Jesus is saying, but not in the living out of our Christian life!

To illustrate his point, Jesus tells a parable about two very different people who build their houses! Remember, as a carpenter for fifteen years, Jesus would have known something about building houses, because he must have built some! So, he tells this parable based on his experience to help lead people to God.

One of the builders, whom Jesus describes as a "fool" built his house on sand! When the winter floods came, and the winter gales blew, the house was washed away, and destroyed! It didn't stand a chance, because it was built on sand!

The other builder, Jesus describes as a "wise" man built his house on a solid foundation! It too had to bear the cold blast of the winter floods, and gales, but it stood firm, because it was "built on rock" so it was not destroyed!

People who listen to Jesus' words, but don't put them into practice, are the builders "on sand" in their spiritual lives! On the other hand, those who listen to Jesus, and act upon what they have heard, are the builders "on rock" in their spiritual lives. These are the "wise" ones in the Kingdome of God!

Of course, life is seldom an either or proposition. We tend to build our spiritual lives on both, on sand, and on rock, as the parable suggests! Even though we honestly take to heart the teachings of Jesus, and try to put them into practice in our daily lives, we still fail! Some of us fail too often.

But there is encouragement for us in today's 2nd reading to the Romans, where Paul says, "we have all sinned, and we are deprived of God's glory." A better translation would be, "we all have sinned, and we have "fallen short" of God's glory!" In other words Paul is saying, "not one of us always shows forth God's glory, as we should, the glory that is our, as God's children!"

But we need not lose heart. In another letter Paul explains that he himself is not perfect, yet! He admits he has not achieved the ideal that Jesus sets before him in the Sermon on the Mount! But he says he hasn't stopped trying, and that he will keep on trying to the very end! Whatever else, Paul was not a hypocrite! And, if we keep on trying, even though we sometimes fail, neither are we hypocrites, we are human and sometimes fail!

The Christian life is not a matter of personal achievement, it's not something we can accomplish all on our own, rather it is something that is achieved only with God's help and God's grace! As today's responsorial psalm states, "it is God who is our rock of refuge - it is God who is our mighty stronghold!"

And that is why, as long as we try to live out our faith, and at the same time, trust in our merciful God, we have every reason to believe, one day, at the end of life, we will meet God face to face. And as Psalm 37 puts it, "God's face will shine on us, brimming with love over us, and God's voice will gently welcome us by saying, "My son, my daughter, welcome. Because you kept trying and trusting in me you have built your spiritual life on solid rock and now the Kingdom is yours! "Enter it with joy!"

10th Sunday "A" Matthew 9:9-13, 18-26

In today's gospel, Jesus saw a fellow Jews named Matthew collecting taxes for the Roman occupiers. As a tax collector, Matthew was disdained by the Romans and hated by the Jews, who considered him to be a schemer, a quisling, and a cheat. Yet Jesus calls him to be one of his disciples!

Jesus lived in a society where there were barriers between the classes, the races, and other status groups. So, there was a strict taboo on any social mixing. You don't share a meal, talk to, or socialize with people who belong to a different group! You never eat, or drink with a person of a lower class, or with a person considered to be an outcast, or a sinner.

No wonder the Pharisees criticized Jesus! He not only ate, and drank with tax-collectors, and sinners, he invited one of the tax-collectors, Matthew, to be one of his 12 disciples. What a scandal!

And so here we have Jesus saying that for him barriers between people should not exist! In fact Jesus had a habit of disregarding barriers for example by touching the "untouchable" leper, by healing a pagan's servant, and curing a foreign woman's daughter, and telling the story in which a "hated" Samaritan turns out to be a "good" neighbor to a Jewish merchant robbed, and left half-dead on the road to Jericho.

And here in today's gospel, Jesus is at it again! His eating and drinking and partying with tax-collectors and sinners leaves no double about his message! There are no barriers with Jesus! No one is excluded from the love of God – no matter how bad they are or have been and all the "Matthews" down through the ages are welcomed to the banquet, as long as they decide, like Matthew, to follow Jesus, even at the last moment!

In Eugene O'Neill's wonderful play "The great God Brown," a man named Billy is on his death bed and he's very frightened! At his side is a woman who has become something of a "mother" figure to him in the last moments of his life. So, she speaks to him as though he were a child, saying, "go to sleep, Billy, It's all right." And he answers "yes, mother!" Then Billy starts explaining what he experienced in life. "it was dark, "he said," and I couldn't see where I was going, and they all picked on me." The woman says "I know, I know, Billy. But you're tired now! Go to sleep." And he asks, "when will I wake up?" She replies, "The sun will be rising." Then Billy interrupts and says in all seriousness, "will God judge the living and the dead?" and then with great fear he adds, "I don't want justice, I want love!" The women replies quietly, "there is only love!" And as he is dying, Billy begins saying the only prayer he knows, "Our Father who art in heaven". For sinners like Billy, and Matthew, there is only love, at least according to Jesus who sat down and broke bread and ate with them!

The gospel story about Matthew's call to follow Jesus says that Jesus also stands ready to call us sinners to his banquet. He does so, because "there is only love" in his heart focus! Paul tells us that we have all sinned, and we are deprived of God's glory. A better translation would be that we all have sinned, and we have fallen short of God's glory! And here stands Jesus who really does love us, and wants us, disease and all. Yes, the Matthew story is our story! Like Matthew we find ourselves at this banquet of the Mass today with Jesus, and with the rest of the sinners here in Church!

At communion time today as you reach out to receive the bread of life, and the cup of salvation, do so with the humility and gratitude Matthew must have felt! And rejoice the fact that Jesus has not come to call the righteous, but to call the sinners. And that at this Mass we have answered Christ's invitation to be transformed, like Matthew was, from sinner, to Apostle!

11th Sunday "A" Matthew 9:36-10

You go to the school dance with your friends. No one really dates yet. It's only the eighth grade. A group of teenage girls bunch up against the wall at the dance. They travel in packs for safety. They giggle together, they go to the restroom together, and stand together. It would be much simpler if they could just dance with each other! They are mortified at the thought of one of the boys asking them to dance. But they are also afraid none of the boys will ask them to dance. Finally, one of the boys crosses the no-man's land of the dance floor. He approaches the group of girls, which one of you will be asked to dance? You all pretend to be disinterested. You are afraid! So is he! Do you remember when he smiled, and reached out his hand to you? Do you remember how that felt?

Or, you are the smallest kid on the playground. You cringe when the teacher suggests that two of the bigger boys choose sides for a game of basketball! You know the drill everyone else will be picked first. You will be embarrassed, standing all alone after the other kids have been chosen. But then the unexpected happens! The big kids picked you first!

When they call out your name, you are not even listening when they repeat you name, you can scarcely believe it! They called your name! How did that feel? Ah, the delight, and joy of being chosen! And it still feels great in adulthood, doesn't it? For example when the company selects you to represent them at the trade show, or when you are chosen for a promotion, doesn't that feel great? Whether you are invited to join the team, or attend a party, it still feels wonderful to be the "chosen" one.

Israel experienced that same joy of being chosen. Let's listen to our text today, for God extends the same grace of choice to us through Jesus Christ. "You are God's chosen people!" Isn't that terrific? But just what does this mean? Israel didn't win a spiritual beauty contest when God chose them to be God's special people. In fact they were often stubborn, rebellious, and unfaithful to God. Israel was not chosen because they were a powerful, wealthy nation. In fact, they were a nation of slaves, and gypsies. Israel was not chosen because they deserved to be chosen. Israel was chosen because it was God's delight to choose them. It was sheer, undeserved, grace.

In a sense they were the awkward girl asked to dance, or the short kid picked first for the team! Listen to the beautiful language of God's love for Israel in today's readings. God called them up on eagles' wings. They were precious to God. Isn't this good news for us today? We are also the delight of God's heart. God cherishes us like a most prized possession. God is like a parent eagle nurturing and protecting its young.

God also called Israel a "nation of Priests." What does this mean? Certainly, to be a nation of Priests suggests that all the people will enjoy a special closeness to God. But this calling as Priests carries with it the responsibility to do the work of a Priest in the world! God did not just choose Israel so that they could enjoy God all by themselves! God chose Israel to be priests so that they would lead the rest of the world to intimacy with God. This is the work of a Priest!

Priests are reconcilers between God, and humanity. The very word "Priest" comes from the Latin word "Pontifex", a bridge builder. "Pontiff" comes from that word. God calls Priests to stand in the gap that we humans have created between ourselves and God. Priests build bridges across that chasm.

So here we are. God's chosen people! God's Priests! You may not wear a Roman collar or a vestment but you do bear the mark of election through your baptism! When you see any need, meet it! When you encounter injustice, fight it! When you sense a loss, rescue it! You share in Jesus Priesthood through your baptism, and confirmation. It's true! The Lord always gives away the best of God's gifts. As God's chosen people, and as Priests, so must we! So, rejoice that God's hand stretched out to choose! Imagine, God picked you, God smiled at you, and wants to dance with you! But having been chosen yourself stretch out your own hand to others. Invite them to the dance too. God's grace always comes to us on its way to another. So, pass it on! Without cost you have received, without cost, you are to give.

12th Sunday "A" Matthew 10:26-33; Matthew 10:24-39

In today's gospel, Jesus calls us forward to be witnesses. And like any good attorney, Jesus prepares us in advance for the task. What does it mean for us to be witnesses for Christ? Today's readings give us some good insights to help us understand our role as witnesses for Christ.

First of all, as a witness for Christ, you don't need to be afraid to step forward! Fear no one Jesus tells us. After all, as a witness for Christ you are not the one on trial; Jesus is, and his teachings!

Notice – in our first reading from the Old Testament, Jeremiah did not need to be afraid. It was the corrupt world around him that was on trial – not the Prophet Jeremiah.

And in the gospel, Christ calls us forward to be the witnesses on his behalf – not on our own behalf. He also tells us the task will not be easy! Our witness may not always be well-received by those who hear our testimony, but Jesus assures us not to fear because he (Jesus) will be with us! And if Jesus is with us we do not have to be afraid of any "cross examination" coming from the world!

Another thing to remember is that a witness in a courtroom trial does not have the burden of convincing the jury, or the judge. That is the attorney's job. The job of the witness is simply "to tell the truth – so help me God." A "good" witness can't make up or embellish the facts. Witnesses are simply to tell the truth, as they know it from their own experience!

In fact, in a courtroom trial, the witness is not even allowed to speak about the case from "hearsay" evidence –what a 2nd or 3rd person has said. Their testimony must be from their own personal first-hand experience – from their own personal life story! That is what makes their testimony so powerful, so moving, so compelling, and so believable!

That is what we are called to do as witnesses of Christ in the world. It is pretty simple – just tell the truth about Jesus as you know it; and as you have experienced Christ in your own personal story of salvation. Pope John Paul II put it this way; If you have met Paul he would say that we have all sinned, and we are deprived of God's glory. A better translation might be we all have sinned, and we have fallen short of God's glory! Christ – live Christ –and live with Christ. Proclaim Christ in the first person as St Paul could have said, for me, life is Christ. It is no longer that I live, but Christ lives in me. I know nothing else but Jesus Christ and he was crucified. That is the liberation, to proclaim Jesus free of ties. Proclaim Jesus living in men and women, who are transformed, and made into new creatures"

The most effective witness to Christ is often done without words – but only with our actions. As St. Francis of Assisi once taught – we must always bear witness to Christ's love, but use words only when it is absolutely necessary. So, if you truly believe that God is love, and that God wills the salvation of the entire world –and if you have experienced that love through the person of Jesus Christ; proclaim Christ's love to the world by the way you live! Actions speak louder than words. This is what a witness for Christ does.

In a homily preached in Chad, June 30, 1990, Pope John Paul II gave some practical examples of how we can witness of Christ today. I quote: "When you help your neighbor, you proclaim the Good News of Christ, which makes universal brotherhood and sisterhood possible."

When you visit a sick person, you are a sign of Christ's mercy toward those who suffer.

When you forgive your worst enemy, you are the sign of the forgiveness of Christ, who never nourished hatred in his heart.

When you refuse to accuse someone without proof, you proclaim the coming of the kingdom of God and God's justice, and witness to the truth that no one is excluded from God's kingdom.

When as Christian spouses you remain faithful in marriage, you are the encouragement to all, and a sign of the eternal covenant of love between God and humanity.

When as a young man or young woman you save yourself for the one you will marry, you are a testimony to the sacredness of human love.

When you call evil that which is evil, and refuse to practice it – you are the witnesses of Christ's light in the world! He ended his homily with this prayer: "May the Lord of peace help you to be for your brothers and sisters – people of light, and authors of peace and reconciliation. People who can be builders of a more just and loving world. And what is our reward for being witnesses? Everyone who acknowledges me before others will be acknowledged by my Father."

13th Sunday "A" Matthew 10:37-42

The Pastor received a letter marked "Please give to Harry, the usher." It was handed over to Harry, and this is what it said: "Dear Harry, I am sorry I don't know your last name, but then you don't know mine either. I am Gert at the 10 o'clock mass every Sunday. I am writing to ask a favor. I don't know the Priests all that well, but somehow feel closer to you.

I don't know how you got to know my first name, but every Sunday morning you smile and greet me by name. We exchange a few words, how bad the weather is, how much you like my hat, or how I am late on a particular Sunday. I just wanted to say "thank you" for taking the time to remember an old lady, for the smiles, and for your thoughtfulness.

Now for the favor. I am dying, Harry. My husband has been dead for 16 years, and the kids are scattered. It is very important to me that when they bring me to the church for the last time that you will be there to greet me and say "Hello Gert, good to see you." If you're there, Harry, I'll feel assured that your warm hospitality will be duplicated in my new home in heaven. With love and gratitude, Gert."

Today's readings are about hospitality. In the ancient world hospitality was essential for survival. There were no malls, nor did 7-11s open all night, so travelers depended on the goodwill of others for food, shelter, and necessary supplies while traveling. Some people even believed that divine beings roamed the earth searching for examples of human kindness. In Hebrews (13:2) we read: "Do not neglect hospitality because you may unknowingly be entertaining angels."

Our 1st reading describes how the Shunemmite woman showed hospitality to Elisha, the Prophet; and for her act of kindness she was promised a son. This promise was not merely a gesture of gratitude from Elisha (as the reading says) – "The woman's husband was getting on in years." So, this son to be born would eventually care for her in her old age. She had provided for the prophet by giving him a place to stay on his journeys, and the prophet in turn provided for her future care.

We find the same theme in today's gospel. Jesus is instructing his followers (the early Christians) on the need for hospitality; but it is hospitality from a particular point of view.

The woman in the 1ˢᵗ reading opens her home to a Prophet, a "holy man of God." Jesus is talking about openhearted hospitality extended to the apostles as ministers of the gospel. As representatives of Jesus, he identifies himself with them so much so that he tells them that if someone receives you then they receive me also. The "little ones" Jesus mentions in the gospel are not the little children, but the,apostles, who are to be humble and unassuming as little children in receiving hospitality from others.

But, Jesus tells the apostles that following him will not be easy. They will have to make great personal sacrifices. They will have to be ready to sever close family ties if they are ever called to choose between Jesus and their own family. That is what it means when he tells them that whoever loves their parents more than they love him is not worthy of him and that whoever finds his life will lose it; and whoever loses his life for his sake will find it." What did Jesus mean by that? A story can help us understand.

The company threw a lavish dinner party to honor its CEO on his retirement. His rise to the top was amazing; his management of the company through good times and bad times was flawless. Everything he touched turned to gold. Through his tireless efforts he made himself the company's senior manager; and the stockholder's very wealthy people.

After dinner, the CEO addressed his remarks to the young up-and-coming executives: "I know each one of you wants my job –and I'll tell you how to get it. Last week my daughter was married –and as I walked her down the aisle I suddenly realized I didn't know the name of her best friend, the last book she read, or her favorite color. That is the price I paid for this job. And if you want to pay that price –you can have it."

Sometimes it takes a "stopping to smell the roses" moment to discover what we are missing in life; when amid our wealth and success we see how poor we really are! Jesus's words in today's gospel are echoed in the CEO's sad remarks to his young executives. We can sometimes become so absorbed with building a career that we fail to develop our full potential as human beings. We become so focused on "making a living" that we don't have a life "worth living."

Christ calls all who would be his disciples to "lose" the obsessive meaningless life, and petty pursuits, in order to "find" a life fully human and alive, filled with hope and joy!

14th Sunday "A" Matthew 11:25-30; Matthew 11: 16-19-25-30

Have you heard the story about the doctor who completed a man's examination, despite the constant chattering of the man's wife?

After the examination, he called the wife aside for a private talk. The doctor told her: "Your husband needs lots of peace and rest. Here are some sleeping pills." She asks: "How often should I give them to him?" The doctor replied: "The pills are for you – not for him."

In today's gospel, Jesus invites all who are weary, and find life burdensome, to be at peace and refreshed. Whatever are the burdens we bear, Jesus invites us to come to him for peace and rest. He tells us that his yoke and burden is easier and lighter than ours.

In Jesus' day a "yoke" was a wooden device that paired two oxen together and made them a team as they worked in the field together. So, in a sense, Jesus is inviting each one of us to become his "yoke-mate" so that joined together with him we will find our burdens much lighter, and our problems shared.

Jesus is telling us that the weariness of life, the fears or anxieties we may encounter in life need not drag us down, or overwhelm us, because Jesus is willing to shoulder our problems with us.

I don't think God ever intended people to "go it alone." We need someone to talk to, to share our secret fears, and anxieties with; someone to help us carry whatever it is that weights heavy on our hearts. Such a person could be a wise and trusted friend, a teacher, a relative, a neighbor, a counselor, or a spiritual advisor. And Jesus is saying he wants to be included in that select group of supporters!

In today's gospel, Jesus promises to "reveal" things that perhaps may be hidden from us. Things like a lack of awareness of the kingdom of God among us; or we may be carrying the heavy burden of some sin, or some anxiety about the future, or we may feel the weariness of searching for God, or for true happiness! But Jesus is the only one who has the power to free us from our burdens!

The "rest" that Jesus promises to give us is the love, the healing, and the peace of mind with God! Sometimes some so-called "religious" people portray God as a vengeful, condemning, spiteful God, needing to be appeased. But this is not the God Jesus has made known to use in the gospels!

Life is meant to be shared – not only with people, but also with God. If you think about it, that is the true meaning of prayer. Prayer is not just asking God to give us certain things; or asking God to get rid of our problems! No, prayer is the giving of ourselves and our problems over to God; and allowing God to come into our lives. Prayer is a mutual sharing between ourselves and God! We give our weakness to God and God, (in turn), gives us God's strength to help us carry our burdens.

Let me give you a good example. When Martin Luther King Jr. was leading the struggle for civil rights his burdens became so heavy he could hardly carry them. Friends and family feared he might break under the strain.

While making speeches and leading peaceful demonstrations everyday across the country his life was often threatened by anonymous letters or phone calls. But he never broke down under the tremendous strain.

He explained how he was able to carry such a heavy burden. One day in the quiet of his room, he prayed aloud and said something like this, Lord, I am here taking a stand, but I have come to the place where I cannot face it any longer alone. And somewhere (deep in the recesses of his heart) he heard an answer to his prayer: "Martin" (the voice seemed to say), "stand up for the truth – stand up for what you know is right. Don't worry, I am with you at your side." From that day forward King said that he would never know fear again.

When we find ourselves weighed down by life's burdens, Jesus' invitation and assurance is given to use: "Come to me all you who labor and are burdened, and I will give you rest! Take my yoke upon you, and learn from me; for I am meek and humble of heart; and you will find rest for yourselves! For my yoke is easy, and my burden is light." (Matthew 11:28-30)

15th Sunday "A" Matthew 13:1-23

A woman once had a strange dream. She dreamt she was shopping at the mall when she spotted a new store she had never seen before. It was called "Dreams-R-Us." She walked in, and much to her surprise God was working behind the counter!

She asked God: "What are you selling here?" "Everything your heart desires," God replied. It was incredible. She was actually talking with God; and God told her she could have anything she desired. "Well, (she said), I want lots of love; and happiness; and peace of mind. I want wisdom; and forgiveness; and freedom from fear." Then, almost as an afterthought she added: "Not just for me, but for everybody in the whole world."

God smiled and said: "I don't think you quite understand. We don't sell the finished product here – we only give away the seeds. You have to take the seeds of God's love and plant them wherever you go! Only then, will your dreams; and my dreams for the world, be fulfilled."

In today's gospel, Jesus tells the story about a farmer who went out to sow seeds in his field. But, not all the seeds would germinate, and grow. Some would be quickly eaten up by the birds. Some would fall on hard ground, or among thorns, which would eventually choke it. But some seeds would fall on "good soil" and would produce an unbelievable harvest – some 30 fold; some 50 fold; and some even 100 fold!

While Jesus was telling this story, he looked into his listeners' hearts. He knew that some of them already rejected him; and would walk away shaking their heads, thinking he couldn't possibly be the Messiah! Others would follow him for a while until they found someone else more interesting; or somebody else less demanding.

But, he also knew there would be some who would make a choice to follow him – a choice that would change their lives forever! They were the "good soil" upon whom his words would fall – and they would produce a rich harvest of goodness! The story he told was about them; and his story is also about us today!

Jesus is challenging us to make a decision; a choice to follow him. He is asking us what kind of disciples do we want to be. Shall we live productive, fruitful lives – allowing God's word to take root in our hearts; and thus allowing the Holy Spirit to produce a rich harvest of grace for ourselves, and others? Or, shall we live only for ourselves?

We never know when we are "good soil," and what the result might be. We leave all that up to God. The Lord just gives us God's seeds of love to plant!

The children to be baptized today will someday be asked to make a decision to be "good soil" – so that the word of God might take root in them; and produce an abundant harvest in their world. That is our prayer today.

16th Sunday "A" Matthew 13:24-43; Matthew 13:24-30, 36-43

The bottom line of the weeds and the wheat story Jesus told us is this: "Let both of them grow together until the harvest!" (Matthew 13:30)

We tend to divide the world unto two different kinds of opposites; either black and white; young and old; male and female; rich and poor; the insiders and outsiders; the strong and weak; heterosexual and homosexual; sacred and the secular; clergy and laity; winners and losers; wheat and weeds; "them" versus "us"; and "us" versus "them." And those whom we deem to be "the other" or "the opposite" automatically become "the enemy." And we know what happens when this kind of thinking pervades society – it often results in racism; sexism; anti-Semitism; ageism; and homophobia!

Today's parable challenges us to ask ourselves the question: "Who are the "them" of the "others" versus "us" in our society today? "Are they the Muslims; the Iraqis; the Iranians; democrats; republicans; progressive Catholics; conservative Catholics; the "good old boys"; or the feminists? (Just to name a few). Whoever "they" are; the parable of the weeds and wheat tells us: "Let both of them grow together, until harvest."

The unusual use of the parable of the weeds and wheat comes from the time of the Protestant Reformation. During the 16th century in Germany, (in both Catholic and Lutheran churches), paintings of this parable were a popular theme.

For example, in St. Mary's Lutheran church in the town of Wittenburg, (where Martin Luther lived and taught), there is a painting that interprets today's gospel. The scene is set in the middle of the night; and the Lutheran Reformers are fast asleep by the side of the field, (which represents the church).

The Pope and the other Catholic leaders are sowing weeds in the Lord's field! There was no doubt in their minds whom the "weed-planters" were!

But, in some other Catholic churches in Germany; artists have portrayed the Pope and Bishops asleep beside the field. Luther and the other Reformers are the enemy, (sneaking in late at night) to sow weeds in the Lord's field – (the church)! So, the parable can be seen both ways. The weeds and the wheat......Them and us......Us and them.

Hans Christian Anderson's story of the "Ugly Duckling" shows what can happen when we call the other people "weeds…" or when we exclude certain people. The Ugly Duckling's siblings said to their ugly brother: "If only the cat would get a hold of you – you're so hideous!" But, in time, however, the "ugly" duckling grew into maturity – and found acceptance as a majestic; graceful and beautiful swan!

In today's parable, when the slaves asked the farmer: "Do you want us to go and pull up the weeds?" The farmer replied: "No! If you pull up the weeds; you might uproot the wheat along with them! Let them both grow together until harvest time; then separate them." Good advice!

This parable invites us to look beyond our small perceptions of reality – and to embrace; and appreciate the "bigger" picture of life. God sees the whole picture! God's acceptance and generosity are beautifully brought out in today's gospel.

Just as the farmer was willing to wait for the harvest to separate the weeds from the wheat – so God gives each one of us the time to grow; to change; to be redeemed and transformed by God's grace – to become the person God intended us to be! Yes, God sees the "bigger picture"; and allows us the time to grow and reach our full potential! No one should be prevented from "growing" to "full maturity" until harvest time!

This list would include the "elderly" – even when their aging bodies make it difficult to get around; or their forgetfulness makes them "difficult" to care for. This includes the "ill" and "disabled" – even when their physical or mental disabilities may have "diminished" their quality of life!

This would include the "unborn" – whose chance to grow is denied them, because someone else is expressing their own "freedom of choice." Pope John Paul II expressed it this way: "Human life must be respected from its dawn to its natural sunset."

It also includes people who are in prison; or who are on "death row." People who are often "written off" as "unsaveable, because of their repeated or serious wrongdoings. Jesus seems to be saying in this parable – they are "redeemable"; they also need time, (with God's grace) to experience a conversion; to repent; and to be reconciled to God; to themselves; and to society.

The good news about this gospel is that a loving and forgiving God will be the final "harvester" – not us human beings! When the time comes for the Great Harvest at the end of the world – I am sure, some of those gathered into heaven will surprise us! And, (I suspect), we may be a big surprise to them, also!

Saint Peter – Saint Paul – Matthew 13:44-52; Matthew 13: 31-33, 44-52

Today, the church celebrates the two great saints – St. Peter and St. Paul. One was called to discipleship by the Sea of Galilee, and the other on the road to Damascus. One a blue collar fisherman and the other a learned scholar. Both were founding apostles of the church.

We celebrate them today as any country, corporation, or organization celebrates the people whose genius gave the vision, who supplied the witness and hard work to make a contribution. They both literally gave their lives to begin the church!

Here are some facts that you may not know: We know for sure that Peter and Paul did not establish the church in Rome. It was already there when they arrived; founded earlier by the other disciples of Jesus. But we know for sure that Peter and Paul later on went to Rome to preach the gospel. They both died there as martyrs – one crucified upside down, and the other beheaded. They gave their lives for the ONE who gave his life for them! Paul was buried beneath the church we today know as "St. Paul's outside the city of Rome," and Peter is buried under the St. Peter's Basilica in Rome.

Why do we celebrate the feast day of these two saints on June 29th? The early Christians chose that day because June 29th was already being celebrated as the day Rome was founded by Romulus and Remus. The message intended by choosing June 29th was that if Romulus and Remus had founded the Roman Empire – so also, St. Peter and St. Paul laid the foundation for a new spiritual empire to be known as the "Christian" church. Rome would be called the "Eternal City."

Here are some of the other things that we know about Peter and Paul: They were both flawed men whose names were changed – something that had deep meaning in those days. Changing one's name signified a dramatic conversion; a calling to a totally different vocation; an extreme make-over of character.

For example, Peter was weak and a sinner; something he admitted the first time he met Jesus. "Depart from me," he said, "for I am a sinful man, O Lord." But "Simon" was summoned by Christ to go beyond his weakness, and Simon was given a new name, "Peter" – the "rock," on which the church would be built. And "Saul" was summoned by Christ to go beyond his hatred as a persecutor of the church – to become "Paul," the apostle to the Gentiles.

Both men would become great saints, but not the stereotyped idea of what many people may have about saints, that they be perfect, flawless, and without any weakness. Peter was a good man, big hearted, and enthusiastic, who loved the Lord. But, he was also impetuous, hot-headed, inclined to act recklessly, and proud. Remember that extraordinary boast he made the night before Jesus died: "Even if all the others run away, I will not." Well, we know what happened to that boast – he ran away; and even denied three times knowing Christ, just a few hours later.

Then there is Paul. His greatness, his willingness to travel anywhere and endure anything for Christ is beyond question! But, his letters reveal he wasn't always the easiest guy to get along with. He was passionate and fiery, outspoken, touchy when people questioned or criticized him, and he openly argued with Peter about some polices he disagreed with. He had serious differences of opinion with his traveling companion and fellow preacher, Barnabas. They parted company, and as far as we know, never traveled together again.

Yes, Peter and Paul were great saints, but first of all they were human beings. And this is a good lesson for us.

Being human with human failings is not a drawback to holiness! On the contrary, being true to the nature God has given to us is the first ingredient in becoming holy. Being human, Peter and Paul had their weaknesses – they sometimes got scared, they argued, took offence. They were impatient and frustrated, and sometimes took the easy way out – just like us!

What was it then that made Peter and Paul saints? One word – Jesus! And how can we regain their vision of holiness? Again, one word – Jesus!

Peter put it this way: "Lord, to whom should we go? We have come to believe that you are the Christ, the Son of the living God…..Lord, you have the words of eternal life."

And Paul explained his holiness when he said: "It is no longer I that live – but Christ lives in me." And when he said: "I am determined to know nothing else, but only Jesus Christ, and him crucified." Jesus was the center of their lives!

So, today as we honor these two great saints, let us remember that Jesus also accepts us, and uses us as he did with them. He accepts us just as we are – a mixture of the good and not so good, of strengths and surprising weaknesses. It seemed to work with Peter and Paul. I know it can work for us as well.

17th Sunday "A" Matthew 14:13-21

A Catholic high school basketball team had just celebrated mass in preparation for their going to the state tournament. During the homily, the priest said that 10 years from now the important thing about their basketball season will not be whether they became state champs, or not. The important thing will be what they became in the process of trying to win the state title. Did they become better human beings during the course of the season? Did they become more caring, more loyal to one another, more committed? Did they grow as a team and as individuals?

After mass the priest was in the sacristy talking off his vestments when he heard the coach say to the players: "Sit down a moment. Father said something that made me think. I wonder what I have helped you become in the process of trying to put together a winning season. If you did become those things father talked about, then we are a success, regardless of what we do in the state tournament. But if not, then we have failed God, we have failed our school, and above all, we have failed ourselves."

In our gospel Jesus compares the kingdom of God to a search for fine pearls and a buried treasure found in a field. The pearl merchant and the lucky finder go and sell all they have and buy it. It's the most important thing in their lives. Jesus' point is this – nothing in this world should take priority over God's kingdom and our pursuit of it. Nothing!

What really counts when we come to the end of our lives is not what we have acquired, or what social status we have attained, or what great things we have done, or how well-known we are – but what we have become in the process of searching for the kingdom.

Most of us realize the important things in life and are not the going to school, or getting married and having a family, or becoming Catholic and being a member of a parish, or the career or job we have. No, the more important thing is what has happened to us along the way, in the process of doing these things. Am I a better person? Am I more loving, more unselfish, more compassionate and forgiving, more tolerant of others, more prayerful, because of these things?

So, Jesus tells us in the gospel, the kingdom of God is not the goal but what we have become in the process of searching for that kingdom. That is our goal in life. Like the priest who talked to the basketball team, we can ask ourselves: Are we becoming better human beings, more loving, more loyal to God and one another, and more committed as Christians? If we are, then the kingdom of God is truly at hand. In doing so, the kingdom of God not only comes alive in the world around us, it also comes alive within ourselves. The Kingdom of God is within you!

18ᵗʰ Sunday "A" Matthew 14:13-21

Today's gospel tells us how Jesus fed a hungry crowd on which he had taken pity. All through scriptures, God will not allow us to forget the starving people in the world. Six times in the gospels there are various accounts of Jesus feeding large groups of people.

In today's account, look at the actions Jesus used in handling the food: "Taking the 5 loaves and the 2 fish, and looking up to heaven he said the blessing, broke the loaves, and gave them to the disciples, who in turn gave them to the crowd." These are the actions and the language he used at the last supper institution of the Eucharist. Matthew is saying there is a connection between this miracle and the Eucharist.

Jesus is ministering to the crowd's physical needs, but he is also asking them for their faith in him at the same time. Everything Matthew is saying points to the fact that Jesus wants to give himself to us also, in the sacrament of the Eucharist.

But, notice the challenge he gives to the disciples: "There is no need for them to go, give them something to eat yourselves." (Matthew 14:16) His disciples shrug their shoulders and raise their hands in dismay: "But we have nothing here but 5 loaves and 2 fish." Yet, Jesus forges ahead. The disciples thought they were off the hook; given the size of the crowd (20,000) in relation to the meager amount of food they had. But, Jesus put them back on the hook! He involves the disciples in the distribution of the food he blessed; and in the clean-up of the leftovers!

Is there a lesson here for us today? Yes! It means that if we want to be disciples of Jesus, we also must be willing to feed our hungry world by responding to his command to give them something to eat ourselves.

According to the stats compiled in 2008 by the Bread For The World Institute; 854 million people out of the entire world population of 6.55

billion are hungry. As a result, almost 16,000 children die from hunger, (or from hunger-related causes) every day. That is one child dies every 5 seconds somewhere in the world!

With our eyes fixed on these alarming facts, and our ears attuned to the word of God, we are compelled to act quickly and decisively. Apathy toward the hunger of another person by simply raising our hands in dismay; or foisting the responsibility for the world hunger on the shoulders of others is not permissible! And prayer alone is not enough if it is merely "wishes" another well, but does nothing to translate our good "wishes" into food.

The issues of global hunger are so overwhelming that it is hard to know where to begin, or what to do. We may be just as doubtful as the disciples were; but the gospel proclaims that God can, and will, accomplish miracles – even though our efforts are meager and limited.

Here is what one man did: In the 1930s a short Italian immigrant with the nickname of "the Little Flower," was the mayor of New York City. His name was Fiorello LaGuardia. He was an inspirational leader riding on fire trucks with those who served the city's safety.

As a young boy growing up in Tacoma, Washington, I even remember hearing that during the newspaper strike he read the funnies to the children over the radio every Sunday. He also befriended many orphans – taking them to the Yankee baseball games, when he could.

One night, at the height of the "Great Depression" in 1935, he went to one of the poorest areas of the city. He entered the courthouse and gave the judge the night off. He took over as judge and listened to the first case of the evening.

An elderly woman was accused of stealing a loaf of bread. She admitted her crime. "Yes, I did steal the bread," she said, "to feed my grandchildren. Their father had run off, and their mother was sick. They were hungry and I had no money to buy food for them."

The mayor appealed to the store owner for mercy; but he refused. He said it would lead to a reputation of leniency, it would encourage others to shoplift, and it would ruin him in the neighborhood.

Judge LaGuardia knew the store owner was probably right. The fine was $10.00 or 10 days in jail. So, he imposed the $10.00 fine. Then he took off his hat, put the $10.00 in it, and said: "I am fining everyone on this courtroom here tonight 50 cents.......for living in a city that forces a grandmother to steal a loaf of bread to keep her grandchildren from starving!"

So, the hat was passed around to all, including the red-faced store owner. $49.50 was collected from the petty criminals, the police, attorneys, and the reporters, and it was given to the grandmother. Then everyone gave the mayor a standing ovation.

Is this not the same kind of miraculous behavior to which we are all called to do? As Jesus told his disciples, so he tells us again to give them something to eat ourselves.

May Christ give us the grace, the courage to carry on the same mission. Jesus feeds us with his own Body and Blood in the Eucharist at every mass we attend; that we might go out into the world to help feed others.

19th Sunday "A" Matthew 14:22-33

In the gospel according to Charlie Brown; the parables of the Peanuts' book contains a cartoon story in which Linus and Lucy are watching an infant crawling across the floor: "How long do you think it will be before Sally starts to walk?" Linus asks. "Good grief! says Lucy, "What's the hurry? Let her crawl around for a while... don't rush her – she has got all the time in the world."

Lucy stops to reflect for a moment....then she says: "Once you stand up and start to walk – you are committed for life."

In today's gospel, Jesus wants Peter to stop "crawling around" with his faith. Jesus wants Peter to stand up in faith and start to walk. Jesus wants him to be fully committed to Him in faith – for life.

Peter watched intently as Jesus walked across the stormy water. Peter shouts out to Jesus: "Lord, if it is really you, tell me to come to you on the water." Faith was beginning to stir in Simon (Peter). He was starting to believe that he could do the things Jesus called him to do. He was even willing to do the impossible – to step out of the boat and walk on water! All Jesus said was "come" and Peter took the first step.

To his surprise he did not sink. He was actually walking on water! He took another step. It was the moment of triumph. It was a victory of faith. Peter, perhaps for the first time, began to realize that faith involves venturing out and doing things he had never dreamed of doing; trusting that God will take care of him. Faith is not simply a "passive" trusting that God will come to us when we are down and out. No. Faith is an "active" process of living a full vital life – going places we would never go; loving people we would never love; living life to the fullest because we have met the Lord, in faith.

There are times when our effort to do the right thing or do a good job seems as difficult and frustrating as trying to walk on water.

For example, trying to be a good father or mother or trying to get parents to understand; trying not to hold a grudge; trying to cope with the "system"; trying to kick some awful habit; by not taking that first drink or smoking that first cigarette; or trying to stick to that low-fat diet; trying to come to terms with the terrible loneliness and grief that follows the loss of a loved one. It is almost like trying to walk on water! You feel nothing solid underfoot. You have the terrible feeling of being sucked down into the darkness below.

I think Peter experienced that same feeling as he began walking toward Jesus on the water. Because he took his eyes off Jesus, and began to concentrate on how strong the wind was, and how dangerous the situation was, he began to sink. Truly frightened now he cries out: "Lord, save me!" And Jesus stretched out his hand and caught him saying: "Man of little faith, why did you doubt?"(Matthew 14:31)

Several years ago I remember talking to a man who was attracted to the gospels, and who had been coming to church for several months. I asked him if he was interested in joining the RCIA and perhaps eventually being baptized. He said his whole experience of the church had been like climbing up on a train and asking the conductor: "How much?" And he heard the conductor say to him: "Your life." "When I heard that I got scared." The man said: "So I went and hid in the caboose, and I have been hiding there ever since." Well, he did decide to come out of the caboose and was baptized the following Easter.

When Jesus invited Peter to walk on the water, he was calling him out of the caboose where it was safe and secure, but Peter became convinced, in the middle of his walk, that Jesus had asked the impossible. I think that is what most of us feel when Jesus calls us out of the caboose, and into the ministry of being a baptized Christian. We feel like "mission impossible." We feel like we are in over our head. But when we begin to falter and lose faith, there is Jesus reaching out to save us and to calm the waters.

Jesus always comes to us in our hour of need. He invites us to step out in faith, trusting Him. If we just keep our eyes fixed on Him – he will never, never let us down!

Like Lucy says: "Once you stand up and start to walk – you are committed for life."

20ᵗʰ Sunday "A" – Matthew 15:21-28

Religion spends a lot of time defining boundaries: Who belongs and who doesn't; who conforms, and who doesn't; who is like us, and who isn't; who can receive Communion, and who can't; who is going to heaven, and who isn't.

But religion must also be universal and inclusive, journeying across limits and boundaries and encouraging the "outsider." As the New Testament writings show, Christianity came to be by constantly reaching out to wider and wider circles – beyond its Jerusalem base. Faith grows and expands as it meets the new and different.

Today's gospel describes how Jesus and his disciples dealt with such an "outsider," a non-Jewish, pagan woman who begged Jesus to cure her daughter tormented by a demon.

In the popular musical, "My Fair Lady," Professor Henry Higgins speaks a song that offers a commentary on today's gospel story of Jesus and the Canaanite woman. The song is: "Let a woman in your life." "Let a woman in your life and your serenity is through. She will redecorate your home from cellar to dome, and then go to the enthralling fun of overhauling you!" In the song, Henry Higgins claims to be "an ordinary man of no eccentric whim…..just an ordinary man."

The woman he lets in his life, however, is the extraordinary Liza Doolittle; an uneducated flower girl whom he teaches to speak proper English, and act like a proper lady. But in the process of "overhauling" Liza, the professor himself is "overhauled."

In today's gospel Jesus and his disciples are presented as typical "ordinary" males of their day, who grew up with a sense of prejudice against all non-Jews. The Canaanites had occupied the land before the Jews invaded and took control of it. So, they were considered public enemy number one!

Knowing this background helps us to understand the harsh responses Jesus makes to the Canaanite woman's plea for him to cure her daughter. First, Jesus gives her the silent treatment; he totally ignores her; not even answering her. Then, he reminds his disciples that he was sent only to the "lost sheep of the House of Israel." His mission was to Jews first, not to the gentiles – that would come much later. Finally, he replies to the woman's plea with a racial slur. He refers to her and her people as "dogs" – the ordinary term by which Jews referred to all non-Jews.

But the Canaanite woman, like Liza Doolittle, is feisty and determined not to take "no" for an answer. She made up her mind to "overhaul" the engrained hostility of Jews to non-Jews, and she was determined that Jesus would heal her daughter!

It was then that Jesus said to her with a smile and twinkle in his eye: "It is not fair to take the childrens food and throw it to the house dogs."("dogs" meaning non-Jews). (Matthew 15:27)

The Canaanite woman counters with a witty response: "Come on, Lord, even the dogs get the scraps from your table." Jesus immediately saw the truth and honesty of the woman's comment and replied: "Woman, great is your faith." Jesus makes an exception to his policy of ministering only to Jews; and heals her daughter. He is impressed by her love for her daughter, and her faith in him!" Her persistence paid off.

This gospel asks the question: Who are the contemporary Canaanites in our society? Are they people in our community or parish, in our work places and schools whom we would like to "send away?"

As the disciples wanted the Canaanite woman to be sent way, are we really convinced that there is no race, no culture, no gender, and no religion that has a monopoly on God?

Our former Pope John Paul II reached out in love and dialogue to Christian and non-Christian religions. He was the first modern head of the Catholic Church to visit a mosque, to pray at the Temple Wall in Jerusalem, and attempted to reopen dialogue with the Orthodox tradition.

One of the most profound contributions to his Papacy has been seeking to heal the ancient wounds between Christianity and Judaism.

It remains to be seen what will be done with his dream of reconciliation; and whether we will make it to Isaiah's "holy mountain" to offer our sacrifice of praise together.

Prayer for "all people" seems very, very far away, but we must be persistent like the Canaanite woman and keep asking for a miracle!

In a few minutes we will receive the Eucharist. Jesus comes to crumble the walls of prejudice in our hearts. He comes to build bridges of love and service to all people. When we let Jesus come into our lives, he comes to "overhaul" us to heal us - and to refresh and renew us.

21st Sunday "A" Matthew 16:13-20

"You are the Messiah, the Son of the living God," was Peter's answer to Jesus' question: "Who do you say that I am?" And Jesus' response to Peter identified who Peter was: "Blessed are you Simon, son of Jonah; for you are Peter, and upon this rock I will build my church, I will give to you the keys to the Kingdom of Heaven." (Matthew 16:17-19)

Peter was an important and vital figure in the early church. Yet, the scriptures record some rather negative things about him. He had a dark side. At times he was impetuous, insensitive, hot-headed, and undependable, and one who would eventually deny even knowing Jesus 3 times, publically!

But that denial would be the turning point in his life. It was then that Peter honestly asked himself the question: "Who am I?" He realized what he had done, and was sorry. He realized he was a much better person than his 3 denials. And he realized that Jesus was, indeed, the Son of God, and his friend, who loved him very much!

Peter Marshall, in a famous sermon, spoke of St. Peter as "the rock that moved"; as a "shaky foundation" and as an "unsteady base" for the future building of the church."

But by contrast, in today's gospel, Peter is courageous, confident, and competent. But God apparently uses flawed, sinful people to build up the kingdom of God, and to proclaim the gospel.

What is the lesson for us? Obviously, it's important for us also to profess our own faith in Jesus as "the Son of the living God." And, we who profess that faith, are also "blessed" by God, because we are called to continue the work of Christ –as Peter was called in his day. The story of peter forces us to realize how the most unlikely people can teach us; and can touch us with the power of God! We may be surprised at the various ways God speaks to us today.

Peter's story of his conversion reminds us that Christ's friendship does indeed change us. We can't remain the same after being in his company. Peter changed drastically... and so must we!

God loves us in spite of all our faults and failures. The message is clear that God's love is unconditional even for those who believe themselves to be too "broken" to be mended.

A priest friend of mine thinks we should have two kinds of reconciliation rooms side-by-side. The one on the left should be for penitents to confess their sins, and the "penance" always given would be to go to the other reconciliation room immediately and there to confess honestly all the good things they have done; and confess the signs of God's love and presence within themselves.

The reason for that (my priest friend says), is that God always looks at us as we are already, the people God wants us to be; and as the people we might someday become! That is the way Jesus treated Peter. He looked beyond his failures and human weaknesses, and saw his great potential for goodness. In fact, to make up for his 3 denials, Peter was asked the same question three times. That question was if Peter loved Jesus and the answer was yes all three times by Peter. That was good enough for Jesus.

Every day for years a man visited his wife in the care center. She suffered from Alzheimer's disease. Each day she seemed to get a little more forgetful. Every day he would feed her lunch. He would sit with her and show her pictures of their children; telling her the latest family news and stories; which she would forget as soon as she heard them.

He would patiently remind her who he was, that they were married 52 years, they had 2 daughters and a son, and 5 beautiful grandchildren. Before leaving he would give her a kiss and tell her how much he loved her. But she would never realize, or remember later, that he had even been there.

Some of his "well-meaning" friends would ask him: "Why do you keep going when – when she doesn't even know who you are?" And he would always answer them by saying: "I go because I know who I am!"

This man came to realize who Jesus was, and accepted the true meaning of the gospels; and in the process, came to understand who he was, and what gave meaning to his own life.

So, today Jesus is asking us: "Who do you say I am?" Yes, who is Jesus to us? He is the clearest picture of God that we have ever seen! He is also a picture of you and me – the person God intends us to be, and by God's grace, the person we will someday become!

22nd Sunday "A" Matthew 16:21-27

Since this is the Labor Day weekend, and school is beginning again, I have been thinking about my first day of school.

For many of us that first day was probably one that we would like to forget. Very likely, it was a day of much anxiety, if not downright fear. When I was growing up my family rented a house owned by the parish, just across the alley from St. Patrick's grade school in Tacoma. Even though my twin brother and I lived so close to the school, we were scared to death of the first day. There we were in first grade; torn from the security of our home; wrenched from the reassuring presence of our parents and family; and thrown into a room full of strangers with one towering nun (Sister Alma) who kindly, but very firmly, told us when to sit and when to stand; when to talk; when to eat; and when to go to the bathroom! We could hardly wait for 3 o'clock when we could tell mom we were NOT going back to school! But, of course, we did.

If we think we had a terrible time that first day of school, let's consider the trouble St. Peter had. For the sake of this homily, let's pretend that today's gospel is a school scene...Jesus is the teacher...his disciples are his students.

Jesus starts his first lesson by talking about the tough, terrible, and traumatic times he is about to experience. Far worse than having to go to school; Jesus has to go to Jerusalem, the capital city of his country. There he will "suffer greatly...to be put to death, and raised up on the third day." And we thought we had problems!

Now, Peter, the student, does not like this kind of tough talk, so Peter proceeds to disagree with Jesus, hoping that his teacher will talk about good and happy things – like power, prestige, victory, and glory. He didn't want to hear about suffering and death, or taking up the cross.

But Jesus is not about to change his lesson plan. So what does Jesus do? He promptly throws Peter out of the class! Jesus tells Peter: "Get out of my sight you Satan!" (A small "s" meaning an adversary or opponent). So, Peter has to leave the classroom. How is that for a first day of school experience? We can be sure Peter never forgot that day.

To make sure that his students did not forget the first lesson, Jesus continues to teach them, and us, our spiritual ABCs. "A" stands for "after" as in "come after me." "B" stands for "begin," as in "begin to follow in my footsteps." And "C' stands for "cross," and "carry" as in carrying our cross as we follow Jesus, our teacher. Jesus wants his students (and that includes all of us here today) to learn this primary lesson, namely, that we are enrolled in the original "school of hard knocks!" Following Jesus often means sacrifice, suffering, ridicule, rejection….perhaps even death."

Suffering and the cross are part of life. We can't avoid it. We can't deny it. The cross takes on meaning only when we are willing to carry it in union with Jesus…..then our cross becomes a prayer – then it becomes redemptive – and salvific!

So, as we begin another school year, and as we celebrate another Labor Day, let's resolve to renew and continue our love of learning about the Lord of life! Jesus is our teacher….the parish is our school….and we are the students; ready, willing, and eager to get back to our classes for another year!

23rd Sunday "A" Matthew 18:15-20

According to an old Chinese story, a wise teacher asked his students to identify the most satisfying thing in life. There were many good answers given such as: "Having a happy marriage," "making lots of money, having "good health," and "close friends." But the teacher said they all failed to give the correct answer. "The most satisfying thing in life," he said, "is to see a child confidently walk down the road on his or her own, after you have shown the child the way to go."

Today's gospel reminds us that we are responsible to each other and for each other; to help each other do what is right. I am my brother's and sister's keeper. What I do affects the lives of others for good, or for evil. No man or woman is an island; and we don't go to heaven alone….we always take someone with us.

As Christians we must be different; if not, we won't make a difference. If we don't make a difference, the people around us will remain unchanged; the world will remain the same old place; and the gospel will go un-preached. There are some people in my life who have made a difference for me. 1) I remember when I was in first grade we had a test to write the numbers 1 to 100. After #10 I got confused. I was sitting in the back of the class next to my twin brother. He was stuck too. So I snuck a book out of my desk and began copying the numbers page by page. I was doing just great when all of a sudden Sister Alma was standing behind me glaring. Nuns must take glaring classes. She was looking right through me! She simply closed the book I was using and quietly said: "George, I am really disappointed in you! I expected better things from you. I expected you to be honest." I never did that again. That little incident taught me a lesson that stayed with me for life. (Of course, I also had to write 'I will not cheat' 100 times)! 2) Another time that someone made a difference was when I was in college in the seminary.

That summer I was working in the CYO summer camp (Camp Don Bosco) driving the supply truck and running "Chaplin's Hour," a religion class for the kids at camp. I was seriously thinking of leaving the seminary because some of the professors thought I did not have a vocation – my self-image was not so good. I felt unwanted and depressed. I had a hard time making a decision. The camp director was Gordie Hamilton. He must have heard what was going on. While driving one day with him he asked me if he could give me some advice. He told me he thought I should return to the seminary. He had observed me all summer, and thought I had some real good qualities and talents that I could use in the priesthood; he also told me I was too lazy, and too easy-going; I needed to grow up and mature; and be more positive about myself!

That little talk really helped me decide to return to the seminary. Someone believed in me, and took the time to encourage my vocation, and be honest with me.

Who are the people in our lives who need our prayers; our example of faith lived out in our Christian values; our support, and encouragement? "All that is needed for evil to prosper," said Edmond Burke, "is for good people to remain silent."

Who are the ones we can put on the right road and show which way to go? We can make a difference!

Remember, we are not along in our endeavor – Christ is with us helping us to love each, and be reconciled. But we often fail to recognize his presence.

Jesus reminds us in today's gospel that if two or three are gathered together in His name, then He is in their midst.

Jesus is present in this Eucharist as we gather here in his name. He is present in all of our relationships; whether in our family, our neighborhood, or at work. He is present in the good times; and the not so good times; in times of peace, and in times of conflict, and disagreement. Be aware of him! Invite him into your life; into your marriage, and family life!

Karl Barth, the famous Lutheran theologian, tells a great story about himself. He was on a streetcar in Basel, Switzerland. A tourist climbed on board and sat next to him. The two men began chatting. "Are you new in the city?" "Yes," said the tourist…

Barth: "Is there anything you would especially like to see?"

Tourist: "Yes….I would really like to meet the famous theologian, Karl Barth."

Barth: "Well, as a matter of fact, I gave him a shave this morning." This delighted the tourist, and he went back to his hotel saying to himself: "Imagine that! I met Karl Barth's barber this morning!"

We sometimes treat Jesus the same way. Christ dwells among us; and within us – in all of us. But how often we sit next to one another; eat with each other; sing with another; pray with another; or work with another, and fail to see in each person the delightful presence of the living Christ!

Our Prayer is "Lord, help me to recognize the presence of Jesus in all of my relationships. Give me the grace to show others the road leading to you."

And that is the most satisfying thing in life!

24th Sunday "A" Matthew 18:21-35

Today is the 10th anniversary of the tragedy that has become known as 9/11. The air is still full of sadness and remembering. Special memorials will be held; and people will visit the World Trade Center site; the Pentagon; and the field in Pennsylvania. We will remember the heroes of that day; and once again tell their stories; for there is healing in the retelling, and in the allowing the sadness to speak!

But amid all the anguish; and despite the anger and feelings of revenge, the church challenges us today to have forgiveness "in our hearts" even for those who attacked us!

Some may be inclined to rule out any forgiveness; citing the enormity of the offense; and the lack of remorse on the part of its perpetrators! Others may still be overwhelmed by grief that finds a certain comfort in a desire for revenge. Nevertheless, forgiveness "from the heart" is the message of today's readings.

The book of Sirach counsels us against anger and vengeance. It is our willingness to forgive others that opens us to the healing forgiveness of God. "Wrath and anger are hateful things…the vengeful will suffer the Lord's vengeance. Forgive your neighbor's injustice that our own sins will be forgiven."

In the gospel, Jesus is approached by Peter with a very generous offer: "Lord, how often must I forgive someone who has sinned against me? As many as seven times?" Jesus explains to him that not only should you forgive 7 times but 77 times 7. In other words, there is no limit to your forgiveness! Forgive as often as you are offended!

In the parable he tells, Jesus' point becomes very clear. We who are sinners have been forgiven a huge and unpayable debt like the servant in the story. We have been forgiven time and time again by God! Having been forgiven so much ourselves, how can we behave less generously toward one another?

But words are just words; and translating our words into actions remains a constant challenge for us. To whom shall we all look for inspiration? It is believed that Mahatma Gandhi, (a Hindu), once said that if you take an eye for an eye then the whole world goes blind! When this holy man was shot 3 times by an assassin, he is reported to have raised his hands in a gesture of forgiveness. His last words before he died were spoken to his assassin: "I forgive you - I love you - I bless you!"

Likewise, the young Jewish girl, Anne Frank, although her death in a Nazi concentration camp at the age of 15 was preceded by years of hiding, often near starvation and daily in fear of being discovered – she nevertheless (without a hint of vengeance) wrote in her diary to keep her ideals because, (in spite of everything), she still believed that people were good at heart.

Nearer to our times, the actions of Lawrence Jenco are also a witness to the possibilities of forgiveness. Jenco was held hostage in Lebanon for 14 months; during which time he was kept in isolation, beaten, starved, humiliated, chained to a wall, and threatened almost daily with death!

He wrote a book about his ordeal called "Bound to Forgive" (Ave Maria Press, Notre Dame, Ind – 1995). He wrote the book because he himself was a forgiven Christian; so he felt he had no other option than to forgive his captors. His faith and his personal relationship with Jesus demanded it!

Today, the scripture readings remind us that we can do no less! Our faith and our relationship with Jesus, who died on the cross for the forgiveness of our sins, permit us no other option then to forgive.

Like Gandhi, Anne Frank, Jenco, and Jesus, we are to forgive without holding a grudge; without hatred or revenge; without deciding on the worthiness or unworthiness of the one forgiven.

As we are forgiven, so must we forgive – fully, freely, and "from the heart." Only then will the grief and bitter suffering of this anniversary of 911, be transformed by the fresh air of forgiveness!

Two former survivors of a Nazi concentration camp met years after their ordeal: "Have you forgiven the Nazi's?" one asked the other. "Yes, I have," he replied to the other. "Well, I haven't, and never will!" replied the other." "I'm still consumed with hatred for them!"

"In that case," his friend gently said; "they still hold you in prison!" In today's gospel, Jesus is trying to tell us that those who refuse to forgive others build their own prison, where they are held captive by their own hatred, and bitterness. But those who are willing to forgive others, (because God has so often forgiven them), are set free to be the "ambassadors" of God's love, and reconciliation in the world!

25th Sunday "A" Matthew 20:1-16

If this parable puzzles us, at least we have been warned by Isaiah in our first reading that says Gods thought are not our thoughts and your ways are not my ways.

So, when we hear this parable we cry out: "This is not fair!" But parables are told to make a point –and the point here is that salvation is God's total, free gift. It's something we have to earn.

This parable has nothing to do with just wages, union contracts, or affirmative action. The landlord was generous on several levels, with different workers. With the first group he hired he was just! With the second group he was just, and generous. And with the third group he was just plain generous. People can demand justice, but not generosity; because generosity is a totally, free gift!

The parable bothers us because we feel "it's just not fair!" Perhaps it takes us back to our childhood days when our brothers and sisters seemed to get a bigger piece of cake, or a nicer bike, better grades, or more love and attention. Or it reminds us of those times we weren't picked to be on a team; or not chosen by a teacher or boss for some honor. "It's just not fair!" We say.

It reminds me of the story about the cab driver and a priest who arrived at the "pearly gates" at the same time.

Paddy, the cab driver, was driven to a large, beautiful mansion for his home. And the priest, Father Kelly, was dropped off at a small, run-down, one bedroom, condo. Father Kelly complained to St. Peter: "It's just not fair! I preached hundreds of sermons to God's people!" St. Peter explained: "Yes, but, Father Kelly when you preached, people slept! But, when Paddy drove them in his cab, people prayed!"

The key to today's parable is found in the first sentence – "The kingdom of heaven is like……." This is not about economics, politics, money, or labor relations. The parable ends with the conclusion: "The last will be first – and the first will be last."

When Matthew wrote this parable in the early church – there was a feeling of distinction between those who had followed Jesus from the very beginning; and those who were "recent" converts. But, Matthew was telling the community of believers that there should be no distinction between the "early" and the "later" converts.

Some of the faithful thought that somehow religion was a matter of a reward; or something that had to be earned by them. But, Jesus is telling them "NO!" Religion is a free gift given by God to various people –at different times.

Perhaps a modern day example can help us understand. Here, in our own country we live in a land rich with immigrants and descendants of immigrants; but the idea still exists that those who are "new" somehow don't fully belong. After all, we were here first! So, some resent the "new" immigrants as "outsiders" as taking our jobs away. They don't "deserve" the same rights and benefits we "old-timers" have taken for granted, and have "earned" over the years.

The kingdom of God is not a matter of reward, but a matter of rejoicing in the fact that all people are invited into God's kingdom – the first as well as the last; the faithful as well as the sinner; the old-timers as well as the newcomers!

Jesus told the "good" people of his day (those people like us), that their faith cannot be measured by their own human ways of thinking; but by God's way of thinking.

God is more generous, more loving, and more forgiving then our limited human minds could ever imagine. God will not be outdone in generosity!

Like the landlord in today's gospel, God's generosity is available to all of us, all of the time; at the beginning of the day – at the middle of the afternoon – and even at quitting time. That's the good news!

And no matter what sort of a mess we have gotten ourselves into that day; God's invitation will keep coming to us: "You, too, come into my vineyard." And we know we can count on the generosity of our loving God!

26th Sunday "A" Matthew 21:28-32; Matthew 21:23-32

The original meaning of today's parable is clear. The first son stands for the tax collectors and sinners in Jesus' day. Their lives seemed to be a refusal to have anything to do with God, but then (when Jesus came along), they listened to him; they repented, and changed their lives.

The second son stands for the Scribes, and the Pharisees, (the religious leaders of the day). They considered themselves to be holy and saved, because of their superior knowledge, and their love of God.

Proof of their holiness came from their claim they kept all 1,300 laws of Moses, perfectly. Yet, when Jesus (the Son of God) came, they refused to have anything to do with Him! They totally rejected Him, and (in the end), they would even crucify Him!

But, (in a practical way), what meaning does this parable have for us today? Both sons in the parable are us. One son promising his father to do good, but (in the end) not doing it. The other son, (at first), refusing to obey his father…..but then he changes his mind and decides to obey his father's request to go work in his vineyard. This parable is about us.

That is how we often act with God. We go through life experiencing exactly what these two sons experienced. It is a universal condition, (the psychologist William James) once described as "the divided self" condition.

For example, most of us find it difficult to "always" be good – to "always" do the right thing. So, we shouldn't be surprised that our "doing good" is not always constant – not always steady – and is not unwavering. We often feel like we are in a kind of spiritual "tug-of-war" with ourselves; being pulled this way and that way by contrary attractions. Life, therefore, becomes a struggle for us. We have to decide what is right and what is wrong; between what is better and is the best thing to do; or trying to figure out what is the lesser of two evils. And sometimes our decisions are made on the "spur" of the moment without enough thought, or reflection.

The typical spiritual journey of a soul toward God is usually not a direct, constant, straight like, always propelling us toward God – like a rocket. No! It is rather like a series of zig-zags; constantly being on and off course; following one tendency for a while, but then changing course when another tendency takes over.

St. Augustine gives us the classic picture of the wandering soul, when he wrote: "Oh Lord, you have made us for yourself! And our hearts are restless until they rest in you! Lord, you are the beauty, so ancient, and yet so new…." (Then he sadly admits): "Lord, I have loved you too late!" Seeing the experience of such a great saint as Augustine – we should not be too surprised at our own inconsistent and wavering love of God. (I guess that is one reason why Jesus gave us the sacrament of confession!) To help us to be more steady.

Today's parable is about a son who said "no" to his father, but then changed his mind and said "yes." That is the pattern of my own spiritual journey; trying to change my "no's" to God into "yes's."

There are plenty of examples of "no" to "yes" in conversions or transformations in the gospels. For example: In the parable of the Prodigal Son, his habitual "no's" to his father became a definite "yes" as he turned back to God!

Peter denied even knowing his best friend, Jesus three times, but then later on repented with a definite "YES" "I love you" - for the rest of his life!

And the doubting Thomas went from the "no" of doubt, to the "yes" of belief in Jesus' resurrection, (in his famous act of faith), when he humbly professed: "My Lord, and my God!"

The point of these stories, for me, is that even the worst "no's" in my life to God can become one, big, glorious "YES" to God – as long as I don't give up the struggle; and I am willing to accept the grace of God's love and mercy.

In today's parable, the father said to both sons: "Go, and work in my vineyard today." The question we have to ask ourselves is: Are WE ready to go out and work in God's vineyard, and put our "yes" into action today, and every day?

27th Sunday "A"

In today's gospel, Jesus tells a story about a wealth landowner, who planted a huge vineyard, which he leased out to some tenant farmers to take care of! Then, at harvest time, the landowner and the tenant farmers would together share in a successful, rich harvest.

Does this story have any meaning for us today? Yes…the wealthy "landowner" is God the Father; the "son" of the landowner is Jesus; the "vineyard" is the Kingdome of God planted here on earth; and we, today, are the "tenant farmers" invited to work in God's vineyard, the church. God expects a rich, spiritual harvest in return from our efforts!

Once we are united to Christ through our baptism and the other sacraments, we are able to become "little vineyards" of the Lord ourselves… able to produce a rich harvest of grace. Jesus once told us, "I am the vine, and you are the branches, bearing much fruit."

God has done great things in our lives, but God also expects something in return. We OWE God a debt of gratitude for God's blessings and gifts! What are some of the things God expects in return from us?

I think the Lord also expects husbands and wives to love each other, and to treat each other with respect, and that they are good examples of faith for their children.

I think the Lord expects that we work together to help remedy some of the social injustices of our time, and that we pray for and work for true peace in our family, in our church, and in our community!

I also think the Lord expects that children and young people listen to their parents, and that they respect the rights and property of others!

I think the God expects men and women to value one another as their equals, and that men and women see each other as brothers and sisters in the Lord!

These are just a few examples of the type of the work God expects of us as "tenant farmers" in the Lord's vineyard here on earth. In today's second reading (Phil. 2:11), St. Paul gives us some more sound advice of how to act: "Brothers and sisters, your thoughts should be wholly directed to all that is true, all that deserves respect, all that is honest, pure, admirable, decent, virtuous or worthy of praise." Then, he ends by saying: "Live according to what you have learned and accepted"!

Over the past year in his homilies and speeches, Pope Francis often described what it means to be a true Christian today! I thought I would share with you some of his quotes over the last year:

On one occasion, he explained that a true Christian is someone who finds that their joy is not born of having many possessions, but their joy is born in having encountered a real person – Jesus – in a personal way!

On another occasion, he described Jesus as a "roped guide climbing a mountain, who, on reaching the summit, pulls us up to Himself and leads us to God, our Father!

Another time, he said that being a Christian is not just about obeying the laws, but it also means being in Christ, living in Christ, thinking like Him and loving like him! True freedom is living in Christ.

Another time he wrote that you shouldn't be afraid of being a Christian and living as a Christian! Have the courage to proclaim the Risen Christ, who has given you His peach and forgiveness by His death on the cross and by His resurrection!

To some young people, he said that they should pay attention! He told them to go against the current and swim against the tide! We Christians were not chosen by the Lord to do little things, but to do bigger, more noble things with our lives!

In a sense, these quotes from Pope Francis are a good "job" description for all of us today, who are invited to work in the Lord's vineyard – the church!

What reward or what payment can we expect from working in the Lord's vineyard? In the second reading (Phil. 4:6-9), Paul tells us if we work at being good Christians, by our prayers, and by doing good to others, we will have "no anxiety, and God's peace will be with us."

A few years ago, someone gave me a plaque which I have hung in my kitchen. It reminds me of what I can look forward to. It says "working in the Lord's vineyard doesn't pay much, but he retirement plan is out of this world!"

The one lesson I learned from this parable of Jesus is that our God is a generous God – a God who will never be outdone in generosity!

28th Sunday "A" Matthew 22:1-14

I can remember one time in my life when I wasn't dressed properly. Like the man in today's gospel who was invited to the wedding reception. It happened when I was a young priest, and when Archbishop Connolly was in charge. He was very strict about certain rules, and regulations. One of his rules was that the priests should always wear their clerical clothes; i.e., black suit and shoes, the Roman collar, and black hat, wherever they went.

On one occasion all the priests were at the seminary for a retreat. Of course, we all wore our clerical garb. The retreat ended on Friday after lunch. I decided I would play golf on the way back to the rectory; so I put on my golfing clothes and left by the rear entrance thinking I could sneak out undetected! Well, our course, I ran right into Archbishop Connolly! "Where are you going dressed like that"? He demanded. "I am on my way to the golf course to play golf." I explained. "You know the rule about wearing your clericals," (he persisted). "Now go back to your room and change into your proper clothes! You can change into your golf clothes at the golf course." "Yes, Archbishop" I obediently responded! I then waited a few minutes until he got into his car and was driven away, then I left for the golf course without my clerics.

In today's gospel story, Jesus compares the kingdom of heaven to a wedding banquet filled with music; dancing; good food and drinks; laughter and fun with family and friends. He seems to be saying that the kingdom of heaven is also filled with happiness, joy, and celebration! It's a place we want to be with our family and friends! Heaven is not a somber, serious, boring place where we "have to go, or else."

All people in the entire world are invited and welcomed to "come to the feast of heaven; and have a good time!" But Jesus's story doesn't have a happy ending; at least for one of the invited guests. Something went wrong with one of the guests. What happened? What went wrong?

It was the custom in those days that wedding garments were handed out "free-of-charge" to all the invited guests as they entered the banquet hall. To refuse to wear such a garment was an insult to the host, and hostess – a serious breach of etiquette! So, the king throws the man out of the wedding feast because he is "not properly dressed." He is not wearing a wedding garment. And it is the man's own fault. He knew better; (like I knew better not to leave the seminary dressed in my golf clothes. I knew it was against the rules).

What can we learn from this story? Well, all of us have already received our "wedding garment" when we were baptized as infants, or as adults. Part of the baptismal ceremony includes placing a white cloth (or baptismal gown) on the one baptized with the words: "You have become a new creation, and have clothed yourself in Christ! See in this white garment the outward sign of your Christian dignity! Bring that dignity unstained into the everlasting life of heaven."

So, in baptism we "put" on the garment of God's grace as a "free" gift. It's the sign of God's love for us; and our love for God! It's also a garment we can put on or take off anytime we want. But, if we expect to enter the external banquet of heaven, we need to be wearing it!

God invites everyone to the kingdom of heaven! The banquet is not just for the elite; for the educated; or for the "good" or "religious people." It is not just for Catholics or other Christians – but for all people of good will who listen to and accept God's invitation to come to the banquet!

For us who are Christian, Jesus tells us we must wear our "wedding garment" of baptismal grace. As St. Paul reminds us – we are to "put on Christ from within, accepting His feelings; His gospel values, and His attitudes! We must clothe ourselves with God's justice and peace; with holiness; and good works. That is the challenge of today's gospel story. I just hope God is more understanding than the king in today's gospel story, and much more lenient than Archbishop Connolly was to me!

29th Sunday "A" Matthew 22:15-21

On July 6, 1535, (473 years ago), Thomas More, (one of the most admired Englishmen of his day) stood at the foot of the scaffold on Tower Hill waiting to be hanged! Condemned to death for refusing to take the "oath of supremacy" which would have been to acknowledge King Henry VIII as "the only supreme head of the Catholic church in England." He simply could not do that in conscience. Thomas More was a scholar; a devoted public servant; chosen by Henry VIII himself to be his chancellor. He was a much-loved family man; deeply attached to his wife, and children; and above all, a loyal Catholic!

He had told the judges who condemned him at his trial that he prayed that he and they would "all meet happily in heaven!" And even as he was mounting the rickety ladder to the scaffold he kept his customary sense of humor: "I pray, Lord Lieutenant, (he jested) "see me safe up!...but for my coming down, let me shift for myself." Then after a few words of encouragement to the crowd, he declared he was about to die as "the king's good servant...but as God's servant first!" Those words sum up what Jesus is saying in today's gospel.

The Pharisees ask Jesus a loaded "gotcha" question: "Is it lawful to pay the census tax to Caesar...or not?" If Jesus says "yes," then it would have been absolutely insulting to most Jews, who hated Caesar, and who considered God as their only divine king. If he said "no," he could then be accused of stirring up civil disobedience; even rebellion against Rome; and that could be grounds for treason, imprisonment, or even death! But Jesus sidesteps the dilemma by telling them to repay to Caesar what belongs to Caesar; and to God what belongs to God.

Since the coin for paying the tax had the image of Caesar on it, legally the coin belonged to the emperor. By reminding the crowd of this, Jesus simply indicated that the coin was Caesar's anyway – so why not give it back!

In giving it back Jesus was saying something important about our own relationship to God. Jesus was saying that we must be as careful about our obligation to God, as we are to Caesar. So, the question is this: "Are we as careful about our obligation to God, as we are to the state"?

We pay our taxes. We follow the speed limit. We obey the civil laws, and we vote. For the most part we do our best to be good citizens. But are we as obedient, and as compliant with God? Are we good citizens of the kingdom of heaven as we are of the civil kingdom here on earth?

Many people today tell us we must separate our religion from our political views. If we bring our religious values or motivation into political discussion, we are quickly dismissed! "Keep the church in churchly things," we are told. And they will remind us of the sacred national creed called "the separation of church and state."

Sadly, many of us accept this separation of church and state as some divinely revealed truth; and therefore we leave our religion at home when we enter the workplace; the classroom; or the political arena. If we have been doing this, we must ask ourselves: Which kingdom is more important to us —earth's or heaven's?

If Jesus is truly our king, then everything we feel, think, or do must flow from that central truth. Our faith and gospel values must "form" our political lives.

People will also tell us that we should not "force" our religious views on others. I agree. But that does not mean we have to abandon our religious views because they may differ from someone else's. In order that the government can function, there must be toleration and respect, but not to the extent that we have to turn our backs on our baptismal beliefs!

So, we don't look to the state as our moral guide. For example: Civil law may allow abortion; or the sale of arms to oppressive regimes; or may encourage capital punishment; but the fact that such activities are "legal" does not make them morally right! And if ever there is a genuine clash between our duties to the state, and our duties to God's law, we know God's law has the last word!

The trap of separating "church and state" is now set before us. What is our answer going to be…..God or Caesar? Can we say with Thomas More: "I am the king's good servant…but God's first!"

30ᵗʰ Sunday "A" Matthew 22:34-40; Matthew 22:34-46

In loving us so completely, God expects three things in return:

First, God expects us to return complete love back to God!

Secondly, God expects that we will love one another as God loves us!

Thirdly, God expects us to love ourselves!

Self-love has a very important role to play in keeping the greatest commandment. I say that because before we can even begin loving God and our neighbor, we have to love ourselves FIRST. For example: If I don't see myself as God sees me as a beloved child of God; as redeemed by the death of Jesus on the cross; as a temple of the Holy Spirit; and as especially chosen by God to live with God for all eternity, then I will never see others as God sees them. I will not see the great potential for goodness in everyone, or respect them as my brother or sister in Christ. Yes, self-love and a good image of myself are vital to loving God and one another. If we cannot see these traits in our own lives, how can we see them in others?

I recently saw a poster of a young child, bruised and battered, clearly the victim of physical abuse. Under the picture were these words: "I know I'm somebody – because God don't make no junk." "Yes, God don't make "no junk" because God makes everyone in God's image and likeness…all of us; each one of us; with no exceptions. And what a variety of people we are.

A young foreign-exchange student was filling out an application for college. When he got to the question about his ethnic background, he seemed confused. None of the categories seemed to fit him. So he asked his mother: "Mom, what do I put down here? What am I?" Even though the young man had a Hispanic name, he never thought of himself as Hispanic. His mother said: "Well, I suppose you could just tell them that you are a child of God."

And that is exactly what he wrote. I can imagine the registrar putting that answer into the computer!

Someone like Tiger Woods (for example), could also fill out his application the same way. His father was ¼ Native American, ¼ Chinese, and ½ African-American. His mother is ¼ Chinese, ¼ Caucasian, and ½ Thai. For marketing purposes, Tiger is an African-American in the United States, but he is considered Asian in China and Japan.

The point is that we are all different. But Jesus calls us to love all people, everywhere, all the time. No one is excluded. Some of us may be inclined to dismiss that simply as pious "church talk." It may be good homily material for Sunday morning, but the rest of the week in the "real" world, it doesn't make much sense. It is just not very practical.

I know there are certain people whom we feel we can never love. We probably know some of those people the best. We can tolerate them if we leave them alone, but we really don't like them. What then is the meaning of the Christian "mandate" to love all people without exception? "You shall love your neighbor as yourself" is a "mandate," a "commandment" from Christ. It is not a matter of choice for us. It is something we must do as Christians.

This commandment takes us out of the realm of feelings and emotions. No one can command anyone to "feel" affection for another person – not even Jesus. We cannot even command ourselves to do that. The fact is Jesus does not expect us to have warm and fuzzy feelings about everybody. He did not command us to "like" everyone, but to "love everyone," i.e. to respect them; to accept them as children of God to treat them as equal, and to see the potential for goodness in them. The true meaning of Christian love is that it is a conscious decision to do something good for others – whether we "like" them or not. Love is something we do, not something we feel.

The last story Jesus ever told was his parable of the Final Judgment. It all had to do with how we act, not how we feel about others. Feelings are completely omitted from the story. Jesus does not say: "I was hungry, and you felt sorry for me. I was in prison, and you were embarrassed for me. I was sick and you had sympathy for me." All that might have been nice, but Jesus did not ever mention it. The only thing that counted for him was that the hungry were fed, the naked were clothed, and the sick and prisoners were visited.

The early Christians practiced this type of love, which they referred to as "agape" – a "love feast." The non-Christian historian, Aristides, described the way Christians acted when he wrote these words to the Emperor Hadrian:

"Christians, truly love one another." They never fail to help widows. They save orphans from those who would hurt them. If one of them had something, they give freely to those who have nothing. This is really a new kind of person. "There is something divine in them," he wrote. What a tribute! What would Aristides write about us Christians today? Would he see in us a new kind of person? Would he perceive in us something of the divine? Today's liturgy is an opportunity to express our love for God by loving the people in our lives during the coming week. Remember, Christian love "agape" is a decision to do something good for others. It is not something we feel.

31st Sunday "A" Matthew 23:1-12

In the "holy" gospel according to Peanuts; Linus has just made a drawing of a man, and Charlie Brown is looking at it. Charlie Brown says: "I see you have drawn a man with his hands behind his back…and that tells me that you are "insecure."

Linus replies: "I didn't put his hands behind his back because I am "insecure"; I did it because I can't draw hands!

This story forces us to ask ourselves a couple of questions: "Do we tend to judge other people's motives? Do we tend to set ourselves about others? Or do we tend to pass judgment on others that are unkind or unfair; as Charlie Brown did?

For example: Criticism of the Catholic Church, and some of its bishops and priests abound today. The sexual scandals involving the priesthood are sadly true. As Catholics, we need to be honest about that! Above all, we have to make sure this never happens again in our church! We must remove and prosecute those who have caused these scandals. We need to compensate and offer healing to the victims, and their families. But perhaps we also need to get a broader perspective of these scandals.

Two priests met for lunch; and one of them had just read a biography of a certain American bishop. The priest was angry and upset at all the politics in the church; the "cover-ups"; and the self-seeking ambition of this particular bishop.

He told his priest friend: "If these are the church leaders today; why should I continue being a priest, or even continue believing in the church?" His priest friend then reminded him of the obvious: "You cannot judge from this one book that all bishops act that same way! All church leaders are not bad!" Then, he added: "You know, maybe you should read more books."

When I was pastor of St. Madeline Sophie Parish in Bellevue in 1997, I got a letter one day. Inside the envelope was a small article cut out of the PI paper. It was about a 66 year old priest from the Archdiocese of Chicago. The article went on to mention he was a known pedophile priest, who was transferred to the Seattle Archdiocese! Printed on a small piece of paper were these words: "Could this be you?" It was unsigned.

When I read the note, I thought it was a joke. But then it hit me. Whoever sent this really thinks I might be the pedophile priest; and I had just celebrated my 66th birthday!

Then I got angry! I was hurt and upset! The following Sunday I read the letter at all the masses; and gave a rousing homily about rash judgments, and unfair accusations! And I challenged whoever sent me the letter to see me after mass. No one showed up.

There are many good people in our church today, (both laity and clergy), whose lives bear witness to the simple gospel truths that Jesus taught. A few bad priests or bishops does not mean that all, or the majority, are bad! In fact, the priesthood and the hierarchy are not the whole church. Remember, this church that is torn by such internal strife today, is also the proud church of saints and martyrs. The same church has a long history as the servant of the poor and needy!

The church is like any ordinary family where moral weaknesses and tensions can arise; where mistakes are made, and disappointments happen! Any family can become fragmented – as its members go their separate ways. But any family can also come closer together, and even become stronger by listening to one another; by saying: "I am sorry" or "I forgive you." That is when true healing and reconciliation can take place. Only then can a family once again become one and united….by celebrating their good times; and grieving together over their bad times; by acknowledging their failures and weaknesses; and by rejoicing over their strengths!

The same thing is going on in our church family today. There are many problems and tensions facing our church today. Of course, the sexual abuse scandals; the lack of religious and priestly vocations; the role of women in the church; the alarming number of Catholics leaving the church, to name a few!

These problems and tensions can be painful. They can make us feel as if we are falling apart. They can perhaps make us feel distrustful of one another; and of those in the church who are trying to do good!

When differences or scandals threaten to divide us as a church family; we need to gather around the basic truths of the gospel that we can all agree on.

Listen to what Jesus tells us to do in today's gospel: Practice what you preach! Don't rash judge one another! God alone is your Father! Jesus alone is your teacher and Master! Those in authority among you must be your servants! And all of us are to be servants to one another! That makes for a happy and holy church family! Good advice for all of us!

32nd Sunday "A" Matthew 25:1-13

Today's gospel reminds me of something we used to do in the seminary. The night before a big exam many of us would stay up most of the night cramming for it. We used to refer to this practice as "burning the midnight oil."

I remember on one such occasion about 2 a.m. turning to my roommate (blurry-eyed) and saying: "This is ridiculous! Are you getting anything out of this? We both said "NO"! So we turned out the lights and went to sleep. We realized it was too late to prepare for the exam.

The story of the wise and foolish bridesmaids can teach us some important spiritual lessons. First, it teaches us the necessity of being "prepared" for the coming of Jesus into our lives; and preparation for his final coming cannot be left to the last minute! It may be too late!

A large part of a parent's life is spent making sure their kids don't go out into the world "unprepared." "Wear a sweater; take enough money for your lunch; don't forget your backpack." "Be careful crossing the street; drive carefully; and be home by midnight."

Today's gospel story is about the five foolish bridesmaids who went off to a weeding unprepared. They went out into the night to greet the bridegroom without enough oil for their lamps! They were unprepared! The wise ones, of course, came prepared with extra oil. As the night drew on, those who were unprepared had no light by which to see the honored guest.

The point of this story goes far beyond the need to be practical, organized, or a better time manager! Jesus is the bridegroom! The preparation Jesus is urging us to make is a spiritual preparation. This parable asks the question: Have we gathered enough oil or fuel to keep our "inner" light burning? It is not the kind of oil or fuel that we can borrow from others. It is the kind we need to have ourselves! The "oil" in the parable is our good deeds! In our culture it is easy to let our "inner" light be dimmed – or even burn out.

For example: Most of us don't have the time to wait for Jesus to come. Jesus may be coming on Judgment Day, but the clothes need to get to the cleaners; and dinner has to get on the table. We are just too busy! What can parents do to help nurture their children's "inner" light? Why not say a prayer together the next time you gather for dinner and ask for the ways Jesus can be invited into your home and hearts.

Another lesson we can learn from this parable is that we must be ready to "seize" the opportunity when it comes! It is like when you call someone on the phone and get their answering machine…. "at the beep, give your name, number and a message so I can get back to you…..Beep!!" If you do not "seize" the opportunity to leave a message – that moment is lost forever!

And so it is with God's invitation to enter the kingdom! If we do not respond immediately, or soon after the "beep" we may lose that opportunity; and it might be too late to respond!

God leaves lots of "beeps" for us to answer. "Master, open the door for us!" But he answered: "I tell you, I do not know you." In other words, he is saying: "You never responded. You never even left your name and number!" Yes, we must be ready to "seize" the opportunity when it comes. There is a Latin phrase that warns us: "Carpe Diem," in other words, "seize the day, or seize the moment!"

We sometimes hear about an "understudy" who becomes a star overnight after going on stage to replace a leading actor or actress or some little known reserve football or baseball player (who because of an injury to a first-team player), has the chance to play….and takes that position!

But the fact is that the "understudy" did not wait until that moment to learn the part; and the reserve player did not wait until that moment to be trained and in good physical shape! By hard work, practice, and diligent preparation thinking were ready to "seize" the chance when it came!

The greatest event in our life is that someday we will stand in the presence of God at the end of our life! For that we must make ourselves prepared and ready! That is what Jesus is trying to say in this parable.

The story is told of an old Scotsman that when he was drying, someone offered to read the Bible to him. To their surprise he did not seem very eager for this, although they knew he loved to read the Bible all his life! When they asked him why he didn't need the Bible read to him, he answered: "I thatched my house when it was warm weather, so when winter came it was prepared." So, now I am ready to die. In other words, his whole life was a preparation for meeting Jesus in death! He was able to recognize Jesus in his life; so Jesus now could recognize him in his death! There is a short ditty that captures that same idea.... Whenever I go by a church, I stop to make a visit; just so when I am carried in.....Jesus won't have to say – "Who is it?"

33rd Sunday "A" Matthew 25:14-30

The whole attention of today's parable is centered on the "unworthy" servant who was given just one talent to invest for his master while he went away on a long journey.

So the question is: "Who does the "unworthy" servant stand for? He stands for the Scribes and Pharisees; the religious leaders in Jesus's day!

Their one and only aim in life was to keep things just the way they always were in Judaism. They wanted to build a fence around their Jewish religion, and protect it from any change!

But Jesus came preaching some new (and they believed) radical ideas about God; about what it meant to be "holy"; and he even challenged some of their ancient traditions. They in turn totally rejected these ideas, and accused him of blasphemy, which finally led to his crucifixion!

Is there a lesson in this parable for us today? Yes, and I think it is this: In our Catholic faith, there must be steady developments; new revelation from God, who is still is the God of surprises! We must be open to learn new ideas about God, and our rich traditions. New ideas about what it means to be "holy" today; and the new interpretation and meaning of scripture!

But, (as we see in Jesus's day) the whole tendency of "orthodox" religion is exactly the opposite. It is so easy to worship the past; to look back on the "good old days," we believe to have been the "golden" age of faith; instead of looking forward to any possibilities of discovering new revelations of God! That is why, as Catholics, we need to keep learning more and more about our faith; and then to follow the prompting of the Holy Spirit, wherever the Spirit may lead us!

Have you ever thought what would have happened to medicine if doctors were not allowed to use the new discoveries made since the 18th century? The same is true in the life of the church. There is something wrong if, (over the last 100 years), people have not learned more about their faith! And there is something wrong about an individual Catholic whose faith remains exactly the same at the age of 20 as it was at the age of 10; or at 40 as it was at the age of 20.

Yes, the "unworthy" servant in today's parable could also be us – if we bury or hide the spiritual gifts and talents given to use at baptism! This parable is challenging us to be creative by investing and increasing the worth of our spiritual gifts until our Master Jesus returns!

Notice the "unworthy" servant was not punished because he was bad or sinful, but because he gave up, and he never even tried. The Master was angry and upset: "Should you not then have put my money in the bank; so I could have got it back with interest on my return?" he asks. But the servant gave up and didn't even try. After all, he was given just one talent, and it wasn't even worthwhile to invest it!

We know our world is not just composed of talented and "extraordinary" people like Steve Jobs of Apple; or Bill Gates of Microsoft. They are the exceptional! For the most part, the world is composed of ordinary people (like us) – people of ordinary talents, who do ordinary jobs. But, these "ordinary" jobs have to be done – if the world is to continue to go on; and if God's plans are to be accomplished in this world!

I think it might have been Mother Teresa who inferred that God doesn't want "extraordinary" people to do extraordinary things but rather He wants "ordinary" people to do ordinary things – extraordinarily well!! And Abraham Lincoln once mused that evidently God loves the common man because He made so many of us. So, that tells me that the world really does depend on the person with just one talent!

Today is Stewardship Sunday; when the church is asking us to give our "fair share" of money, time, and talents back to God, and to our parish." True stewardship giving has four elements: 1) It must be "planned" – that is, it must be prayed about and thought out. 2) It must be "proportionate" – that is, based on how much God has blessed us. 3) It must be "sacrificial" – that is, there must be some element of sacrifice in our giving. 4) It must truly be a gift – that is, it must be given with no conditions, or strings attached!

Let me give you an example of true stewardship: An old man was sitting in a bus, holding a beautiful bouquet of freshly-cut flowers. Across the aisle was a young woman, whose eyes (from time to time), glanced over at the man's flowers, in appreciation. The time soon came for the man to get off the bus. When he stood up to leave he gave the flowers to the young woman! "I can see you love the flowers, (he said); and I think my wife would like you to have them! I will tell her I gave them to you, and I am sure she will understand!"

The woman gratefully accepted the flowers and then watched the old man get off the bus and walk through the gate of a small cemetery!

That is what sacrificial giving is! When you sign up for your financial commitment to the parish this year – I hope you will do so with the same attitude; and feelings of the old man in this story!

Look at your commitment as your special gift to God!

Thank you for your past generosity and support of our parish – with your time, talents, and treasure!

Solemnity of Christ the King "A"
Matthew 25:31-46

One of the interesting things about Jesus' parables is that we usually can find ourselves somewhere in the story. So, my question to you today is: "Where do you see yourself in today's parable? Do you see yourself in the group of the "non-helpers" on the left; or in the group of "helpers" on the right side of Jesus?"

An honest answer would be that we find ourselves in both groups. There have been times when we helped the poor, the homeless, the sick, and the hungry. But there also have been other times when we have turned our backs - and walked away!

All of us belong to both groups – a little bit. So, what is the meaning of this parable? In order to find out, we have to take a closer look at the story. The message is so simple, that we may be walking right past it, and may be missing the point!

There are not just two groups of people in the parable –there are actually three groups. There are those who helped; there are those who refused to help; and there are those who needed help! This third group is the one we usually have overlooked.

It is strange that we would overlook those who needed help, because these are the people with whom Jesus chose to identify himself! He is telling us that to help those who are in need was to help Him; and to neglect them was to neglect Him! I think this is the real message of the parable. Jesus took his stand with the poor and needy of the world. I believe He is saying that He belonged to them; and they belonged to Him. This is where He lived and that was where they would find Him. He completely identifies with them as His suffering brothers and sisters, in whom He lives!

So, these people were not just "another group," separate, and apart. No! Their hunger was HIS hunger. Their need was HIS need! He spoke of them not in the third person, but in the first person, because He and they were one and the same!

Let's face it; this is the group where you and I also belong. It is not an exclusive club! In fact, everyone in the world is a member, because at some point in our lives we will find ourselves "in need" of something only others can give!

None of us are self-sufficient. We depend on each other. Someday I may need your help; and someday you may need mine. The only "outsiders" to this group are those who refuse to participate – and even they are "in need," whether they realize it or not!

The New York Times recently had a short article that read: "Witnessed on a New York City street: A homeless man sitting on the curb near St. Patrick's Cathedral. He has set his hat in front of him for donations. A shabbily dressed "bag lady" dragging a cart filled with bags of her only belongings walked by. She pauses in front of the man. Deciding that he was worse off than she was – she takes out of her worn ripped coat pocket, two crumpled dollar bills, and places them in his hat! It is a random act of charity that goes almost unnoticed by the world.....a snapshot of compassion that both inspires the spirit, and breaks the heart!"

Anything you have done for one of my least brothers, or sisters, you have done for me, was what Jesus believed. We cherish those words of Jesus; and we do want to help the hungry and the thirsty, the lost, the sick, the homeless, and imprisoned!

But it is so hard for us to get beyond our own needs; our own poverty; our own disappointments; our own problems; and unrealized dreams! Oh, we would like to help – but it always seems to be a bad time, especially now with the economy in the dumper; the struggle to make the mortgage, and tuition payments; and not knowing how long I will have a job!

The poor woman in the front of St. Patrick's Cathedral manages to put aside her own hardships to embrace Christ's compassion in the homeless man she meets! She doesn't even know his name. All she knows is that he is "in need." In today's parable Jesus is saying: "That is holiness; that is discipleship; that is being a good steward!"

Today we celebrate the Feast of Christ the King! Christ the Shepherd - King calls us to care for one another; to see the suffering Christ in the poor and the needy; (and above all), to help establish Christ's Kingdom of Justice and compassion in our own time and place, by helping the less fortunate.

Exaltation of the Holy Cross (A-B-C)

The cross is everywhere in Christian life! In our church, in our art, the jewelry we wear and as a sign traced on ourselves.

Protestant churches favor the cross without the Body; a reminder that "He is risen-He is not here." Catholic and Orthodox Christians favor the image of the Crucified One, perhaps to say, "Yes, He is risen" – but He is still here present among us; sharing in the pain of the world, sharing in the suffering and passion endured by so many!

At one time, the cross was one of the most hated signs in the world! – similar to the electric chair, the guillotine; firing squad; the hanging noose, or lethal injection. Even St. Paul described the cross as "an obstacle to the Jews; and us madness to the Greeks and Romans!

But what originally was a sign of punishment and death is now, today, a symbol of abundant life! The early Christians first began to honor the cross because of its close association with Jesus's redeeming death! The cross today is still a sign of pain – but the pain it represents is the price of Jesus' own victory over sin, suffering and death.

It's a little strange that we call today's feast the "Exaltation of the Holy Cross" because "Exaltation" has overtones of winning and conquering.

The "Exaltation of the Cross" means that Jesus broke through death to Resurrection and New Life. It teaches us that "good" always prevails over "evil," and that Jesus transforms our weakness into strength! Therefore, the "Exaltation of Jesus' Cross," then, becomes the "exaltation of our own Crosses," too!

Every year, a small college in the mid-west invites one of its faculty to give what is called "The Last Lecture," ……the wisdom a professor would give the students, as if it were his or her "last lecture." Last year, Randy Pausch accepted the challenge! The irony was that it really would be his last lecture; as he had been diagnosed with pancreatic cancer, and had just a short time to live! When he agreed to give the lecture, Professor Pausch expected that maybe 50 or so students would attend – but it was standing room only in the 400 seat auditorium! The lecture was not about his cancer! Rather, he spoke about honesty and truth, of perseverance, of gratitude, and of his passion for life! He urged the students to live their dreams, and to help others realize theirs. He reminded them that good things happen when you do the right thing; that people will eventually "come around" if you are patient enough; and there is NO substitute for hard work! He also spoke of his love for his wife, Jane, and his three young children. He said he decided to give his "last lecture" for them – to leave a "message in a bottle" for them to discover when they grew up." Much of his talk was about how he managed to scale the "brick walls" that stood in the way of achieving some of his own dreams. "The brick walls," he said, "are there for a reason! They are NOT THERE to keep us out! NO, they are there for a reason! The "brick walls" are there to give us a chance to share how badly we really want something!

"In the time left to me," he said, "The most important thing is my family! The metaphor I've used is this: Someday in the future, bad times might push my family off a cliff – and it breaks my heart that I won't be there to catch them! But, before I die, I still have the time to set up some safety "nets" to help break their fall! So, I have a choice to make – either I could curl up in a ball and cry; and feel sorry for myself; or I could get to work on putting up those safety "nets."

"We tend to think of our "crosses" as burdens or obstacles that demand so much of our time and energy. But, just think of what could happen if we viewed our crosses as "opportunities" – as rich sources of "hope and joy; of discovery of resurrection and New Life – for ourselves and others!"

Professor Pausch embraced the cross of his illness; and in so doing, transformed it into an "opportunity to teach, inspire, and to enlighten himself and others!

The RCIA Program, The Rite of Christian Initiation for Adults, is beginning soon in the parish! The RCIA Program is for ANY non-Catholic adult interested in becoming "Catholic," or for any Catholic adult who has, not as yet, received the sacrament of Confirmation.

All Saints "A"

There are some events we would give anything to attend! Who wouldn't want to be invited to and have the best seats in the house of a Super Bowl, or a World Series, or the installation of a Pope? Although these are very different events, they are big occasions and invitations to them are hard to get! One has to be "in the loop" in order to be invited to attend!

Today, we celebrate the most important event to which we will EVER be invited to attend; the great gathering of the saints in heaven! The invitation has been extended to all women, and men from every nation; race, people and tongue! But, what kind of a ticket does one need to get in? One must be marked with the "seal of the servants of GOD." And what is that seal? The blood of the lamb…the blood of Jesus who died on the cross for us!

In ancient Pagan mythology, the highest mountain was thought to be the dwelling place of the major Pagan god. Israel took this idea over; claiming that its god (the one true God), did indeed dwell on the highest mountain! Eventually, the hill on which their temple was built was considered to be this sacred place, where God dwelt in Jerusalem.

Today's responsorial psalm asks the question; "Who can ascend the mountain of the Lord or who may stand in God's holy place?" The answer is given; "The one whose hands are sinless, whose heart if clean, one who desires not what is vain!"

This means that access to God is not limited to celebrities, or those who might have connections! Everyone can "be in the loop," as long as they have *the right attitude*."

The Beatitudes found in today's gospel remind us that *the right attitude* needed to approach God is not found in obeying a bunch of laws and regulations! Rather, it is found in our relationships with others; in how we treat on another.   It calls us to be meek and merciful; it challenges us

151

to hunger and thirst for righteousness; and to work for peace! Those who live in this way have access to God; they can "ascend the mountain of the Lord!" They make up the multitude who stands "before the throne of God and the Lamb! They are the saints of God!

We all know people in this world who are living examples of this kind of holiness! They are the ones who stand tall in times of crisis; who step forward in times of need! They are the women and the men of principle. They are the members of our family; neighbors; friends among whom we live; possibly with whom we work!

There is seldom fanfare when they practice virtues – but their virtue leaves its mark on the lives of others! These are also the saints we celebrate today, the ones still living, who have accepted God's invitation to be holy NOW; even in this world! My favorite definition of a saint is: "A saint is a sinner who keeps on trying." I once attended a Cursillo Weekend, when someone made a name tag that said: "Hello, my name is John.….and I am a saint; in training!"

It reminded all of us during that weekend of our true calling as Christians! It also reminded us of the dignity of the People who surround us – the people we live with; work with; or the people we pray with!

So, happy feast day to all of you – because all of us, truly are "saints – in – training!"

Assumption Day "A"

A few years ago, a newspaper described some new and different guest suites at the Grand Hotel on Mackinac Island, Michigan. The hotel was unveiling five new "First Lady Suites" - in honor of five of the former Presidents' wives! Lady Bird Johnson, Betty Ford, Rosalyn Carter, Nancy Reagan, and Barbara Bush each provided advice on the décor for their suites. Each suite has the official White House portrait, and an autographed book from the First Lady, after whom the room was named. The colors used in each suite reflected the individual taste of each of those First Ladies!

Well, today, we celebrate the day when God brought our "First Lady," the Blessed Virgin Mary, into the heavenly suite, prepared for her for all eternity. Mary IS the "First Lady" of the Church, because she is the mother of God's own Son, JESUS. We might wonder how her heavenly suite is decorated. Is Mary's official portrait there? NO! There are not any paintings of her that we know of! Are there any autographed books? NO. Mary never wrote any books during her lifetime, as far as we know.

But Mary's suite in heaven is decorated with what she, herself, has left us! It's something that best expresses the meaning of her life here on earth! It's in a sense, her legacy – the marvelous song of praise and thanksgiving that we just heard in today's gospel! We call that song "The Magnificate" which was taken from the first words in its Latin version: "My soul magnifies the Lord."

Yes, Mary could sing that song everyday of her life, because her soul truly was like a magnifying glass – making God's Presence so clear and so evident, for all to see!

Her song of praise continues with these words: "The Lord has shown great power, and has scattered the proud in their conceit! The Lord has cast down the mighty from their thrones, and up the lowly! The Lord has filled the hungry with good things, and the rich have been sent away, empty handed!

Mary's song is not about herself – it's about God's work done in and through her – for the salvation of all humanity.

God raised the humble Virgin Mary to the heights of heaven in her assumption; so God wishes to raise all people, whose lives magnify the Lord God, as Mary did!

The promise of Mary's Assumption is that all of Jesus' brothers and sisters will come to eternal life, if they remain faithful till death, as Mary was faithful!

Mary is generous, God-bearing, God-giving. Besides being our "First Lady", the Church on this feast of her assumption, applies to her the title from today's responsorial psalm – since now she has her reward: "on your right, oh Lord, stands the Queen, in garments of gold.

YEAR

B

First Sunday of Advent "B" Mark 13:33-37

Most of us know what the work "Advent" means. It means "coming" or "arrived." We know that Advent is the four weeks preparation for Christ coming into the world at Christmas. Most of us have celebrated advent many times, and are quite familiar with its meaning. So, that should end my homily for today, but, wait a minute, what we fail to realize is that the coming of Christ is a three-dimensional idea (concept). We tend to limit advent to only one or two meanings at the most. We usually think of Advent in terms of the Christmas story. This is when we pause to look back across the centuries and remember that the Son of God came into the world as a little baby, born of the Virgin Mary, in a stable. That is the classic and historical meaning of Advent. At other times we turn our faces to the future, remembering that Jesus has promised to come again at the end of the world. We refer to this as the "Second Advent" or "Second Coming" of Christ. Both of these meanings have been celebrated and proclaimed through the history of the church. But if we stop with these two meanings only and go no further, we will miss the coming of Christ into our daily lives. So, we need to open our minds to one more meaning of Advent. We need to recognize that Christ not only has come in the past, and shall come in the future, but he does continue to come now in the present. This, it seems to me, is the meaning of our Gospel reading today. Jesus told a story about a man who was getting ready to travel abroad....and Jesus is that man. Before leaving, he turned the responsibility of his household over to his servants…and we are the servants! To each of them he gave a specific task; and this final word of instruction, "You do not know when the master of the house is coming. Do not let him come suddenly, and catch you asleep…so be on guard, and watch!"(Mark 4:35-37) What is the message of this parable? I think Jesus is trying to tell us about his final coming at the end of time…but he is also trying to open our minds to the truth of his coming to us in the events and experiences of our daily lives! Surely, he is never far from us; and we should look for him, not just in the clouds of tomorrow; but in the streets of today. Perhaps the first thing we need to do is to think of his coming, not as a threat, but as a promise. His instruction to be alert and watchful; does not mean we should be fearful, or over-anxious; but that we should be joyfully expectant! After all, the one whose arrival we anticipate is not a policeman with a search warrant, but a loving friend who knows us better than we know ourselves; and who loves us more than we can imagine. I think of Jesus' coming to the home of Martha and Mary while they were in the midst of mourning the death of their brother, Lazarus. They could see him down the road, and Martha, being unable to wait, ran down the road to meet him. Mary remained in the house, but when she saw Jesus was there, she also hurried to his presence. Their only regret was that he had not come sooner. That is how Jesus' friends acted when he visited them. So how can we ever think of his return as something to dread, or to fear?

Jesus has not changed! He is the same yesterday, today, and forever. We are not that much different than Martha and Mary. It was just that they had found a faithful friend, who had taught them the meaning of love and forgiveness and trust in God. If we could just learn that then we will see his coming as a promise, not a threat. Next, we should look for Jesus, not just in the big events of life, but in the small things as well. In the parable, the master gave each of his servants a job to do, and then told them while doing it to expect his coming at any time. The two seemed to go together – their work, and his return. A doctor once told me, "I don't see how anyone can witness the birth of a baby, and not believe in God." Now, there was a man who had learned to see the coming of the Lord in doing his daily work! How about us? Do we think our work is too drab and ordinary to ever find God there? What about Jesus? He wasn't a doctor, he was a carpenter. Simon Peter? He was a fisherman. The servants in the parable? They were doing household chores and taking care of the farm. To experience the presence of Christ in doing our daily work depends not so much on the type of work we do, but the attitude of the worker. If our heart is right and our mind is joyfully expectant, we will find Christ in many places—in the face of a child; in the need of other people, in our joys, and even in our sorrows! The Advent Season speaks to use of the Christ who has come as the Son of God, and as the Son of Mary. It speaks to us of the

Christ, who shall come as the King of Kings! But it also speaks to us of the Christ who comes as a friend, to walk with us in the pain and gladness of our daily lives, and even in the hectic preparations for Christmas during this Advent Season!

Second Sunday of Advent "B" Mark 1:1-8

Who is this strange figure the gospel brings to our church today? He's dressed in a garment of camel hair, and a leather belt around his waist. He kind of looks a little weird to me! Shall we invite him into our community? Yes, it's John the Baptist – the great Advent figure who describes himself as "A voice crying in the wilderness; prepare the way of the Lord." He has an important message for us, who find ourselves in our own "wilderness" – The "wilderness" within, and all around us – The wilderness of our forgetfulness of God! We live in a sinful world, full of darkness, in a world too busy to recognize God's presence. And John the Baptist offers us a way out of the wilderness – by preaching a fiery word out of the wilderness as he proclaims, direction." It's not just casually saying, "I'm sorry, pardon me, or excuse me" for accidentally bumping into someone. It's a deep awareness of the need we have for God's cleansing presence in our lives! Because we continue to sin, and fail in our lives; repentance is a daily experience for most of us Christians. God's faithful love and mercy reach out to us every day. That's why we begin every Mass with a confession of sins and absolution. "Prepare the way of the Lord" -- John the Baptist calls on each one of us today to stop in the middle of our frantic preparation for Christmas to "hear" the message of Advent: The voice of one crying out in the wilderness, "Prepare the way of the Lord, Make his paths straight. Every valley shall be filled and every mountain and hill shall be made low, and the crooked shall be made straight, and the rough ways made smooth, and all flesh shall "see" the Salvation of God."

Third Sunday of Advent "B"
John 1:6-8, 19-28

I saw a bumper-sticker the other day that brought a smile to my face! It read: "There is a God; and it's not you!" It's amazing how a bumper-sticker can (not only be amusing, but at the same time), can be so profound. In fact, this bumper-sticker captures the dual message found in today's gospel! John the Baptist was one of the most famous men of his time…a charismatic preacher and a powerful prophet! His church was the rugged outdoors in the Judean desert! His dress and diet were certainly odd (to put it kindly!), his message was fiery – demanding repentance of sin; a conversion of life! Great crowds came out to hear him and be baptized! Why did they come out to such a harsh setting, to hear such a harsh message from a harsh-looking preacher? What was the attraction? It was his message! He announced to the people that there is a God who loves them! A God who is engaged in the world! A God who still is in charge and a God who was soon coming into the world in the person of the Messiah! And, in fact, the Messiah was already in their very midst as one they did not recognize. Imagine how that must have made the crowd look around at one another and wonder, could it be possible, could the Messiah be here among us? This is the exact same message we are hearing on this 3rd Sunday of Advent. Yes, there is a God, who still lives among us! Our God is closer than our next heartbeat and more current than tomorrow morning's newspaper. But in order to "see" God, we have to learn to look with the eyes of faith, not with our physical eyes, and we have to learn how to listen to God with our hearts, not just with our ears! We also have to learn how to slow down to quiet down long enough to repent of our sins, to prepare for Christ's coming, to expect miracles, and to believe God is here among us, and God still loves us! Perhaps the biggest obstacle preventing us from recognizing God in our midst, is the temptation to act as though we were "god" (with a small "g") to act as though we are in control of our lives, and of our "little" universe, to act as if our security, our possessions, our decisions, and our very destiny were all in our own hands! But actually, we know that our lives and the entire universe is in God's hands – not in ours! And no matter how successful we may be or how many awards and titles we may have, no matter how much of God's abundance we have or how many people blog onto our website, we are <u>not</u> God (with a capital "G"!). In today's Gospel, a group of people ask John the Baptist a direct question, "Who are you?" They wanted to know how John saw himself and what he regarded his role in life to be. John answered, "I am the voice of one crying in the wilderness – make straight the way of the Lord!" What a beautiful way for John to identify himself! God had called him for a purpose – to point out the Messiah among the people and to prepare them for his coming! That was his job and he was doing just that. Public opinion tried to make John into somebody other than who he was! He rejected that temptation! Some thought he was Elijah, or some other great prophet from the past who had returned to earth. Many others even thought he was the Promised Messiah, the Son of God he preached about, who would come down from heaven! But John denied these titles. He accepted himself for who he was ("I am the voice of the one crying out in the desert -- make straight the way of the Lord."). Pretending to be someone else is "make-believe" a game children play, and when adults play that game, it's called insanity or being delusional. Today's gospel also describes John as "A man sent by God." That same title applies to you and to me – to all of us! I'll show you how -- it can apply by doing a little "editing" to today's gospel verse! Take a pen and cross out "John" and write in your own name. If you are female, cross out the word "man" and write the word "woman." The verse will then read "There was a man named Joe - (Bill or Mike) sent by God;" Or there was a woman named Diane – (Helen or Rose) sent by God!" When we do that, then that gospel verse is no less true of John the Baptist than it is true for us now today! Our lives also have a divine calling to point out Christ to others. John the Baptist was in a sense the advance "P.R." man for the Advent! His mission was to point Christ out as the Promised Messiah and to prepare the people for His coming into the world! The good news is that we can do the same thing by the words we speak, the things we do, and the attitudes we show. We, too, can help the world to be a little more receptive to Christ's coming this Christmas! We believe God is in the world still living among us. But we have to look for God where we least expect to find God – especially among the poor and powerless, the humble and the outcasts, among children, the sick, the handicapped, and the forgotten. But there's one place we need not look – and that's in a mirror! As the bumper-sticker says, "There is a God, and it's not you!"

Immaculate Conception "B" December 8th

I don't know how many of you remember that famous Super bowl game – I think it was between the Dallas Cowboys and the Pittsburg Steelers in 1973 – when Terry Bradshaw, with a few minutes to play, threw up a "Hail Mary" pass to the end zone. The football was batted around by two or three players and was finally caught by Lynn Swan for a touchdown, and a Super Bowl win! The announcer referred to the play as the "immaculate Reception". It was truly a miraculous catch!

Today, we celebrate that feast of the Immaculate Conception, which simply mean that Mary was preserved from all sin, from the moment of her conception to the moment of her death.

When you think about it, it's fitting that God should have preserved Mary from all sin. After all, she was chosen from all eternity to be the mother of the Promised Messiah – the Son of God!

I don't think it does much good to get too technical or theological in explaining what the title of the "Immaculate conception" means. I think that Mary's holiness and greatness comes from one fact – that she was chosen to be the mother of Jesus – all the other titles or honors come from that.

What is important is that Mary is our spiritual mother; she is still the channel of God's grace to the world and she is still at work in the world performing miracles.

I know this from my own experience…When I was first ordained (a hundred years ago), I was assigned as an assistant pastor at St. Matthew's parish in North Seattle (next door to Jackson Golf course). One of my duties was to take care of four nursing homes by bringing the patents communion, hearing their confessions and given them the sacrament of the sick, then referred to as "extreme Unction", or the "last rites", only to be given in danger of imminent death.

One day, I got a call from Norton's Nursing home about 2 a.m. the nurse said the man in room 211 was very ill and was not expected to make it through the night. He wanted to see a priest. "Could you come to anoint him, hear his confession and give him communion right away?"

I was there in 20 minutes. I was surprised that his room was dark and he was fast asleep. When I turned on the light, he woke up with a start. He didn't seem that ill and seemed surprised to see me.

I introduced myself and said I would pray for him and give him the "last rites." His eyes filled up with tears and he began praying in French, his old hands tightly holding on to his rosary beads.

When I finished my prayers, I anointed him and gave him communion. He asked me who had called me to see him, because he had not requested a visit. About that time, I noticed the room number above his bed – it was room 212, not 211. I had gone to the wrong room and anointed the wrong person.

Then he told me his story in broken English. He was born in France. He attended a French convent school, where he had finished the fifth grade. He ran away from home when he was 14 years old and became a Merchant Marine. He traveled all over the world. He was now 82 and he had not been to church in over 70 years.

One of the sisters who taught him I the 5th grade, made him promise that he would say a "Hail Mary" every night before he went to sleep to pray for a happy death. She said if he did so, he would receive the "last rites" and blessing of the church before he died. He told me he never missed a day.

I blessed him and went next door to room 211. The next day I dropped by to see the Frenchman. The nurse told me he died about 3 a.m. that morning.

I became a believer in the power of prayer. I also became a believer in the powerful intercession of Mary. Mary is a model for our own journey of faith (Advent Preparation). She wants to help us just as she helped the Frenchman. She is not only the physical mother of Jesus, but our spiritual mother as well.

Let's close with these words from a hymn to Mary. These words make a fitting conclusion to this homily:

"Mother of Christ – Star of the Sea – Pray
for the Wanderer – Pray for Me."

Fourth Sunday of Advent "B" Luke 1: 26-38

She was the most unlikely person to spark a revolution but what Rosa Parks did that afternoon of December 1, 1955 in Montgomery, Alabama, transformed America! Rosa Parks was a 42 year old black seamstress at a department store. At the end of a long day, she boarded a city bus to go home. A white man demanded her seat (and by law), he was entitled to it, but something stirred inside the soul of this quiet, humble woman that said, "Enough, I have just as much right to this seat as this white man." So, she politely refused to give up her seat. Rosa Parks was arrested, jailed, and fined $14.00. Her arrest triggered a year-long boycott of the Montgomery City bus system organized by a young little-known Baptist minister...the Rev. Martin Luther King Jr., and the civil rights movement in the United Stated had begun! It is light years from the days of the Jim Crowe laws of peaceful marches, of arrests, and of beatings and the killings. Many Americans are too young to have remembered those terrible days. And half a century later, it's difficult for us to fully understand how courageous it was for Rosa Parks to remain seated on that bus! At the news conference on Rosa Parks death a few years ago, Julian Bond said, "She is properly thought of as "the" mother of the civil rights movement because when she sat down, she really stood up for the rest of us!" Coretta Scott King said of Rosa Parks' dignified act of civil disobedience: "It was a moment when the woman, and the "hour" met on that bus in 1955 when the Holy Spirit brought Rosa Parks to meet her "hour." She responded by bringing the first light of a new day of justice and equality for all Americans! In today's gospel, God calls another woman, Mary of Nazareth to meet her "hour" by accepting God's call to be the mother of the Promised Messiah! Her saying "yes" to God was the beginning of humanity's re-creation in the love and life of God! And Mary said to God, "Let it be done to me as you say." Her saying "yes" to God began the world-wide "Jesus" movement that would transform all of humanity! Through Mary's "yes", the Eternal Son of God was conceived in her womb by the power of the Holy Spirit…and God is born on earth! This Jesus would free all people from the "slavery" of sin. He would be the light that would dispel the darkness of despair. Jesus would restore the friendship with God lost by our 1st parent's sin! He would redeem (or buy back) our salvation with the terrible price of his own death on the cross and this Jesus would guarantee to all people the final victory over sin, suffering, and death by his own Resurrection from the dead! Yes, Mary met her "hour" of decision, and all humanity has benefitted! Isn't this really the mystery we celebrate at Christmas? Christ is born in us as well and God is living in us, as God once lived in Mary! And like Mary, we are invited to say "yes" to God… "yes" we welcome your Son into our lives, into our "sacred place" made holy by the God who dwells within us! So, during this Advent Season, may we, like Mary, have the same trust and faith in the providence of God to meet "our hour" of decision – whenever and wherever that time may come. Then we will be ready and willing to bring the transforming hope of the Gospel of Jesus to our own time, and our own place. Our Advent prayer is the same as Mary's prayer: "Lord, let it be done to me; as you say."

Christmas Day "B"

One of the most meaningful Christmas stories of all is told about Father Flanagan, the founder of Boys Town. On this particular Christmas, Father Flanagan had become so busy trying to find gifts for his homeless boys and preparing and decorating the church for Christmas that he found himself scrambling on Christmas Eve to write a homily.

He thought to himself: "If only I have time for some peace and quiet, I could write the best Christmas homily ever." But as you might expect with a house full of boys, peace and quiet wasn't to be found that Christmas Eve!

He had no sooner sat at his desk when he heard a knock at his door. It was Sister Mary, one of his staff members, who exclaimed, "Father, it's Paul! He's under his bed crying and he won't come out." "Just tell him that everything is alright", Father Flanagan suggested. "Tell him not to be scared. Tomorrow is going to be a great day, and there will be something for him under the tree!" "I'll try…but he's really upset" Sister Mary said.

It was only minutes later that Sister Mary was back at Father Flanagan's door, sounding more frustrated than before. "I told him what you said Father, but he only sobbed the more. He just won't come out!"

Putting down his pen and glasses, Father Flanagan resigned himself to leave his Christmas masterpiece and go to see Paul. Sure enough, he found Paul just as Sister Mary had described…hands over his head, arms covering his eyes and sobbing! As he looked at Paul, he remembered that Paul was the boy who hadn't had any visitors in over two years. He remembered the sadness in Paul's eyes every time he saw someone else have a visitor.

As he remembered, Father Flanagan crawled under the bed in the darkness and began to cry with Paul! They cried for the longest time together and when they could not cry any longer, Father Flanagan and Paul embraced and together they came out from underneath the bed arm in arm!

"It's really going to be ok", Father Flanagan reassured Paul. "I'm going to tuck you into bed and stay with you until you fall asleep ad when you wake up in the morning, I'll be here…I promise."

Father Flanagan went to bed that night, filled with wonder and awe, for when he least expected it, he had discovered, once again, the true meaning of Christmas!

For you see, all through the Old Testament God had told the people how much He loved them. God sent word after word through the prophets. He was telling us how to live,because this is who He is,and this is what it means to be His people. But the people of the Old Testament remained hiding in the darkness under their beds, afraid and unsure of themselves.

But on that first Christmas, God changed all of that. God didn't just send mere words; God became the "Word"… the "Word" made flesh! God crawled under the bed of humanity and entered the world. God became one with us. God shared our pain, embraced our weakness and led us from the darkness of fear into the wondrous and glorious light of a Father's love.

And that is why we celebrate tonight (today)… God giving Himself totally, God embracing our life; God taking away our fear and showing us the depths of His love – not in words only – but by God's presence! Just think of it – God so loved the world that God became one of us! Our human nature would never again be so privileged!

I don't know about you, but I come to this celebration tonight (today) ready and longing to be embraced; to be nourished; and to be loved in order that my life might "re-tell" the Christmas story through my own loving actions; by daring to give myself to others in such a way that others might know that love and mercy of our wonderful God!

My friends, Father Flanagan never had to write a homily that Christmas Eve, for you see, Paul's new-found peace, his joy, his experience of being lived and understood, proclaimed the Christmas message of love and hope in that house on Christmas Day! May our lives proclaim and reflect to all in our house and in the world, that on this night (day) we rejoice and remember that unto us "there is born in Bethlehem a Savior, who is Christ our Lord!"

I wish you and your family, a happy and holy Christmas and a wonderful New Year!

First Holy Family "B" Luke 2 22-40

The Feast of the Holy Family is intended to be part of our Christmas celebration! It points out the fully human condition of Jesus! He didn't come into the world a fully-formed adult, but he was born into a family as an infant. He needed a family to take care of him, to teach him, to share faith with him, to enable him to grow and develop day-by-day and year-by-year just as we all do! There an old proverb that says – No family can hang out a sign that says, "There's nothing the matter here." The fact is, being human, even the best of families has, as least "something the matter with it." Sometimes it may be family arguments or holding old grudges, there may be some sort of domestic violence, financial problems, health problems, divorce, or a host of other problems that families have to face! But, what about the Holy Family of Jesus, Mary, and Joseph whose feast day we celebrate today? Surely, they could have proudly displaced such a sign on their front lawn "There's nothing the matter here!" After all, 2 of the 3 never even committed a sin! There was no sibling rivalry! Wasn't this the perfect family? They had it all together didn't they? Weren't they "problem-free" and "worry-free?" Weren't they considered the model family for all time? Yes, they are the "Holy Family" and they are the model for all families to follow – but, being human, even they had some serious problems to deal with! For example, it's no secret Mary was an unmarried, pregnant teenager. Surely, it was no less a struggle and a social problem in the 1st century, as it is today! I'm sure her parents, family, and friends weren't buying her story about the angel appearing to her and asking her to be the mother of the promised Messiah! And poor Joseph, he didn't know what to believe! At one point he decided he would divorce Mary quietly and not bring any legal suit against her. And he wasn't even sure he really wanted to raise a son, who was not his biological child! Yes, the Holy Family had some problems to deal with! The Holy Family lived in an occupied territory, under an oppressive foreign government. They were forced to begin their early married life as "refugees" fleeing the persecution of a local official – (King Herod) an appointee of Rome. When Herod heard about the birth of a "newborn King" in Judea, he feared that child would someday replace him as King, so he murdered all the male babies 2 years and younger, who were born in Bethlehem! As a result for a few years, the Holy Family was an "Exiled Family" living in a strange land—as countless families are doing today in our own time! We just heard the wonderful gospel account of Joseph and Mary taking their 1st born son to the temple to offer him back to God, as was the custom for all families in those days. They must have been elated to hear Simeon's stunning revelation that their son, Jesus, was indeed the promised Savior for all, but then they must also have been troubled to hear the dire prediction that their son, Jesus "was destined for the fall and rise of many in Israel and that he will be a "sign that will be contradicted!" What did these words mean for their son? Then, Simeon made a prediction about Mary, "You yourself a sword will pierce – so that the thoughts of many hearts may be revealed", ominous words that painted a troubled future for them as a family! Just these few glimpses into the life of the Holy Family make us realize they were very human indeed, and were not exempt from suffering, sadness, or struggles. In our own society, there's much complaining and handwringing over the decline of the family and family values! But, has there ever been a "golden age" of the family? No! Not really! Families have always and will always live together under pressure and they will experience some form of trouble or conflict. That's just the human condition of family life! Today's gospel gives us an insight into how the Holy Family survived these challenges! The Holy Family teaches us an important lesson that where the family lives, or what the stresses are a family faces, or what problems a family must encounter – these things are not nearly as important as the "spirit of love" that exists between the members of that family! It's this "spirit of love" based on mutual trust and respect that will carry them through any challenges they have to face as a family! Today we gather as God's family around the sacrament of God's love for us in the Mass and in the Eucharist! An our prayer today is that God the Father teach us how to be good parents, that God the Son teach us how to be good children, and that God the Holy Spirit teach us how to be good lovers!

New Year's Day "B"

One of my resolutions for the New Year is to begin painting again. When I retired 10 years ago, I took some watercolor painting classes; and I was pretty good! When I painted my "masterpiece", an iris, I hung it in my condo hallway and even signed it "By George." Then I retired from painting, but now that I have converted my 2nd bedroom into a studio, I'm going to start painting again! To paint in 08'. Today, the New Year lies before us like an empty blank canvas, just waiting to be painted. There are so many possibilities and opportunities waiting for us – much more important thing than those resolutions we usually keep until the kick-off time of today's 1st football game. But, a whole New Year of time lies ahead of us! Time is a wonderful gift from God! A New Year is always a New Beginning, and since God's graced abounds in us, spiritual growth will always be possible for us. To put it another way, this New Year we will be invited to another stage in our lives, perhaps to a deeper involvement with the Holy Spirit, or to a more personal conversion to the person of Christ, or to the challenge of being a better person at the end of 2008 than we have been at the end of 2007. We Christians believe that God has sanctified acute lymphocytic leukemia (ALL) time in God's master plan of creation, especially since the time of the birth of God's own Son into the world. So, may this New Year be truly "new" for each one of us – a time of spiritual renewal; a time for making this year a "year of peace" in our heart, in our homes, and in our parish, and a time for becoming the people of love and compassion, God is calling us to become. Any may we always remember that every day can be a new beginning, that God helps us to always begin a new canvas and that we can erase the crooked lines and clashing colors….to begin a new and a better work of art. We have more masterpieces to paint.

On this 1st day of the New Year, we celebrate the feast of Mary, the Mother of God! Mary is one of God's many masterpieces; since she is the mother of Jesus, the promised Messiah. She is also our model to copy, to pain, to imitate and follow in the New Year.

The great theologian, Meister Eckhart preached that we are all meant to be mothers of God because God is always waiting to be born in us, as Jesus was born in and through Mary! God seeks to be born today in our own humble mangers and in our forgotten caves; God wants to come alive in the Bethlehem's of our fears and hopelessness, and God wants to make a dwelling place in the Nazareth of our homes, in our schools, and workplaces. Only we can make that happen and so on this 1st day of 2008, we honor Mary as the Mother of God, who gave her Son to the world. In our baptism into the life of Mary's child, we also give Christ to our world by bringing Christ's light and love to others. Our average lifespan is about 25,000 days. Some of that time has already been used up, but a New Year wipes out all the yesterdays and offers us 365 brand new, shining tomorrows in which to be holier, more focused, and more faithful Christians. Of course, life last year, it's only an offer, an opportunity. To accept it, has to be one of the most important New Year's resolutions we make.

Epiphany "B" Matthew 2:1-12

The Magi story is our story and that is why we're so taken by it! Their timeless story follows the storyline of everyone!

In a very real sense, we are all born with a vocation, a calling, a goal! It may be to become a mechanic, a teacher, an engineer, a dancer, a priest, or whatever! The goal may be to find one's true love; or to find the jewel in the eye of the idol; or to find the Emerald City as Dorothy did in the Wizard of Oz; or the Holy Grail, for Indiana Jones; or to find the sorcerer's stone for Harry Potter; or to fine the "King of the Jews" for the three Wise men! And beneath all these symbols, is the human ache to search for God…the search we all share with the Magi!

On any journey, there are always obstacles. For the Magi, there was Herod, (the wicked king) who sweet-talked a lie to them. "Please, go find this adorable child you are seeking, and by all means, come back and tell me where he is, so I too, can adore this newborn king! On this feast we can ask the questions what are the obstacles to our goal of searching for God in our lives? Could it be the sweet-talking "lies" of the commercials that try to convince us we are what we purchase and what we buy makes us what we are? Or, perhaps it is the world preaching that we don't need to have any spiritual goals, that all we need for happiness can be found here and now in this world? Or could it be the world telling us that real happiness can be found in a bottle, in drugs, or in the lure of exciting sex on the internet? The big lie is that there is no need to be on a spiritual journey, that all religion is "pie-in-the-sky" and that it's all an illusion! Such obstacles are the spiritual steroids that puff-up our own self-importance that inflate our desire for power and make us blind to the gospel values!

But, on our journey of faith, there are helps too! For the Magi, help came in the form of an angel who warned them not to return to "sweet-talking Herod" but to "take another path!"

For us, we have our "moral" heroes, and heroines—our parents, grandparents, teachers, priests, religious and our real friends – who have taught us by word and example "to take another path" – the path of Jesus and the path of faith. These people have taught us who we really are—people made in God's image and likeness, redeemed by Jesus' death on the cross, created to know, love, and serve God in this life and to be happy with God forever in heaven! Another source of great help in our search for God can be found right here in our faith community in the parish staff, your fellow parishioners, the religious teachers, the liturgical ministers, those who serve on the various committees, and groups in the parish! We also have the inspiration of the saints, both those canonized and those living in our midst, also, in our community worship, in prayer, and the sacraments! The helps far outweigh the obstacles on our journey of faith! But, what happens at the end of the journey? For the Magi, it was to engage the sacred, to look into the face of Christ, and falling down to offer him their gifts, and to worship him!

It's the same for us; to offer our gifts, and talents and to minister to Jesus – which we do whenever we feed the hungry, give drink to the thirsty, or shelter the homeless. When we do these things for the very least of humanity, we are doing them for Jesus himself.

The reason the story of the Magi resonates so well with us is that deep down in our hearts, we recognize ourselves! That we are the Magi en route on the same journey, and that recognition forces us to reexamine where were are right now, on our own spiritual journey, to ask ourselves the question, "What risks have we taken, or are we willing to take in our search for the Kingdom of God?" Or to ask ourselves the more basic question, "Have we given up the search, or has our search for God been replaced by some of the false idols of this world?"

John Henry Hopkins Jr. was 37 years old when he wrote the lyrics to the hymn, "We Three Kings of Orient Are." He gave the world an enduring Christmas carol that has been sung for the last 150 years! Hopkins was the son of an Episcopalian bishop. He wrote the words and the music to the hymn while teaching at the theological seminary in New York City. He later was ordained as a priest. The familiar words sing of the Epiphany we celebrate today, "O star of wonder, star of night, star with royal beauty bright, westward leading, still proceeding, guide us to the perfect light."

Baptism of Jesus "B" Mark 1:7-11

You first heard it was as a child that tiny whisper of a voice deep within you. You wanted that cookie in the cookie-jar so bad, or you wanted to fight with your annoying little brother, but you heard that voice saying; "No! Don't do it! You know what mom told you!" But you heard it and you know you did! As you got older, the voice spoke more critically, telling you something like: "That was a dumb thing to say, or do." "You really came off looking like a jerk, or "What were you thinking?" But the voice could also be encouraging and affirming saying "Nice job" or "You'll be glad you did that!" or "You didn't deserve that remark." Sometimes the voice would prod, nudge, or even clobber you! But, as you grew up, you knew the voice was usually right. Eventually, we try to make friends with the voice. We don't just listen to the voice, we converse with it by asking it questions like, "I'm not sure what I should do here?" or "What was that all about?" or "How can I make things better?" "Shall I take the high road, or take the low road?" Usually you and the voice (together) found a way to move on, to work it out, or put things back together, and then over time, we begin to hear the voice speaking more comfortably and consoling words like "You are loved", "You belong", or "You are mine!" In the Christian tradition, there's a name for that voice. It's our conscience—or a better definition is that it's the voice of God, God speaking to us in the events of our everyday lives, in people we love, in the various and sometimes difficult decisions we have to make as Christians! At the baptism of Jesus in the Jordan River, Jesus heard that same voice, the voice of God, his Father, speaking to him! It's a message of tender love and encouragement, "You are my beloved son; with you, I am well pleased." Today, we also recall our own baptism. Through the waters of baptism, we are also God's son or daughter. That's who we are! Knowing our true identity tells us not only who we are, but also what our mission in life is. We are to be like Jesus in the world; to bring healing and light to the darkness! Today's feast is about our own self-identity; it's about who we are as baptized Christians! Today, we hear a lot about the miracle of medical transplants for the human body; for example, a kidney or heart transplant gives the patient a chance to live. In a sense, when we are baptized "into" Christ, we also receive a "spiritual transplant", a total "identity" transplant." At that moment of baptism the three Persons of the Trinity take up their dwelling in our souls! We can't see it happen but we are totally transformed. We become adopted children of God; we share in God's own divine life! We can truly call God "Abba" Father, Jesus is our Brother; and the Holy Spirit is our close friend! That's what I mean by getting an identity transplant. In baptism, we "put on" the garment of God's grace, which totally transforms us from being paupers into becoming God's Princely (Royal) people! St. Paul knew this well He wrote in (Galatians 2:20) "I live now, not my own life- but the life of Christ, who lives in me!" On our spiritual journey we gradually come to realize we're not just living our own life. We realize that someone else is living in me and through me – and that we are a part of a much bigger mystery! We're just a drop in a much bigger ocean and what's happening in that ocean is happening within me. Again, St. Paul defines who we are as baptized Christians in (Col. 3:3-4): "You are hidden with Christ in God and Christ is in your life!" he says. Jesus' baptism by John is a defining moment for Jesus! The birth of a child, a life changing retreat, or the death of a loved one in which we have sensed God's loving. Mark tells us: On coming up out of the water Jesus saw the heavens torn open and the Spirit like a dove descending upon him, and a voice came from the heavens telling Him that He was the beloved Son and His Father was pleased. Today's gospel invites us to recall some of those important events in our lives – (our baptism, confirmation, wedding day, presence and hearing God's voice saying to us that we are His beloved son or daughter and He is delighted in us. Such moments are the ones that energize us to continue the healing mission entrusted to us through Jesus – and empowered in us by the Holy Spirit!

Ash Wednesday "B" – Matthew 6:1-6, 16-18 – 2 Corinthians 5:20 – 6:2

The story of the Prodigal son is a story of returning – and that makes it an ideal Lenten Parable. In my own life, I have come to realize the need for returning over and over again! My life drifts away from God…and I have to return. My heart moves away from loving God, and my neighbor as I should…and I have to return. My mind wanders when I'm trying to pray and I have to return. Yes, returning is a life-long struggle that is renewed each Lent! The wayward son had rather selfish motivations for returning to his father. He returned simply to survive. He had discovered that his way of living was leading him to death. He realized he had sinned but this realization came only because sin had brought him to ruin! I'm moved by the fact that the father didn't require any motivation for returning. His love was so total, and so unconditional that he received his son back, whatever his son's motivations might have been! For me, this is a very encouraging thought. God does not demand a pure heart before welcoming back and embracing us! In fact, God doesn't even care why we want to return. Even if we return only because following our own desires has failed to bring happiness – God will take us back! Even if we return because drifting away has brought less peace than being faithful. God will still receive us. Even if we return because our sins didn't offer as much satisfaction as we'd hoped – God will take us back. Even if we return because we could not make it on our own – God will welcome us back with open arms. God's unconditional love does not ask any questions. God is simply glad to see us home and wants to give us all we desire; you will receive the ashes today with these words: "Turn away from sin; and be faithful to the gospel." As you receive the ashes tell God: "Yes Lord, I want to return to you." And then let the open arms of God the Father, be the image you carry in your heart during this Lenten Season!

First Sunday Lent "B" Mark 1: 12-15

Noah and the Ark

Dorothy singing "Somewhere Over The Rainbow" to Toto remains one of the most magical moments in film history. It touched something deep within many people's hearts. In many ways the only thing more magical is the look on a child's face when he or she sees a rainbow for the first time! What is it about a rainbow that is so special for young and old alike? The first time I saw a rainbow my mother told me there was a pot of gold at the end of it just waiting to be found! Then she said the rainbow is a sign from God! God is saying "I love you." The reason of Lent is supposed to be an austere time for prayer, penance, and conversion – but it begins with the bright image of the rainbow! I wonder if Jesus saw a rainbow as he prayed in the desert for 40 days! Like Jesus, our 40 days in the Lenten desert will be filled with temptations; and wild beasts bent on drawing us away from reconnecting ourselves with God. But God promises that God's loving presence will always be with us! God makes a covenant with us, and the rainbow is a sign of that promise, but the funny thing is when we go searching for rainbows, we seldom find them. They seem, rather to find us; to appear when we least expect them to! This Lent, perhaps it would be better not to spend our time in the desert scanning the horizon. We might be looking in vain for what is already present in our own hearts! Our friend, Noah, had been cooped up on board an ark for 40 days and 40 nights with every kind of animal on earth, as well as his own family. His neighbors and friends were all gone! The world (as he had known it) had disappeared! He was having to start all over again. That was Noah's story – but sometimes it's also our story! What do we do when the waters are rising around us, and the world around us is rapidly changing and life seems dreadfully frightening? We find ourselves today standing on the brink of war. The economy is in serious trouble, within our own church the sexual abuse scandal of some priests and the cover-up by a few bishops continue to disturb us! What are we to do? For one thing, we can see that beyond the rising water there is always a rainbow -- the rainbow of hope! Storms do not last forever. Grief subsides, and time heals. Most people who lose their jobs usually find another. Single moms or dads do make it through somehow and when doors are slammed, other doors of opportunity always seem to open! The God of Abraham, Isaac, and Noah, turn rain clouds into rainbows and the God we worship can do the same for us! So, if the waters around you are rising these days, bring your concerns to the one who can put a beautiful rainbow in the heavens – as an eternal promise that the water will never overwhelm us. We can trust the Lord with our lives no matter how difficult the test seems to be! Flood waters symbolize (for many ancient people) what a mushroom cloud symbolizes for us today – death and destruction. Because a flood brought about ultimate annihilation – it is fitting that the waters of baptism for us Christians became a symbol of salvation and eternal life. The God who changes sin into grace and death into life now transfigures the symbol of water from destruction to redemption and salvation! We see the results of such a powerful symbol in the life of Jesus! As mark tells it, no sooner was Jesus baptized than "the Spirit drove him" into the desert to confront the temptations of sin but Satan had no power over him! In the second reading today, Peter tells us Jesus now sits at the right hand of God with angels and power subject to him but we are here on earth where things are not so harmonious! We have a long way to go to make amends with our planet, and a farther way to go in making peace with our fellow humans. But the power of our faith compels us, and the strength of our baptism empowers us! Mark tells us that Jesus was not alone in the wilderness. After his temptations "angels came to minister to him!" Angels came to strengthen him and give him courage! That's how it will be with us. Life puts us to the test, but when the test seems the hardest expect help, because it will surely come! Jesus made that promise when he let us know that He would be with us always, even until the end of the world. Maybe that's the pot of gold we will find at the end of the rainbow! Have a happy and hopeful Lent.

Second Sunday of Lent "B" Mark 9: 2-10

The word "honeymoon" has an interesting history! The two words that compose it, tell the story. The first few months of the marriage are the "sweetest" – that's the "honey" part of the marriage! But then comes the "moon." At first it's full, bright, and beautiful, but eventually it begins to wane and so does the initial affection of a married couple, thus comes the saying "The honeymoon is over." It's just like the first months of a newly elected president in the office – when he and congress are cordial to each other, or it's like a new manager, who is all smiles at first – but then "the honeymoon is over" as differences of opinions arise! The same can apply to a new pastor of a parish or a Lay Pastoral Minister. But, most of us know, life isn't lived only on the "top of the mountain." It's mostly lived below in the foothills of monotony, in the fields of everyday work and disappointments and on the plateaus of quiet devotion, love, and sacrifice! It's there that a couple's love really grows, deepens, and matures, as the years go by. When we meet devoted golden jubilarians, we know what real love is like. Yet, there's always the temptation in marriage to settle down in a sort of "fantasy land" to dream of always remaining young or of being lulled to sleep by thinking problems and difficulties will never happen to us. It's the temptation to the stay and live on the "top of the mountain." In the gospel we just heard, Peter succumbed to that very temptation. Dazzled by the mountain-top transfiguration of Jesus, he blurts out "Let's settle in here and build 3 tents so we can live here happily ever after." But, it was not meant to be! It could not be! Then Peter was hit with the most realistic words in today's gospel, the words that say: Suddenly, when they looked around, they no longer saw anyone but Jesus, alone with them! That was it. Just like that, then it was all gone – it was over. The 2 celebrities, Moses and Elijah, were gone. The voice from the cloud, the dazzle and strobe light were all gone. Only Jesus was left and he matter-of-factly spoke of his suffering and death as they came down the mountain. Yes, the honeymoon was over for them! As they talked, I can imaging Jesus telling them to take up their daily cross to follow him; to make the difficult decisions to be faithful and chaste, to be honest, and trustworthy; to be just, merciful, and forgiving in the everyday event of life. And he probably warned them to beware of the false prophets who might promise them endless honeymoons and constant mountain-top highs. He told them God's life, God's grace, and redemption are lived and gained on the plateaus of daily living. On May 19, 1953, Edmond Hillary and his native Serpa guide were the first people ever to reach the top of Mt. Everest. He was knighted by Queen Elizabeth and became an overnight celebrity and a household name. Edmond Hillary could have tried to live in his little success and glory for the rest of his life, but he knew better. He knew that life is not lived at the top. So, what did he do? He went back to little out-of-the-way Nepal to live. Back to the Serpas whom he had grown to know, and respect, appreciate, and love. And he used his fame and fortune to help them. A few years after his expedition, an elder from the Serpas told him, "Our children lack education. They are not prepared for the future. What we need more than anything else is a school." Hillary set up a trust fund and in 1951 a 3-room schoolhouse was built in Khumjung. Since then, the trust fund has built 27 more schools, 2 hospitals, 12 medical clinics plus numerous bridges and airfields in that area. Many people there don't even know Edmond Hillary. He's no longer a household name – he's certainly no match for Paris Hilton, Brittney Spears, Jennifer Lopez, Brad Pitt, or George Clooney, but his monument is written in the countless hearts of many happy children! The 2nd Sunday of Lent reminds us to be a better and more noble person, to given alms, to visit the sick and forgive our enemies, to be transformed. We really don't need another sweater, or the latest CD. Why not give that money to the poor? That's a surer and better way to spiritual maturity and holiness. So, what's the bottom line of today's gospel? It is that the honeymoon is wonderful, but the moon will soon wane. The mountain top is exhilarating, but the plateau is where it's really at. Hobnobbing with celebrities, like Moses and Elijah is nice, but serving our neighbor gets us to heaven. Our mountain top experiences are wonderful and they can bring us great joys, but coming down the mountain and being alone with Jesus – that's priceless!

Third Sunday of Lent "B" John 2: 13-25

The pastor of a poor parish got a call from the I.R.S. (Internal Revenue Service). "Are you the pastor?" the voice on the phone asked. "I am" he replied. "Do you know a Bob Weaver?" "Is he a member of your parish?" "Yes, he is." "Did he donate $10,000 to your church?" "No, but he will!" responded the pastor. In Jesus' time, the temple was maintained with a tax charged to every Jewish male over 19 years of age. There were also many different currencies accepted in Palestine at that time – but the temple tax; the buying of animals for sacrifice; or any other purchases made in the temple had to be paid for with Jewish shekels. As a result, there was a brisk business of money-changing going on in the temple all the time. The problem was that the money-changers were charging sky-high exchange rates and were fleecing the worshipers, especially during Passover time; thousands of pilgrims were being unjustly exploited in the name of religion. So, when Jesus came to pray he shouted at the money-changers to leave his temple alone. In today's gospel, we shouldn't picture Jesus as knocking tables over like someone in a bar-room fight, or as though he went totally berserk acting like someone on a rampage! His anger was more of a symbolic action – the kind of things prophets did when, for example, they would take a piece of pottery and break it to show how Israel had broken the Covenant with God. Jesus, most likely in one small area of the temple spilled some coins and turned some tables on their side and shooed away some animals with his whip, But he did it to teach that the temple needed cleansing – to make room for prayer and God's presence there! St. Paul reminded the early Christians in Corinth: (1 Cor 3:15): "Do you not know that you are the temple of God; and that the Spirit of God dwells in you?" Lent is a time when we "cleanse" our own temple. It's something we have to do every once in a while. It's something like spring cleaning. We clean our homes all year round, of course, but there are some times when we do some "heavy-duty" cleaning. We move the sofa in the living room, the refrigerator in the kitchen to clean behind it, and move other large pieces of furniture. We take down the curtains and wash them, and even clean the windows. When we do that, we notice things we hadn't noticed before. We see how worn the carpet is because the part that was under the sofa looks so different, and with the curtains down, we notice that the windows really needed to be washed, and with the curtains down and all that sunlight coming in we see the cracks in the paint on the walls we hadn't seen before. So Lent is a time when we move the furniture in our lives; take down the curtains and wash the windows. It's not just a matter of getting rid of the dirt. It's re-arranging things; finding new ways of creating more room; of making a neater and a more beautiful space, then we can see ourselves differently and make more room for God in our lives. Jesus purified the temple and during Lent he invites us to purify the temple of our hearts; to uncover the obstacles, which keep us from living our faith to the fullest. So Jesus is asking us today: "What are the things in your life that are keeping me out? Get rid of them if they are blocking your path to me." And once we see where we need to be purified, Jesus will hand his whip of cords to us so we can drive those obstacles away – the things in the temple of our heart that need "driving" on this Lent. The RCIA "elect" and candidates are moving closer to their baptism, confrontation and 1st Communion at the Easter Vigil. In these final days there are 3 "scrutinizes" along the way. The 1st takes place this weekend; the 2nd and 3rd "scrutinizes" on the next 2 Sundays. The "scrutinizes" are rituals conducted during the Mass. They are a soul-searching kind of a "spiritual house-cleaning", by which the RCIA candidates become more aware of any possible sin; and the need for God's forgiveness and God's saving grace. They come before God who is like a physician, searching (scrutinizing) them for whatever needs healing. The entire congregation prays intercessions for the "elect;" then the "scrutinizes" end with an "exorcism" – a prayer for their spiritual protection; deliverance and the God-given freedom of the "elect" before they receive the Easter sacraments.

Fourth Sunday of Lent "B" John 3:14-21

In the first reading from Chronicles we read: "Early and often" God sent messengers to the people to warn them not to sin. However, the people despised God's warnings and scoffed at God's prophets. So God allowed their enemies to triumph over them, but once the people had repented, they were allowed to return to their loving God and to their beloved Jerusalem after 70 years of exile.

"Early and often" as our first reading suggest, we also know where our actions are taking us. We know for example, that violent means do not lead to peaceful ends. Yet we pursue them over and over, hoping the laws of human behavior will change this time, just this once, for us.

Yes, "early and often" we observe. Anger does not make for a satisfying or successful lifestyle, nor does surrendering to addiction, to selfishness, greed, the blame game or self-righteousness. Each time we try these strategies, they fail us – yet we persist in them because they are so familiar and after all, we tell ourselves "everybody is doing it."

The theology of original sin might be viewed through this lens: "Early and often" humanity chooses against the primary law of loving God and neighbor, and in the process suffers the effects of that decision in a world of darkness, corruption, and death. Just think there are more than 6 billion people on this planet and that a lot of people and also a lot of sin and darkness into which we are born.

But the extent of God's merciful love is recounted in today's gospel: "For God so loved the world that God gave us God's only Son, so that everyone who believes in Him might not perish but might have eternal life." Jesus was sent into the world to save it, not to condemn it! God seeks to draw all people out of darkness into light and to save them from their own sinfulness.

When Jesus came to earth, "early and often" he preached forgiveness, conversion, and salvation> But we so often continue to make choices of unforgiveness insisting that people will never change and therefore they deserve to be punished or ignored. So, we continue to identify people as our enemies (when Jesus said we should love them); and we find ways to isolate and label them, and in extreme cases, even to sentence them to death. In this regard, we much more prefer the God of Chronicles, who first warned the people to change their ways, if they refuse then God allowed them to be conquered, crushed, and swept into exile. Now that kind of God appeals to us and makes sense to us! That kind of God does what we ourselves often do, or would like to do. That God, frankly, is as moral as we are and doesn't challenge us to go beyond an "eye-for-an-eye" moral yardstick.

But what about the God that St. Paul describes for us? A God who is rich in mercy, with great love for us; a God who encounters us even when we are "dead" in our sins, and wills to raise us up to new life through grace! Paul talks about God's "kindness" and the pure gift of salvation. We are God's handiwork, not the shame of our creator. After acute all, God does not make junk! Which view of God is the right one? Both are true – yet the verdict, Jesus tells us in today's gospel, has already come in; in favor of salvation! God's light has come into the world!

Many survivors of the Holocaust recount how they were brutally taken from their homes to the horrifying concentration camps, where so many died. For some the journey to the camp was a living hell. Those who did not live near the train stations were forced to walk, or even run many miles without stopping.

At nightfall they were jammed into homes, or barns of other who were already taken ahead of them. Afterwards they remembered those homes where it appeared as if the people who had lived there might return at any time. It looked as if they had gone on a vacation, but so few ever did return. All that was left of the homes were the dreams and memories they carried away with them. The worst part of the exile for many of the survivors was to find they had no home to go back to! Some of them just wandered around. Some fought to create a new homeland in Israel. Others came to the shores of America.

During Lent we realize we are in an exile of sorts. The difference is we cause it ourselves through our own sinfulness. Sin tears us away from our true home, the community of faith in which we live and we wander in darkness.

During Lent, we search for the light. We gather around Jesus and find what it truly means to be home. But we are not done with Lent yet! We are still wandering in the desert waiting for that light to be lifted up and that will happen on Good Friday, when Jesus is lifted up on the cross; the day that God's merciful love is fully revealed to us.

Fifth Sunday Lent "B" John 12: 20-33

One of the worst things that can happen to the Church is for it to get disconnected from life. Someone once said, "The Church is always answering questions that no one is asking." That is a serious indictment! If it is not true, there is no reason to get upset about it. But if it is true, we need to take it to heart. Just look at history. Over and over again, religion has turned inward and become absorbed with itself. This was the sad state of affairs with the Jewish religious leaders in Jesus' day. They would spend endless hours debating fine points of doctrine and the law. They were zealous about keeping the rules that had little or nothing to do with life, and the result was that most of the common people lost interest in religion. They did not oppose it – they simply ignored it. From time to time, the same thing has happened to the Catholic Church. That's why it was necessary to have the Vatican II Council in 1963. The Church was not answering the questions the world was asking. We were more concerned about being "Catholic" than being Christian. What questions is the world asking? What answers is it seeking? This is not to say that the world should set the agenda for the church; no, not at all. But, the world is our clientele. Christ has commissioned us to win over this world to Him. If we are to do that with any measure of success, we must listen to what the world is saying to the Church. What do they want from us? What do they expect from us? Those Greeks, who came to Philip in today's gospel, answered that question long ago. They said to Philip, "Sir, we would like to see Jesus." That is what the world wanted from the Church back then, and that is still what the world wants from the church today! They are not very interested in the theological defense of our creek. They could care less about our debates between the liberals and conservatives. But, if we could somehow give them a clear vision of Christ of who Christ is, most people would be interested in Him. Of course, the only convincing way for us to do that is by personal example. We must live in such a way that His qualities can be seen in our attitudes and actions! In a hospital in the Middle East, a young American nurse watched as a Turkish man was bought into her ward and placed under her care. She recognized him at once as the one who killed her mother and father…and he also recognized her! The man lived in constant fear, waiting for the revenge that was sure to come. At mealtimes, he expected a lethal poison in his food. In the night, he would startle at the slightest sound, expecting a dagger in his back. But day after day, the young woman cared for him patiently and kindly, as if he were a brother. Finally, the man could stand it no longer. He said to the woman, "You know who I am. You know I'm the one who killed your parents. Why have you been so good to me?" The nurse was quiet for a moment, and then replied "I am a Christian, and Christ has taught me to love my enemies and forgive them." Now it was the man's turn to be silent. After a long pause, he said "I never knew there was a religion like that." There in that hospital ward, a young woman had answered an ancient request – "We should like to see Jesus." That's what the world wants from the church, not pious sermons; but personal testimonies of faith! We cannot take people by the hand and lead them into Christ's presence, as Philip and Andrew did. But we can help people see a little bit of Jesus shining through us. John is the only one of the Gospel Writers who tells this story and he leaves us wondering what happened. Did Jesus talk with them? I think we can assume that he did, but we don't know what was said. Did the conversation lead to anything? Did these anonymous seekers become disciples? All such questions are left unanswered. But the important thing is to us that these Greeks were there; for in a sense, they are representatives. They are a delegation from the world, talking to the Church. Most of the time, we envision that conversation as the Church talking to the world. We think of the Church's message to the world, but this is the world's message to the Church and we need to listen! It's important for us to know what the world really wants from the Church. It's the same request the Greeks asked of Philip, "We should like to see Jesus."

Palm Sunday "B" John 12: 12-16

In his painting called the "Lifting Up of the Cross" the Dutch artist Rembrandt portrays the final moments of preparation before Jesus is hoisted upon the cross. In the painting, the man raising the cross is dressed in contemporary clothing of the artist's time. Those who knew Rembrandt recognized the man in the painting immediately...it was Rembrandt himself! Rembrandt's making himself one of the actors in Jesus Passion, is an act of humble faith; a recognition that each one of us plays a role in the crucifixion of Christ, that is repeated around us in the arts of violence; injustice, and hatred. As we relive the story of Jesus' final hours and his passion and death during this Holy Week, we can consider the role we have played in the agonies, betrayals, condemnations, sad crucifixions going on around us. May our prayer this Holy Week be that God will give us the grace not to be "judging" Pilates; but become Josephs of Arimathea, offering Christ a peaceful place of rest. May we pray that we not seek to melt into the crowd of onlookers; but become Simon of Cyrene; helping Jesus take up his cross in those who are oppressed! May we become Veronica's, who offer Jesus a towel to wipe his bloody face...that we have more courage than the disciples, who abandoned Jesus in his hour of need and be one of the compassionate women, who came early in the morning on Easter to complete the burial of Christ. Let us not be builders of crosses, but be angels, who roll back the stone and proclaim the Good News of Christ's Resurrection. This coming week is called "Holy Week" because Holy Thursday, Good Friday, and Holy Saturday are the "high Holy day" of the year. Come to these services to keep alive the wonderful story of your redemption...and to experience once again Jesus' unconditional love for you!

Easter "B" Easter Sunday John 20: 1-9

A man walked into a local cemetery. It was late at night and he was "under the influence." He stumbled into an open grave and fell fast asleep. When he awoke the next morning, he was puzzled, to say the least. He slowly climbed to the top of the grave, looked around at all the tombstones, and muttered to himself, "My God, it's Resurrection Day and I'm the first one up!" Yes, today is Easter, Resurrection Day, and a time to resurrect ourselves! Easter's good news is that we don't have to wait until we die to share in Christ's resurrection and new life. We can begin to do it right now, today, at this moment, at this Mass! We share in the power of Christ's resurrection now in this world. Every time we begin loving once again after having our love rejected we share in the power of the resurrection; every time we begin trusting once again; after having our trust betrayed and we share in the power of the resurrection NOW, and each time we begin hoping once again, after having our hopes smashed into pieces! Yes, the good news of Easter is that nothing can destroy us anymore – not pain, not sin, not rejection, and not even death itself. The good news of Easter is that every Good Friday now always ends with an Easter Sunday! In fact, life doesn't make sense unless we can make sense of death, and death makes no sense without belief in Christ's resurrection. Belief in the Resurrection is not something added onto the Christian Faith; it is the core and the very center of the Christian Faith! The gospels do not explain the resurrection; no, the resurrection of Jesus explains the gospels! We search for examples that make resurrection real – to make it clear that the Risen body of Jesus was not the same body that was placed in the tomb. Resurrection is not "apparent" death like coming out of a "code blue" in the emergency room; it is not our old life, merely resuscitated and brought back to life. It is a death; going to the other side, and returning with a new glorified body, like Jesus did! The early Christians painted colorful butterflies on the walls of the ancient catacombs in Rome, to grasp the true meaning of resurrection! The early Church saw the butterfly as a symbol of the resurrection of the Risen body of Christ. The caterpillar forms a cocoon and remains in it for a time – as if in a dark tomb, then it emerges with a totally different body, as a brand new, beautiful butterfly! We no longer recognize it as a caterpillar any more than could Mary Magdalena recognize the Risen body of Jesus. She thought it was the gardener. We tell the wonderful story of the resurrection over and over again. Even so, as it was on that first Easter morning, things had not changed that much: The Roman soldiers still ruled, babies still died, violence, and injustice was still everywhere. But what did change the world and what has changed the world today, is the message of Easter – that Jesus lives and that death has died, that evil can never win, that the word of God cannot be imprisoned, that goodness and God's love has triumphed and that all humanity has been redeemed! There's a very famous icon that depicts the Risen Christ standing on the battered-down door of hell. He is extending his hands to a man and a woman, representing Adam and Eve, emerging from their tombs. The two figures look surprised; a little confused and anxious. If you look closely, you can see that Christ has Adam and Eve firmly clasped by the wrists and is forcefully yanking them out of their tombs into the freedom of the resurrection. Adam and Eve, our first parents, represent all of humanity now freed by Jesus' death, and resurrecting, so we can enter into heaven! So this Easter, let Christ grab you out of the grave you may have dug for yourself and fallen into! With the Risen Christ, we have the power to transform our lives from fear into hope; from brokenness into wholeness; from darkness into light; and from death into New Life! Happy Easter!

2nd Sunday Easter "B" – John 20: 19-31

The 20th chapter of John's gospel describes the search for faith in the early church. Upon discovering the empty tomb, John says the Beloved Magdalene met Christ in the garden but didn't recognize him until he called her by name and then he believed! The apostles were huddled in the upper room behind locked doors; frightened by all that had happened, then Jesus appeared to them, and showed them his wounds; only then they believed, Thomas, however, was not there. Only when Jesus came back, and Thomas saw him and touched his wounds did he believe by saying, "My Lord and my God." Faith is a search; a life-long quest! Faith is also a struggle because faith involves growth – and growth is never easy for us. Examination of conscience books, in listing possible sins, will often ask the question, "Did I doubt my faith?" I think that question has caused a lot of misunderstanding. It really should ask, "Did I refuse to face the doubts I have about my faith?" I say that because the decision to believe – to live by faith is the decision to live in the midst of much doubt. Doubts about God, about religion, or about faith are commonplace. It's part of being human! Like Thomas, we have doubts about the credibility of witness. We wonder if the gospels are true. Is Jesus divine and human at the same time? Is Christ really present under the form of bread and wine?

Our emotional doubts surge over us in times of trouble, when we wonder where God was when my child was killed, or when my husband died, or when my son was in an accident that left him paralyzed – especially when I have been so faithful, couldn't God have treated me better? It was the same thing with Thomas! It was all right up to a point – but when his best friend and mentor, this peaceful, innocent man who went around doing good was cruelly arrested, beaten, and horribly crucified – how could Thomas believe in God anymore?

The world was surprised when Mother Teresa's diary was made public and people read about her painful doubts she had all through her life. Was her work caring for the dying and the poorest of the poor, the work God really wanted her to do? Does God really care for the poor? Is there a kind and loving God after all? It turns out that this holy woman, now on her way to sainthood was plagued with many religious doubts.

We doubt for many reasons! We doubt because we want scientific proof that something is true, like Thomas demanded. We doubt because we know there is more to life than we know right now. And we know we don't know all the answers. Like St. Paul, we see dimly as in a clouded mirror. We are aware there is always a new angle; always a new question that arises; always more to learn; that there is always something we never thought of before.

One thing we do know is that doubts are good and necessary for our spiritual growth! In fact, our faith needs doubts in order to grow and develop. Faith is never meant to be something static and finished; and doubt is something like the hunger pains is our body. With hunger pains, we wouldn't eat and be nourished with the food we need to grow and be strong. Sometimes a plant doesn't grow very well because it has too much light. It needs some darkness to grow. The same is true of our faith. We need both light and darkness! But we have to have the courage to admit the darkness. Before Karl Wojtyla become Pope John Paul I while he was the Cardinal of Krakow, he requested permission to build a church in the new town of Nova Huta, which was to be a model communist community.

The communist official denied the request and lectured the Cardinal telling him that with communism in power, all religion will soon disappear and there will be no need for a church. All the myths and superstitions the future Pope believes in will disappear! Some doubts entered his mind, as he wondered if religious freedom would ever return to Poland, but he never gave up, he trusted in God's Providence.

One Christmas Eve, several thousand people gathered to celebrate midnight mass in a makeshift church – a warehouse. A young soldier confronted the Cardinal and arrogantly told him that only a few people could attend the mass. But after the young soldier heard Wojtyla's homily about peace, nonviolence, and God's love for all people, the young soldier had a change of heart, and allowed the rest of the people to enter the church.

At the end of mass, as the Cardinal blessed the people, he noticed the young soldier make the sign of the cross…a powerful and symbolic sign of faith and hope for the future. Faith defeated doubt on that Christmas Eve mass and the communist official who berated Cardinal Wojtyla has long been forgotten. And Thomas came to believe by seeing Jesus' wounds of love and we come to faith by daring to face the doubts that surround us, then we will hear Jesus say, "Blest are you who have not seen; and have believed."

3rd Sunday Easter "B" Luke 24: 35-48

Easter proclaims the Good News that: "Jesus is risen" in accordance with the scriptures! This message assures us that Jesus is not only raised from the dead, but that he also lives in our midst now. He has conquered death and offers us peace and hope in our own resurrection. But where do we find Jesus living in our midst now? Today we don't have the luxury of seeing the Lord "face to face." We can't put our hand into his side, (as Thomas did) or eat fish with him on a beach at sunrise! Or can we? The question is where will we find the risen Christ today? For many this may be a big challenge – yet it's not as difficult as one might think! Jesus once promised that he would be with us, even to the end of time! If we take his word seriously then we should be able to encounter the Risen Lord each day! In fact, we should expect to meet him often! We know we can find him at mass in the "breaking" of bread and in the breaking open of God's word in the scriptures! But the Risen Lord is also present in other ways as well. But Where?

The clue to answering that question can be found in today's gospel! Jesus appears to his disciples and asks them a simple question, "Do you have anything here to eat?" They gave him a piece of cooked fish, which he took and ate in their presence – to prove he was indeed the same Jesus who lived with them, who died on the cross, was buried, and now had risen from the dead!

Now picture yourself being asked a similar question! Most likely it would not be in the exact same words as in today's gospel, but it would be a request from someone in need! Actually the words might sound more like this, "Mom I'm hungry!" "We got anything to eat?" And you hear those words with the same love, caring and joy, as if it were the Risen Christ asking you for a response! And the Risen Lord is their present in a child's request!

Or, you're hurrying down the street to your next appointment and suddenly a dirty hand reaches out to stop you in your tracks. "Hey pal, got any spare change for a cup of coffee?" You immediately feel upset at this imposition of your time and money – and there stands Jesus (with his nail-marked hand) reaching out to you for some help!

Or, (for you younger people) you and your buddies are about to choose up sides for a game and you hear someone ask, "Can I play too?" and you tell him "No, we don't need you!" You're too young or you're not good enough. Or you and a couple of friends are about to head for the mall and as you're about to leave you hear the question, "Where are you guys going?" "Can I tag along too?" You stop and turn to tell the little kid or the guy who seems to be a little strange or different to get lost! And there stands Jesus – once again, rejected and excluded!

We encounter the Risen Christ in the people living around us! We become true witnesses of Christ's resurrection by recognizing Him in our family and friends and in our neighbors, in the poor and needy, and in the people we work with! Even in our enemies and in the people who are different than us, in those who disagree with us or even dislike us!

After his resurrection, Jesus appears to his disciples as a human being – with "flesh and bones" and that is the way the Risen Lord remains present in the world today – in the "flesh and bones" of one another!

By asking his disciples for "something to eat" he is asking us to have compassion and generosity for the cries of the poor, and the needy in our midst!

We all experience hunger in our lives – not just physical hunger, but the hunger for a sense of belonging; a hunger for the reassurance that our lives do matter; that our lives have meaning; that there is a point to my existence besides just existing!

Often, it's we ourselves who are hungry and sometimes it's those around us who are hungry, who hunger for our affirmation and our acceptance, for our forgiveness, or for our compassion and generosity!

"Do you have anything here to eat?" is the question Jesus is asking of us today...we who are now the witnesses of his resurrection in our world.

4ᵗʰ Easter "B" John 10: 11-18

In today's gospel, Jesus draws a comparison between two different kinds of shepherds! One is a "hired-hand" and the other he describes as a "good shepherd!" The difference between the two is in the level of their commitment to their task as shepherds. Now, there is no suggestion that the "hired-hand" was a bad shepherd. As far as we know, he performed all his duties well, keeping the flock together and leading them to find adequate shelter, food, and water! That is what he was paid to do but a hired-hand was not paid to lay down his life for the sheep. So the difference between them is revealed at the time of crisis – when the flock would be threatened by wolves attacking the sheep in the lonely desert, a time when not only the sheep, but the shepherd himself would be in serious danger of his life! The "hired-hand" (Jesus said) would flee in order to save his own life. But the "good shepherd" would stay and if necessary, (even would be willing to die) protecting the flock. Jesus identified himself as the "good shepherd" who would lay down his life the sheep.

That kind of dedication only comes voluntarily from the heart, out of love! Money can't buy it, no law can demand it! And that is what Jesus (the Good Shepherd) is saying of himself. "I lay down my life!" No one is taking it from me, I lay it down freely!" When Jesus went to Calvary to die for our sins, he was functioning in a realm totally above and beyond the call to duty. I wonder how many of us today have discovered that level of loving and living!

For example, an employee is expected to show up for work at a particular time, remain on the job for a certain number of hours and do certain things while there! Every employee is expected to perform at least at this level!

It's the same expectation in all areas of life – whether we are a student, a teacher, a parent, a politician, a priest or parishioner, a police officer, or a fire-fighter, we all have certain duties we are expected to perform!

But our true greatness in life doesn't lie in just doing our basic duties as Christians (like the hired hand) but lies in the realm beyond the call of duty....where the "good shepherd" was willing to go! That's the message of today's gospel!

Jesus is remembered, and honored as the Good Shepherd because he voluntarily took on himself that which no one could possibly have demanded of him! It is in this sense that his cross deeply touches our lives and inspires us to imitate him by becoming "good shepherds" ourselves!

A student discovers the joy of learning only when he places demands on himself – that no teacher could even require. Family life takes on a whole new dimension or beauty, and meaning. Only when parents, husband, wife, and children begin to give themselves in ways no law on earth could ever demand! And a person's work becomes a privilege and pleasure only when he or she stops thinking of the "minimal requirements of the job," and begins to function in the realm that is above and beyond the call of duty, in fact, all genuine Christian living consists in breaking free from (and rising above) all legalism, to do what no law can require, or no person can demand, to do the right thing, to always take the high road! This is the very essence of the life and teaching of Jesus, our Good Shepherd!

Jesus expressed it in this way when he once told us to go two miles instead of one if you were compelled by someone to do so. He compelled us to love those who love you because what reward can you expect otherwise. Even though tax collectors and sinners do as much He told us to love our enemies, even love the ones who hate or persecute us. In other words I believe that Jesus is telling us to do something above and beyond the call of duty; do something more than is required; or expected of us!

Jesus, (the Good Shepherd), calls us to look beyond our own expectations; our own needs, and fears in order to become "shepherds" of compassion, of peace, and charity to others! To be a disciple of Jesus is not simply to be a "hired-hand", who acts only to be rewarded! The real followers of Jesus realizes that every person belonging to the "one-fold" of Christ possesses the sacred dignity of being a child of God; and rejoices in knowing that in serving others we serve God!

And by embracing the Gospel values of comparison and love for the sake of others – (in laying down our own lives in service for others). Our lives will one day be "taken up again" in the Father's Easter Promise!

5th Sunday Easter "B" John 15: 1-8

Sometimes we Christians tend to separate our lives into two "boxes" – either into the "church" box, or into the "world" box. And one box has nothing to do with the other! Their lives are divided into separate compartments into my "church" life into my professional "work" life, or my "entertainment life" – into separate little "boxes" that seldom touch one another and are not connected! So, they become (in Jesus' metaphor in today's gospel) like branches, cut off from the Vine! And even though they may look "successful" they soon wither and die! They are like "dead men walking" because they are not connected to Christ, or to the world wide community in which they live! Jesus warns against this in his parable of the Vine and the branches! He is in the Vine and we are the branches. He urges us, "To remain in Me; as I remain in you! Just as the branch cannot bear fruit on its own, unless it remains on the vine, so neither can "you bear" spiritual fruit, unless you remain in me." In short, he is saying; "Be connected with Me, and be connected with one another!

The great Christian truth is that we are connected to someone and to something much larger than ourselves!

For example, we are connected to the millions of people suffering from hunger, AIDS, or ethnic cleansing in Africa and in other parts of the world! We are connected to those who have died, or been wounded in the wars, and in other acts of violence in Iraq or Afghanistan! We are connected to the children in the world who suffer abuse and neglect. We are connected to all non-Christians in the world, and all other Christians who worship the One and same God as we do, but believe and worship in different ways! We are connected to the earth, which we dare not pollute by our selfishness and our greed! We are connected to nature – to all of God's creation.

St. Francis of Assisi reminded us of this when he spoke of "Brother" Sun, and sister "Moon" and when he preached not just to people but also to the animals. Yes, we are one, big interconnected human family! We truly are our brother's and sister's keepers; we are part of a larger global community – and our actions or our inactions really do have consequences! As Christians, we believe that we are a "people of God" that we are "The Mystical Body of Christ" in the world we believe that Christ is the Vine and we are the branches! We know we should not live our lives in separate little "boxes" separating our beliefs from our actions; separating our "church going" from our "church living", or separating our own lives from the lives of others! Therefore, what you and I do and say here in church today – should be the same, as what we do and say when we leave church to go home; go to work or go to school!

There's another way to look at Jesus' words which say that He is the vine, and we are the branches. We could take the word "branch" in the same sense as the meaning of a "branch" office. In the business world, there's a main headquarters – and then there are it's "branches" that are supposed to reflect the same product and philosophy as the main corporation! In that sense we are all "branch" offices of Jesus in the world! We are supposed to reflect his values and His mission! We are expected to be Christians all the time, 7 days a week, not just on Sundays! People should be able to know we are Christians by the way we act. So let us do something beautiful for God – together!" All of us are united with Christ, our true Vine!

6th Sunday Easter "B" John 15: 9-17

In today's gospel Jesus tells his disciples and us "Remain in my love!" Contained in these 4 little words is a "hidden" treasure! I say that because "remaining in his love" means that we are already there --- "in his love." In fact, we have always been "in his love" from all eternity – even before we were born! And we will always "remain in his love "forever! Even the worst sinner in the world is still loved by God! Mother Teresa put it this way, "When we look at the cross, what do we see? We see Jesus' head bent down to kiss us! Look at his pierced hands – they are saying to us "I love you! We see his arms stretched out on the cross, as if to embrace us! We see his heart opened wide to receive us!"

In today's 2nd reading, John gives us the best definition of God – "God is Love." And John begins today's gospel by telling about God-the-Father's love for Jesus! The love within the Trinity is a mystery – totally beyond our understanding! It's not a trivial or a sentimental love – but a love that is deep personal and truly self-sacrificial! This is the love Jesus wants to share with us, "As the Father has loved me, so I have loved you."

In the gospel, Jesus describes how much he loves us by telling us that no one has a greater love than this – to lay down one's life for one's friends. Then he lets us know that we are all his friends. His love is a sacrificial love! That's why Jesus is often referred to as "The Man for others." He proved his love for all humanity by freely accepting death even death on a cross! But that's the same type of love Jesus is asking of us, when he says, "Remain in My love." Have the same type of love that nailed me to the cross! Have a love that doesn't count the cost! A love that is sacrificial, unselfish, and unconditional – a love that includes everyone!

Is such a love even possible? It seems so unrealistic, too spiritual, too far above me, too impossible! But Jesus doesn't think so! He says to love each other as He loves each of us. He thinks it's possible, yes, perhaps difficult, but certainly not impossible! Let's go back to those 4 little words again when Jesus told us to remain in his love.Those words are the "hidden" treasures, I was talking about, the key to loving others, as Jesus did! "To remain in my love" means to see others as Jesus sees them! That's the "difficult" part of Christian love!

At last count, the You-Tube video of Susan Boyle singing on the show "Britain's Got Talent" has been seen by millions of people! Ms. Boyle is an unemployed, unmarried, middle-aged woman, from a remote village in Scotland, a Catholic, who has spent the last few years quietly caring for her ailing mother, who recently died at 91. And when she strode onto the stage to sing "I Dreamed a Dream" (a beautiful song from "Les Miserables"), the judges visibly smirked – that is, until she opened her mouth in song! She silenced them with her glorious voice! What is it that attracts such astonishing interest in Susan Boyle for millions of people? Is it that such an unlucky person has finally been given a lucky break? Perhaps! But, there may be more!

I think the way the viewers see Susan Boyle is like the way God sees us! God sees us as worthwhile, special, talented, unique, beautiful and loveable, because we are created in God's image and likeness!

The world usually looks down on people like Susan Boyle; if it sees them at all! Without classic good looks, without a job, without a spouse, living in a small town – people like her, may not seem to be very "important" or even "worthwhile."

But, God sees the "real" person and the value of each person's gifts and talents – rich or poor, old or young, single or married, matron or movie star, lucky or unlucky in life, saint or sinner! God knows each one of us – really knows us and still loves us. God looks beyond our sins, and failings – and sees our goodness, or our potential for goodness!

That's how Jesus wants us to see and love one another – the same way God sees and loves us! That type of Christian love is possible. That's something that is "do-able"! Difficult yes, Jesus tell us, "but not impossible." Let's try it this week. It just might work!

The Ascension "B" The Ascension of the Lord – Mark 16: 15-20 – Acts 1: 1-11

The final days of John Paul II's life were a witness to everything he stood for; to everything he had preached during his life. Even his final illness became a sermon in silent suffering; telling the world that every life is of supreme importance and has infinite value! On his final Easter Sunday (2005), just a week before he died, unable to speak the words of the Easter message, he stood at the window and read it silently, while another voice spoke the words. Then, raising his hands, he gave his final blessing to the world. This final act was his personal witness to the truth of the gospel – to the truth that John Paul had written (about 10 years before in 1995) when he wrote his letter called "The Gospel of Life." In that letter he wrote these words, "The just man does not seek to be delivered from old age, and its burdens…but accepts from God the need to die…and he trusts in God." John Paul II did exactly that! In so doing, he was a witness to the good news about life – the good news that Jesus Christ is the King of Glory; that he has conquered evil; he has conquered death itself, and that Jesus Christ has ascended to heaven, and where he has gone, we hope to follow.

On this feast of the Ascension, we recall the great mystery of Jesus Christ – that he died on the cross. He was buried in the tomb; He rose from the dead and ascended into heaven. This is the story of Jesus Christ – and this is our story too! Where Jesus has gone, we too, by His grace, will follow. The pattern of His life now becomes our pattern too!

The bride loved flowers and she planned her wedding bouquet carefully – white roses were her favorite, blue iris her fiancé's favorite and green ivy representing hope for their future.

During the wedding reception, one of the guests, a woman the bride didn't know very well – a friend of her mother-in-law, came up to her holding some ivy, "This fell out of your bouquet when you were on the dance floor" she said.

The bride thanked her and began to reach for it but the guest asked, "Would you mind if I keep it?" The bride was startled at first but then smiled graciously and said, "Sure, go ahead and keep it." Then returned to her other guests.

A few months later, the doorbell range at her new home. The bride opened the door – and there was the wedding guest. "I have a wedding gift for you" she said and held out a small planter with a thick, healthy foliage. "It's the ivy you dropped at your wedding. I took it home and made a cutting and planted it for you." She went to explain "When I was married some years ago, someone did the same thing for me. It's still growing -- and every time I see it, I remember my wedding day. I hope you enjoy it."

That happened 20 years ago. Today that bride – now the mother of three sons – looks forward to including a cutting of ivy in her future daughters-in-law's wedding bouquets.

On the feast of Ascension, the Risen Christ invites us to continue to nurture the seedlings he first planted in our hearts at baptism – the seedling of his teachings; his works of healing and the seedlings of his own passion, death, and resurrection! Like the gift of ivy from one generation of brides to the next, we are called to continue to plant and grow the Gospel of life – to carry on the work of Redemption begun by Christ that was the work of the Apostles; that was the work of Pope John Paul II; and that is the work entrusted to each one of us today.

Today we hear a lot about the "DaVinci Code" and a group in the Catholic Church called "Opus Dei" translated from the Latin "Opus Dei" simply means "the work of God."

We are all "Opus Dei" members through our baptism into Christ – when we are called to continue promoting the "work of God" in our everyday life – whether it be in our family, in our relationships at work, at school, in our church, in all of society. "Opus Dei" is not a secret society with a limited membership – it's open to all Christians who love God and who want to carry on the work of Christ. Yes, it's Ascension Day once again! And Jesus is telling us, "Go out to the whole world. Preach his gospel and heal the sick." The real question today is not, "Where did Jesus go?" The real question to contemplate is "Where is Jesus asking us to go?"

Pentecost "B" John 20: 19-23

Today's readings describe 2 different accounts of the Pentecost Event – one found in the book of Acts, written by St. Luke; and the other found in St. John's gospel. Both describe how the Holy Spirit formed the followers of Jesus into a community of faith, which we today call "the Church."

In Acts, Luke pictures the Holy Spirit descending on the disciples in the form of a powerful wind and in the form of tongues of fire! Wind and fir are suitable metaphors for how the Holy Spirit works in our lives. Wind is powerful, but invisible. Fire is intense and bright. God's fire lights the way for us and brings us warmth and comfort!

John's gospel describes the 1st Easter night. The Apostles are hiding in fear, behind locked doors, when the Risen Jesus suddenly appears and "breathes" on them thus giving them the gift of the Holy Spirit! "Receive the Holy Spirit," Jesus tells them and then gave them the same power to forgive sins, as he himself had! The Acts account of the disciples along with the Apostles receiving the Holy Spirit, takes place 50 days after Easter on "Pentecost" Sunday! The Greek word for 50 is "Pentecost." All the followers of Jesus gathered together in Jerusalem on Sunday! Jesus had already ascended back to heaven and these men and women felt alone and lost; they were confused and undecided – having no idea what to do next! Even the Apostles are terrified, because they are "marked" men – considered to be followers of the disgraced Nazarene, who claimed to be "The King of the Jews." But then the Holy Spirit "blows" through their locked doors! Like a powerful wind, the Spirit drives them out of their safe, hiding place into the streets to being the work of proclaiming the Risen Christ! The Spirit of God, the very "breath" of God, is "breathed" into their souls – giving them new life, transforming their fear into purpose; their despair into hope and their disgrace into peace!

So, here is the question for us on this Pentecost Sunday, will we allow the same rushing, powerful wind of God to "breath" freely into our lives; to blow away all that keeps us from being close to God; from being good disciples? Will we allow the rushing "wind" of God's Spirit to rearrange our lives? To adjust our own plans, and our priorities? To rethink or reconsider our own ideas of what's right or wrong? Or will we rush to close the widow and shut the door to protect our own arrangement of the clutter in our own lives? Sometimes, we find ourselves locked in that same room, afraid, not knowing what to do next! Struggling to find Easter peace, trying to experience Pentecost courage; or to find some direction, but we need the Holy Spirit to drive us from our comfortable hiding places and from our "safe" isolation – in order to do the work of discipleship! The Holy Spirit empowers us to put aside our fears, and our doubts – to be God's agents for peace and reconciliation in our own time and place!

I recently came across a modern-day "Pentecost" story of hope. It took place during these difficult economic times; at a grocery store in Minnesota! It's a true story that was reported on NBC's "Nightly News" program.

A woman was waiting in a check-out line, when she was passed an envelope from the person in front of her. Someone had written on the envelope, "There's $50.00 in this envelope for your groceries." Take it if you need it, if not, pass it on." the woman passed it on to the person behind her. She then watched it go through the line – then on to the next line and the next and so on. What struck her most, was not that people passed the envelope on – but that several people actually added money to it!

The Spirit of God moved through those lines of shoppers in an envelope! Any time, any place; where compassion, generosity, and love compel people to do what is right and just – the Spirit of God is moving among them!

The feast of the Pentecost is the celebration of that same Divine Spirit dwelling within us – within us collectively, as a church, or as a nation; or within us individually as baptized Disciples of Christ.

It's that same Spirit of God that brings two people together as husband and wife, to be witnesses of God's love to the world; it's the same spirit that forges strong and lasting friendships between friends and families, or between nations, races, and religions! The Spirit of Pentecost enables us to "pass on" God's love to others. To "breathe" into our world the love of a God, who first loved us enough to become one of us to die for us and to rise for us! And Jesus so loved us, that he "passed on" to us his most precious gift, the Holy Spirit! That's what we celebrate today!

The Holy Trinity Sunday "B"
Matthew 28: 16-20

The story is told about a country preacher who announced to his congregation he would preach about Noah and the Arc on the following Sunday. He gave the scriptural reference for the people to read ahead of time. A couple of mean-spirited boys noticed something interesting about the story of the flood in the Bible. They slipped into church and glued two pages of the preacher's bible together. On the next Sunday the preacher got up to read his text. "Noah took himself a wife" he began, "and she was …." (He turned the page to continue). "30 high cubits, 50 cubits wide, and 300 cubits long." He paused, scratched his head, turned the page back and continued reading then he looked up at the congregation and said, "You know, there are some things hard to believe, and hard to understand in the Bible."

One of the truths difficult to understand or believe in the Bible is the teaching on the Trinity ….that there is One God, but Three Divine persons in the One True God. It's difficult to explain the relationship between the Father, The Son, and the Holy Spirit and ourselves.

There are many things in our human life that are difficult to understand, or explain, at least for me! For example: How can we Fax a message, or a picture anywhere in the world in 30 seconds? Or how do we transmit the sound of our voice to a tiny village in Ireland over the phone? Or it's difficult to understand why certain human relationships work and others just don't work. For example, why do I like certain people? What is it that attracts me? A good relationship is not necessarily built on logic or reason; it's not just emotional or psychological attraction either. It is a mystery! I can't explain it or even understand it.

One thing I do understand is that when I'm with people I like, I experience warmth, acceptance, and love. While with them, I can say or think anything I want without fear of being rejected or laughed at. I'm simply loved unconditionally. So, in a sense, in that type of a relationship, I can experience bits and pieces of other relationships. I can experience the love of a mother, or father, the sense of loyalty and closeness that exists between brothers and sisters; or that certain spirit of growing up in a loving family and even though our human relationships are imperfect (and never will be perfect) – yet they are life-giving and bring happiness.

Today is the Feast of the Holy Trinity – we celebrate our relationship with God the Father, God the Son, and God the Holy Spirit. It's a deep mystery; we will never understand it! But we human beings can experience that relationship ONLY through the human relationships we experience.

For example: We experience God's love through a loving mother or father. We experience a closeness to God because we have had that same closeness with a brother, sister, or a close friend. We experience God's acceptance and forgiveness because of a loving family, a community, or a support group. God's love is a gift freely given. We don't deserve it; we can't earn it. All we have to do is accept it like any relationship.

On this Feast of the Blessed Trinity we can ask ourselves some basic questions like: "What is it that attracts God to us?" Or who are we; or what do we have that makes us so lovable in the eyes of God? We are loveable to God because we are baptized into the very life of God The Father, Son, and Holy Spirit. We become adopted children' able to call God "Abba" (i.e. Father, Dad, Jesus, our Brother). We automatically inherit all that belongs to God through our baptism. Humanly speaking, there are no mirrors in heaven, and because there are no mirrors, God needs some way to see Himself! So the Trinity focuses on people who are created in the image and likeness of God. We humans become the mirror reflecting God's love! When God wants to see what God looks like, God simply looks at us, and at the various ways we love each other. Conversely, John says, "No one has ever seen God, but as long as we love one another, God will live in us; and God's love will be complete in us. (I John 4:18). Now Do you understand the trinity? Neither Do I!

Corpus Christi "B" Mark 14: 12-16, 22-26 (The Body and Blood of the Lord)

Do you remember the last time you had dinner at a nice restaurant? Perhaps it was to celebrate a birthday; an anniversary; or some other important event. Special events like these almost demand a special meal! And often, that special meal is shared at a "table-for-two"...perhaps just you, and your spouse and you, and a good friend, or a family member, or someone you are dating! There's something intimate about a "table-for-two!"

Such is the intimacy, the warmth, and love of the Last Supper meal of Jesus, and his 12 very close friends! We know the story so well because we share in it every time we attend Mass! There in the upper room is Jesus and his disciples. There is the bread and the wine, and the words. Those haunting and transforming words of Jesus: "Take, and eat; this is my body broken for you and over the wine. Take, and drink; this is my blood, poured out for you and for many!" My fear is that we know the story so well, we have failed to know it deeply and personably.

What if today, (on this feast of the Body and Blood of Christ), we could experience Holy Communion, (this sacred meal with Jesus), in a new and more personal way. What if you came to Mass today – because Jesus has personally invited you to dine with him – at this altar at his "table-for-two!" And there you "rediscover" what it really mean to eat this bread and drink this cup!

But, (you may ask), how can such a personal meeting with the Risen Lord happen for me? The first thing required is a proper preparation on our part! If receiving communion is truly a meeting between Jesus and us – have we taken the time to prepare a holy place (or a sacred space) in our souls for that personal encounter?

The second thing required to make communion more personal is to visualize that there's a "table-set-for two" at a certain time and place, at the altar – for a meal with Jesus and you're invited!

Sometimes people tell me they wonder why they can go to church week after week and they receive Holy Communion but they leave church feeling just as "malnourished" as when they came! Again, it's the lack of preparation, the lack of reflection on who the Eucharist is and a failure to rid themselves of all those distractions that keep us from meeting Jesus IN A PERSONAL WAY!

Have you seen the cell phone commercial on TV, where the young couple is sitting in a nice restaurant at a "table-for-two" when the man glances down at the screen of his phone to check the score of a game? His girlfriend questions him about it—she's upset that he would find anything more important at that moment – than just being with her!

Of course, he denies that he's that shallow, but then (at that moment) his cell phone beeps to announce another update on the game he was secretly viewing!

Sad to say, we often treat our time with Jesus in that very same way; especially at Mass, and at communion time when Jesus longs for so much more from us! We gather at mass without much preparation. We say the prayers and the responses without much thought. We hear the scriptures read without really listening, and we put the holy bread and consecrated wine to our lips with little wonder and awe. Doesn't Jesus (the Bread of Life come down from heaven; our loving Savior, and our best friend) deserve better from us?

I have three suggestions how you can make your communions spiritually more fruitful. First, use your God-given gift of "imagination" when you come to church. While preparing to receive Holy Communion, think about the fact that Jesus truly longs for and desires to dine with you. You and I, are not "after-thoughts" or "second-best" guests at his table! No! He sets a place at this table just for you – because he wants you to dine with him!

Secondly, as you listen to the readings at mass, ask God to speak to you personally through those sacred words. And as you sing the hymns and responses and during the quiet moments of the liturgy, renew your desire to know God's will and to follow it to the best of your ability.

Thirdly, (here is something that helps me focus on the true meaning of Communion), I like to "visualize" Jesus as standing, alone, outside my closed, locked door - wishing to enter into my life!

He just stands there, patiently waiting for the door to be opened in welcome to him! And once the door is opened he joyfully enters as a friend – accepting me as I am and bringing me his love and forgiveness! He then sits down at my table and dines with me! That is what Communion means for me! Remember that your table-for-two is always reserved!

2nd Sunday "B" John 1:35-42

I think Andrew is one of the most attractive characters in the New Testament! For one thing, he was content to play second fiddle to his brother, Peter! For another, he simply couldn't keep the Good News of Jesus to himself, he had to share it with others and he seemed delighted to introduce people to Jesus!

The New Testament mentions Andrew 3 times, and each time he is introducing someone to Jesus! (1) He brings the boy with the 5 loaves, and 2 fish to Jesus; and Jesus feeds 5000 people with the boy's gift! (2) He brings a group of inquiring Greeks, who want to talk with Jesus and (3) (as recorded in today's gospel) he runs after and gets his brother, Simon, to meet Jesus! When they met, Jesus looked at him and said, "You are Simon son of John; you are to be called Cephas'-- meaning Rock." (John 1:42) When Jesus looks at people he sees (not only what we are) but also what we can become with God's grace! In today's gospel, John the Baptist sees Jesus walking by and he tells Andrew, "There is the Messiah, the Lamb of God!" (Andrew and another disciple of the Baptist) follow after Jesus and ask, "Where are you staying?" Jesus invites them to "come and see" and they stayed with him that day! Imagine spending the entire day talking with Jesus, and asking him questions. Andrew is convinced that Jesus truly is the Messiah, and he immediately runs to find his brother, Simon, to share the Good News! "We have found the Messiah" he excitedly tells Simon, and then the gospel says, "He brought him to Jesus!"

This gospel is a perfect example of the most common type of "evangelization" – one based on the personal sharing of Good News with another; not one based on the preaching, or teaching to someone "about" Jesus. St. Francis of Assisi explained the difference between the two types of evangelization when he said, "We are call to preach the gospel at all times; when necessary, use words!"

213

Another example of this form of "evangelization" comes from Mother Teresa! Most of the people she and her sisters worked with were either Hindus or Muslim. Asked why she decided to accept the award "in person" she replied, "I myself am unworthy of the prize! I do not want it personally! It is on behalf of the poor that I have come. We all have reason to be happy because we have Christ with us – Christ in our hearts; Christ in the poor we meet; Christ in the smile we give; and Christ in the smile we receive!" She went on to say, "In the more wealthy developed countries, there is a poverty of intimacy! A poverty of spirit! A poverty of loneliness! And a poverty of lack of love! There is no greater sickness in the world than that! She finished her talk by saying, "You can do something I can't do! So let us do something beautiful for God – together!" All of us are united with Christ, our true Vine!

That's the best way they could introduce Jesus to others and perhaps bring them to Jesus!

Let me tell you a true story about a very young evangelist. Her name is Josephine; she is 8 years old, and she is in the 3rd grade!

Every day the school bus would pick her up and drop her off at her home. In her case, when the bus dropped her off at her home, her brother was always waiting for her by the fence that surrounded their house. He was a year or so older than Josephine, but he didn't go to school.

Some of the students on the bus used to look for him and when they saw him they would laugh! They laughed at him because somehow they saw that he was "different." The kids laughed at him because they didn't know or understand why he was different. They would wave at him, and sometimes call out to him and he would wave back, only making them laugh all the more!

But when Josephine got off the bus, her brother would jump up and run to meet her and to the other kids' surprise Josephine didn't seem at all embarrassed; even though she knew the kids on the bus were having a great time! She would greet her brother and hug him, and after that she would throw both arms around her brother! And then, hand-in-hand, the two of them would march into the house together!

At a young age, Josephine had learned the very human lesson of love and acceptance! When the other kids asked Josephine about her brother; she should simply say her brother was "slower" than other kids and he would never be like them, but he was her brother and she loved him.

Over time, the other kids on the bus began to understand a bit more-and their "mocking" began to stop. They still continued to wave at Jimmy but now it wasn't mockery; it was with a sense of kindness and compassion and Jimmy would always wave back! What was it that changed the attitude of the kids on the school bus? It was the image of Josephine embracing her brother and accepting him the way he was.

In a sense, Josephine was doing what Andrew was doing and what Mother Teresa (and her sisters were doing), introducing people to the Good News of Jesus!

By her love for her mentally handicapped brother, she was introducing those kids on the school bus to Jesus' love and his compassion. She truly was a little "evangelist" without even being aware of it! She was "preaching" the gospel of Jesus' love to them – just by her example! Words were not necessary! Her actions spoke volumes!

The moral of this homily is obvious! No matter how young or how old we are (8 or 80 years old), each one of us can become "evangelists" without saying a word, just by our example of living the gospel values. There's an old saying that says, "No one goes to heaven alone; we take other people with us; the ones we introduced to Jesus in our lifetime!

3rd Sunday "B" Mark 1: 14-20

It was 30 years ago, January 18, 1982, that I decided to quit smoking. I was 51 years old and my golfing buddies had quit smoking six months before. I was tired of being short of breath and stuffed up all the time. I really felt good about my decision and wondered why I hadn't quit years before! In fact, I felt so good and confident about my decision I decided to announce it to the congregation the following Sunday at all the masses. I told everyone I needed their prayers and support. I knew I was just one cigarette away from starting all over again, and I needed them to remind me of that.

Quitting smoking is a big decision and it's not easy to do! But I thought of what I really wanted. I wanted freedom. I was a slave to smoking. I loved it and hated it at the same time. Smoking ran my life. I was not free to quit or even cut down as long as I continued to smoke. So I began living my life in a new way, living "as if" I had never smoked before, "as if" I was always a nonsmoker. I began living each day "as if" I didn't need to light up every time I had a cup of coffee, or talked on the phone, or drove my car. (All this ties in with today's readings). What does all this have to do with today's reading? In today's gospel Jesus is telling us to behold because the Kingdom of God is at hand. He wants us to repent and believe in the gospel. He is saying live "as if" Jesus and the Kingdom of God, are the most important thing in your life. Live "as if" nothing else mattered in this world. The entire gospel is a call to live as "as if" Christians.

In our first reading, the Pagan Ninevites listened to Jonah the Prophet and they repented. They turned away from sin and accepted the God who set them free from the worship of false gods and they were willing to pay the price!

The early Christians heard the good news of the gospel and responded to Jesus' invitation to "come, follow me."

We see James and John turn their backs on their fishing boats, and their fishing nets (the source of their income) and they even left their father to follow Jesus. They experienced a true conversion! They began living "as if" people, "as if" nothing else mattered but Jesus Christ, and they were ready to pay the price!

St. Paul turned out to be an "as if" Christian when he could say, "It is no longer I that live…it is Christ who lives in me."

The decision to stop smoking is not a "one-time" decision. It's a decision that is made time and time again. In fact, I have to make a confession to you. Six months after I announced my non-smoking decision to the congregation, I began smoking again! I thought I could just smoke one cigarette, but I couldn't, so I had to confess my failure to the Parish. Likewise, the decision to follow Jesus is not a "one-time" decision made at our baptism, but a daily decision, which involves struggle, temptation, failure, and sin. But we have to be willing to pay the price! Conversion is an ongoing process, which constantly invites us to a deeper, more personal relationship with God. The essence of our Christian faith is this, to keep on repenting, and keep on believing in the good news of the gospel, and to keep on following Christ, even though we might fail.

But how do we do that? St. Paul tells us how in the second reading, he says this, "Make use of the world "as is" not using it." He is saying that jobs, homes, cars, money, clothes, even relationships are not the most important things in life, but Jesus Christ is the most important. Once I believe that, then I'm free to listen to Jesus. I'm free to allow Him to come into my life and lead me back to the Father.

So, each day Jesus is inviting us "to come, follow me." In order to respond we have to live as "as if" people. We are a Pilgrim people, not attached to this world, but free to follow Jesus wherever He may lead us. So, during this New Year, let's pray for each other, and support each other in our daily decision to follow Christ and to live "as if" that is the most important thing.

4th Sunday "B" Mark 1:21-28

The healing miracles of Jesus are signs of our own need for healing! When we read about Jesus curing the blind, the crippled, the paralyzed, and the deaf – or (as in today's gospel) casting out an evil spirit, we can apply these miracles to ourselves. After all, what is worse? A paralyzed body or a paralyzed heart, eyes that cannot physically see, or a mind plunged in total darkness? Ears unable to hear or a heart deaf to the very people they love?

Christ came to set us free from all the evils in our lives, to heal us, to make us whole and well – in mind, soul, and in body! All of us have some form of paralysis, some hint of blindness or deafness or something we might call a "demon or evil spirit" that needs casting out!

In today's gospel, Jesus is confronted by a man with convulsions. His sickness is attributed to an "unclean spirit" or "demon." The man was thought to be possessed by the devil. For Mark, (who wrote this gospel), the ungodly power of Satan is the cause of this poor man's sickness.

So, a classic confrontation is set up between goodness (Jesus) and evil (Satan). Jesus proves his power evil by a simple word of command to be silent and come out of him. Immediately, the man is cured!

In our own personal lives, there's a need to get rid of certain "demons" that may possess us! Demons, which make us less human! Demons, which can break down, or even destroy our relationships! Demons, which separate us from each other by building up walls of fear and hatred.

For example, perhaps there's a tremendous amount of anger hidden away within our hearts. We get angry with all sorts of people, with the government, from the president, the governor, the Mayor down to the local dog-catcher or we get angry with the boss, or the people we work with and even the people we are closest to, our spouse, our children, our in-laws, and neighbors! We get angry with the church in general, with bishops and priest in particular. We even get angry with God at times!

So often we fail to recognize the anger within us. Only when we can put a name on the "demon" anger or identify it, and see it for what it is can we begin to handle it and deal with it! Anger, and resentment, are often the underlying causes of other evils!

Jesus once asked a demon, "What is your name?" The answer came back, "My name is Legion, for we are many. But once we can recognize and name our demon, only then we can begin to have power over it. Only then can blind eyes begin to see once again; only then can deaf ears be opened to hear the word of God! Only then can broken hearts be mended and begin to love once again!

Nineteen year old Keshia Thomas didn't intend to become a hero on that June afternoon in 1996. The black teenager was one of 300 protestors, who assembled in downtown Ann Arbor, Michigan to protest a rally of the "Ku-Klux-Klan."

The anti-Klan protestors spotted a white male spectator wearing a Confederate flag on his T-shirt! Keshia wanted to yell at him, "What did I ever do to you?" but before she did, one of her friends hit him with a sign and a swarm of angry demonstrators began beating on him! Appalled, Keshia threw herself over the fallen man, shielding him from the kicks and punches!

Thanks to Keshia, police were able to step in and rescue the man, who suffered only a bloody nose! It was learned later that the man was not even a member of the Klan. Keshia told the angry crowd, "You don't beat up a man just because he doesn't believe the same things you do."

A 19 year old student changed a lot of minds and hearts that day, even including some of the members of the Ku-Klux-Klan!

As Jesus casts out the "unclean spirit" from the poor man with a word of compassion, Keshia Thomas cast out some "demons" of racism and violence by her act of bravery!

There are "unclean spirits" and "demons" all around us (and within us) that can be cast out by us with a simple act of kindness or generosity. Demons can be silenced by a peaceful word or can be transformed just by doing the right thing!

219

5th Sunday "B" Mark 1: 29-39

In today's gospel, Jesus came to Simon Peter's hometown (Galilee) for a visit. He spent the morning in the local synagogue preaching and teaching! Then he went to Peter's home for lunch where he cured Peter's mother-in-law, who was ill with a fever. That evening, the whole town gathered at Peter's door – the blind, lepers, the sick, the lame, and those possessed by demons, asking Jesus for a cure. He cured many of them the gospel says. "And rising very early before dawn, Jesus went to a deserted place, alone, away from the crowd where he prayed to his Father in solitude! But Peter, and the others pursued him and found him and said, "Everyone is looking for you!"

This is an unforgettable scene! Jesus is seeking solitude in prayer in a "deserted place" far away from the clamoring crowd, but the people track him down and his time of being "alone" is over!

It has been said that, as human beings, we have two basic needs, the need for solitude, and the need for community. As a human being, Jesus was no exception! But sometimes these needs clash, as we see in this scene of the gospel. Jesus gives up his time of prayer; his precious time to be apart from the crowd because there is much work to be done; the work given to him by his Father. So Jesus tells Peter, and the others, "Let us go elsewhere, to the neighboring country towns, so that I can preach there too, because that is why I came." (Mark 1:37-39) In other words, He was saying that he hadn't come just to perform miracles of physical healing! Rather, He came to preach and teach about the Kingdom of God, to bring "spiritual" healing to the world, to establish peace and justice for all, to free the poor from oppression, to tear down the walls that divide us, to set the captives free!

The selection, in 1977, of Oscar Romero as Archbishop of San Salvador delighted the country's powerful and wealthy oligarchy as much as it

220

disappointed the social activist clergy of the Archdiocese! Known as a pious, distant and rather conservative Bishop – there was nothing in his background to suggest that he was the man to challenge the "status quo" of the brutal government.

No one could have predicted that in three short years he would become a powerful "voice of the voiceless" or as one priest called him "a gospel for El Salvador!" Nor could anyone foresee that he would be denounced by his own fellow bishops as "subversive" because they felt he was substituting politics for religion! Nor could anyone have foreseen that he would earn the hatred of the rich and powerful, and that he would be targeted for assassination, or that he would be the first Bishop slain at the altar, while saying Mass, since St. Thomas Becket in the 12th century England!

What was it that changed him? That interrupted his solitude and drew him out of staying in his own deserted place? Within weeks of becoming Archbishop, he officiated at the funeral of Fr. Rutilio Grande, a Jesuit Priest of the Archdiocese, who was assassinated because of his commitment to social justice for the poor. Romero underwent a profound transformation – a real conversion as astounding to his new friends, as it was to his enemies. From a once timid, shy, non-engaged bishop, there emerged a fearless, outspoken, champion of justice! His weekly sermons, broadcast by radio to the whole country denounced the violation of human rights, casting the glaring light of the gospel on the many abuses of the day!

Yes, Romero was seeking solitude in his own "deserted place" – but the people track him down and his time of being alone was over. And, like Jesus, he would go and proclaim the "good news" of the Kingdom to all the people, to the rich and powerful, as well as to the poor and abused! And, like Jesus, he would lay down his life in sacrifice.

On March 24, 1980, while saying Mass in the Chapel of the Carmelita Sisters' Cancer Hospital where he lived, a single rifle shot was fired from the back of the chapel. Romero was struck in the heart and died within minutes.

Romero was immediately acclaimed by the people of El Salvador as a true martyr and a saint! For Romero, who clearly anticipated his fate, there was never any doubt as to the meaning of such a death! In an interview, just two weeks before his assassination, he said, "I have frequently been threatened with death. As a Christian, I do not believe in death, but in the resurrection. If they kill me, I shall rise again in the Salvadoran people!"

He went on to say, "Martyrdom is a great gift from God that I believe I have not earned, but if God accepts the sacrifice of my life, then may my blood be the seed of liberty and a sign of the hope that will soon become a reality. Yes, a bishop will die, but the Church of God (the people) will never die!"

6th Sunday "B" Mark 1: 40-45

For Jesus, no one (absolutely no one) was considered an "untouchable." Sinners; tax collectors, prostitutes, the poor, and foreigners not considered "untouchable," nor were the sick; not even were the lepers looked upon as "untouchable."

It's as if Jesus wanted to show God as one who loves to touch, and heal all of creation as something basically good. Isn't this the way that Michelangelo painted God on the ceiling of the Sistine Chapel…as a God always reaching out to give life through the gift of touch?

In Jesus' day, lepers were considered sinners and outcasts. They were excluded from society and even banned from public worship in the synagogue. There was a law that forbad anyone to touch a leper. But Jesus stretched out his hand and touched him, commanding him to be clean. Therefore he was made clean and Jesus restored an untouchable leper back to society.

Personally, I have never seen a leper standing in rags announcing, "Stay away, I'm unclean, do not touch me," but I have seen individuals with AIDS, whose family and friends refused to visit, let alone touch them. I have seen people with mental illness or some form of handicap struggle to be accepted and respected. I have known parents who disowned their children because they married someone of a different race or religion. I have seen a man refuse to exchange the sign of peace with a fellow parishioner at mass who was indicted for a (possible) crime.

So, who are the modern-day "lepers" in our society? They are those who stand in front of us in the grocery store check-out line with their food stamps. They are the aliens (legal or illegal) whose entry into our country is resented as them getting a free ride—as people who are taking our jobs. Other modern-day lepers are the people who want to build a halfway house in our neighborhood or the people living in a tent city. But whoever these modern-day "lepers" might be, they are often judged to be unclean, untouchable, and unwanted.

Today's "lepers" are quite aware that we resist standing near them, that we hope they'll choose another row to sit in or another street to walk down. We caution our children not to speak with them, and we try to distance ourselves from them.

In our second reading today, Paul has some good advice for all of us. "Never do anything offensive to anyone." Maybe we need to ask ourselves the question, how do we treat today's "lepers" in our society? For example, how do we treat ex-prisoners or even their innocent families? How do we as a community behave toward the divorced and remarried? Do we make them feel accepted, or unwanted. Are homosexuals or lesbians welcome to worship here? What's our attitude toward former priests or religious leaders, or toward priests accused of sexual abuse? How does Jesus treat them?

Leprosy is a real physical illness, even today, but it can be seen as a metaphor for all sorts of disfigurement in our own lives and in our society.

We are "disfigured" in many ways as a society by our refusal to confront the evils of poverty; the lack of medical care for millions of people, allowing abortion on demand, and capital punishment. We are a society that accepts violence and war as a solution to its problems, and there are enormous gaps between the rich and the poor. All these "sores" on the body politic of our country are a form of "spiritual leprosy," And should we choose to look deep inside ourselves, we may find that place within us where our own unique "leprosy" is still in need of healing…our own sins and limitations that embarrass us, where we might find some forms of prejudice or religious elitism, judging who can be saved and who cannot be saved, who can belong to my church and who can't, where we find festering sores of holding onto grudges or refusing to forgive past hurts.

Perhaps humbly kneeling before Jesus, as the leper did, we will recognized that in our own deep secret darkness, we and the leper are one, and we are in need of cleansing. And in that discovery, then we might be willing to widen our circle to include those we've kept at arm's length as untouchable, for whatever reason.

Only then can each one of us (like the healed leper in today's gospel), have something really worthwhile to proclaim to everyone…the good news that "Jesus touched me, and I have been made clean."

7th Sunday "B" Mark 2: 1-12

There's a lot going on in today's gospel. First, Jesus and the Pharisees get into a big fight about who can forgive sins, and the paralyzed man becomes the center of the controversy.

Jesus is making the point that he is the promised Messiah sent by God, his Father, not just to heal bodies but more importantly, to heal souls, to restore the broken relationship between God and humanity caused by sin, to mend the brokenness and separation afflicting all the people of God. So that's why, before Jesus heals the man's physical paralysis, He first forgives the man's sins and heals his soul of his spiritual illness (paralysis).

But the Scribes and Pharisees strongly complain that <u>only God</u> can forgive sins. Jesus agrees with them but then to prove he has the power to forgive sins as the Messiah and as the Son of God, he heals the paralytic with a simple command, "I order you, pick up your stretcher and walk." (Mark 2:12) The man got up, picked up his stretcher and walked away, much to everyone's amazement.

The second thing going on in the gospel is about the four friends who brought the paralyzed man to Jesus. Consider them to be among the unknown saints of the gospel. Look at what they had to do. First, they had to carry their friend through the huge unruly crowd, which had gathered to see and hear Jesus preach. When they say that what they were doing wasn't going to work, they decided to go to Plan B. They devised a new and bolder plan. They carefully hoisted their friend up onto the roof of the house where Jesus was preaching. By pushing aside the thatch and tiles, they made a large hole in the roof through which they lowered their friend ever so gently and carefully to Jesus. It must have been quite a sight.

Imagine how the crowd must have reacted to this sudden and shocking intrusion. Can't you just hear their angry remarks and grumblings? What is all this noise and distraction going on while we are trying to listen to Jesus? Who do they think they are to be destroying private property? It's not fair that this lame man gets a front row seat, right in front of Jesus. He should have gotten here earlier and waited in line like the rest of us. But the four friends of the paralytic were so determined to bring their friend to Jesus for a cure. Nothing was going to stop them.

What extraordinary love and concern for another human being they showed. Just think about it, Jesus could not have healed the paralyzed man if the man's friends had not brought him to Jesus. It was their faith and their confidence in Jesus' compassion that caused this miracle to happen.

The four friends in today's gospel are often referred to as "roofer" friends. These roofer friends teach us what true friendship and what Christ-like friendship is all about.

"Roofer" friends don't get stuck in their own self interests or in what other people say or think. They find joy in lifting up one another's mat and to carry their friend whenever he or she is wounded, broken, or in need. "Roofer" friends never have to be asked to help...they just seem to know. They are willing to stand with one another both in times of crosses and times of resurrections.

Sometimes, we may feel like the paralyzed man in today's gospel. At times, we may feel we are even powerless to help ourselves. It's then that God sends us grace in the form of friends, true friends, whose care leads us to find help or to help us find wholeness for ourselves.

I once had such an experience. It was my last year in the seminary. The rector and I never seemed to get along. One day, he told me he was seriously considering not ordaining me. In his estimation, he felt I didn't have the right qualities to be a good priest. He then suggested I not return to the seminary after the Christmas break.

I felt devastated. I felt alone and helpless. Doubts about my own vocation filled my mind. I began to think, maybe he's right, maybe I don't have a religious vocation after all. I was upset and confused, not knowing what to do. I felt paralyzed like the man in today's gospel.

But that all changed. A few days before the Christmas break, the rector called me into his office. He told me he had changed his mind. He decided to allow me to be ordained after all. He told me what changed his mind. About 3 or 4 of my classmates, without telling me, went to the rector and told him I would make a good priest. They pleaded my case. They had faith in me, believed in me, and stood up for me. When the rector told me I would be ordained that year, I felt like the paralytic in today's gospel when he heard Jesus say to stand up, take up your mat and walk.

These classmates were my "Roofer" friends who took away my doubts and fear, who healed me of my spiritual paralysis, and who gave me back my self confidence and my self esteem once again. Thank God for friends like that. They truly were a grace sent from God to heal me.

8th Sunday "B" Mark 2: 18-22;
Mark 2: 13-22 (Common Lectionary)

In today's first reading, Hosea compares Israel's relationship with God to a marriage covenant. Israel is the bride, and God is the groom. But Israel turned out to be an unfaithful bride, leaving the one true God to worship other false gods. Hosea warns Israel there will be a divorce if she continues her sinful ways, and even though God was extremely angry at Israel's unfaithfulness, God, like a husband madly in love with his wife, was willing to take Israel back if she would only change. If she refused, she would be lost forever.

God's plan for reconciliation with Israel is captured in these tender words, "I will lead her into the desert and speak to her heart. She shall respond there as in the days of her youth, when she came up from the land of Egypt. I will espouse you to me forever." In this reading, God is pictured as the ever hopeful husband who believes that with the right amount of love, forgiveness, and caring, his wife will return to him and fall back madly in love with him once again. But Israel refused God's offer. She was satisfied with her newfound wealth and all those things that led her to adultery in the first place. So, unwilling to change, the northern kingdom of Israel was conquered by Assyria and was lost to history forever.

Hosea was writing from his own experience. His own marriage was a failure. His wife left him for a life of prostitution in the pagan temple, and she never returned, despite his many efforts. He was left with three children, a broken heart, and a ruined life.

How could he possibly continue to be a prophet, speaking to the people in God's name? He felt unworthy to be a prophet. His life was ruined because he was such a failure. And yet, this is precisely the point at which God enters his life in a very special way. At the point of his greatest heartbreak and his worst personal failure, God reveals a word that Hosea could only understand in the light of his failure. That revelation became the central message of Hosea's ministry, and it is summed up in this one idea. Our failures do not have to be the final word about us. God does not stop loving us or using us when we fail. God's unconditional love will never let us go, and God never gives up on our ability to change and therefore to stay in a relationship with God.

I hope you have found this remarkable truth. After all, who can better understand forgiveness than the one who has sinned? Who knows the value of family better than the one who has lost theirs or who knows the blessings of food more than the one who has experienced hunger? Are you in a dark place in your life just now? If you are, or someday, if you find yourself there, feel around in the darkness. You may find there the most important discovery of your life as Hosea did. You will find a God who does not forsake you in your failure or in your sins. Just ask King David, whose psalms and poetry sang out God's praise after his adultery. Or ask Paul who persecuted the early Christians but met Christ in his blindness to become the greatest Christian missionary of all time. Or ask Simon Peter who, after denying Jesus three times, was appointed by Jesus to be his vicar on earth. These sinners were used by God to bless the church after they had failed, and we can add to their names all of our own names.

I believe God continues to speak through us, to act through us, and to bless through us; not because we are good and holy, but because God is good. That's good to remember the next time we're tempted to ignore or throw away someone who has failed, or to feel useless for God when we experience brokenness. Jesus would announce the same good news some eight centuries later. He would come to say that God will never give up on us. Even when God is the jilted lover. God continues to woo us, and love us. Yes, God is love…that is who God is. And because that is who God is, we can be <u>more</u> than who <u>we</u> are. And that is good news indeed!

229

9th Sunday "B" Mark 2: 23 – Mark 3:6

When I was growing up the Sabbath, or Sunday, was a special day. We went to mass as a family, and we usually had breakfast together after mass. It was a day of rest from all hard manual labor except wiping the dishes, which Mom said was essential work. We never went shopping on Sundays unless we ran out of milk or ice cream or something as important. It was a day for us kids to go to a movie, of course if it was approved by the Legion of Decency. On Sundays in the summer, we often went to the farm in NE Tacoma to spend the afternoon on our 5 acres of land on which Dad had built a one-room shack. We always ended Sunday with a big family dinner of pot roast or chicken and listened to Jack Benny, Kate Smith, Bob Hope, and Steve Allen. Sometimes, my two brothers and I would serve benediction at 4 p.m. in the parish church.

Those days are gone forever! We live in a very different world today. We seem to have lost the meaning of the command to keep holy the Sabbath, and why it is still important today! The Sabbath is a gift from God in order to bring order and meaning to our hectic lives. Just think about your life this past week…burning the candle at both ends, staying up late, getting up early, rushing to work, fighting the traffic, coming home, rushing to church. You make the beds, brush your teeth, get the bills in the mail, answer your E-mail, call your voice mail, shop and cook, pickup the kids from soccer and get them to swim class…and on and on it goes. Life is just one big blur! It's often meaningless and exhausting, without a chance to slow down and think, without time to relax and pray. God knows how tired you are, how hard you are working, and how long your "to do" list is. God knows going to church is often just another thing to add to your list of things to do. A young mother was asked what she wanted most for Mother's Day. She replied, "a nap!"

God understands this. The Lord wired us for work but also for rest. The Sabbath is God's way of slowing us down. Too many action verbs and piled up adjectives are wearing us out. For example, we are spending less time eating together today than we used to. More of us are eating "on the run," either at work or at our computers than ever before. We're getting less sleep than we need, causing us to show the effect of aging sooner.

What's wrong with this picture? We have overlooked the Sabbath. We need a nap. We need to slow down the RPMs of our racing lives. We need to keep holy the Sabbath.

The Sabbath is also a gift from God to help us focus on relationships rather than on accomplishments. It's a day set aside to focus our minds and hearts on those we love. It's a time to worship God of course, but Sunday is also a time to spend with children, calling friends, visiting the sick, or touching base with relatives.

In the gospel today, Jesus was criticized by the religious leaders of his day, because he spent Sabbath time relaxing with his disciples, his friends. They were eating grain and talking with each other enjoying the day, just "hanging out" with each other but pulling off heads of grain and eating them was seen as work, as harvesting, and therefore a very serious violation of the Sabbath law. Later on the synagogue, Jesus healed a man, because the Sabbath is a good day to focus on helping others. Jesus told them that the Sabbath was made for man, not man for the Sabbath. The Pharisees accused him of breaking the Sabbath law, because healing was also a form of work. Jesus taught that the Sabbath is like any day of the week when a kind act of healing can be done.

All days, even days with long "to-do" lists, are holy, not just the Sabbath. So, here we are on a day of worship and rest. What will we do with this gift of God? Will this day be wasted on chores or invested with our children and family? Will we spend time on trivial pursuits or adore the God who gave them all to us in the first place? Is it the day to go back to the office, or stay at home and work on your relationships? Perhaps "keeping holy the Sabbath" is an old gift from God worth rediscovering!

10th Sunday "B" Mark 3:20-35

Jesus faces two accusations in today's gospel. The first one comes from some of his own family members, who were considering some sort of family "intervention." They were worried about his mental state.

Jesus was preaching some rather "far out" and strange things like offer no resistance to injury, if you are struck on the right cheek then let the left be struck also, love and pray for all your enemies, be good to those that hate you, and forgive the ones who harm you.

No wonder some family members thought Jesus might be "going out of his mind!"

The second accusation came from his enemies, the Scribes. They charged that Jesus was casting out demons by using the power of Satan and not by using any divine powers given to him by God.

Jesus told them how absurd and illogical their accusation was. It made absolutely no sense. Jesus asked them a simple question: "How can Satan cast out Satan? If a kingdom is divided against itself, that kingdom cannot last."(Mark 3:24-25)

Evil never overcomes evil. Only goodness can overcome evil. When evil is responded to by another evil, nothing can ever get resolved. All that does is sets up a never-ending cycle of more and more evil.

When bitterness or hatred is met with hatred, it only sows more seeds of hatred. So, on and on the cycle of evil will continue to go, until someone decides to return a good act for an evil act.

The so-called "insane" and "far out" message of Jesus' preaching centered around love and forgiveness. He talked about turning the other cheek; walking the extra mile; loving everyone, even your enemy, and forgiving others… as God forgives us our sins.

Jesus totally believed that the only way to stop the vicious cycle of evil is to respond to evil by doing something good. What a different world this could be if nations, religions, various races, the poor and the wealthy men and women really respected and loved one another. Imagine a world without revenge, injustice or war. But it all depends on each one of us, on how we respond to evil in our own little world.

If we want to accomplish anything good in our lives, we have to try to leave this world a little bit better off than when we found it; and the only way to do that is to try to live as Jesus lived. We do that by trying to turn the other cheek; to love and forgive those who hate us; to respond to any harsh words, with soft spoken words; and to be willing to respond to evil by doing good.

Perhaps this may sound a little "insane" to some people, but it's the only thing that will ever work. That's what Jesus is telling is in today's gospel.

11th Sunday "B" Mark 4: 26; Mark 4: 24

My dad was raised on a farm in Iowa along with 3 brothers and 6 sisters. He attended a German-speaking convent school until he finished the 5th grade, and that ended his formal education. The nuns taught him well, because his Catholic faith was very important to him his entire life of 91 years.

After he left the farm, he was a bartender in Montana until prohibition laws made drinking illegal. Then he became a policeman for the Milwaukie Railroad, which got him out to Tacoma. There he worked a few years at the Tacoma smelter and then some 25 years at the Centennial Flour Mills until he retired in 1950. In retirement, he spent much of his time donated to working at the St. Vincent de Paul store on Tacoma Avenue.

Dad was always a farmer at heart. Wherever we lived, we had a garden in the back yard along with some chickens. Each one of the 5 kids was responsible for a portion of the garden. He taught us how to prepare the ground, plant the seeds, how to water, and care for the plants and flowers once they grew. Above all, he taught us how to be patient. He would often say, "You just can't rush Mother Nature."

I think that's the message of today's gospel. Jesus is telling us to be patient with God—you can't rush God. In today's gospel story, Jesus may have been speaking to the party of the Zealots (those belonging to the Jewish sect that sought the political restoration of Israel from Roman occupation). Many Zealots were radical terrorists, using rebellion, violence, and murder to destabilize the Roman government. Under the military leadership of the Messiah, they believed that these foreign Roman occupiers would be driven into the sea. That was their idea of the Messiah. Jesus, however, is telling them to be patient, to see their true identity as God's people not in terms of military and political might, but as a people of deep faith and spiritual openness to God's will and love.

Christ is asking us to have that same kind of patient faith, the faith of the sower to plant the seeds of peace, love, reconciliation, and justice wherever and whenever we can, that in God's good time, our plantings will result in the rich harvest of the kingdom of God here on earth. This type of patience is what Jesus would call "mustard seed faith." It is the conviction that from the smallest acts of kindness, compassion, and justice, the kingdom of God will take root and grow.

Since today is Father's Day, I thought I would use my father as an example of being patient with God and allowing God to do "God's thing" in God's own time and place. When we were kids, Dad asked us one day to pray for his brother, Uncle Herman. We never met Uncle Herman, because he lived on a farm in Iowa and never came to Tacoma to visit. So, we prayed for him every day at dinner and in our night prayers. Dad never told us why we should pray for him. He simply said, "just pray for him that God would take care of him." Then one day, after a long time, Dad announced at dinner that we didn't have to pray for Uncle Herman any longer, that he had died. However, before he died, Aunt Clare wrote that he came back to church. He called for a priest who anointed him, heard his confession, and gave him communion on his death bed. Dad was so happy and thankful that our prayers were heard. Dad was patient enough just to plant the seed of prayer and then to get out of the way and let God's grace work the miracle of conversion.

The message of the parable of the seed is, be patient. God's work in the world is like a seed that grows slowly in the ground. It's a mystery, pure and simple. Who can explain that little spark of life, which enables a tiny seed to grow into a big plant or into a giant tree? I certainly can't. Jesus simply says "the seed sprouts and grows without the farmer even knowing how."

So it is with God's working in the world. It's a mystery of grace. God is constantly working among us in His own mysterious ways, in His own time and place. So Jesus is telling us, be patient; let the Lord do His thing. Then watch the miracles of grace happen.

12th Sunday "B" Mark 4: 35-41

Today's readings point out the awesome power of God over raging waters. In the first reading, God penned up the ocean waves as easily as we would plug the water in our sinks. In the gospel, Jesus subdues the storming sea the way a mother calms a child by commanding it to be still The wind ceased, and then there was a great calm. Jesus spoke to the wind, as Mark Twain once described it as the confidence of a Christian in a poker game holding four aces.

Jesus knew he had an unbeatable hand, and besides that, he knew he was safe in the hands of his Father. This was the Jesus who was fond of saying that we should not be afraid because we are of more value than many sparrows. And we can be sure that Christ will always be there for us in our times of crisis. Christ is always above the storm.

Christ was with the disciples when the storm hit. Even though the storm was raging, he was in the boat with them, and he is also there with us in our storms today. The middle of a storm may seem like a strange place to find Jesus. We are more inclined to look for him in some quiet calm harbor and of course, he is found there also. But if we are looking for Christ, and if we really want to find him, the storm is a good place to begin the search.

Jesus is right at home in the midst of chaos and hard times. We know he grew up in a village with a bad reputation. The one-liner, put-down-of-the-day was "can anything good come out of Nazareth?" Jesus spent much of his time with the outcasts and losers of his day, people who were mentally, physically, or morally sick, and Jesus' life seems to have ended in total failure; rejected, abandoned, and condemned to a horrible death by crucifixion.

You and I will never encounter any frightening experience that is unfamiliar to him. Yes, Jesus has seen it all, right down to that black hole where even God seems to have abandoned us at times. Jesus knows all

236

about storms, literally and figuratively. That's why we can trust him to get us through, because he has been there before us, and he will be there again and again for us.

The disciples were experienced seamen. Some were fishermen by trade. But despite their best efforts, the boat was on the verge of sinking, and they feared for their lives. Meanwhile, Jesus was in the stern, sound asleep. Finally in desperation, they shook him awake and shouted, "Teacher, doesn't it matter to you that we are going to drown?" In other words, "Don't you care what happens to us?" Who can blame them for asking such a question? We have asked it ourselves and will most likely ask it again in our lifetime.

It's one thing to ask that question when you're standing on dry ground, safe and sound, but it's another thing to ask it in a boat being tossed about by violent winds and waves, when we are in mortal danger. The most serious questions about God come not from theory but from tragedy. When we are caught in a storm from which there seems to be no escape, then the question becomes real and relevant, "God, don't you care about me?"

The gospel message today is this, don't dodge that question and don't be ashamed of asking it. The one who asks is at least being honest and is dealing with reality. We live in a tragic world. If we are going to believe in God, we must hold onto that faith in the midst of doubt and tragedy. We should be able to see ourselves in today's gospel story. We often think that people are most inclined to believe in God when life is beautiful and easy. But that's not the experience of the disciples who, in their doubt and fear, found out that Jesus <u>really did</u> care for them, and the gospel ends with the disciples asking another question, a question of awe and wonder. "Who can this be that even the wind and the sea, obey him?"

Look at the example of Jesus himself. He saw his heavenly Father in the flowers of the fields and in the birds of the air, but that wasn't the place where his faith reached its height. That happened at Calvary where doubt was strong and faith was hard. It was there that he wondered why even God had forsaken him. But it was also there that he calmly spoke his final words of faith asking God to commend His spirit into His Fathers hands.

Does God really care for me? As long as we live in this world, we will never get finished with that question. But the very experiences that cause us to ask it will be the place where we find our answer. It's a strange paradox, but faith reaches its height in the midst of doubt and adversity, where we discover God really does care about us.

237

13th Sunday "B" Mark 5: 21-43

Today's gospel story is about a 12 year old girl who was on the brink of death from a serious illness. Her father, Jairus, was desperate.

Jairus was the high-ranking synagogue leader in his town. Since no one else was able to cure his daughter, when Jesus came to town, he turned to him for help. In doing so, he was taking a big risk. The established religious leaders of the day considered Jesus as a radical extremist rabbi to be avoided. But Jairus was desperate.

His plea to Jesus was heartfelt and sincere. "My daughter is at the point of death. Please come lay your hands on her that she might get well and live."

While on their way to Jairus' home, the chilling news came, "Your daughter has died. Why trouble the teacher any further?" But Jesus assures Jairus, "Do not be afraid; just have faith. (Mark 5:36) Why all this commotion and crying? The child is not dead but asleep." (Mark 5:39-40)

When they arrived, Jesus took her by the hand and said to her, "Little girl, I tell you to get up." (Mark 5:41) and she arose immediately. They were all astounded.

This gospel proclaims that Jesus has power over human sickness and even death itself and that through his own death and resurrection, Jesus has given us the final victory. He is telling us that when we are in our darkest hour, not knowing what to do, when we are desperate like Jairus, when we have nowhere else to go, then come to Jesus with faith and humility, and the dawn of God's presence will break into our lives giving us hope and meaning.

Jenny Bastian was 12 years old when she died. She and her sister, Teresa, helped with the childcare at the noonday mass that Sunday morning in June. That afternoon, Jenny called a girlfriend to go biking with her to Point Defiance Park, but her friend decided to go shopping instead, so Jenny went alone. Her parents told her to be careful and be back for dinner. She never returned. Her body was found 3 weeks later, next to her bicycle in a wooded area off the 5 mile drive in the park. She had been murdered.

What do you say to Jennifer's parents? There are no words that can console them, no logical reasons can be given to explain such a terrible tragedy. It is so unnatural that parents should have to bury their own child. But children do die. They are taken from us by sickness, accident, or violence, and the parents with other family members who survive, carry with them the memory of a life that ended much too soon.

Perhaps today's first reading from Wisdom 1:13-24 can help us better understand the tragedy of a child's death. The author of Wisdom tells us

1. That God did not make death.
2. That God created us in God's image and likeness to be imperishable, that is to live with God forever.
3. And that death entered the world by the envy of the devil.

In other words, we are created by God for life and for relationships. Death came into the world through sin and evil, and having faith in Jesus tells us we human beings are immortal. When the time comes for us to die, no matter at what age or what circumstance, Jesus will raise us up to live forever in God's presence. This is the good news Jesus wants us to know about death.

It's interesting to note what Jairus asks of Jesus for his daughter, that she may be saved and live. On a deeper spiritual level, his request could be understood to mean, that she may be saved, and raised up to have eternal life.

In Jenny's case, my faith tells me that's what happened when her life was violently taken from her. I can picture Jesus coming to her at that moment, as he did in today's gospel, taking her by the hand and saying, "Little girl, I say to you arise" and Jenny immediately began walking around in heaven with the saints and angels, with Jesus at her side. I truly believe that's what happened.

At this Eucharist, we gather to celebrate our belief in the risen Christ. We come together to proclaim Jesus' resurrection and our own and to acknowledge that all life is sacred and therefore must be respected. Oh, we will still grieve over the loss of a loved one. We will still have the fear of facing the possibility of being separated from one another. Yet, we continue to reach out for the kingdom of God with a sense of longing for the time when we will all someday be united. That's what Jesus was trying to tell Jairus in today's gospel. It's the same message he has for us today.

14ᵗʰ Sunday "B" Mark 6: 1-6

Alice Walker is a contemporary writer from the south. As a young black woman, she grew up during the 1950s in the midst of poverty and prejudice. Much of the power of her writing comes from her own experiences. She wrote about herself.

One of her novels is called "Meridian." It's about a young black girl growing up in the segregated south. In the chapter entitled "Gold," the young girl, Meridian, finds a heavy metal object all covered with dirt and rust. So, she files and scrapes away the layers of dirt and rust, and to her amazement, she realizes that she has found a bar of pure gold. She rushes home to tell her mother, who is sitting on the back porch shelling peas. "I've found gold," she excitedly shouts, "real gold," and proudly places the heavy bar on her mother's lap. "Don't bother me now," she says. "Can't you see I'm busy trying to get these peas ready for supper?" "But it's gold, real gold!" the girl insists. "Just feel how heavy it is. Look and see how bright and shiny it is. It's gold, and it can make us rich!" But her mother was not impressed. Neither was her father, her family, or any of her friends. Meridian has something wonderful to share, but she is rejected. No one is interested in sharing her joy.

So the young girl took the bar of gold, put it in a shoebox, and buried it in the backyard near the apple tree. About once a week, she dug it up to look at it, but as time went on, she dug it up less and less, until she finally forgot to dig it up at all.

Perhaps, at some time in our life, we have experienced the pain of rejection. How awful it is when others don't believe in us or won't allow us to share with them the good things we do have to offer. It's especially painful when the rejection comes from those whom we love the most, our own family, our close friends, from those who know us best.

This is the pain Jesus experienced in today's gospel. He has just returned to Nazareth, the home town where he grew up, to proclaim the good news, to share his love, to heal the sick, to minister to the people he grew up with and loved so much, but they rejected him. "We know this guy," they said. "He's the carpenter's son. Isn't Mary his mother? We know his relatives and his friends. Who does he think he is preaching to us? And where did he get all this knowledge anyway?" Mark tells us, "They took offense at him."

The townspeople reduced Jesus to their own narrow understanding of who he was and refused to see who he had actually become. Mark tell us that "Jesus was amazed at their lack of faith," so amazed and disappointed in their rejection of him, that he was unable to perform any great miracles there.

What is the lesson for us in today's gospel? I think it is this; we all have a treasure to share with others. In fact, our very life, our own life experiences, and our love, can only improve by sharing them with others. In a sense, we can see that our life is like that chunk of metal the little girl, Meridian, found—rusty, tarnished, covered with dirt, and in need of improvement. So we begin to work at it. We file and scrape away the dirt and the rust until we find that we do have something unique and something good and beautiful to share, something rich that shines before others encouraging them to share and to shine as well.

As I look over this congregation, I see a lot of gold. Oh, there are some rusty layers on some of that gold that still needs to be filed away, and I'm sure you can see that I have a lot of filing to do myself. But, the key for all of us is to focus not on the rust, but on the gold; not to judge or reject one another but to accept one another; not to bury our goodness but to share that goodness with others.

In the novel written by Alice Walker, the little girl, Meridian, buried her treasure because she felt rejected but in real life, even though Alice Walker was often rejected, she refused to bury her treasure, her God-given talent for writing. She used her talent to bring happiness and hope to countless other people. Her writing ability was internationally recognized when at a very early age, she received the Pulitzer Prize in literature!

I tell her story because she teaches me what true success in life is. True success in life is the ability to find and uncover the goodness buried deep within yourself and then to have the courage to share that goodness with others despite any opposition you may have to overcome. That's what Alice Walker did so beautifully.

15th Sunday "B" Mark 6: 7-13

What a strange gospel we have just heard. Jesus is talking about evangelization. He sends his disciples out to prepare the way for him, but his instructions are a little puzzling. Take no food, no traveling bag, no money, not even a change of clothes. What kind of a sendoff is that? No comb, no toothbrush, no extra cash in case of an emergency? Stay at the home of whoever may invite you, and if people don't welcome you or listen to you, "leave there and shake off the dust of your feet in testimony against them." That doesn't seem to be very friendly.

But wait! It all makes sense if you add in one more factor. The people at that time believed that the end of the world was very near. Therefore, there was a necessary urgency and haste about the business of evangelization.

In a sense, the time for evangelization is always urgent, especially in our troubled times. The trouble is that most of us think that the work of evangelizing belongs exclusively to missionary priests and religious, or we think that evangelization means bringing the gospel only to pagans in far-away foreign lands or to the unchurched or to those who have fallen away. We think of someone like St. Isaac Jogues who left his native France to evangelize the North American Indians.

The truth is, we are all called through our baptism to share the faith and to announce the Good News of Jesus to others. But we tend to resist that idea by saying let someone else do it and besides, we don't want to impose our faith on others. That mistaken idea often prevents us from doing the work that rightly belongs to all who are baptized.

Most of you are familiar with the name Harriet Tubman from your early American History. She knew how precious freedom was. Her grandparents were kidnapped from Ghana in 1725 and sold into slavery. Harriet was the third generation in her family to live as slaves in the United States. She was born as a slave in Maryland in 1820. She was convinced that God intended all people to be free, so Harriet decided to escape, which she successfully did. She traveled mostly by night and hid in the fields and barns during the day. There were designated stops along the way at the home of sympathetic people who believed in the cause of freedom. Her destination was Canada where many escaped slaves lived.

Once freed, Harriet chose to return hundreds of times to the south to lead others to freedom on the "Underground Railroad" to her home in St. Catherine, Ontario, Canada. In doing so, she risked recapture, prison, beatings, and even death to help others escape from slavery. But she never got caught, even though there was a $40,000 bounty on her head. She died at the age of 93 in 1913.

Like the 12 disciples in today's gospel, Harriet felt she was also sent by Christ on a mission of love and mercy. She was a true evangelist and preacher of the gospel. Once, while speaking to a church congregation, she said, "I freed hundreds of slaves, but I could have freed hundreds more if they just had realized and known they were slaves." I think this quote says something important to us about evangelization today.

First, evangelization means bringing the good news of Christ to others, including our fellow Catholics but especially first of all to ourselves. Too many people today don't even realize they are living in some form of spiritual slavery. For example, a New York Times survey concludes that Catholic Americans have much of the same views as most other Americans on important issues such as abortion, the death penalty, euthanasia, preemptive war, nuclear weapons, welfare, poverty, divorce, assisted suicide, premarital sex, global warming—you name it.

If there is very little or no difference from other Americans in the way we look at critical issues, then we Catholics, in a sense, are slaves to the culture, slaves to "group think," accepting and living by its values. Evangelization means looking into our own religious values and lifestyles and those of our fellow Catholics, and announcing the good news that there is more to life than what we currently embrace.

Each one of us has been given our part to play in the drama of God's redemption. We have been given the good news to share. What is the good news? Seek ye first the kingdom of God, pray without ceasing, do not repay evil with evil but with goodness, bear one another's burdens, be kind to one another, forgive one another as God forgives you, love all people, love even your enemies, be merciful as your Father is merciful. Jesus promised that living the truths of the gospel is what will set us free.

I think the beginning of evangelization lies in recognizing our own slavery and our own need of deliverance. It means living fully the message Jesus handed on to us, not changing it to suit our needs, or watering it down to please others. The time for evangelization is as urgent now, today, as it was back in the time of Jesus.

16th Sunday "B" Mark 6: 30-34;
Mark 6: 30-34, 53-56

This homily is based on today's second reading of St. Paul's words to the Ephesians. "My brothers and sisters in Christ Jesus; you who were once far apart have become near by the blood of Christ. For Christ is our peace and our reconciliation. He has made us one. He has broken down the dividing walls of enmity by his death on the cross, putting our enmity to death by it."

One of the most unforgettable moments of Pope John Paul's visit to Jerusalem was when he prayed at the Western Wall of the ancient temple in Jerusalem. This wall is a very holy site for Jews, for Muslims, and for Christians in a divided city. At this sacred wall, Jews come from all parts of the world to pray. They pray

1. For the redemption of Israel
2. For the unity of God's people
3. And for their own personal petitions.

At this wall, Pope John Paul offered a bold prayer, asking forgiveness for the sins of the church against the Jewish people in particular and sins against humanity in general. It was a holy moment indeed. With that prayer at the wall, you could almost hear the crumbling of the invisible walls that have divided people of faith for centuries. It's really hard to crack a wall built of stones of resentment, of hatred, national pride, and fear. It makes you wonder, why do we have walls at all? Why do people build them and then hide behind them?

Perhaps St. Paul answers those questions in the letter to the Ephesians in today's second reading. Paul described the redemptive work of Jesus as the tearing down of walls and barriers that had separated humanity from God

246

and separated people from each other. According to Paul, Jesus has broken down the walls of hostility, making us all one body and united with one God. In a sense, Jesus takes the rubble from the broken walls and builds bridges with them instead.

Christ did not die and rise again for the isolated individual. No, he shed his blood to break down the barriers of hostility that separate race from race, class from class, young from old, men from women and religion from religion. He died to tear down the walls that keep people apart.

Of course not all walls are bad. For example, the Vietnam Memorial wall in Washington D. C. was built as a place of healing and as a bridge building for Vietnam veterans and their families. Any day of the week, you can see middle-aged men reaching out to the touch the names etched in the granite wall. People come to the wall as if on a pilgrimage to make peace with a tormented past, to say good-bye to friends and comrades, and to find solace in the gratitude of a nation. Such a wall causes us to remember a terrible scar in American and Vietnamese history, but this wall now is a place of healing.

Some walls, though, are meant to be torn down, to be destroyed by the bridge-building work of Christ. Many walls are monuments we build from our own fears and from our own insecurity. We build them high and wide to protect our valuables from thieves. We build them with our legislation to exclude, and our zoning laws to protect the purity of our ethnic or economic neighborhoods. Walls are often testaments of our hostility, and our distrust.

Imagine the incredible effort by the ancient Chinese dynasties to build the Great Wall of China, guarding thousands of miles of Chinese border from intrusion by outsiders. What does it say of a nation whose national symbol is a wall? And what about the Berlin Wall? For decades, this barrier divided a city and a nation, and became the symbol of the Cold War between Russia and the Western Countries. Walls like this need to be destroyed.

Somewhere today, a missionary is locked up behind the thick walls of a Chinese prison. He serves a sentence for the crime of spreading the Christian faith in a country where such religious activity is against the law. When he looks at those cold stone walls, what does he see? Certainly, he sees the concrete expression of that nation's fear of Christian truth. But might he also see the hope that one day (whether during his lifetime or not), those walls are going to come tumbling down? For no wall can hold back the powerful tide of the love of Christ. The eternal hope of the church is this promise of Christ, that the very gates and walls of Hell cannot withstand the power of God.

Walls, visible or invisible, divide the human family into races, nations, religions, and fortunes. These walls may look thick and high and permanent, but they will all crumble to dust one day before the reconciling love of Christ and on that day, all that will be left standing will be the bridges of love and acceptance.

17th Sunday "B" John 6: 1-15

I love this gospel story about the little boy who was willing to give his entire lunch to Jesus in front of all those people. He didn't stop to think it might not be good enough to feed that big crowd. He simply gave it to Jesus, what little it was, and to everyone's surprise, it was more than enough. The point of the story is to show us what the master can do with our small offering when it's freely given in love and trust.

A small Bible study group was looking at this passage, and the leader asked them what they thought it meant. Was it just another miracle story about Jesus' amazing powers, or does it have some deeper meaning for us today? After much discussion, one woman said, "Maybe the story is saying that what God wants is for us to be just who we are." This suggestion generated some different reactions. For some, it was a new and interesting idea, but others said that they had been taught to believe that the opposite was true, that the worst thing you can do is be just who you really are in front of God. After some more rather heated discussion, someone quoted Mr. Rogers, who for many years hosted that wonderful television show for children. She recalled that Mr. Rogers often told children, "God loves you just the way you are." That ended the discussion. After all, nobody wanted to argue with Mr. Rogers.

Jesus wants us to come to him just the way we are, as this little boy did, with complete trust and confidence that Jesus will accept us and use our gifts, no matter how insufficient and small they seem. Jesus wanted all people... adults, children, Jews, Samaritans, sinners, tax collectors, all people to come to him just as they were. He always accepted people, regardless of their weaknesses, their sins, or their failures, and God treats us in exactly the same way today.

But does it seem like something is missing here? Yes! And it's this; Jesus not only accepted the boy's lunch as it was. He also transformed it into a feast for the multitude. Perhaps Mr. Rogers' statement that "God loves you just the way you are" doesn't go far enough. What needs to be added is this. God loves you and wants to transform you. That's what happens in the Eucharist. We offer ordinary bread and wine to God, God accepts it, Jesus transforms our gift into his real Presence, and in the process, we are transformed by receiving communion.

This gospel story tells us something else about God; that with God, no situation is hopeless or impossible. That is what John was assuring the early church by telling this story, that despite going through a terrible persecution, the church will prevail. And if we will listen, God will give us the same assurance today.

What do we do when we get to the end of our rope, when we have done the best we can, and that's not enough? Today's gospel answers those questions. Come to Jesus as you are, in your humanity, in your weakness, in your fears and failures, and Christ will meet you there. Offer him whatever little gifts you have, no matter how meager, and then trust in him for a solution.

When our resources are not enough, God will always make up the difference. I'm not saying everything is going to turn out right, just the way we wanted. But when we do our best, and then turn our lives over to Jesus, miracles begin to happen.

Isn't it strange to say we believe in God without expecting some marvelous results; to say on Sunday, "I believe in one God, the Father Almighty," and then go out on Monday, and not expect anything wonderful to happen?

Sometimes, we are overwhelmed with the huge problems of the world—hunger, AIDS in Africa, natural disasters that cause poverty and starvation, and we wonder how our small donation could make a difference.

The story of the boy in today's gospel reminds me of another little boy who was walking along the shore and throwing back into the sea the starfish stranded on the beach. An old man asked him what he was doing. "I'm saving these fish," he replied. "Saving them?" said the old man, "but there are thousands of them. What you're doing can't make a difference." The little boy tossed another starfish back into the water and said, "Well, it's going to make a big difference for this one." If only we were prepared to do the "little" that's in our power, and then leave the rest in the hands of the Lord.

18th Sunday "B" John 6: 24-35

And Jesus told the crowd, "Do not work for food that cannot last, but work for food that endures to eternal life."(John 6:27) What was Jesus telling the crowd in today's gospel? He was telling them a very sobering thought—that everything; everything we now have will be gone someday—your home, your computer, your money, your clothes, your cell phone, your CDs, everything you and I own will be gone, passed on, worn out, used up, destroyed, gone. It's a truth we simply can't deny or avoid.

In today's gospel, the wise and caring voice of Jesus is warning us not to cling to such food that "perishes," not to put our identity there, but rather, to work for something that is not perishable—something that endures both here on earth and into eternity.

What is the "food" that endures for eternal life that Jesus is talking about? Love, justice, truth, forgiveness, mercy, fidelity, and compassion. These are some of the enduring things Jesus had in mind. These are the things that give us joy here on earth and are our passport to heaven, but that may sound a little too vague or a little too unrealistic.

So perhaps a story could make Jesus' truth more attractive and understandable. I found it in the latest movie called "Up," a delightful animation from the wizards of Pixar. The story is told during the first 4 or 5 minutes without a word of dialogue. A quiet, shy kid named Carl meets Ellie, a real go-getter, in grade school. They both dream of being explorers someday, of going on great adventures to faraway places. Eventually, Carl and Ellie grow up. They fall in love and marry. They transform a fixer upper house into their dream home. Over the years, they save their loose change in a glass jar for their dream trip, but real life gets in the way—work, home, car repairs, medical bills etc., but they are happy and in an instant, it seems they

251

are celebrating their 50th wedding anniversary. All too soon, Ellie succumbs to cancer and dies leaving Carl alone and lost.

After Ellie's funeral, Carl finds the scrapbook Ellie had kept since they were children. She named it "My Adventure Book." The first pages are filled with the silly, funny little treasures and memories of childhood. Then there is a page Ellie has labeled, "stuff I'm going to do." On these pages, Ellie planned her dream trip with Carl. Carl is stung with remorse that he never kept his promise to Ellie to take her on such a trip, but as Carl turns the page, he sees that Ellie has collected pictures of their life together—their wedding, working side by side on their dream home, the simple joys of going out for ice cream, and the family get-togethers. Under one of the last pictures taken together, she had written, "Carl, thanks for the great adventure. Go and have a new one. Love, Ellie."

Carl then realized that he and Ellie had indeed shared a great adventure. They dreamed together, they faced and survived disappointments together, they had happily grown old together, and they realized that love and friendship truly are life's great adventure.

Carl and Ellie discovered that life doesn't have to be exotic and exhilarating to be lived to the fullest. A life of true joy and meaning is not driven by perishable material things and fleeting experiences but by the nonperishable values and the truths of God.

Yes, Jesus is right when he says without exception, everything we now own will be gone someday, and since we will be left with nothing material we now have, maybe we should ask ourselves an important question. What will be our spiritual legacy?

In the final judgment, Jesus will not ask about our material possessions and portfolios. He will ask questions like, did you feed the hungry, give drink to the thirsty, clothe the naked, visit the sick or the imprisoned? These are the questions that resonate here on earth and rebound in heaven.

Today's gospel invites us to make a place in our homes and in our hearts for the Bread of Life, for Christ the true bread who came down from heaven. He tells us as he told the crowd, "I am the Bread of Life." Whoever comes to me will never hunger, and whoever believes in me will never thirst. Do not work for the "food" that perishes, but for the "food" that endures to eternal life.

19ᵗʰ Sunday "B" John 6: 41-51

As I was writing this homily on the Eucharist, I thought about the time before Vatican II when there were no lay Eucharistic ministers. In those days, only the priest was allowed to give communion at mass or take communion to the sick. I remember when I was at St. Joseph's parish in Vancouver, Washington. I would spend every Monday taking communion to the sick. I really looked forward to it, because it would take most of the day to make the calls. It was a special time for me, because I could spend the day with Jesus. It was a time to pray, to talk over my problems with the Lord, to mull over any parish concerns, or just listen to the Lord. So I really looked forward to our time together. I often thought what a privilege it was for me to bring Jesus to the ill, the elderly, and the dying. Communion was such a comfort to those unable to attend mass. Some of these people were really suffering from loneliness, depression, fear, or pain. But they were a real inspiration to me, because they not only received, they believed in the Lord's real presence in the Eucharist.

I remember bringing communion to a woman in her 90s who lived out in the country. As a child, she recalled a priest riding horseback who would say mass once a month in the very same farmhouse she was now living in. He gave her catechism lessons in the front room, and here I was some 80 years later bringing holy communion to the same home, to the same person.

Another woman lay paralyzed in bed. Her 12 year old son accidentally shot her in the back with a 22. She would never walk again. She always greeted me with a smile. Receiving communion was the high point of her week.

Another young woman was confined to bed with a disabling disease that was slowly killing her. Over a number of weeks, I noticed how much weight she had lost. She finally confided in me that she was deliberately starving herself to death. She told me she was doing it out of love for her husband and children. She felt they would be much better off if she were to die. We talked about Jesus laying down his life for all of us, but that he wants us to take up our cross of suffering to follow him, to join our suffering with his for the redemption of the world and how God is the giver of life, and only God can take it away. After thinking and praying about it, she chose life. She began to see that there really was some purpose to her suffering.

I guess the point of my homily is this—when we receive Christ in the Eucharist week after week, we do more than just "take communion," we also must take and receive the message of Jesus, especially those hard-to-swallow teachings he taught, those outrageous things he said that got him in so much trouble.

The people in today's gospel were outraged at Jesus. Who does he think he is, telling us that he is the living bread that has come down from heaven? What about being the Bread of Life; whoever eats this bread will live forever. What are his qualifications? We know his mother and father, so how can he say that he has come down from heaven? Their know-it-all attitude totally rejected him.

Let's be honest. When we hear Jesus say certain outrageous things, we're also ready to question his qualifications for telling us how to live. We don't mind it when the Bible tells us, don't murder, don't steal, don't commit adultery don't worship false idols. We kind of like that kind of preaching, but when Jesus tells us to love our enemies, and pray for those who harm you, that's a little hard to swallow. Who is this Jesus? Who does he think he is, telling us what to do? Or when we are told to forgive those who harm us not 7 times, but 70 times 7 times. How about when we hear things like you cannot love God and money at the same time, or to take up your cross daily and follow me if you would be my disciples. Or, don't judge unless you want to be judged. We hear things like, if you would be first, you must be the last of all and servant of all. Things like If you would be perfect, go sell what you have and give it to the poor, and you will have treasure in heaven.

Who is this Jesus anyway? Jesus answers that question in today's gospel by telling us that He is the Bread of Life, and that whosoever believed in Him would have eternal life, and be raised up on the last day.

Communion Is not just receiving the bread and wine; communion is to believe in the message of Jesus and live it. That's what brings us true happiness and the gift of eternal life now and will give us the final victory over sin, suffering, and death itself. All of us are Eucharistic ministers. Our job is to bring the Christ we have been receiving to others, to share the Good News with all we meet.

20th Sunday "B" John 6: 51-58

In today's gospel, John reminds us that bread is not just bread; it's life. Bread also represents hunger, our hunger for God and God's hunger for us. Many people today sadly know physical hunger. So much of the world doesn't have enough to eat. But all people know spiritual hunger. Maybe that is why you came to church today, because you're hungry and will be disappointed if you're not fed.

When people say, we're not being fed in this or that church, they don't mean there's not enough pancake breakfasts or potluck dinners; they mean their souls are not being nourished. There's not enough nourishment in the preaching, the music, the liturgies, or parish activities to sustain them through the week.

I think the number one question parish staffs must keep asking is, are the people being nourished? Are we so out of touch that we fail to fill their hunger? If so, how can we do a better job? Maybe staffs don't listen enough to people's needs or perhaps they don't remind people enough of what <u>is</u> nourishing in the parish.

Let me list some of the "nourishments" that people can find in a parish.

o The first source of nourishment is found in the parish community itself, in the people who already belong; some people you know, some you don't. Some are lifelong members, some are visitors. But all, for one reason or another, decided to come to church today. We are saints and sinners, young and old, the rich and poor, the successful and the failures, the humble and the proud, but all of us are equal here right now. We've left all our distinctions outside the church doors, and here we are; all of us like beggars standing before the Lord pleading to be fed. This odd mix is your parish family, your fellowship in the Lord. These other members are the ones who pray with you and are present with you, but there are millions more of them all over the world doing the same thing. So every time you come to church, you are part of something much larger. You are a branch on a vine, a living stone in the building, a member of the mystical body of Christ. And remember, you belong—no matter where you stand, no matter how out of sync you may feel physically, spiritually, sexually, or emotionally. You belong! This congregation, even the strangers are your brothers and sisters in Christ. You should be nourished by that fact. Your hunger for family and for meaning should be met here.

o   Secondly, you are nourished by a 2,500 year old scripture. You listen to an ancient wisdom that has nourished Moses, David, Mary, Joseph, Peter, Andrew, Cosmos and Damian, Augustine, Ignatius, Catherine, and Mother Teresa. The word of God, the very same gospel story you heard today, was heard by billions before you who have been comforted by its message of hunger satisfied. Jesus is letting us know that He is the living bread come down from heaven; whoever eats this bread will live forever. Whoever eats my flesh and drinks my blood has eternal life, and I will raise them up on the last day.

o   Our third source of nourishment then is the Eucharist. Two thousand years ago, at the last supper, Jesus broke the same bread and shared the same cup as we do, and he tells us to do this is memory of me, and so we do. Through this Eucharist, we are connected with him and with one another, and that makes us an ancient people bound together by an ancient ritual. We continue to be fed with Christ's real presence, as countless believers have been down through the centuries.

o   These are the "nourishments" found in a parish that can feed our spiritual hungers, but there is one more powerful hunger, perhaps we may not even be aware of, and that is God's insatiable hunger for us. God has been described as the "Hound of Heaven," the stalker, the shepherd, who leaves the 99 and searches for the one lost sheep, the seeker, the finder, the God who is madly in love with us, the God who hungers for our love and our companionship. Jesus spoke to his disciples at the last supper telling them that they had not chosen

Him but that He had chosen them. But we so often fear God. We fear God's love for us. We even fear God's hunger for our hearts and souls, that hunger, which has swallowed up so many people from Francis of Assisi to Dorothy Day. We are both fascinated and frightened of God's love and yet by coming to church, we flirt with it, and we are exposed to the deep mystery of God's love for us.

So here we are on a Sunday that talks about our spiritual hunger, and I thought it would be worthwhile to review the nourishments we do find here, the nourishment of each other, scripture, the Eucharist, and the amazing fact of a God who hungers for our love. Every time we come to church, we move closer to God and to one another.

21st Sunday "B" John 6: 60-69

It would be interesting to know why the people in today's gospel decided to leave Jesus. But I'm more curious to know why the 12 disciples decided to stay with him. Jesus gave the 12 the chance to also leave him when he asked them if they wanted to leave Simon Peter wondered where they would go because Jesus had the words of eternal life. They had come to believe and were convinced that He was the Holy One of God.

Perhaps the disciples (on occasion) may have thought about the possibility of someday leaving Jesus, and they may even have talked about it amongst themselves, but when the critical moment came, their minds were already made up. They all decided to stay. Why? I can think of only one good reason why they decided to stay. It was because of what they had come to believe about Jesus. It was not so much that they held on to him, as much as the fact that Jesus held onto them. Jesus had a grip on their minds, on their hearts, on their very lives; so strong a grip that they could not easily shake loose. Perhaps that's what we are missing in our spiritual lives. What kind of a grip does Jesus have on us?

When faced with the decision (either to stay with or leave Jesus), the twelve made a surprising discovery, that Jesus had taken hold of their lives with a gentle grip that could be so easily broken if they decided to leave. But they found out that being thus "captured" by Jesus was the most liberating experience of their lives.

Being "captured" by someone, or by something can sound rather confining or even oppressive. It seems to imply the loss of freedom or independence, but that all depends on who the captor is, or what it is that holds one captive. For example, Bach was captured by the beauty of music, but it released all of his creative musical powers. Michelangelo was captured by the fascination of art, and it brought out all of his artistic genius.

It was in that sense that the disciples were captured by Jesus and by his teachings. They were "possessed" by someone so much greater than themselves. He taught them truths about God, about themselves, and about the true meaning of life. That set them free! What they learned was so real and so wonderful that there was no way to cast that aside, or walk away from him. Perhaps today is the time to ask ourselves the question, what kind of a hold does Jesus have on us?

For most of us, Jesus is more than a lofty, pious man who once lived 2000 years ago but now lives far away from us in heaven. No, Jesus still lives here with us today…in the church, in the sacraments, in our hearts, and in one another. He is the center and the very meaning of life. Whenever we think of truth, we think of him because he told us that he was the way, the truth, and the life and that no one would go to the Father except through Him.

And whenever we long for validity, we think of something he once said or something he did while he was on earth. Perhaps we even ask ourselves the question, W.W.J.D.…What Would Jesus Do If He Were In My Shoes, Facing Some Important Decision?

So, like the disciples in today's gospel, we would probably find it difficult to ever walk away from Jesus. With Peter, we would say, "Lord to whom would we go? You have the words of eternal life."

For example, where would we be without the Golden Rule or the 8 Beatitudes of the Sermon on the Mount or his stories and parables like the Good Samaritan, the Good Shepherd, and the Prodigal Son? If we ever would consider walking away from him, we had better (at least) wonder who or what we would put in his place.

The 12 disciples were ordinary people; simple and hardworking, who at times were slow to understand and even sometimes were sinful. But they became great, because they belonged to someone great (to Jesus), and they were "captivated" by something greater than themselves (by his teachings).

The message of today's gospel is that even ordinary people (like you and me) can also be "captivated" by Jesus and his teachings, and that being captivated by Jesus is the most liberating experience a person can know.

Just ask St. Paul the secret of his great life, and he would answer, "I have died with Christ, and the life that I now live is not my own but Christ living in me." And the great St. Augustine (whose feast day we celebrate this Tuesday), once said this about Jesus, "My heart is restless until I find my rest in you." St. Augustine and St. Paul were "captivated" by Jesus. They would never leave him.

22nd Sunday "B" Mark 7: 1-8, 14-15, 21-23

It happened at a board meeting of one of the leading producers of dog food. Sales were way down and slumping badly, and the chairman of the board was angry. "I don't understand it" he shouted, as he pounded the table. "We have the best dog food money can buy. We have the most expert brains in nutrition advising us on the content. Our art department has designed award-winning labels for our product. Our advertising people are second to none in putting together an aggressive marketing campaign. So, why are sales down? Can anybody tell me, huh?" There was silence around the table as the various members of the board wilted under the chairman's glare. Finally, from the back of the room, a voice piped up with the answer. "The dogs don't like it."

This story reminds me of today's readings. The only difference is the subject. It is religion and not dog food. In both cases, it's the quality inside that counts. With the dog food, it's the quality of meat inside the can that counts. In the case of religion, it's the quality of love inside the heart that counts. The number one temptation in religion is to think that following certain rules, doing certain things, or saying certain prayers, or performing magic ceremonies will automatically guarantee holiness and salvation. But the Lord does not look for quantity but quality. The readings basically speak of two different kinds of religion; one is a camouflage religion, the other is a religion of the heart. Jesus describes camouflage religion as he speaks to the Pharisees the "experts of the law." They got hung up on the ritual washing of hands before eating and made that an essential part of religion; so much so that in their minds, Jesus' disciples were committing serious sin in neglecting this tradition. Their self righteous attitude allowed them to judge Jesus and his disciples as unfit for the kingdom of God. Camouflage religion enables people to hide under, or camouflage, their true way of living with empty

261

ritual, mere human traditions, and empty words. The religion of the heart comes from acting on the word of God, caring for the poor and abandoned of the world, and following our conscience as we worship God. Religion of the heart is based on a relationship of love and not on an obligation to a law.

Some of us go through life asking the question, "Do I have to? Do I have to wash my hands before dinner, or brush my teeth before going to bed? Do I gotta do my homework?" Those are a child's questions, but we adults do the same thing when it comes to religion. For example, we know how late we can come to mass or how early we can leave and still have it "count." Or if we attend a wedding mass Saturday night, we ask "Does this fulfill my obligation?" Or, we call a priest and say, Father so and so said it was a sin to do such and such; I just wanted to call you and get a second opinion. Behind such questions hides the desire to do the least we have to do in order to stay on the good side of God. It's a minimal approach to God and religion.

People who are really in love don't have to ask the question, "Do I have to?" People truly in love with each other are happy to express their love with generosity and self sacrifice. That other person is really the center of their lives. I think that is what Jesus is telling us in our gospel, to put God at the center of your life and put love back into your heart and don't get hung up on a bunch of man-made rules and regulations. Make religion truly a religion of the heart.

23rd Sunday "B" Mark 7: 31-37; Mark 7: 24-37

There's a well-known painting of Jesus reaching out to touch and heal a blind man. His disciples are looking over his shoulder closely watching the healing miracle. That painting reminds me of another image, the image of a senior doctor making his rounds in a hospital surrounded by young interns; following closely, watching and taking notes, trying to figure out how he or she works their magic healing.

That image says something important about our own ministry of healing. Jesus expects us to carry on his healing. In that sense, we are called to be Jesus' interns of healing in the world today. By that I mean that we all have the power to heal, to lighten a burden, to share a sorrow, or to speak a word of hope, encouragement, or comfort, and therefore to heal a heart. Our healing usually happens quietly, almost unnoticed, and often takes place when we least expect it.

I have two stories about ordinary healing to share with you today, not spectacular ones, but small unnoticed healings caused by two unlikely people, a baseball manager and a woman who works at Starbucks. Both stories are true. The first story is about a 15 year old boy who ran away from home and joined a Nazi gang. His parents never complimented him for anything good he did at home or at school. They never asked his opinion about anything, and they didn't seem to care about what he said or where he went. He felt isolated and unloved, so he ran away from home and joined a Nazi gang.

They took him in. They accepted him and seemed to like him. The White Supremacists poisoned his mind with hatred and disdain for anyone who wasn't a member of the pure, superior white race. The run-away boy now had a purpose in life. But after a few years, all that changed. A conversation and a true healing began to take place when he went to a Starbucks for lunch, and a black woman waited on him. At first, he was going to walk out, but then he decided to stay. He sensed that she knew who and what he was. His tattoos and shaved head gave it away that he was a White Supremacist, more commonly known as a "skinhead." But despite this, he was surprised that she was so kind and so respectful to him. When he came to pay for his lunch, the woman noticed a swastika tattooed on his finger. Then holding onto his hand and looking into his eyes, she kindly told him, "You're better than that. These four simple words began his healing process.

He left there thinking about her kindness and her compassion to him. He began to question why he was taught to hate people like this woman, just because of the color of her skin. Hatred and prejudice no longer made any sense to him. Today, he has set up a website to help other White Supremacists to follow his example. Healing can even take place at a Starbucks.

The second story is about the former New York Yankees manager, Joe Torre. While walking into the stadium one day, he was stopped by a young man who said, "I met you 20 years ago when I had cancer. I was 15. The doctors thought I was terminal. I was scared. You came to the hospital to see me and gave me a pep talk, and I never forgot it. You were playing for the Mets then, and I never said thank you. You really helped me!" He was pleased by the story and was happy the young man was now free of cancer.

Later on, in telling someone about the incident, Torre said he only had a vague memory of the incident but went on to say, "It makes you realize what all of us can do with a word of encouragement here, a pat on the back there, or a visit, a phone call. We all can have a tremendous effect on people."

Joe Torre didn't put his finger into anyone's ear or touch anyone's tongue like Jesus did in today's gospel, but in his own little way, he was effective in healing a young boy's fears in a troubling time.

I share these stories, because when we talk about healing, we usually think about dramatic big ones that make the news. But far more common and far more within our reach is our power of healing with simple words and gestures like, I'm here for you, I need you, I love you, or just a hug, a pat on the back, a phone call. These are not the dramatic stories of scripture, but they are real healings nevertheless.

Yes, the healing ministry of Jesus is now in our hands. All of us are called to be miracle workers, to be interns of Jesus' healing in the world today. It's simply a matter of knowing our own power and using it.

24ᵗʰ Sunday "B" Mark 8: 27-35

A man was on his first trip to Australia. He got a taxi at the airport. He was surprised and shocked when the cab driver asked him, "Did you come to Australia to die?" He thought that was a strange question for the cabbie to ask him, so he said, "Excuse me?" The cabbie elaborated by saying, "Did you come to Australia to die or yester-die?"

In today's gospel, Jesus tells his disciples that he, as the Messiah, has come to earth to die and that he must suffer many things. He will be rejected by the elders, the chief priests, and the teachers of the law and then be killed and after 3 days, rise again.

The disciples were stunned and horrified at what Jesus told them. They were in disbelief. Peter began to rebuke Jesus for even mentioning the possibility of him dying. Jesus then looked Peter in the eyes and sternly rebuked him. "Get behind me, Satan. Because the way you think is not Gods way but mans." (Mark 8:33)

When the rhetoric calmed down, Jesus called the crowd and disciples together and told them something strange, that only those who lose their lives for his sake and the sake of the gospel will truly find their lives. Losing and finding go hand in hand. Both are necessary elements for a successful spiritual life.

Jesus taught as much in paradox as he did in parable. He said things that seemed contradictory but were true. Perhaps his most widely quoted paradox is the one that appears in today's gospel; "For anyone who wants to save his life will lose it, but anyone who loses his life for my sake, and for the sake of the gospel, will save it." (Mark 8:35-36)

When Jesus spoke these words, he was not just giving us some beautiful religious theory or some pie-in-the-sky teaching. No, he was telling the truth

265

about life. That's the way life really is. Try to hang on to it or hoard it, you will lose it, but let loose of it, share it, or give it away, and you find it.

This conflict lying deep within each one of us is the question we all have to answer. Am I going to be self saving or self losing. Our natural inclination is to hold on to life tightly and keep it for ourselves. But Jesus is saying the way to true life and happiness is the way of self losing.

Jesus has the right answer. Forget yourself, lose yourself, and give of yourself. We become our best selves only when we get self out of the center and put God there. It's a paradox, but it's true and it's real. Just think about it; the healthiest and happiest people we know are the people least preoccupied with themselves.

In today's gospel, Peter confesses belief in Jesus as the Messiah, but in a Messiah of victory, of power and domination. But in contrast, Jesus speaks of a Messiah who will suffer rejection, suffer pain, and be put to death. Peter strongly objects.

Peter's reaction to a suffering, failing, dying Messiah perhaps mirrors our own feelings. We also prefer to follow the popular, the successful, the miracle-working, healing and comforting Jesus. But we tend to back away from the suffering, humiliated, rejected, and unsettling Jesus on the cross.

Yet, Jesus tells us we cannot be his disciples unless we embrace his spirit of self sacrificing servant hood, taking up our own crosses, however heavy the wood or however steep the road leading us to our own Calvary. "If anyone wants to be a follower of mine, let him renounce himself and take up his cross and follow me." (Mark 8:34)

In October 1971, Pope Paul VI stood at the altar of St. Peter's as a procession moved down the aisle. The occasion was the beatification of Father Maximilian Kolbe, who was arrested by the Nazis in 1941. He was sent to Auschwitz concentration camp. While there, ten prisoners were chosen for execution as reprisal for the escape of one other prisoner. One of the ten chosen for execution was a young sergeant in the Polish army who was married and had children.

Father Kolbe knew him and stepped forward and offered to take his place for execution. The offer was accepted. Kolbe and the other nine were put to death by starvation and dehydration.

Leading the procession down the aisle of St. Peter's on that October Day 1971 was Cardinal Jozsef Mindszenty of Poland. Beside him walked a white-haired man who wept as he was embraced by the Pope. He was the prisoner, the one whom Father Kolbe saved from death by willfully laying down his own life in sacrifice. In the homily that day, Paul VI quoted the words of Jesus, "There is no greater love than to lay down your life for a friend."

Self survival is the first law of nature, but there is a higher law that leads to life. Father Kolbe lived by that law. If you and I would find life, we must also do the same.

We most likely will never be called upon to die so dramatically as Father Kolbe, but in the day-to-day routine of living, in small little ways, if we hold onto life selfishly for ourselves, we lose it. But if we give it away generously, onlt then we will find it.

25th Sunday "B" Mark 9: 30-37

A debate broke out among the disciples as to who was the greatest among them. I'm sure each one of them thought he was the greatest.

Jesus overheard their argument and told them how to settle it. "If anyone wants to be the first," he told them, "he must make last of all and servant of all." (Mark 9:35) Here we have another one of those paradox saying the disciples failed to understand. So to help them understand what he had just said, Jesus places a little child in the midst.

In the ancient world, a child was considered as a social non-person, as someone without any legal rights or any social status. Then Jesus, putting his arms around the child, said to them, "Anyone who welcomes one of these little children in my name welcomes me; and anyone who welcomes me welcomes not me but the one who sent me." (Mark 9:36-37)

Jesus is identifying himself with this child, a "nobody", and with all who are considered the least of society. The receiving of such least ones with dignity and value is equal to receiving Jesus himself and his heavenly Father. That's a profound idea. Every human being has inherent worth and value, especially the least among them.

So, to be truly great in the kingdom of God, Jesus is saying one must become a servant to all the least ones. In fact, the child that Jesus embraces in today's gospel is a metaphor representing all the poor and needy, the forgotten, the lost, the rejected and marginalized people in the world. Only by putting ourselves in humble service to them can we hope to claim a place in God's kingdom.

Let me tell you a story to help you better understand today's gospel. A monk prayed many years for a vision from God to strengthen his faith. But it never came. He had almost given up hope when one day it happened. The old monk was overjoyed. Then right in the middle of the heavenly vision, the monastery bell rang. The ringing of the bell meant it was time to feed the poor who gathered daily at the monastery gate, and it was the old monk's turn to feed them. What was he to do? If he failed to show up with some food, the people would leave quickly thinking the monastery had nothing to give them that day.

The old monk was torn between his earthly duty and his heavenly vision. But before the bell stopped ringing, the monk made his decision. With a heavy heart, he turned his back on the vision and went off to feed the poor. Nearly an hour later, the old monk returned to his room. When he opened the door, he could hardly believe his eyes! There was the vision still waiting for him. As the monk dropped to his knees in thanksgiving, God appeared in the vision telling him that if the monk had not fed the poor then He would not have stayed.

Like the disciples in today's gospel, the old monk learned the most important spiritual lesson of his life. He learned that the best way to serve God is not necessarily by giving up everything and going to the monastery, or by spending long hours in prayer or contemplation. No, the best way to serve God is to do something more basic and more important. The best way to serve God is to be a servant to others, especially those gifted less than ourselves.

Who are the greatest people in your life? Most likely, they were the people who were your servants> People who took care of you when you couldn't take care of yourself, people who taught you how to read and write, and taught you right from wrong, people who spent time with you when you were lonely or afraid, people who gently corrected you when you went astray, people who encouraged you when you were down or depressed.

As I look back on my own life, these have been the greatest people in my life.

26ᵗʰ Sunday "B" Mark 9: 38-42, 47-48

Part of the problem in the world today is the phrase "us versus them." The "USES" are the people we consider okay, and the "themes" we consider not okay.

This "us versus them" attitude is often the cause of much of the division in our politics, in our religions, and in our international relationships.

So, there's "us," and there's "them." We're right, and they're wrong. We know the truth; they don't know the truth, because they are so ill informed. We're concerned about the common good; they're out to grab whatever they can get. You can trust us, but not them. We're all created equal, but some of us are more equal than others. We are all God's children, but we are God's favorites. We are the people of God, and we pray for those others who are not.

Today's readings present us with two difficult questions. Who belongs to Christ, and should anyone ever be excluded from Christ? Jesus answers both those questions in today's gospel when he tells John, "Anyone who is not against us is for us." (Mark 9:40)

Today's liturgy invites us to become more aware of the Spirit of God at work in others, especially those others we would least expect to find the spirit.

In the first reading and the gospel today, the disciples of Moses and Jesus are complaining that some others not of their company are acting as if they have received the Holy Spirit, and they are speaking in God's name, working miracles of healing and acting as prophets. "Shall we stop them", they ask Moses and Jesus, "since they don't belong to our group"? Again, this is a classic "us versus them "scenario". It's the same old tension between thinking of the church either as an elite club for saints, or as a hospital for sinners.

The answer from Moses and Jesus to the disciples' question is the same; "No, don't stop them." Welcome them, encourage them, cheer them on.

They're doing God's work. God works in mysterious ways. Sometimes, God takes away the spotlight from us and gives it to others.

Because Christianity is divided into so many different churches and beliefs, it's been difficult for the various denominations to say good things about each other. For example, some Protestants thought of Catholics as "idol worshipers" because of their veneration of statues of Mary and the saints. In turn, Catholics considered Protestants as heretics. This "us versus them" mentality existed between Christians for a long time. If Christian churches through the centuries paid more attention to today's scripture, efforts to find moral and religious common ground would not have been so long in coming.

The disciples in today's gospel thought they had a monopoly on the truth, so they tried to stop a stranger from casting out demons in Jesus' name, because he was not one of the twelve; not one of us but one of them. Jesus simply told them not to stop him. Later on, he would tell them, "I have other sheep that do not belong to this fold" (John 10:16).

Apparently, Jesus didn't limit his friends just to his close inner circle of followers, and neither should we. Jesus' response to his disciples is one of tolerance and one of acceptance. Jesus welcomed as a friend any person who even does the most menial act of love. He once said, "If someone gives you a cup of water to drink because you bear the name of Christ, will by no means lose their reward." (Mark 9:41)

And in his description of the final judgment, Jesus numbered among his friends those who fed the hungry, clothed the naked, visited the sick or imprisoned, and sheltered the homeless. He explained because they had done this to the more unfortunate it was the same as doing it for Him.

Jesus also considers as his friends the members of other non-Christian religions. The second Vatican Council taught that God's Spirit resides in all religions, not just in Christianity. These other religions have a share in God's revelation of divine truths.

So, we Christians today can say to the Buddhist and the Jew and to the Hindu and the Muslim, we respect your faith in God' it's a valid faith. We believe there is one God, and we all belong to God's family. Therefore, we are truly brothers and sisters. In fact, we can share with each other some new ideas and insights into God's presence in the world and new ways of looking at our worship, and our prayer life.

In today's gospel, Jesus is calling us to put an end to the "us versus them" mentality that divides us. Jesus has come to build his Father's Kingdom, a community based on humility, respect, love, and understanding for all. No one is excluded. He is telling us to reach out to all peoples without condition, without prejudice or fear, and without judgment.

27th Sunday "B" Mark 10: 2-16

Today is Respect Life Sunday. As a society and perhaps even as a church, we have lost our sense of childlike wonder at the value of human life. In Jesus' day, a child had no legal rights; a child was powerless, poor, totally dependent, even dispensable. In today's gospel, Jesus takes such a child and holds him up for our example. "Whoever does not receive the Kingdom of God like a little child, will never enter it." That child in today's gospel is a symbol of all people who are marginally on the fringe of our society, people who are considered dispensable, people who are poor and powerless, people judged to be of no use to society—the elderly, the ill, those in prison, even the unborn. The modern novelist, John Updike, warns us what can happen when we lose touch with the younger members of God's family. He says, "If we adults do not keep on speaking terms with our children, we cease being human and simply become machines for eating and making money." The modern novelist, John Updike, warns us what can happen when we lose touch with the younger members of God's family. He says, "If we adults do not keep on speaking terms with our children, we cease being human and simply become machines for eating and making money."." When our sense of childlike wonder of life begins to die, then our sense of prayer and worship, and then our sense of respect for all human life will begin to die. On Respect Life Sunday, we celebrate the sacredness of all human life. We proclaim that all life is a precious gift from God. For it is the unconditional love of the child, with Downs Syndrome, that teaches us to trust each other without fear or apprehension. It is the halting steps of the elderly and the disabled that reminds us to praise God for good health and for energy. It is the criminal languishing on death row in our prisons who calls us to reflect on the mercy of God and God's willingness to forgive the sins of the most hardened and callous among us. It is the poor in our midst who remind us that charity is not sharing from the over-abundance of our tables and the excesses of our material possessions, but that true Christian charity is giving from our scarcity and our need. These are the gifts of life we must treasure, value, protect, and celebrate. And if we are to celebrate, then we must first pray—pray to God who is the creator and sustainer of all life. So this is a day of prayer and reflection. We must pray to see in the gift of a child an answer to the cynicism and despair we find in the world.

We must pray for those who, in the difficult circumstances of their personal lives, cannot find the strength to sustain the new life they have created. And we must pray for our own sins of omission in failing to support or share their burdens. On this day, we must pray in a special way for those who use their medical skills and healing gifts for the destruction of human life, rather than for its preservation and enhancement.

We must pray for those who make civil laws that violate the laws of God, those whose legal short-sightedness help create a system in which life is cheap and dispensable. On this day, we must pray for a world, which has come to accept violence, military power, and the stockpiling of arms (to the tune of 1.8 million dollars a minute) as the solutions to its problems.

The U.S. Bishops' powerful statement is a real challenge for us (1995). "Increasingly, our society looks to violent measures to deal with some of our most difficult social problems: Millions of abortions to address problem pregnancies, euthanasia and assisted suicide to cope with the burdens of old age and illness, and an increased reliance on the death penalty to deal with crime. We are tragically turning to violence in search for quick and easy solutions to complex human problems. A society, which destroys its children, abandons its old, and relies on vengeance, fails fundamental moral tests. Violence is not the solution; rather, it is the most clear sign of our failures. We are losing our respect for human life! How do we teach the young to curb their violence when we embrace it as the solution to social problems? We cannot teach that killing is wrong by killing." What a powerful statement!

Albert Schweitzer was right; "The tragedy of life is what dies inside us while we live."

28th Sunday "B" Mark 10: 17-30

The scene in today's gospel paints a rather strange picture. It pictures a rich man kneeling at the feet of a poor man asking him for something. Usually, it's the other way around. It's usually the poor who beg from the rich.

The poor man in the scene we know well. His name is Jesus. The rich man is not so well known. The story leaves him nameless. Perhaps he represents all of us. He is asking Jesus for some advice. "What must I do to inherit eternal life?" (Mark 10:17) "You know the commandments; you must not kill; you must not commit adultery; you must not steal; you must not bring false witness; you must not defraud; honor your father and mother. Then Jesus, looking at him, loved him and said, "There is one thing you lack Go and sell everything you own and give the money to the poor, and you will have treasure in heaven; then come, follow me." (Mark 10:19-21) The man's face fell, and he went away sad, because he had many possessions.

Jesus was trying to tell him that the demands of love are always greater than the demands of keeping the law. It's one thing to avoid hurting others… the law demands that. But, it's another thing to voluntarily give of one's self, sacrificing for the benefit of others. Only love can require that.

In his encounter with the rich young man, Jesus demands of him what he is not prepared to give. Jesus is asking him not just to help the poor but to become poor, to find the treasure of heaven, by giving up his earthly treasure.

Jesus is speaking to us, you know, and that is the lesson of today's gospel. We too, like the rich man in the gospel, are "good people," but we can do better. Jesus loves us too much to let us settle for just being "good people." Hey, Jesus is telling us, you can be better and do better.

This gospel is not about riches or wealth per se, but it's about us asking ourselves, what is it we must let go of in our lives that will better help us find the Kingdom of God, that will help us find a greater love and a richer spiritual life?

Here are some modern-day parables to think about. They might help us understand today's gospel better. A college baseball player went to Jesus and asked, "What must I do to inherit eternal life?" Jesus replied, "Go to the local playground and help set up an after-school program for kids who are poor or who are at risk." The baseball star's face fell, and he went away sad. His only focus in life was making the majors.

The owner of a small business asked Jesus, "What must I do to inherit eternal life?" Jesus replied, "Go and create job opportunities for those who have lost their jobs and whose families are struggling. The business owner's face fell, and he went away sad, because he was barely keeping his own company going. He was afraid to take a chance.

A woman who had recently buried her husband, who died of cancer, asked Jesus, "What must I do to inherit eternal life?" With great compassion for her loss, Jesus said, "Go, put aside your grief for your husband and give your time to help raise money for cancer research." The woman's face fell, and she went away sad, because the loss of her husband was still too painful.

Perhaps we now know how the rich young man felt in today's gospel. Yes, sometimes Jesus seems to ask a lot from us as a price to pay for being a disciple. But Jesus asks for only what we have, not what we don't have.

Each one of us has certain gifts, talents, skills, resources, and assets that have been given to us by God for the work of making the Kingdom of God a reality in this world.

In the gospel, it was the rich man's possessions that Jesus was asking him to give up in order to make him a better disciple, but "he went away sad."

What is it in my life that Jesus is asking me to give up, that will make me a better disciple: Is it my anger, my laziness, my prejudice, my pride, my being too judgmental, my selfishness? It is a question each one of us needs to ask ourselves. Jesus is waiting to hear my answer, or will I sadly also walk away?

29th Sunday "B" Mark 10: 35-45

In today's gospel, James and John ask for seats at the right and left hand of Jesus in his glory. When his kingdom comes, they don't want to miss out on any of the perks. They were asking for the highest places of honor in heaven, to have important roles to play in the Kingdom. But Jesus tells James and John that true greatness in his Kingdom is not measured in power, status, or control over others, but by humble service. And the more servant-like the service, the greater the genuine stature of the disciple. So, the only way to aspire to greatness in the kingdom is to serve the rest.

This type of servant-like leadership Jesus himself modeled for his disciples at the Last Supper when he humbly washed their feet. He explained that since He, as Lord and Master, had washed their feet they must do for each other. That's why in today's gospel, he tells them, "For the Son of Man himself did not come to be served but to serve and to give his life as a ransom for many." (Mark 10:45) True greatness in the Kingdom of God is something you have to earn; it cannot be given, and it can only be earned by a life of love and service. What is the good news in all of this? I think it's this: If greatness in the Kingdom of God can only be earned, then all of us have a chance to be great by serving the needs of others.

In today's gospel, Jesus tells the twelve disciples, "You know that among the pagans their so called rulers lord it over them, and their great men make their authority felt. This is not to happen among you. No; anyone who wants to become great among you must be your servant, and anyone who wants to be first among you must be slave to all. "(Mark 10:42-44)

When Bishop Kenneth Untener was installed as the bishop of the diocese of Saginaw, Michigan, he began his homily by appearing in the pulpit with a waiter's towel over his arm, holding a pen and paper in the other hand, ready to write down a dinner order. His first words to the congregation were

"Hello, my name is Kenneth Untener...and I'll be your waiter." What a beautiful way to establish a relationship between a bishop and his diocese. He comes as a servant to serve them.

I remember the first time I met Archbishop Raymond Hunthausen. It was in 1975 when he was appointed as Archbishop of Seattle. It was at a social gathering to welcome him. We talked a few minutes and as I was leaving, I noticed he was holding an empty coffee cup. I asked if I could get him another cup of coffee. He smiled and said, "No thanks, George. I prefer getting my own cup of coffee, but thanks for the offer anyway."

I was impressed and pleasantly surprised. Here was an archbishop who didn't want to be served. It was a small thing, and I never forgot it, and that's the type of leader he turned out to be.

A few years ago, I had the privilege of attending a priest's retreat Archbishop Hunthausen was giving. In one conference, he was talking about how we priests sometimes can misuse our authority as pastor and mistreat people. "Be kind, use your authority with humility; after all, you have to come to serve, not to be served," he said. He went on to say one of his nephews gave him a present when he became Archbishop. It was a Mickey Mouse watch. He told us it turned out to be a great grace in his life. Whenever he was tempted to think he was important or indispensable or that he was some sort of a powerful leader, he would look at his Mickey Mouse watch, and he would come back to reality. Any sense of false pride or any inflated image of power or authority would immediately leave him. He even wore it when he was called to Rome for the investigation of his so-called liberal views. "How can anyone who wears a Mickey Mouse watch take himself that seriously," he said. That watch kept him sane during those difficult times.

Archbishop Hunthausen has been an inspiration for me and for my priesthood as I have tried to live out this gospel. Greatness in the Kingdom of God cannot be given to anyone. Even Jesus could not give greatness to two saints like James and John. They had to earn it by their love and service.

And the good news is that true greatness is within the reach of everyone; even Jesus wasn't just speaking to bishops and priests. He was also speaking to anyone holding positions of authority; to parents; teachers; politicians; police officers; judges; C.E.O's; or those in the military; to anyone seeking true greatness..

30th Sunday "B" Mark 10: 46-52

Healing Mass

There's a real contrast in today's gospel between the disciples of Jesus and Bartimaeus, the man born blind. The disciples were physically able to see, but at times, they were spiritually blind, like when James and John asked Jesus to be number one and number two in his Kingdom, or when Peter rebuked Jesus for saying that as the Messiah, Jesus must suffer rejection, be condemned to death, and die and then rise from the dead on the third day, or when the twelve argued amongst themselves which one of them was the greatest in the Kingdom of God. At times, they totally misunderstood who Jesus was, and what he was teaching them about the Messiah. Truly, they were at times spiritually blind.

Bartimaeus, on the other hand, is physically blind, but spiritually and morally, he was full of insight. We know this by the way he answers Jesus' question, "What do you want me to do for you?" He answers, "Lord that I might see." He speaks the truth from his emptiness, his incompleteness, from his own identity of who he was as a blind man. He wants Jesus to meet him in his humanity and in his weakness. He needs a Savior.

Let's pause for a moment. What would your answer be? What do you want Jesus to do for you now, today? Perhaps to win the lotto, or to get that raise, to regain your health, to be rich and famous, to be happy? Jesus is asking you tonight, "What do you want me to do for you?"

Most healings in the gospel are done anonymously. We usually are not told their name. The exception is this gospel. We have a name for the man who is cured…Bartimaeus. But why did the gospel writers remember his name and not the others?

Perhaps, he was the only one who gave an honest answer to Jesus' question, "Lord, that I might see." He wanted to see physically, yes, but he also wanted to see spiritually. He wanted to see what life was all about. He wanted to see how to live his life. He wanted to see the hand of God in the confusion, in the unfairness of his life, to see beyond his physical blindness. He was, in a word, asking for the gift of faith, for goodness, for moral and spiritual insight.

Would that be your request, your response to Jesus' question? I have written a kind of examination of conscience for us. I ask you to close your eyes and pretend that you are blind, like Bartimaeus, and respond by saying, "Lord, we want to see," when I say, "and so we pray." Respond in your own name, in the name of the church, or in the name of society. "Lord we want to see."

Some of us are blind to our own sins and faults…and so we pray, "Lord we want to see."

Some people are blinded by their addictions to pleasure, money, or self promotion…and so we pray, "Lord we want to see."

Some of us rarely acknowledge many of our blessings…and so we pray, "Lord we want to see."

Some people are blinded by prejudice and hatred…and so we pray, "Lord we want to see."

Some are blinded by pride and ambition, and step all over other peoples' feelings…and so we pray, "Lord we want to see."

Some are blinded by arrogance, which makes them think they are the center of the universe…and so we pray, "Lord we want to see."

Some wallow in their own self pity and never notice God's mercy…and so we pray, "Lord we want to see."

Some don't have their prayers answered and need to see the meaning of the crosses they have been given…and so we pray, "Lord we want to see."

Now you can open your eyes. Yes, Lord, we really want to see. Like John Newton, who had a conversion experience and became a priest in the Church of England and devoted the rest of his life to serving others, he was converted from being a slave trader to becoming a priest, from being a pagan to becoming a Christian. While in the darkness, he saw the light of God's grace and love. It was John Newton who wrote the famous hymn, "Amazing grace, how sweet the sound that saved a wretch like me. I once was lost but now am found, was blind, but now I see."

That's the kind of sight Bartimaeus was asking for, to see as Jesus sees, to see what's really important. Once Bartimaeus "saw" what was important, he began to follow Jesus as a disciple. He was changed from merely being a man born blind to a man being born again in faith.

The story of Bartimaeus is our story. At times, we have been morally or spiritually blind, but we have met Jesus on the way. Once we begin to see the many little miracles of healing the Lord has given us, then we can joyfully follow Jesus down the road as his disciple.

So, Jesus is asking us tonight, "What is it that you really want me to do for you?" He's waiting for your answer.

31ˢᵗ Sunday "B" Mark 12: 28-34

In an election year, especially in the last days before voting, political candidates try to reduce their message to 30-second sound bites or to a bumper sticker. The truth is, we tend to remember catchy phrases more than complex ideas anyway, but it's hard to reduce a message without sacrificing some of its meaning. But that's what the teacher of the law was asking Jesus to do in today's gospel.

The scribe was asking Jesus to reduce the 613 commandments in the Old Testament to the one law that was the most important and the number one law to follow. "Teacher, he asked, "which commandment is first of all the others?" In other words, he was asking Jesus to give him (and us) a bumper sticker slogan. And to his amazement, Jesus does just that. But in the process, Jesus gives him more than what was asked for.

Jesus' answer was simple. "This is the first; Listen Israel, the Lord our God is the one Lord, and you must love the Lord your God with all your heart, with all your soul, with all your mind and with all your strength." (Mark 12:29-30)

The first law came from Deuteronomy, our first reading, and the second law came from the book of Leviticus. But what's really important is that Jesus made these two laws into one.

In a sense, Jesus is saying that our love for God and our love for our neighbor must be in the form of a cross. Our love must be vertical; that is, it must reach up all the way to God, and our love must also be horizontal; that is, it must reach out all the way to our neighbors.

We cannot choose to love God only and at the same time be unconcerned for humankind. Likewise, we cannot choose to be involved just with social justice issues and then substitute that concern for our love of God. These two loves cannot be separated. If they are, then our love is incomplete.

When you come to think about it, love is a strange command. Other commandments are precise. We know what it means to steal, to lie, to kill, to commit adultery, but the command to love God and our neighbor is so open-ended, it's kind of vague. It's hard to put love into precise rules and regulations. We need some images of loving that can guide and help us understand the ways of love.

Let's ponder some of the images of love from Jesus' own life; when he changed water into wine at a wedding reception to save a bride and groom's embarrassment for running out of wine, when he blessed the children to make them feel welcomed and accepted, or eating and drinking with outcasts and sinners, to tell them of God's love and forgiveness, or when Jesus was often at prayer with his father, to show us the importance of prayer, or on the cross when Jesus asked his Father to forgive those who were crucifying him. "Father, forgive them, they don't know what they're doing."

Each one of us has the capacity to love as Jesus loved in many little ways. We have all experienced receiving and giving love in our own lives. When we love others, we are loving God, as well. Maybe you and I need to be surprised once again into learning that in the kingdom of God, as in our own life experiences, where there is love, there is God.

Perhaps, by the word we share and the bread we break in this mass, we will draw closer to God and to one another, even closer than the scribe in today's gospel was to the Kingdom of God.

32ⁿᵈ Sunday "B" Mark 12: 38-44

Let me tell you a true story that happened in 2005. It's a modern day parable about the widow's mite story we just heard in today's gospel.

The second collection taken up at St. Lawrence Church in the Watts area of Los Angeles, a collection earmarked for Hurricane Katrina victims, was not much different than the thousands of other collections taken up across the country.

St. Lawrence Catholic Church is an inner city parish of 3000 families, about 80% Hispanic, 20% African American. "They are people of very modest means," said Father Peter Banks, the pastor.

The total normal parish collection per week is about $6,000, but on this weekend, the second collection was itself $7,000. Plus, there was a stunning gift left by an anonymous donor…a woman's wedding ring. That eventually was sent to a New Orleans church that was hit by the flood waters of Katrina.

The money counters showed Fr. Banks the church donation envelope with its hand printed messaged in Spanish. It simply said, "For the victims of the hurricane. I did not bring any money, but this should be of some value. It is given with all my heart." It was unsigned. When Fr. Banks opened the envelope, he saw a gold wedding ring with small notches on the outside. "It just touched my heart," said Fr. Banks. "My immediate reaction was, what incredible kindness and charity this woman had. She obviously was not giving out of her surplus but out of her want. This woman had nothing, and she reached down on her hand and took off her ring. This was all she had, and she gave it with all her heart."

For several days, Fr. Banks carried the ring with him in his shirt pocket close to his heart to remind him of this woman's generosity. But he knew the ring and it's story had to be shared. So the following weekend, the priest shared the amazing story with his parishioners, many of whom had Louisiana relatives.

"I wanted the people to know what happened," Fr. Banks said. "Watts has this bad image of poverty and violence, but Watts is full of goodness. There are saints living here in our midst. Our parishioners do relate to tragedy and suffering.

Fr. Banks then began searching the internet for a parish in the archdiocese of New Orleans that might need direct help recovering from the storm. He found the Church of St. Gabriel, a church that had been totally flood by water, 8 feet deep.

Today's gospel told me something new about Jesus, something I didn't know before, that Jesus was a people watcher. The gospel tells us Jesus deliberately took a seat in full view of the collection box in the temple and watched the people as they dropped in their money offerings.

Watching people for Jesus meant not only seeing how they physically looked and acted, but also he had the ability to read their minds and to see their hearts. That way, Jesus knew what people were thinking, and what truly motivated them to give.

That's why, when the collection time ended, Jesus pointed out one woman and told his disciples, "Truly, I tell you, this poor widow has put in more than all the others who contributed to the treasury, by giving her 2 small coins worth only a few cents."

Jesus measured the poor widow's giving with a very different kind of bookkeeping, a bookkeeping based on the gospel values. He explains this type of giving in the last verse of today's gospel by saying, the other contributors gave from their surplus wealth, from their leftovers, but she gave from her poverty, from her need. She gave all she had, her whole livelihood.

What is the lesson for us? I think it is to remember that our giving, whether to church or to other charitable needs, is not measured by its size or amount but by its sacrifice, by how much it cost us in our time, treasure, or talent.

When we give a gift to someone, we take great care to remove the price tag, but when we bring our gifts to God, we can't do that. There's no way to conceal the cost or sacrifice from God. God already knows. God knows what's in our minds and what's in our hearts. God also knows that the one who gives the least, in terms of money, often is the one who gives the most in terms of love and sacrifice.

33rd Sunday "B" Mark 13: 24-32

Sometimes, the gospel doesn't seem like good news at all. Mark is describing the end of the world, the end times, when the sun is darkened, the moon disappears, stars are crashing into each other, and Jesus' dreaded return to earth for judgment. It's not a pretty picture. In fact, it's pretty scary.

This struggle between a cosmic doomsday and the return of Christ describe the age-old battle between good and evil, light and darkness. Yes, end-of-the-world themes are as old as ancient Jewish and Greek writings. They are also deeply embedded in the New Testament, from Jesus to St. Paul, and are enshrined in our liturgy. Every time we recite the creed at mass, we say, "He will come again in glory to judge the living and the dead." And in our acclamation after the consecration, we used to say, "Christ has died, Christ is risen, Christ will come again." When Jesus preached that the end of the world would soon come, his intention was not to produce a sense of fear in his listeners but a sense of hope. Fear is not a virtue. In fact, Jesus often preached that fear is useless. Anxiety is not a virtue either. In fact, we pray in every mass just after the Our Father, "Free us from all anxiety." Jesus did not want us to worry about the end of the world. Worry is not a virtue either. Stress, worry, fear, and anxiety are the causes of so many problems in our society. That's not what Jesus intended when he preached about the end times. His message was not a message of gloom and doom but a message of hope and promise.

Jesus wanted us to know God's purpose and final plan for all creation that at the end of time, wars will not have the last word, that poverty and sickness will be destroyed, oppression and injustice, in all its hideous guises, will be destroyed, and even death itself will be destroyed.

Yes, God does have a plan for us. The plan is that we are going somewhere better. Our life has ultimate meaning, and even though we appear to be a tiny speck in the endless cosmos, we are a special child of God, made in God's image and likeness, awaiting redemption and the fullness of love. Jesus also wants us to know that we have an important role to play in God's plan for humanity now. In the Old Testament, God chose prophets to call people back to the cause of goodness. In the New Testament, Jesus called his disciples to go out and announce the good news of the Kingdom. And we today, are assured that God is at work among us to help bring God's dream for humanity to its final fulfillment.

Today's readings may sound like they are about the future, but in reality, they are about the way things are with us right now, today, in the present, especially when we have to face trials and difficulties. Oh, we don't literally see the sun darkened or the stars falling from the sky, but we may say, my world is falling apart, or my dreams have turned to ashes. What we are really saying is that sometimes things just seem to be going terribly wrong. We live in a world that is in a constant state of change and upheaval, a world filled with injustice, violence, and war. Sometimes, it seems that we cannot really count on anything or anyone around us.

I think the challenge from this gospel is how to lead balanced lives in the midst of constant change and upheaval and how to remain unshaken in a very shaken world.

Jesus makes this clear in the parable he tells about the fig tree that lost all its leaves in a drought. He tells us to look at the buds, and suddenly the buds begin to open. The old brown leaves bend, they crack, and they die and fall to the earth. They appear to die. And yet, new life soon appears. A green shoot appears, and new life begins once again. Jesus teaches us how to interpret the signs of the times. Amid the conflicts, the wars, the suffering, and the many dyings we experience, he tells us to have faith and trust in Him. Don't worry, don't be anxious, do not be afraid because He is with us. At the end of time, all will be just fine, and I promise you will be victorious. Heaven and earth will pass away, but my words, of hope and promise, will not pass way.

Christ the King "B" John 18: 33-37

The feast of Christ the King was first introduced by Pope Pius XI in 1925. Pius X1 was worried by what he was seeing in the world. World War I had recently ended in 1918, Mussolini was parading around Italy like an arrogant dictator, and a man named Hitler was gaining popularity and power with his scary Nazi party in Germany. People seemed to be losing their faith in God and their sense of spiritual direction. So, this feast of Christ the King was to remind all Christians what life is really about and to whom they truly belonged.

This feast has nothing to do with crowns or palaces or royal robes, concepts that are foreign to us Americans. Rather, it has to do with one basic question, to whom or to what do we give our allegiance as Christians? It deals with the everyday decisions that we have to make when we leave from church and go out into the world, decisions that reveal where our true allegiance lies.

I can think of two examples of people who chose to pledge their allegiance to Christ the King in some very difficult times. When Hitler rose to power, he and his army overran Europe country by country. There were many heroes who resisted him. One of them was an actual king himself, King Christian of Denmark. One famous story tells of the time when the Nazis ordered all Jews in Denmark to identify themselves by wearing armbands with the yellow Star of David. But King Christian, whose tiny country was occupied by Hitler in 1940, spoke up boldly and said, "No, this is not right. One Dane is the same as the next one. We are all Danes!"

So what did the king do? He himself put on the Star of David armband and let it be known that every loyal Dane should do the same. The next day, almost everyone was walking around wearing the Star of David. The Nazis were confused.

When the Nazis finally decided that all 8000 Jews should be rounded up and sent to the concentration camps, the King again organized a resistance effort that smuggled 7500 Jews to Sweden and to safety. As a result, the Danes saved about 90% of the Jewish population from death.

King Christian chose to follow the principles of justice and charity, preached by Christ the King, rather than to follow the principles of hatred and prejudice taught by Adolf Hitler. The King suffered for his allegiance to Christ the King, by spending 2 years in a German prison. He was freed by the Allies in 1945 but died one year later from the harsh treatment he received in confinement.

Another example of people pledging their allegiance to Christ the King took place a few years ago, in Lancaster, Pennsylvania. Ten young Amish girls were shot by an insane non-Amish assassin. Nine died. But hatred and revenge did not rule here. What did the Amish do? How did they respond? They totally forgave the man. Not only did they forgive him, but they even brought food to his wife and children who lived close to the school where the girls were shot.

To help us fully understand what the Amish did, I ask you to put yourselves in their place for just a few minutes. You have just rung the doorbell of the family whose husband and father brutally murdered your 9 year old daughter, and here you are bringing food and forgiveness for them. It's unreal. It's astounding.

Could we reach that same level of faith the Amish did? These people even went a step further. They asked that some of the money that had been raised for their own grieving families be shared with the family of the man who killed and wounded their daughters. Would you and I, or better yet, could you and I do that? It's a question to think about and pray about on this feast of Christ the King.

Well, we might say, the Amish are different, aren't they? They live apart from us and apart from society, living a strange simple life they believe God wants them to live. But they do take Jesus at his word when he says we should forgive our enemies, as he forgave his enemies while hanging on the cross.

The Amish don't actively try to convert anyone, believing their lives are testimony enough. They accept a core set of rules. They are a people of peace. They don't serve in the armed forces. They don't accept Social Security or purchase life insurance. They do vote and pay taxes. They don't hold public office, they forgive their enemies, because they truly believe they cannot

289

enter heaven if they hate anyone. For them, the matter is simple. Christ, their King, has spoken, and they must follow him.

So, here we have two instances of people who proved their allegiance to Christ the King in difficult times. As we celebrate this feast, let's pray for the faith and the courage to follow their example.

YEAR

C

First Sunday of Advent "C"
Luke 21: 25-28, 34-36

A few weeks ago there was a story in the news about a house that burned down, killing one of the younger children. What made the story even more tragic was that the father, the house's owner, had been planning for two weeks to install a smoke alarm, but did not. The father told reporters that it was something that he kept putting off—because he was too busy with other things. Now one of his children is dead; and there's nothing he, or anyone else, can do to bring him back to life.

That tragic story hits close to home with all of us because it could have happened to any one of us. There are so many things that we want to do, but we keep putting them off—for one reason or another. There are mothers who want to get to know their daughters better; or fathers who want to get to know their sons better, but they keep putting it off. There are husbands and wives who want to deepen their relationship with each other, but keep putting it off—for some reason or other. I think there's a human tendency in all of us to put things off. But a closer look shows that maybe that's not the whole story....perhaps our problem isn't that of putting things off.... Rather, it's that of just missing opportunities. "Why did I get so angry and scream at my son or daughter? I could have been kinder, and more gentle in saying "No.".....or, "Why didn't I offer to do the dishes when I know Mom felt so lousy?" I'm sure the father, who was planning to install that smoke alarm, could have found the time to do it...BUT he simply missed the opportunities.

Advent is the time to make up all those past opportunities for doing good. In his book, "Golf My Way," Jack Nicklaus explains how he prepares for every shot he takes. It's a process he calls, "Mental rehearsal." This simply means he plays every shot in his imagination before he plays it for real.

Nicklaus writes: It's like a movie…First, I see the ball where I want it to finish, nice and white, either on the green, or on the fairway…then I mentally "see" the ball going there; how it lands softly, or with back-up spin. Then there's a sort of fade-out; and the next thing I visualize is the kind of swing I need to turn those images into reality."

That's what the church is asking us to do during this Advent Season…not to play golf, but to visualize what we are to do to prepare for the Coming of Christ—whether it be His coming this Christmas or at the end of the world.

The Season of Advent is like the ancient Roman god, Janus, for whom the month of January is named. Janus is depicted in art as having two faces. One face looks backward into the past; the other looks forward into the future. The Season of Advent is like that. It looks backward into the past to the First Coming of Jesus. It also looks forward into the future to his Second Coming. Today we stand at the midpoint between these two great moments in our history.

Today's readings tell us how best to prepare for Christ's coming. "Be on guard! Watch! Pray! Reform your lives; - avoid sin – but especially do good works!" St. Paul sums it up in our second reading: "May the Lord make you overflow with love for one another, and for all people."

One practical way of keeping Advent is the "Giving Tree," decorated with a variety of different colored "ornaments." These "ornaments" are pieces of paper representing various organizations in need of our help (for example: bring a Teddy Bear for a child at Echo Glenn; socks; underwear; or tee shirts for a man at St. Martin de Porres Emergency enter; buy a toy or a gift for a child attending St. Mary's Christmas party; or give some baby items to the St. Joseph Baby Corner; or write a check to Shanti for support of people living with AIDS, or some other life threatening illness!

Advent is the time to watch for the many opportunities we have, for doing good. It's the time to visualize our swing for making good shots—to help prepare the way for Christ to once again come into our world.

Second Sunday of Advent "C" Luke 3: 1-6

John the Baptist is featured in today's gospel, arriving on the scene as a single, solitary figure, preaching repentance and conversion!

He had no formal education, no endorsement from any religious authority and no financial supporters. His preaching was harsh and demanding—repent and prepare for the coming of the Messiah! And yet, great crowds flocked to the desert to hear him preach and to be baptized in the Jordan, as a sign of their repentance of sin! What was it about this fiery Luke, the solitary preacher that attracted so many.

St Luke gives us the answer in today's gospel when he says: "The word of God came to John in the desert." The people truly believed that and that's what drew the crowds to listen to him! St. Luke goes on to describe John by quoting from the prophet, Isaiah: John is: "a voice of one crying out in the desert." I like Luke's description of John as "a voice of ONE." That phrase: "A voice of <u>One</u> sums up his mission! He truly was an unstoppable army of ONE person!

During this Advent Season, it's good to remember the power of one single voice, a single action, or a single life that can make a huge difference in the world!

Do you remember the Dr. Seuss story about Horton, the elephant? He called it, "Horton Hears A Who." One day Horton, the elephant, heard voices coming from a tiny speck of dust, which turned out to be a very tiny planet, instead of a speck of dust. The microscopic inhabitants of the planet (the Whos) implored Horton to save them from an impending danger!

But when Horton told the other animals in the jungle about the "Whos" and their tiny planet, they thought he was crazy, so they locked him up in a mental hospital! But Horton kept talking to the "Whos!" He told them to shout as loud as they could, with their collective voices, so that the other animals in the jungle might hear them and free Horton, so he could save their tiny planet!!!

So, all the "Whos" (except one named JoJo) joined in one big yell, but the sound was too faint to be heard by the other animals! Finally, the "Who" convinced JoJo to join them in the chorus of yelling to save their planet and <u>this time</u> (with the added voice of JoJo), the sound was loud enough to be heard by the other animals, who released Horton so he could save the planet of Who-Ville, which he did. So:

If you think <u>one single voice crying out makes no difference</u>—don't tell that to JoJo or the residents of Who-Ville and don't say that to John the Baptist either. His voice may have been solitary, but it echoed in the halls of power until kings trembled and it boomed across the desert with the Power of God speaking. It's true—one single voice can pierce the silence, just as one candle can overcome the deepest darkness.

There is also great power in one single life! For example, when Rosa Park refused to give up her seat to a white man on a bus in Montgomery, Alabama that one December day in 1955, her passive act of defiance in the face of injustice, symbolized the struggle for equal rights of millions of others. It was all the more powerful because it was a single act done by one solitary person!

Another example (not as well known) comes from the life and death of Susan G. Komen, who died at the age of 36 from breast cancer and today the "Susan G. Komen For The Cure Foundation" has raised over 1.3 billion toward breast cancer research and cure with over 100,000 volunteers in 125 countries. Just one solitary life, yet what a powerful force for good Susan has unleashed! Make no mistake about it; there is great power in ONE!

One question for all of us to think about during this Advent Season is: "What will be the influence of <u>my </u>life on others?" The good news is that we don't have to do great things—like curing cancer or AIDS, stopping a terrorist attack single-handedly, ending world poverty or hunger, or bringing peace to the world. NO! All we have to do is take care of the people in our own lives—parents, our spouse, our children, relatives, neighbors, people we work with, or attend school with, the poor and less fortunate people we meet during our life time!

We don't have to save the world in general. We only have to give ourselves in a meaningful way, to one person in particular. That's enough! One person at a time.

When we do that (in a sense) we become like John the Baptist, "A voice of ONE" crying in the desert, preparing the way of the Lord to come once again into our darkened world!

Third Sunday of Advent "C" Luke 3: 10-18

A lone gunman stepped out of the car, rested his rifle on the car door, and aimed it at the church. Through the wide-open doors, he could see right down the long aisle to his target—a priest who was just finishing his homily at Mass that morning. A shot rang out and so ended the life of Oscar Romero, Archbishop of San Salvador. It was March 24, 1980.

For the previous three years Oscar Romero had preached the Gospel to his people and had denounced the sins of injustice, the murders and tortures that were destroying his country. Using the Archdiocesan Radio Station, he spoke to all the people and <u>everyone</u> listened to him. To the poor he was the "voice of those who have no voice." To the rich and powerful, he was a Communist, a trouble maker and an enemy of the State---and he was publically denounced as such.

"We have never preached 'violence,'" "Romera once said, "except the 'violence' of love, which left Christ nailed to a cross and the 'violence' we must do to ourselves to overcome our selfishness and such cruel injustice among us."

The authorities tried to jam his radio station, but he gave his sermons faithfully, and the poor people of El Salvador hung onto his every word. Romero once asked, "What kind of a Gospel would it be that did not provoke a crisis in you? Nice, pious words that do not bother people—this is what many people would like. Such a Gospel never hurts anyone, but it never helps anyone either. No!" he went on to say, "the Gospel is courageous and it makes demands on us, even to the giving of our lives." How prophetic!

This was the same message of John the Baptist to the people of his time. The Baptist was regarded by many as a prophet, a messenger from God, but also as a troublemaker, a madman. The good sincere people asked John, "What shall we do to make ourselves ready to meet the Lord when he comes?" John gave them simple Gospel answers: 1) Share with those who have nothing, 2) Do not exploit others for money or power, and 3) he reminded the rich and the military that true wealth and true power are spiritual gifts to be used for the good of the people.

So two thousand years later, in our own time, Romero gave the same message to his people. He said, "The Church says to the rich: Do not sin by misusing your wealth. Share it with the poor and the Church says to the powerful: Do not misuse your power. Work for justice and peace in society."

We know that the abuse of power has brought great suffering to millions of people in the world today. John the Baptist warns the people of his day: "The One who is coming after me is more powerful than I am. He is the one you must face." And that's why in today's Gospel it says: "A feeling of expectation grew among the people." During this Advent Season we can ask two questions: 1) What must <u>we</u> do to prepare for Jesus' coming this Christmas? And 2) Do we have the same feeling of expectation as the people did in John the Baptist's time?

Each of us must answer those questions ourselves. But if we have no sense of God or no sense of justice, or no sense of sharing our gifts, then we will <u>not</u> be expecting anything or anyone this Advent. If we have no expectations, then the Gospel is only a fairytale—just a lot of pious words that mean nothing. It will have no power over us to touch us, to move us, or to bring us to life. That's why we need an Oscar Romero to shake us up, to be a modern-day John the Baptist. Just two years before his murder, Archbishop Romero said this about Advent: "Advent should help us to discover in each brother or sister that we greet, in each worker who wants to use the right to join a union, in each friend whose hand we shake, in each peasant who looks for work in the coffee groves—that we see in them the face of Christ. Then", he says, "it would not be possible to rob them, to cheat them or to deny them their rights. They are Christ and whatever is done to them Christ will take as done to Him! This is what Advent is: Christ living among us."

A bullet stopped that brave heart beating, but it could not still his voice. Oscar Romero is still a voice in the wilderness of worldly greed, a voice that keeps calling to us today. If we listen to that voice, we will ask: "Lord what must we do to prepare for your coming?" And another voice will answer. And it will be Jesus saying come and follow me.

Fourth Sunday of Advent "C" Luke 1: 39-45

There are certain people in our lives who, when we see them or hear their voice, make our heart skip a beat with delight! They are the people who can make us laugh when we are down and feeling blue. They are the people who have strong arms and a soft heart, who instinctively wrap us in a warm hug that makes everything seem right.

They are the wise ones who have weathered many a storm themselves and whose advice to us gives us hope and confidence in the future.

Such is the meeting of Mary and Elizabeth in today's gospel. The moment Elizabeth heard Mary's voice, both her own heart and the heart of the baby in her womb leaped for joy and Mary felt the same.

Oftentimes, we imagine Mary, the much younger of the two, hastening from Galilee to Judea, out of concern and generosity to help her older cousin who is coping with a pregnancy in her advanced age. But, without discounting that aspect of their encounter, I believe Mary had a more <u>personal</u> reason for visiting Elizabeth. It was this: Mary viewed Elizabeth as a wise woman, an elder mentor, as someone who could wrap a bewildered teen-age mother-to-be, in her strong embrace, offering her wisdom and strength during a difficult time. After all, God's timing for both of them was difficult.

How much easier it would have been for Elizabeth, had her child come when her body was more limber and much younger and how much easier it would have been for Mary, had her child arrived after her marriage to Joseph. Sometimes God's timing seems to be off.

In a culture in which a woman was esteemed for the children she bore, Elizabeth likely endured accusatory glances, and unkind remarks her entire life, as people wondered why God was punishing her for not having had any children.

And likewise, in Mary's little village of Nazareth, the gossip about her being pregnant started to fly as soon as her condition was known. Who would believe the story about the angel asking Mary to be the mother of the Messiah? Even Joseph had his doubts!

Elizabeth, who has been totally faithful to God her entire life, despite the suffering she endured, is the perfect companion for Mary. She helps Mary to trust in the mysterious ways of God, as Mary faces the many difficulties and challenges of saying "yes" to God.

On this last Sunday of Advent, in like manner, we carry the mysterious power of God's life of grace within us which enables us to be a source of delight and blessing for others. When we abandon ourselves to the mysterious ways of God, as Mary and Elizabeth did, it's not just for ourselves that the new life of God's grace is given to us. No! We are also meant to be companions of one another, a source of mutual wisdom, strength and joy to others.

Come to think of it, those are the best presents that we can give to one another this Christmas--our friendship, companionship, our love and our joy!

Immaculate Conception "C"

Adopted children often try to learn more about or even to contact, their biological mothers. When they find them, they are often stuck by the differences between their "biological" and their "adoptive" mothers.

In our second reading today (Ephesians), Paul reminds us that we were predestined through our baptism into Christ, to become the adopted children of God. And as "adoptive children," we have the chance to compare our "biological" mother (Eve) with our "adoptive" mother, (Mary).

Eve, the mother of all the living, may be considered our "natural" mother—the mother of our human nature. And Mary, the mother of Jesus, became our "adoptive" mother through our baptism into Christ. By comparing these two women, we may also compare our humanity with the spiritual persons that we are called to be!

Our first reading today (Genesis)tells a rather grim story of failure, shame, fear, and punishment. Adam and Eve have been expelled from the Garden of Eden for their disobedience. Because of their sin, they tried to hide themselves from God, realizing their nakedness.

In contrast, the Gospel today highlights the innocence and transparency of Mary, who was without sin her entire life. Eve, tricked by the serpent (the devil), disobeyed God's will and she became fearful and defensive. Mary, open to God's will, becomes the handmaid of the Lord—willing to follow wherever God was calling her to go.

Eve wanted to know more than what God knew. Her pride and her need to control, separated her from God. Mary humbly subjects herself to whatever God asks her to do.

Perhaps the biggest difference is that Eve is discontent with all that has been given her in the Garden of Eden. Amid all the beauty, the richness and wonders, she is not satisfied; she yearns for more.

But Mary rejoices in what is given her! Even when the gift is hard to understand and accept, or when it doesn't seem to make any sense, when it seems to be contrary to her Jewish customs or traditions...even then she accepts everything, even the mysterious gift of her unexpected pregnancy that turns out to be the Savior Himself!

How often in our lives do we act out of self-interest that we have inherited from our natural mother, Eve. We too, whom so much has been given, long for greater wealth, for more power, for more knowledge, for more independence from God. The gifts the Lord gives us may bring us fear of the unknown future, or a desire for more control. Yet Mary shows us these gifts are precious; they are blessings in disguise; a chance for us to share Christ with the world, as she did.

Mary becomes our spiritual mother when we respond as she did to the call of God: "May it be done to me according to your word." Despite our sinfulness, God is waiting to take the initiative in our lives, too. Are we open to that call today? How will we respond during this Advent Season?

Christmas "C" Matthew 1: 1-25 - 8-25
Holy Family – Luke 2: 41-52

The Feast of the Holy Family scares most of us. We have trouble with the word "Holy." Of course, Jesus, Mary and Joseph were "holy" people. After all, Jesus is the Son of God; Mary, his mother, is the Immaculate Conception, i.e. she was free from all sin her entire life, and Joseph was chosen by God to be the husband of Mary and the foster-father of Jesus. He was the original "Holy Joe!"

So, we ask, how can _we_ compete with all that holiness in our own family?" There's no comparison. We can't even begin to compete. Game over! We don't have a chance, right?

Not so fast! What makes them a "holy" family was not that they were "holy" people. What made them a "holy" family was how they dealt with their family problems. That's how we can imitate them.

Today's gospel shows how they dealt with one problem, most families eventually have to face, and that is when their child began to enter the "twilight zone," that awkward stage between leaving childhood and entering into adulthood. For most families, it usually happens through some experience like going away to summer camp, or volunteering to help at a hospital, or going away to school, getting involved in some youth ministry program like Habitat for Humanity, or in meeting new friends. And suddenly there's a gap between parent and child.

The teen's lament is, "My parents don't understand me." Parents' who once seemed so wise, now seem to be too old-fashioned, too cautious, and too conservative. And to the parents, their "adult-want-to-be child" seems to be too impatient, unrealistic, inconsiderate and ungrateful for all the care, love and protection they have been given.

"Wait," say the parents. "I can't wait," says the adolescent. "You don't know," say the parents. "I _do_ know," says the one who no longer feels like a child.

On this Feast of the Holy Family, Mary and Joseph experienced all the feelings and emotions of raising a child—the astonishment, the anxiety, amazement, the lack of understanding, and the love.

We can only imagine what mixture of pain and joy Mary and Joseph felt as they traveled back to Jerusalem in search of Jesus, who was lost!

Today's gospel says, "Once they found him in the temple, his parents were astonished and his mother said to him, "Son, why have you done this to us? Your father and I have been looking for you with great anxiety."

And Jesus' only response was that they didn't need to look for Him because He just needed to be in his Fathers house. Jesus was upset at their distress. He was in another world—a world he thought they would know about and understand. Jesus was a 12-year-old child, anxious to become an adult.

So, how did the Holy Family deal with this problem? Toward the end of this gospel passage, we read that Mary "treasured all these things in her heart, "until she grew in wisdom to understand and to accept the mission of her son."

And the gospel concludes with these words: "Then Jesus went with them to Nazareth and was obedient to them." And Jesus increased in wisdom and age and favor before God and the people.

This gospel leaves us with the reassuring thought that when family life is a mutually respectful thing between parents and children, both grow to full maturity.

At times it will be the children who don't understand their parent's concern, and sometimes it will be the parents who don't understand their children's need to separate themselves from them, in the attempt to grow up. But when both exercise trust and faith in one another, both will increase in wisdom and in years, and in divine and human favor.

So, today on this Feast, let's celebrate the gift of family and ask God to bless our families with the spirit of loving trust and faith in each other—especially those families <u>now</u> going through some difficult times.

May our parish always be "Family Friendly," and a safe haven for all families, a place where the peace of Christ dwells in our hearts, a place where we love one another as Christ has commanded us. With gratitude in our hearts, may we come to this Eucharist as God's family, as God's chosen ones, truly "holy" and beloved.

Epiphany "C" Matthew 2: 1-12

The magi followed a star in search of the new-born Messiah. They spent two long years in their search and once they found Him, they worshiped Him by offering gifts of gold, frankincense and myrrh.

The gifts they offer are symbolic—the gold was to honor Jesus as a King, the frankincense was to offer worship to this child as the Son of God and the myrrh (a substance used in the Jewish burial rite) was offered to Jesus as a mortal man, a human being who someday would suffer and die and be buried!

The three magi themselves have always been a symbol for us as we make our personal journey of faith to find God. And, like the magi, the star of faith leads us to the most unlikely places. To places where we least expect to find GOD! I'm sure the magi expected to find the new-born King in some big, important city like Jerusalem, surrounded by power and wealth. But the star, instead, leads them to a small, obscure hamlet in Bethlehem. This king is found in poverty, he is powerless and unknown.

On this Feast of the Epiphany, the question we can ask ourselves is this: where are the places we search for God? Do we search for God in the ordinary, hum-drum events of our lives--in our weakness and sin, in the temptations and doubts of our faith, in our humanness and brokenness? Yes, God is there!

And do we search for God in the least of our brothers and sisters—in the poor and oppressed, in those struggling with substance abuse, in those who are terminally ill or those who are in prison or dying with AIDS. Yes, God is there. Do we search for God present in our own sickness, suffering or loneliness, in the crosses that come to us, in our own mortality, in our growing older and in our dying? Yes, God is there!

Perhaps we have been looking for God in all the wrong places--perhaps in power or wealth, in the social status we may have attained, or <u>only</u> in our successes or perhaps in our security and smugness that we are, after all, better than others.

Perhaps we have been looking for God in a church we think should never, never-ever change, or in a set of rules and regulations we hoped would bring us automatic holiness and sometimes we miss God in the false belief that "we can take care of ourselves thank you" attitude. We don't need anyone else to help us. We become so independent that we don't even need God, or a Savior like Jesus. There's a modern-day version of the story of the three wise men. According to the story, they also traveled to the City of Peace, to the modern-day Bethlehem. They sought to offer their gifts as solutions for the world's problems:

1. The first one offered a huge amount of gold, suggesting it would buy all the power in the world.
2. The second, instead of frankincense, brought computers and other electronic gadgets. Their "knowledge" would solve every problem in the world.
3. The third brought myrrh in the form of the split-atom. It would be a weapon against anyone opposing peace.

When they arrived at the modern-day Bethlehem, they met St. Joseph but he refused to allow them in the manger. They protested "But we are offering the means to make every one rich, to solve all the problems on earth, and to destroy all who would oppose peace."

He told the first wise man, "Your gold can provide for many material needs, but you forgot to include the priceless value of Jesus."

To the second wise man Joseph said, "Your modern technology can provide valuable information for all of humanity, but you forgot the teachings of Jesus.

To the third he said, "Your atomic power is awesome, both in what it can do for good and what destruction it can bring, but you forgot to include the Prince of Peace, Jesus. St. Joseph responded to each one. So, the three wise men leave, sadly shaking their heads at St Joseph's foolish words.

The story is a critique of worldly wisdom. The real problem is not with what the modern wise men have brought, but whom they have left out. They

307

have forgotten Jesus! Before all else, Jesus is our way, Jesus is our knowledge, and Jesus is our power! Jesus, the one for whom we search is the only one who can lead us in our search for the living God.

1. Jesus was born in poverty, but the world has more than enough wealth and resources to stamp out poverty, if only nations would share their resources with each other.
2. Jesus is the way, the truth and the life! The ultimate ignorance is not knowing Christ, and his teachings.
3. And Jesus is the Prince of Peace! True peace will come only when the walls of hatred and prejudice are torn down and we love each other as Christ loves us. These are the powerful gifts Jesus brings to us and to the entire world.

Baptism of Christ "C" Luke 3: 15-16, 21-22

Like last Sunday, today's Feast of the Baptism of Jesus, is another "epiphany," another "manifestation" of Jesus as the Christ!

When John baptized Jesus in the Jordan, God the Father proclaimed who Jesus *really* was by saying, "You are my son, my beloved. I am well pleased with you.

Last Sunday the 3 Magi found out who Jesus was—that he was the longed-for Messiah/King. But today's feast pushes us one step further— today, Jesus finds out who *he* really is.

John preached a baptism of repentance and forgiveness and the people responded. But when Jesus went down into the water, it was <u>not</u> to be forgiven (He had no sins), but it was to begin his public ministry, to begin proclaiming that the Kingdom of God has come, to begin confronting the powers of sin, suffering and death and to begin sending the Holy Spirit into the lives of all who would listen and follow him. So when Jesus was baptized, it was not as a prophet or as a teacher, but as the very Son of God, the Word made flesh, who dwells among us.

Today's feast of Jesus' baptism is telling us something very important— that our God is not a distant or absent Creator unconcerned about us, but that God has sent His own Son among us and that God's Holy Spirit is now present <u>today</u> in our world.

Listen to Isaiah's job description for the promised Messiah (the role taken over by Jesus in his baptism): "He will feed his flock like a shepherd, he will gather the lambs in his arms and carry them in his bosom and gently lead the ewes with care."

That was Jesus' job description as the Messiah, the same job description we take on through our own baptism. So, today's feast not only reminds us who <u>Jesus</u> really was, it also reminds us who <u>we now</u> are, through our baptism in Him.

Our baptism is not just a baptism of water, it is a baptism of fire and of the Holy Spirit. We are called to change the world, to create the world anew. "Come, Holy Spirit," we pray, "enkindle in us the fire of your love." Just as the Holy Spirit descended on Jesus at his baptism, so the Holy Spirit has descended on us at our baptism.

Our baptism also calls us to read and listen to the Scriptures (the word of God) not only with our minds, but more especially with our hearts, as something we are to love and cherish. Then, once we have "fallen in love" with the word of God (as baptized Christians) then we are compelled to move and act with conviction—to actually put God's word into action, by living it!

Someone once compared the Bible to a cookbook. A cookbook is just a collection of recipes. But what good are these recipes, if someone doesn't actually cook, or never takes the time to try out the recipes? People don't keep their cookbooks in their living room or bedroom—no, they keep them in the kitchen near at hand, ready to use.

The same is true of the Bible. The Word of God is "useless," if we don't act on what we read or try to put it into action. The ultimate test of the Bible for us is, does the Word of God actually "change" us? Does it impel us to change our values? Does it "change" the way we use our time and money? Does it make us "resolve" to be more compassionate, more loving and forgiving? Does it "challenge" us to find new and perhaps better ways of serving others? If it does, only then can the Bible be useful for us.

We know that a recipe from a cookbook can give us a good meal, at least once in a while. But the teaching of Jesus and the prophets' in the Bible can give us much more; it can give us a good, happy life and can reveal to us the true purpose and meaning of life.

So, in our Eucharist today, let us renew our baptismal promises once again. Remember that it's better to have made promises and broken them, than never to have promised them at all.

So today, give yourself the gift of your own epiphany, as you contemplate what it means to be a "baptized" follower of Christ. If you are willing to commit yourself anew to our common task of building God's Kingdom in our day, I ask you to make this resounding response: "I **do** believe," to the following questions. Please stand for the Profession of Faith.

Ash Wednesday "C" Matthew 6:1-6, 16-18; Joel 2: 12-18; 2 Corinthians 5:20 – 6:2

It may seem that Ash Wednesday and Lent come too soon after the Christmas Season. There still may be some unused presents hanging around the house. It just seems strange that we should be preparing our rice bowls so soon. So the question comes to mind—do we need Lent, now so soon after Christmas?

Lent has an interesting history. The first people to observe Lent were not Christians at all, but were the pagans preparing to become Christian. During Lent, they wore sackcloth and ashes and lived the 6 weeks before Easter as repentant sinners.

But all that changed when some of the baptized Christians noticed something remarkable at the Easter baptisms. They were struck by the sheer joy, and the radiant faces of those just baptized. They, too, wanted to experience that same joy and celebration of new life, new birth and new strength.

Those already baptized realized they had become too "ho-hum" in their faith and decided to do something about it. So the next year some of the baptized Christians joined with the Catechumens in their preparation for baptism on Easter. They also put on the sackcloth and ashes and lived the 40 days before Easter as repentant sinners. This is how Lent gradually spread to the entire Church. It came out of a need to share in the joy of rebirth felt by the pagan converts at their baptism.

Even though Jesus had been baptized by John and was full of the Holy Spirit, he felt the need to go into the desert to fast and pray for 40 days. After the desert and after his temptations by Satan, Jesus realized who he was and what his Father was calling Him to do. He came out of the desert with a gospel and a firm faith in his Father which he would take with him all the way to Calvary.

Today, we are like Jesus, who went into the desert and like the early Christians who felt the need for repentance and conversion. With the early Christians we share a common struggle with sin and temptation. We are driven by the same doubts of faith. We sometimes make bad choices about the most important events in our lives. We live without sufficient reflection, without enough trust and faith, without serious prayer—and without God!

We cannot force Lent upon ourselves. Each one of us must find our own need for Lent. We must find our own need to go into the desert to face our gifts, as well as our own limitations. We all have a need to face ourselves, to face our demons and to face our God.

Even though Lent may seem to come early this year, and it all seems a bit risky and difficult—let's go into the desert together, to find out who we are (like Jesus did) and to find out what God our Father is calling us to do, and to become. Yes, we really <u>do</u> need Lent.

And so today, we will now be signed on the forehead with blessed ashes, in the sign of the cross, that encourages us "to turn away from sin and be faithful to the gospel.

First Sunday on Lent "C" Luke 4:1-13

The desert has always played an important role in Salvation History! In the Old Testament, the Jewish people wandered in the desert for 40 years, searching for the Promised Land. As a pilgrim people they encountered God there in some very special ways:

1. God spoke to them through Moses.
2. God protected them from their enemies.
3. Yahweh led them by powerful signs…a cloud by day and a pillar of fire at night.
4. God fed them with "manna," the mysterious bread from heaven.

In the desert they were also tempted to worship false idols. They melted down their gold to form a "golden calf" which they worshipped. They sinned and turned away from the One True God. But God always forgave them and never abandoned them.

The desert is a dangerous place. It's always changing. Food and water are scarce. It's extremely hot during the day and very gold at night. It's a place in which one can easily get lost. And it is to such a place that we find Jesus in the Gospel today. And here is the big surprise: Jesus is not in the desert because he got lost or because he strayed from the path of His Father's protection. No, Jesus is in the desert because the Holy Spirit led him there. Jesus is there to be tempted by the Devil.

Jesus was just beginning his public ministry. It was a time of discernment and decision in his life. He was trying to understand what his baptism in the Jordan really meant; he was trying to figure out what kind of Messiah his Father wanted him to be and where his Father's will was leading him.

He was also well aware of all the evil in the world—the injustice, the hatred, the violence, the poverty and sickness. Jesus wanted to do something about those social evils—but he was not sure exactly what to do. So, in the desert Jesus comes face-to-face with EVIL in the person of Satan, who tempts him in different ways:

1. Jesus is tempted so he would compromise his mission as the Messiah.
2. He is tempted to be self-serving, and
3. To worship the Devil

But Jesus overcame each temptation!

During these 40 days of Lent, we are also led by the Spirit into the desert. As a pilgrim people, we are "on the move"—searching for God's will and looking for a deeper meaning to life. We are also tempted by those "things" that distract us and lead us away from God. We are tempted to fashion our own "false gods" from the greed of our material possessions. We are tempted to create God in our own image and likeness through our pride or desire for control. Perhaps we are caught in the web of evil that surrounds us by trying to escape into alcohol, drugs, or selfish relationships.

So, what can we do about the temptations in our lives and the evil that surrounds us? Jesus gives us the answer. He tells us to tell Satan to leave us and be gone. We need more than bread alone to live but we also should live on every word that comes from Gods mouth. Pay homage to the Lord your God and only worship Him. It's interesting that the slang word for "money" today is "bread." Jesus warns us not to live by "bread" alone, that is: not to live by money alone and all the things money can buy. We know that money is not evil in itself, but it can become evil if it dominates our lives so much that it becomes a "false god!" We refer to the American dollar bill as the "Almighty Dollar." It's true. The "Almighty Dollar" has the power to dominate us. When it does our motto changes from "In God We Trust," to "In Money We Trust."

There's an old saying that "the best things in life are free." How true. We know we can't buy love, happiness, friendship or peace of mind. Acceptance, forgiveness, good heath, our talents and the beautiful creation that surrounds us are all free gifts from God. But in our materialistic society, it is so tempting to "live by bread alone," and pay little attention to the Word of God!

It's nice to know we are not alone in our personal temptations. Like the Jewish people in the Old Testament and like Jesus in the desert, we are not alone. We are sustained by the power of God, which has already given us the victory over sin and evil!

So, Lent is a time to recognize what we are really hungering and thirsting for. It's a time to stop and think how well we are doing in our worship of the "One True God!" Lent is a time to look at all those "false gods" around us, and say to them as Jesus said in today's Gospel: "Be Gone, Satan." "Get out of my life!" But, like Jesus, we are smart enough to know that the Devil will leave us but only "for a time," and we know that temptations will always be part of our spiritual journey. But we also know that Evil is no match for the Holy Spirit who, from time-to-time will continue to lead us back into the desert, to be tempted again and again.

Second Sunday of Lent "C" Luke 13: 31-35

On this Second Sunday of Lent, the Church takes us to the mountain top, along with Peter, James and John. There we see Jesus transformed in all his glory as the Son of God! God, the Father, gives witness to him by saying, "This is my chosen Son. Listen to him."

One of the most famous "mountain-top" experiences of our time, took place in front of the Lincoln Memorial in Washington, D.C. in 1968. In his famous "I Have a Dream" speech, Dr. Martin Luther King, Jr., challenged and inspired a nation to "dream" with him, about a nation without any barriers of color, of race, of religion or of national origin.

Dr. King had been to the mountain-top with Jesus in prayer and heard Jesus speak to him about justice and racial equality. Then he came down the mountain with Jesus to speak to the millions of people gathered there that day. He shared with them his "vision" of non-violent ways of fighting for justice and racial equality.

As it turned out, that speech was his last; because he was assassinated in Memphis soon after giving it. King's speech made all the difference to the Civil Rights Movement in the days and weeks and months following his death. It prepared the people for the struggles they would have to face in order to eventually win their civil rights. In a sense, his death was some how part of God's plan to bring liberation to a people unjustly treated.

In today's gospel, the disciples were given a glimpse of heavenly glory. It was just before they would have to witness Jesus' shameful death on the cross. Their "transfiguration" experience helped prepare the disciples to face the many struggles they would have to endure after Jesus died. The death of Jesus was also part of God's Plan to redeem all of humanity, and to free all people from their sins.

Notice that Peter suggests they all remain "permanently" on the mountain top. "Let's make three tents here, one for Jesus, one for Moses and one for Elijah." Let's make this a sacred place (like a temple or retreat center) where people could come to encounter God—far away from the struggles and concerns of everyday life.

But Jesus says, "No." Instead Jesus leads the disciples down from the mountain top to the valley below, to a town where people actually lived. It is there that the disciples are called to meet the people and minister to their needs.

Lent also calls us to transform ourselves and each other by the power of God's love within us. The best way to do that is to follow God the Father's advice in today's gospel: "This is my Chosen Son. Listen to him." Listen to him in your prayers and he will tell you what to do. Look for Jesus on whatever hill or valley you might be in on your journey and you will find him. Stay close to him and follow him as a faithful disciple, wherever he may lead you.

The Cursillo Movement has a saying that has helped me as a priest. "Bloom where you are planted." Every assignment became an opportunity to serve in different circumstances. "Bloom where you are planted..." in other worlds, transform the place where you live, be a sign of God's love to those around you there so you can make the world you live in, a much better place.

It doesn't matter if you're single, married, divorced or widowed, whether you're rich or poor, young or old, gay or straight, educated or not, whether you're a leader in the front of the line or a follower somewhere in the middle or you're someone struggling at the very end of the line. The important thing to remember is "to bloom where you are planted!"

The one lesson the Transfiguration teaches me is that religion is not so much about building permanent temples or shrines, but more about healing hurts and bringing liberation to the poor and needy of our society.

Jesus tells us to come down from the mountain, to come out of our church buildings where we feel safe and complacent and to work for peace and justice. Real religion is about changing or transforming ourselves so we can change or transform the world in which we live. The Cursillo Movement says it best, "Bloom where you are planted."

Third Sunday of Lent "C" Luke 13: 1-9

Today's gospel is often referred to as the gospel of the 2nd chance. It's a statement about God's patience with us and it challenges us to give others (including ourselves) a 2nd chance.

There's a famous painting that shows a young man playing chess with the Devil. They are playing for very high stakes…for the possession of the young man's soul. The painting portrays the Devil as having just made a brilliant move. It stymies the young man.

Chess players who study the arrangement of the pieces in this painting immediately felt sympathy for the young man because he has been trapped. He has been put in a hopeless situation. He has been led down a blind alley and there's no way out.

Patrick Murphy, a well-known "world-class" chess player, was intrigued by the painting. One day, while studying the arrangement of the chess pieces, he saw something that no one else did. He saw a way out for the young man. Excitedly he cried out to the young man in the painting, "Don't give up! You still have an excellent move left!"

This story fits in beautifully with the point that Jesus makes in the parable of the fig tree. Like the young man in the painting, the fig tree also seems to be hopelessly lost. But the gardener pleads for the barren tree, asking the owner to give it another year to bear fruit. The owner consents and suddenly hope breaks through. A last minute reprieve is given, a second chance is granted.

That's the way God treats us, Jesus is saying. God (the ever-patient gardener) keeps giving us 2nd and 3rd chances all through our lives, to produce spiritual fruits and because of Jesus, we are never doomed or abandoned! He never gives up on us, no matter how bad things may seem.

According to the parable, the barren fig tree "deserved" to be cut down because it was useless; it was taking up space where something more useful could be planted and it was using up the nourishment given to it, without making any return. Jesus was trying to teach us an important lesson about God and our own spiritual lives.

The story of the fig tree is the parable of the 2ⁿᵈ Chance. The "gardener" is Jesus, who pleads on our behalf, asking the Master (God the Father) that we be given another chance to bear fruit. Jesus is telling us never to give up but always to be living in the hope of God's mercy. God the Father is the ever-patient "Master," who keeps giving us "barren" fig trees the time, the proper care and attention needed to produce a rich harvest.

The story of the young man playing chess with the Devil fits beautifully with the parable of the barren fig tree. Both the young man and the fig tree are in serious trouble. They both seem hopelessly lost and there seems to be no way out. But then, suddenly, a ray of hope breaks through…there s a last minute reprieve and both are given a second chance.

Lent is our opportunity for another "new" beginning, a time to give ourselves a second chance. The death and resurrection of Jesus assures us God loves us, forgives us and never gives up on us—even if we are tempted to give up on ourselves.

What was the failure or the sin of the fig tree? Only that it did nothing, with all the care and provisions it was given. This is the same sin (or "failure") we must examine in ourselves during this Lent. Perhaps our greatest sin may be that we have done too little with the graces and spiritual gifts God has given to us on our journey of faith.

How does this gospel apply to our lives in a practical way? All of us (to some extent) are like the young man in the painting or the barren fig tree.

Most of us (at one time or another) have come to a point in life when it seemed we found ourselves in a "no-win" situation. Perhaps a certain problem has led me down a blind alley, to a dead end and there seems no way out.

If so, then today's gospel has an important message for us. And it is this: Because of Jesus, hope still remains for us, the hope of a second, third and fourth chance, or however many chances it takes, that things will get better, no matter what the situation.

That's the Good News we celebrate in today's Mass. This is the message that God wants us to carry back to the world, this weekend!

Fourth Sunday of Lent "C"
Luke 15: 1-3, 11-32

Charles Dickinson once called the parable of the Prodigal Son, "The most touching story in all literature." Like most of Jesus' parables, it's structure is simple, it's characters are few and are well defined, and it lacks a conclusion; therefore it's up to us to supply the meaning and the ending.

The details of the younger son's sins are not the point of the story, bad as they were. His main sin was not so much what he had done, but where he ended up. Jesus called it "in a distant land," which describes the son's "spiritual condition."

The wayward son had separated himself from where he truly belonged and when the boy got close to home, he found someone looking and longing and running out to meet him. The "apology" speech he had prepared: "Father, I have sinned against heaven and you," was smothered in the embrace of his waiting father.

That would have been a good place for Jesus to end the story. But, Jesus, did not stop there. He went on to point out there is more than one kind of sin and more than one sinner in the story.

For example, there was the sin of the father, who graciously forgave the one son, but forgot to hug his other son whom he had "taken for granted" all those years. When was the last time he had praised his older son or told him how much he meant to him, that he was proud of him, or that he loved him and thanked God every day for him? Never. Not once!

And then how about the decent, faithful, hard working, obedient older son? What were his sins? Well, basically, he had a "bad attitude" toward life. He was deeply hurt, bitter and angry at his father for "taking him for granted. He thought it was grossly unfair for his father to throw a big "Welcome Home" party for the son who had squandered his inheritance on a life of dissipation. He could not even bring himself to call his sibling "brother." Instead he referred to him by using the phrase, "your son."

He also felt sorry for himself and acted selfishly because it didn't matter if his "bad" attitude would spoil the "home coming" party, which he refused to attend. He wanted to be sure everyone knew how badly he had been treated.

And perhaps worst of all, he could not joyfully celebrate that something truly wonderful happened in the family, the momentous gift of grace his brother had received and the generous outpouring of his father's forgiveness and that a sinner had come home and was redeemed. He refused to celebrate that his brother was "dead, and has come to life again; that his brother was lost and now has been found."

The older son believed in the teeter-totter theory" of life—that if someone else "goes up" on the teeter-totter of life, then we automatically must "go down"…and down there, no one cares about us, or thanks us. His refusal to forgive his father and his brother may have fractured the family even more than what the younger son had done.

The older son looks strangely familiar to me. On occasion I have seen him at a family celebration, on a parish staff, or at a Parish Council meeting. I have also caught glimpses of him inside myself. All of us (at least at times) tend to act like the angry, unforgiving older brother.

Anger is a very human emotion. Even Jesus got angry! It's normal to feel angry toward someone who has hurt us. But we don't need to spend the rest of our lives hurting and hiding and hating…just because of something that happened in the past!

The important lesson to learn is that forgiveness doesn't happen all of a sudden—like a miracle. It takes time, sometimes a long time. It takes time to fully appreciate how we have been hurt by someone. It takes time to reflect on it and pray about it, asking God for the grace to let it go and then to forgive that person "from the heart," as God has forgiven us. All that takes time!

Fifth Sunday of Lent "C" John 8: 1-11; Luke 20: 9-15

We all know this gospel story very well. A woman is caught in the act of adultery. This woman in the story, represents, in a sense, each one of us, who has ever sinned, no matter what the sin.

And the words spoken to her are the **same** words Jesus speaks to us when we sin, He askes her if anyone has ever condemned her. She answers that no one had before and Jesus tells her that He does not either. He just tells her to go and don't sin anymore. The real mystery of this gospel story is that we don't know how it ends. Does she go and sin no more? Or does she go and sin **all** the more? We really don't know because St. John doesn't tell us.

But I know how I would like the gospel story to end. I would like it to end the same way as the play, "The Man of La Mancha," ends. Don Quixote falls madly in love with a woman the townspeople know as Aldonza." Aldonza is a scrub woman and a prostitute who is ridiculed and mistreated by the townspeople. But the moment Don Quixote lays eyes on her, he sees only "His Lady, Dulcinea" the name he begins calling her.

At one point in the play Alonza screams at him, "Just once, can't you look at me and see me for who I **really** am?" Don Quixote replies, "All I see is beauty, goodness and purity. You are My Lady. My Dulcinea!" At the end of the play, as Don Quixote is on his death bed, she arrives and says, "This man spoke to me and he called me by a different name (Dulcinea), and it made all the difference. I am now Dulcinea! I also like to imagine that the woman caught in the act of adultery in today's gospel arrived at the foot of the cross as Jesus was dying and when he died, she spoke the same words of comfort to those around her, "This man, Jesus, spoke to me. He called me by name, he saw the goodness in me and he shared with me God's love and God's forgiveness...and it made all the difference in my life."

The reality is we don't know how the woman caught in adultery responded to Jesus telling her about God's love and forgiveness. But we **do** know how we have responded. Each time we gather for Eucharist or receive a sacrament, we celebrate God's love and forgiveness found in the Word of God, in the Bread and wine and in the fellowship we share. But the question we have to ask ourselves is this: as a result of our encounters with Christ at Mass or in the sacraments, are we more loving, more forgiving and more aware of the goodness in others and in ourselves?

Today's gospel centers on the need to change our own hearts before we judge others or demand the conversion of others. God, alone reserves the right to judge others, not us. We are called to judge **only** our **own** actions and to pass sentence on our own lives. In fact, the only way we **can** lift up the "fallen," is by an attitude of compassion, of generosity, justice and forgiveness, rather than through harsh criticism, censure or condemnation.

Jesus had a different approach in dealing with the woman caught in adultery. We wanted to transform her life and to reconcile her with God. The scribes and Pharisees demand she be stoned to death because, according to the Mosiac Law, adultery was punishable by death. But Jesus challenges them to a more lasting, a more permanent, type of conversion.

He tells them to put down their stones of anger and judgment and to look into their own hearts where goodness and evil meet. He tells them to try to understand the despair, the selfishness, the disappointments that can drive us to sin, to realize the hurt, the pain, the destruction others suffer because of our sin and to put aside all our excuses for sinning and embrace the love and mercy of God who knows our hearts better than we do ourselves.

Jesus is telling us that confronting the demons of this world must begin with confronting the demons within our own hearts. In fact, we can't lift up the "fallen," the sinner, until we ourselves realize and admit that we **too** are the "fallen." We can't raise others to hope and to health until we seek our own healing. And we can't pass judgment on others without first judging our own lives.

Palm Sunday "C" Luke 19: 28-40

The Jesus of Luke's gospel welcomes the poor, the outcasts, the sinner and those people considered to be second class citizens of his day. For example, the parables of the Good Samaritan and the Prodigal Son are **only** found in Luke's gospel—two stories of mercy and forgiveness.

The Jesus of Luke's passion account continues that same spirit of compassion and forgiveness. Only in Luke's gospel do we find Jesus healing the severed ear of the High Priest's servant. And Luke doesn't record the fact that Jesus rebuked his disciples for falling asleep in the garden the night before he died. Luke also includes the scene when Jesus, carrying his cross, tells the women of Jerusalem not to be concerned for **him** but to be concerned for themselves and their children.

When Jesus arrives at Calvary, his crucifixion becomes a sacred place of prayer and forgiveness. As he is being nailed to the cross, he prays for his executioners, "Father forgive them; they do not know what they are doing."(Luke 23:34)

In the gospels of Matthew and Mark, the final dying words of Jesus are the words of Psalm 22, "My God, my God, why have you abandoned me?" But not so in Luke's gospel Jesus' final words are not words of abandonment, but of hope and victory. Luke has Jesus pray Psalm 31:5-6, "Father into your hands I commend my spirit"

Luke portrays Jesus as a man of deep love and compassion, who forgives those who betray him, who consoles those who grieve him, and who promises the good thief heaven by canonizing him as a saint, "Indeed, I promise you, today you will be with me in paradise." (Luke 23:43)

As we prepare to celebrate Holy Week (Holy Thursday, Good Friday and Holy Saturday) we not only remember Jesus' passion, death and resurrection, but we try to enter into his own "Passover" from death to life. During this week we struggle to follow Jesus from Jerusalem to the Upper Room, from the agony in the Garden to his trial, from crucifixion to his burial.

May we take up our own crosses this Holy Week and be transformed into Easter joy with Christ!

Easter Sunday "C" John 20: 1-9

We often look at Easter merely as an historical event that happened to Jesus once, a long time ago. We tend to think of Easter in the past tense and not as something that is happening today in our own lives.

But Easter is also a statement about you and me right now, about our possibilities because Easter happens to us every time we find the courage to rise above the past and when we begin to live again. Those are the times we can celebrate the "little Easters" of our lives.

Every year the University of Chicago invites a well-known theologian to give a lecture. One year, the great Dr. Paul Tillich came to speak. Dr. Tillich spoke for 2 ½ hours, trying to prove that the historical resurrection of Jesus never happened, it was false. "Just a story made up by the disciples," he stated. He quoted scholar after scholar and book after book to prove his point. His conclusion was that since Jesus never rose from the dead, then Christianity was useless, just a bunch of emotional mumbo-jumbo. He ended his lecture by asking, "Are there any questions?"

After a deafening silence, an old Southern Baptist Preacher with wooly-white hair, stood up in the back of the auditorium. "Dr. Tillich, I've got a question," he said as all eyes turned toward him. The Preacher reached into his lunch bag and pulled out an apple which he began to eat.

Dr. Tillich (crunch, munch, crunch), "Now I ain't never read those books **you** read," (crunch, crunch), "and I can't quote Scripture in the original Greek," (crunch, munch, crunch) "And I don't know nothing about those scholars you talked about Niebuhr and Heideggar," (crunch, crunch). Then the Preacher finished his apple and began to lick his fingers.

"Here's my question. All I want to know is this: This apple I just ate… was it bitter or was it sweet?" Dr. Tillich answered in a scholarly way. "I can't possibly answer your question because I haven't tasted your apple." The

Preacher dropped the apple core into his lunch bag and looking up at Dr. Tillich he said, "Well, sir, neither have **you** tasted my Jesus." I love that story!

The Easter story Is the story of Jesus rising from the dead, thus giving us the victory over sin, suffering and even death itself. It's not the story of medical science, but it's the story of Faith passed on to us by the Early Church.

The two men in dazzling garments ask the women at the empty tomb, "Why do you search for the living one among the dead? He is not here. He has been raised up."

But we run the risk of putting Easter only in the past. Why do we look in the past for the One who lives right now, today, in our world? The two angels of life speak to us and challenge us to open our eyes of faith, to stop looking for the "Living One" (Jesus) among the dead. So look around you this Easter Day and look for the signs of the "Living One" among us.

Last night during the blessing of the Pascal Candle we sang that, "The power of this Holy Night might dispel all evil, and wash our guilt away and bring mourners joy and that it cast out hatred, brings peace and humbles our pride. This is the power of Christ, the Risen One. He is here and active in the world today. "Taste and see the goodness of the Lord."

Even in our battered and bruised and half-dead Church, the power of the Risen Christ is still here and alive among us.

How do we know? Because Jesus still brings mourners joy. He is still casting out hatred with his love. And in all our turmoil, he still is bringing us peace. That's the power of the One who has risen, the One who is alive, and the One who lives in and among us. This is the Jesus we have tasted and experienced through our faith!

Even the blundering, impulsive Peter, who denied knowing Jesus three times is transformed into a fervent preacher of the Good News. He, and all the witnesses of the Risen Christ, were prepared to lay down their lives for the truth that Jesus rose from the dead.

We, too, all of us who believe, are invited to be caught up in the new life of grace offered by the Risen Christ. So, with our sins forgiven and our lives transformed, we can joyfully sing out our "alleluias" on this Glorious Feast!

Our religion is a faith that demands our constant conversion and transformation, a daily turning toward our Risen Lord. Each Sunday, for us, is a "Little Easter," when we can renew our Baptismal Promises in the presence of the Risen Lord.

2ⁿᵈ Sunday of Easter "C" John 20: 19-31

The disciples were hiding behind locked doors because they were afraid and ashamed of how they treated Jesus. They failed to understand him, they denied him, they abandoned him in his hour of need, and they even betrayed him. But Jesus puts them at ease with his greeting of love and forgiveness: "Peace be with you." He comes to unlock the doors of their fear and shame and to enter their hearts with the gifts of his Easter peace and reconciliation.

Jesus is not concerned about getting through the physically locked doors where the disciples were hiding. He is more concerned about getting through the locked doors of their hearts! He desperately wants them to believe in him, to believe in his Resurrection, to believe in his love and forgiveness.

Today we can ask ourselves this question: "What are the locked doors in our hearts that need to be opened, doors that need to be entered into by the Risen Lord?"

Perhaps it's the door of prejudice which needs to be opened—that's where we put all those people we don't like! We don't want them around. We don't need them. They are a threat to us and to our society. We don't trust them and perhaps we fear them.

They are the people of a different race or culture, people whom we judge to be either too radical or too conservative, people who are poor, the unemployed, the handicapped, those on the fringe of society...homosexuals, lesbians or those who have AIDS, and those in prison. The list can go on and on. These are some of the people we put behind locked doors and perhaps we need Jesus to come and open those doors of prejudice!

Another door that needs to be unlocked and opened is the door of Unforgiveness! That's where we put all those people who have hurt us in some way! We still hold onto certain grudges, perhaps for years, for things that were said to us or about us, or for things done to us in the past. We are in need of healing and reconciliation.

Story: Tommy Clark was drunk when he hit and killed young Ted Morris. Ted was the only son of Betty Morris. The death of her only son left Betty stunned and angry. Tommy pleaded guilty, was convicted and was ordered to give talks to high school students on behalf of MADD (Mothers Against Drunk Driving).

One day Betty went to hear Tommy speak. She heard him say with heartfelt emotion, that he "murdered Ted," and should be behind bars for what he did.

Betty thought, "I don't want my son's death to be totally in vain and in my heart I know that if he could, my son would tell me to forgive Tommy. She did forgive him and today Betty and Tommy are friends.

What locked door in your heart needs to be opened? Is it the door of Fear or the lack of Faith, the door of Worry or some kind of Dependency, or the door of unforgiveness of yourself or others who hurt you…whatever it is, invite the Risen Lord "in" to bring freedom and new life.

A famous artist once held a showing of his many paintings. One very beautiful painting was that of Christ, the Good Shepherd. It pictured Jesus with the "lost" lamb resting safely on his shoulder! Jesus is standing at a door knocking, patiently waiting for the door to be opened.

An art critic noticed a serious mistake in the painting. There was no door latch on the "outside" of the door. The artist explained that it wasn't a mistake because the one who answers the Lord when Jesus knocks can only open the door from the inside and that is why there is no latch on the outside of the door.

Jesus stands at your door knocking, patiently waiting to be invited in. Do you hear him knocking? Are you ready to open the door and let him in?

He wants to tell you how much he loves you; that you are forgiven, that you are loveable, that your life has value and has meaning. Above all, he wants to give you His Easter Peace…a peace the world cannot give!

3rd Sunday of Easter "C" John 21: 1-19

It was a bad time in his life. Peter was a man consumed with shame and guilt. He had denied even knowing Jesus...not once, not twice, but three times. And he had done it at a time when Jesus was most in need of a friend—the night before Jesus was to die.

It was inexcusable what Peter did to his friend, Jesus! Peter was devastated; totally upset at himself for doing such a cowardly thing. But all of this was changed by one meeting and one conversation with Jesus. Peter found healing for his wounds...and so can we! Love can heal all things. In today's gospel, Jesus appears as a stranger on the shore, and he invites Peter and the other disciples to come and have breakfast with Him. Jesus looks at Peter and asks him if he loves him and he asks him three times. And Peter answered each time that he did. That's all that Jesus wanted to know. All three denials are now forgiven!

What a beautiful example for us. People sometimes disappoint and hurt one another and the wounds and the hurt, can often run deep. Two former friends have a falling out, they have a broken relationship and now look at each other as strangers or even as enemies. The only thing that can bridge the gap is forgiveness.

The three most difficult words in the English language to say and to really mean it are: "I forgive you." These three words are hard to say, especially when we have been deeply hurt. But it's also equally hard for the offending party to hear someone say those three words, "I forgive you."

For example, like in today's gospel, it was not a light-hearted thing for Peter to betray his friend and to be so ashamed of doing it and then to be forgiven and taken back as a friend and to be trusted again—that can be the most humbling experience a proud person can have. And we know from the gospels that Peter was a proud man.

Only a few hours before his betrayal, Peter had pledged his unfailing loyalty to Jesus in the presence of the other disciples. "Lord," he said to Jesus, "I am ready to go with you to prison and even to death." But when the chips were down, Peter denied his friendship with Jesus, not just once, but three times.

Yet, here he was being forgiven. He is trusted and accepted by Jesus once again. I'm sure it wasn't that easy for Peter to accept forgiveness. If there had been any other way out from his failure I'm certain he would have taken it. But there was no other way out. The only way out for Peter, and for any one of us, is to have sincere sorrow and to have the humility to accept the forgiveness.

It will work for a husband and a wife. It will work for a parent and a child. It will work for any broken relationship. Any time and any where two people truly reconcile, healing always takes place. When it happens, it's like having a great stone rolled away that has been blocking the heart.

The good news about Easter is that the Risen Christ doesn't crush the fragile sinner. He doesn't reject anyone who is sincerely sorrowful and he doesn't abandon anyone who has ever denied him. Instead, he lifts up the "fallen" through his healing love and it's Easter all over again…a new beginning!

After breakfast, sitting by the fire Jesus had made, Jesus invites Peter to atone for his triple denial he made while warming himself at another fire in the High Priest's courtyard. Now, in the light of this Easter fire, Peter declares three times his complete love and devotion to Jesus. "Yes, Lord," he says to Jesus, "You know that I love you.

And Jesus, the Good Shepherd, passes on the role of forgiveness to Peter and to his disciples and to us. It was a great moment of resurrection and new life for Peter.

The Easter Christ calls us to embrace that same model of forgiveness for each other, to have the "bigness" of heart to forgive or to humbly ask for forgiveness, to rebuild and restore trust with those we have hurt or with those who have hurt us and to be willing to forgive those who have "messed up" big time in their lives.

At the final judgment, I truly believe that Jesus will ask us just one question, "Do you love me?" That's all that Jesus wants to know from us!

4th Sunday of Easter "C" John 10: 27-30

The Allstate Insurance Company is identified by its familiar logo of two outstretched, cupped hands asking the question: "Are you in good hands?" and the implied, correct answer would be: "You're in good hands with Allstate!" That logo offers the reassuring image that it feels good to be safe in strong, caring, protective hands.

Jesus knows that we all have that same need spiritually. That's why he uses a metaphor in today's gospel that appears to be taken directly from the Allstate manual.

Using the image of a Good Shepherd watching over and protecting his sheep, Jesus reminds us we are safe and secure, even in a dangerous world, because he is our Good Shepherd. Jesus is explaining to us that no one can take His sheep out of His hands and that no one can take us out of his Father's hands. Jesus seems to be asking the question wondering if we are in good hands spiritually? And the implied correct answer would be a resounding "yes, if we are in the strong, loving hands of God.

But here is where we may run into some trouble. We hear Jesus' comforting words in today's gospel and we want to trust his good hands—but the world is filled with wolves and all kinds of other dangers for us sheep. So we may be tempted to wonder and question: "What kind of safety is it that Jesus offers when it's obvious that his sheep still suffer and die at the hands of evil people and from natural disasters.

If, for example, we are in the safe hands of Jesus and his Father, why do tornadoes take the lives of innocent children? Where were the hands of God while buildings were crumbling on thousands of victims in Haiti's earthquake last January? Why doesn't the hand of God shield Christian missionaries from martyrdom in hostile countries? And where is God's

332

protective hand when cancer or a drunk driver strikes down a faithful Christian in the prime of life?

These are difficult questions. It's the same question Rabbi Harold Kushner asks in his famous book, "Why Do Bad Things Happen to Good People?"

First of all, suffering is not a sign of God's disfavor. Nor is the lack of suffering a sign of God's favor. We live in a broken world with other broken, sinful human beings, so we are open to being wounded by the brokenness of creation. Yes, it's true. Sometimes good people do suffer and bad people prosper. It has always been that way. We live in an imperfect world.

Secondly, let's carefully look at the words of Jesus in today's gospel. He is saying that we are safe "in God's hands." He doesn't assure us that we are safe in the hands of other people or in the hands of disasters or some terminal disease. Jesus is not offering us an insurance policy against all suffering. The hands of God will not prevent the thief from robbing us nor prevent the staff infection from infecting our body.

So what then does the hand of God do for us? It's this. No matter what happens to us, no matter what evil may befall us—even our own death or the death of a loved one—nothing shall separate us from the safe, loving grip of the hand of God. God is always with us.

Jesus himself did not escape suffering and death at the hands of evil people and God's hand did not spare him from the cross. But the hand of God, his Father, held Jesus, even when his own hands were nailed to the cross and when Jesus' hands fell limp by his side in death. Then it was by the strong hands of God that Jesus was raised from the grave and he now sits at the right hand of God in glory.

If you are looking for hands to protect you from all suffering, even the good folks at Allstate can't guarantee that. All they can offer is the good hands of financial recovery after the calamity strikes. But they can't offer a hand to prevent the calamity from happening in the first place.

But, if you are looking for good, strong hands that can hold you up in your suffering and can carry you over the final passage of death itself—then God's hands, and God's hands alone, are the ones you need.

Are you in good hands spiritually" that is the question Jesus is asking us today. And the answer is a resounding "Yes!" once we take hold of the hand of Jesus, our Good Shepherd with loving trust!

5th Sunday of Easter "C"
John 13: 31-33, 34-35

After giving her catechism class a thorough lesson on the Ten Commandments, the Religious Ed teacher quizzed her students. "What was the first Commandment?" she asked the class. No one answered. So she called on a boy who was staring into space. He clearly hadn't been paying attention to the lesson. The boy thought a bit… "The First Commandment," he said, "Was Eve told Adam to eat the apple!"

In today's gospel, Jesus gives his disciples a new commandment. He tells them to "love one another as I have loved you," explaining to them that "All people will know you are my disciples, if you have this special kind of love for one another."

It was the final night Jesus was to spend with his disciples, prior to his arrest and crucifixion. These were his last words, his last will and testament, as it were, to them. So these words are worth listening to.

It was a one-line command, so simple, and yet so very profound and so difficult to do. Of all the things Jesus might have asked of us, why the command to love one another as Jesus loves them?

Why not command us to go to church every Sunday, or tithe our income, or wear a cross necklace, or fast one day a week? Jesus knew that doing those things were merely the external signs of discipleship, perhaps useful for his followers to do, but they had little or no power to bring about real, spiritual transformation of the world. But to "love as Jesus loves," has the power to make the world stand up and take notice of Christianity. That's why the hallmark of the early Christians was the well-known phrase: "See how these Christians love one another."

When we "love as Jesus loves," in ways that defy common logic, and when we love with a generosity that is "counter-cultural," the world stands up and takes notice. Or, when we love the unlovable, when we forgive the undeserving sinner, when we help the poor and powerless without judging them, or when we tell someone who has hurt us, "I forgive you," (and truly mean it), these are the signs that a greater love is at work within us. It's then that the world wonders and asks the question, "What is the source and the secret of such an unusual and powerful love Christians show to one another and to others?"

There is only one answer to that question. It's not that we Christians are more kind and more loving people by our own power. No! We are simply passing on the transforming love of God that came so lavishly and freely to us through Christ. This is the attraction of the Christian faith to the world. When we truly love others as Christ loves others, then the world will continue to say in amazement, "See how these Christians love one another!"

Each of us has to discover for ourselves the best way to express our love. Usually our love will be expressed in small, little ways, by choosing a kind word rather than a harsh or critical one, by offering a smile or an open hand of welcome, calling or sending a letter to a friend, remembering someone's birthday or anniversary, listening to someone who is lonely, being patient with the impatient or showing interest in someone else's plans.

Franz Kalfa was a German-speaking, Jewish writer who died in 1924. One day, near the end of his life, Kalfa met a little girl in the street who was crying because she had lost her doll.

He quickly explained to her that, although the doll had gone away, he had met the doll and it had promised to write to the little girl. In the weeks that followed, as his tuberculosis slowly overcame him, Kalfa wrote letters to the little girl in which the doll told about its travels and the interesting things it experienced. We can only imagine the joy and happiness that these letters brought to the child.

Jesus understood the importance of loving God and others in little ways—giving food to the hungry, drink to the thirsty, welcome to strangers and clothing to the needy and visiting the sick and those in prison. These "little ways" to love are the stepping stones to heaven and are what makes the world stand up and take notice of Christianity.

6th Sunday of Easter "C" John 14: 23-29

If you could ask just one question about God and knew it would be answered, what would it be? The one question I would ask is this: "Where is the best place to find God?"

God often seems so far away, so inaccessible. If we knew where to look, we could learn more about God. Everyone wants to find God. The problem is, we're not sure where to look.

Most of us tend to think of God as far away. God is at least on the other side of the world. And more likely, God is in another world, like in heaven or on some distant planet. I have heard about some recently discovered planets that are 12 billion light years away! Now that would be a logical place to find God! It's so far away that we can't even begin to imagine the distance. Is God present there in the vast galaxies of outer space? Yes, most definitely through God's Creative Powers. But today's Gospel tells us of a better and more practical place to look for God.

Jesus says, "Those who love me will be true to my word, and my Father will love them. We will come to them and make our dwelling place with them." It sounds to me like the best place to look for God is right where we live. Who would have ever thought of that? God in my own neighborhood, in my own house, in my own little world, God hidden away living within my own heart. But come to think of it, those are the kinds of ordinary places that God most often has appeared.

A peasant girl gave birth in a manager, to a baby boy. That was God appearing in the flesh, but most people did not recognize him as divine. It was all too ordinary.

In the city of Nazareth, a young man worked with saw and hammer as a carpenter. That was God living in the world. But most people did not see God in Jesus. Jesus was too ordinary looking.

A home in Bethany had a frequent visitor who ate with them, talked with them, laughed and cried with them. That visitor was God incarnate! But very few recognized him. He was too ordinary. If we are ever going to find God, we have to stop thinking of God in terms of far-away places and dramatic events. As a priest, I have found God many times in the lives of ordinary people.

One example stands out: It was Sunday afternoon and I was watching the Seahawks getting beat on television. The phone rang and it was Angie. I had been bringing Communion to her husband, John, for the last ten years. "John is dead," she said quietly. "Please come over." John had been totally bed-ridden the last ten years—unable to speak or communicate in any way. He was blind and unable to walk or take care of himself. He would just lie in bed and stare at the ceiling.

Angie was totally dedicated to him. The only time she left him alone was when she went shopping or went to church. John totally depended on her. When I got there, Angie greeted me with her usual smile and a glass of Amaretto liquor. We talked a few minutes, then she said, "Let's go in and say goodbye to John.

She began, "John, the last ten years have been hard for both of us. What I did for you was out of love. I would do it all over for you again, because we promised 'to love each other in good times and in bad, in sickness and in health, until death do us part.' And I know you would have done the same for me, if I were sick. I knew you loved me and appreciated all I did for you, but you were just unable to express it. Goodbye, John. I'll be seeing you soon in heaven." Having said her goodbyes, she said, "Now I'm ready to call 911."

As I listened to Angie, I felt the real Presence of God in that room because God was such an intimate part of their lives and relationship. What a wonderful example of living the Sacrament of Marriage. They found God in their love for each other. So, if you and I will ever see God, it will probably not be in some distant, far-away place, or in some dramatic event—it will be in the courage or kindness of the sacrificial acts of love of ordinary people like you and me.

The Ascension of the Lord "C"
Luke 24: 46-53

To be a practicing Catholic in 16th Century England was dangerous. When Henry VIII insisted on being the sole head of the Catholic Church, Parliament enacted several severe anti-Catholic laws. The celebration of a "Roman Mass" was illegal! Priests were hunted down, arrested and executed. To shelter a priest, to teach the Catholic faith or to give any support or aid to the "outlaw religion" was considered treason—punishable by death.

There were many stories of brave English Catholics who kept the faith alive during that time and paid the ultimate price. Saint Margaret Clitherow of Yorkshire was one of them. This valiant woman was hung in 1586 at the age of 33 for harboring priests and having Mass in her home. She also ran a small, and illegal, school for children in her home. She spent more than 10 years in and out of prison, and finally in March of 1586, a raid on her home found a priest's hiding place in the attic, as well as chalices, vestments and missals.

Margaret was arrested, put into prison and formally charged. She refused to consent to a trial. "Having made no offense," she said, "I have no need of a trial." The Court found her guilty and sentenced her to death by hanging.

From her prison cell the night before she died, Margaret made a final request. She left her shoes to her eldest daughter, Anne, who was 12 years old. The message from mother to daughter was clear: "Follow in my footsteps. Carry on the Faith."

Today is the feast of Jesus' Ascension back to heaven. In a sense, today Jesus is leaving us his "shoes," to carry on his Gospel of compassion, of reconciliation and justice. He entrusts to us his final request—to carry on the work of his life, death and resurrection.

We are to take on the role of witness to all that Jesus did and taught.

What does it mean to be a witness of Jesus today? A busload of teenagers was returning from Mexico. They had gone down there on a mission of love to help the poor. They worked hard that day, then got on the bus which would take them home. They were tired and were very hungry. They crossed the border back to the United States and stopped at a diner in a small town. They waited and waited for the longest time to be served. Finally one of them asked the waitress if they could be served. The waitress said she would serve them, but "they," indicating the 2 black teens among them, "they" would have to eat on the bus. The teens looked at each other in disbelief and sadness, and one of them said to the waitress, "Well, we weren't hungry anyway." And they all got back on the bus!

That's what it means to be a witness to the life, death and resurrection of Jesus. Those teens arrived home hungry, but were filled with the joy of the Holy Spirit that they were able to praise God in a small but very important way!

The 7ᵗʰ Sunday of Easter "C" John 17: 20-26

How often has that scene in our first reading been re-enacted down through the centuries: In the Book of Acts, it is the martyr Stephen and the uninvolved bystander, Saul. While one man suffers injustice at the hands of an angry, mindless crowd, another stands by, doing nothing!

The scene is multiplied thousands of times over. On "Nightline," the other night, Ted Koppel reported there are 45 countries involved in actual war with their neighbors—countries where ordinary citizens suffer and die and innocent people are the victims.

In our own country, the lives of individuals suffer. In this country since the 1973 Supreme Court Decision allowing legalized abortions, tens of millions of unborn children have been put to death as we stand by in silence. They are no less martyrs than Stephen. We still have long lines of the unemployed, the poor, the sick, the elderly, the handicapped—our answer is to cut public assistance even more.

Public indifference is just as effective as Saul's apathy. We, of course, can excuse ourselves because we personally have little control over the shape of our world, and our economy. But our apathy just adds to the problems.

Evangelist Billy Graham begins his crusade in Tacoma this week. In his interviews, people are asking questions that touch their lives…about separation of church and state, about whether or not prayer should be allowed in public schools, whether the Catholic bishops have a right and an obligation, to speak up on nuclear war and the arms race, about persecution and civil rights issues in Russia and other countries. Somehow these questions must be answered in the light of the Gospel and other Christian values. Somehow we have to answer these questions.

Our American political system poses a problem for many people. Our country is committed to a distinct separation of church and state, of the sacred from the secular, of religion and politics. But how far does that separation extend? Should this church be involved in social-economic problems and political issues that affect our lives? Jesus' incarnation makes such hairsplitting difficult to understand at times. He became one of us to embrace us all. He wants to bring His Father a whole, healed, humanity, not broken by hatred and isolation. The one question a follower of Christ <u>cannot</u> ask is, "Am I my brother's keeper?" Cain was the first one to ask that question and he was a murderer. He denied all responsibility.

Everyone who professes faith in Jesus Christ takes on a heavy responsibility. As long as one person suffers from hunger, cold, oppression and injustice, as did Stephen, our work is not complete. Christians cannot stand by in silence, holding coats! Before we separate "sacred" from the "Secular," we must pray with Christ His prayer for unity, "That all may be one, as you, Father, are in Me and I in You. I pray that they be one in Us, that the world may believe that You sent Me!"

That unity is a glorious hope, a shining goal. But it is not an impossible dream—otherwise Jesus would not have prayed for it. But it demands we get our hands dirty and risk rejection and sometimes even a broken heart. But that is the way of life Jesus chose… He gave us the example when He entered into our humanity.

Jesus did not come to our world, to suffer rejection, die and rise to have His deeds discussed in Committee. He came to challenge us to carry on His work of redemption and healing. The gift of ourselves will better the condition of others and bring about that unity He so desperately prayed for. The gift of self is the price of discipleship!

341

Corpus Christi "C" The Body and Blood of the Lord: Luke 9: 11-17

Jean Vanier is one of my heroes. In 1987 he received a special Medal of Honor from Canada for his work with people with disabilities! On the back of that medal is an inscription that reads: "They desire a better country." The medal recognizes the wonderful work and self-sacrifice of the recipient.

Jean Vanier does indeed desire a better country, but he also wants to make this world a better place in which to live, especially for all handicapped people.

Jean Vanier's early life involved him in the business of war, as a trained Navy officer. But he left the pursuit of war in the search for peace.

That journey led him to a meeting with some people who had learning disabilities. That first meeting changed his life! He heard their cry to be loved. They were asking some basic questions: "Am I loveable? Do I have value? Why do I feel abandoned? Do you love me?"

Vanier responded by buying a house and inviting two people with learning disabilities to live with him and this was the beginning of the world-wide organization called L'Arch.

In the course of living with handicapped people, Vanier grew in his own life and understanding of himself. In seeing their pain and brokenness, Vanier discovered his own brokenness and hardness of heart. By reaching out to help others, he helped and healed himself, and in doing so, Vanier became blessed and broken.

When the crowds followed Jesus into a "deserted place" they were also hungering for a better place and a better life. Jesus begins by welcoming them! Then he tells them about the Kingdom of God and God's love for them and then he heals those who were sick.

342

Notice, this is the very same formula that happens at Mass where we are welcomed, where we confess our brokenness, where we are inspired by reading the Word of God and then, Jesus feeds the crowd with his own Body and Blood!

When the disciples told Jesus, "This is a deserted place," they could have been describing the streets of our own modern-day world, where people still hunger for food and other material things and especially for their spiritual needs!

Jesus instructed the disciples to "feed the crowd themselves," with the little food they had and when they finished, there were even scraps of food left over. The little food they had was blessed, broken and shared…and no one went hungry.

This is the kind of world that Jesus creates—a Eucharistic world. He teaches us to give thanks to God for all that we have and we are to break our bread and share it with everyone, especially with the poor and the forgotten. And we exclude no one, because there is plenty for us all.

The Christians in Corinth needed to learn that lesson when they were excluding those who were poor, while having lavish meals themselves. Paul reminds them of what he had learned from the Lord about the true meaning o the Eucharist—bread and wine, blessed and broken. The Body and Blood of the Lord is given to all.

Every time we take part in the Eucharist, we are joining in the suffering and death of Jesus—the rich one who became poor for our sake. We go down into the poverty and suffering of this world (as Jean Vanier did) in order to be raised up together with the Lord.

This way of life is open to all of us—to <u>live</u> the Eucharist, to <u>be</u> Eucharist for one another and to live the life of thanksgiving love. This Eucharistic life involves us with those who suffer.

At times, you may be called to share your life with people who are sick or old, with people who are out of work or homeless, with people caught in the world of drugs or you may find yourself with people who are very angry, who feel abandoned and unloved.

There are so many hungry and suffering people in the world today who have lost their way. They say of life, "This is indeed a lonely and deserted place here." And the Lord says in reply to me and you, "Give them something to eat yourselves."

2nd Sunday "C" John 2: 1-11

Most marriage ceremonies and wedding receptions like the one in today's gospel are happy, joyous occasions. Family and friends gather to wish the bride and groom well. There is eating, drinking, music and dancing. Then suddenly everyone leaves and the bride and groom are left alone!

Someone once described marriage as something wonderful and exciting, but at times as something difficult and boring. After all the planning and the parties, the wedding day, the reception and the honeymoon, reality sets in! It's having the water remain, just ordinary water, 90% of the time and seeing the water change into sweet-tasting wine, only about 10% of the time. It takes a miracle to transfer the ordinary hum-drum events of marriage into the miracle of love!

In today's gospel, Mary, Jesus and some of his friends are invited to a wedding and to the reception. Here is a man who would perform amazing miracles. He would raise the dead to life, calm the wild wind and the powerful sea, feed thousands of people with a few loaves and fish, heal the blind, the sick and the leper with a simple word of command! Yet, he chose to perform his first miracle to prevent a young groom and his bride embarrassment, because they ran out of wine at their reception. Here was a man with a tender heart.

By performing this, his first miracle, I think Jesus is telling married couples of all time that they, too, are called to perform "little miracles" in their relationship. Little acts of love or little miracles that perhaps go almost unnoticed, but bring happiness and joy and give a deeper meaning to their lives.

What are some of these "little miracles" that can change the ordinary "water" of our everyday living into the extraordinary "wine" of joy and happiness? A couple celebrating their 50th anniversary explained it to me this way:

"Marriage," they said, "is taking all that is good in yourself and sharing it with your spouse and seeing that goodness reflected there. And then, as a couple, you can share your love with each other and with others. Your love is bigger than yourselves—it goes beyond you, as a couple, to include others—your children, family, friends, Church and Community."

"Over the years," they went on to say, "marriage is sharing and at times it's not sharing. It's talking and it's silence. It's fighting and it's taking each other for granted. It's forgiving each other and it's saying 'I'm sorry.' It's also remembering the sheer look of joy in each other's face at the birth of a child, it's the sharing of sadness over the death of a friend and it's the laughter you share over a dinner that never did turn out as you planned."

Marriage is being secure in the love of someone who will continue to love you, even when hurts come, or when you get old and fat.

Yes, marriage is also the boredom of sitting across the dinner table with "left over leftovers," having absolutely little or nothing to say to each other and the very next night going out to dinner and falling in love all over again. Marriage is everything, yet nothing more than the love of two dear friends who won't leave each other when difficult times come along!

I often wonder what happened to the young married couple in today's gospel. Were they happy? Did they allow each other to grow in their marriage relationship? Did they learn that marriage is not always champagne, candlelight and roses? That it's also beer, paying the bills and reading the morning paper as well.

I'm sure that inviting Mary and her Son to their wedding made a difference. Jesus not only changed water into wine for them, he invited them, as a couple, to do the same for each other--to change and enrich each other's lives by their gift of love!

Cana is not just long ago and far away. Cana is here and now, at this Eucharist. At the table of the Word, Jesus gives meaning to our lives with the sweet wine of the gospel. At the table of his Body and Blood, he strengthens us to live, not just for ourselves, but for others.

Here at Cana, Jesus is ready to fill us to the brim with the wine of His Presence, and happiness. The advice Mary gave to the servers is the same advice she gives to us today: "Do whatever Jesus tells you!" If we do, then "little miracles" begin to happen.

3rd Sunday "C" Luke 1: 1-4; 4: 14-21

Most organizations have a "Mission Statement" that defines who they are—their purpose, their aim and their focus as an organization.

Our parish has its own Mission Statement: 1. "To proclaim the Good News of God's saving love to all people, 2. To establish and nourish a praying Community of believers and 3. To give practical expression to the Gospel by serving the needs of others and transforming the world."

In today's gospel, Jesus announces his own personal Mission Statement. Luke tells us that, "the eyes of all the people in the synagogue at Nazareth look intently" at Jesus as he read from the Prophet Isaiah: "God has sent me to bring glad tidings to the poor, to bring freedom to captives, to lead the blind, and to free the oppressed." Jesus then sat down and explained to them that today this Scripture passage is being fulfilled in their hearing. Jesus was telling them that He was the longed-for Messiah sent by God, the Father, and anointed by God, the Holy Spirit, to bring wholeness, salvation, justice, peace and healing to a broken world.

In our second reading today, Paul reminds us of who we are and what our Mission Statement should say. We are the Church, the Body of Christ, in the world today. Our Mission Statement, therefore, is the same as Jesus'…to bring healing, peace justice and love to wherever we are planted. Every time we imitate the selfless life of Jesus, we fulfill his gospel.

We make Isaiah's vision of Jesus, as the Messiah, a reality in our own "little part of the world" with every act of kindness and love prompted by God's grace, whether it be planting trees to transform a barren landscape, listening to and giving comfort to a trouble friend, making sandwiches at a soup kitchen or tutoring a child struggling with math.

As baptized disciples in the Church, we also are given the Holy Spirit's call to bring "glad tidings to the poor, to the imprisoned, to the blind, the oppressed and the helpless."

In this week's Progress, Fr. Tom Belleque was interviewed and was asked what his greatest joy as a priest is. He answered, "Empowering others to fully respond to their gift of baptism." Then, he went on to say, "This is the prayer I begin each day with and it's my personal Mission Statement, if you will: "Lord, help me to live this day joyfully, courageously and gratefully, that by imitating your self-emptying, I may share in the building of your kingdom."

If you, as an individual or as a married couple or even as a family, were to make your own personal Mission Statement this week, what would it say? Try it. It might surprise you! I'm sure it would make you a better person, a better spouse or a better family member!

4th Sunday "C" Luke 4: 21-30

Two employees at a retirement home stood side by side at the serving line in the cafeteria. As the residents file by with their trays, one of the servers silently dropped the food on the plate and swiftly moved on to the next.

The other server smiled at each resident and served a portion of food as if to an honored guest at a banquet. Essentially, both employees were offering the same service—both were feeding the hungry, but one did so in a manner that deprived the one being served of his or her dignity, while the other (who acted in love) bestowed honor along with the food being served.

This is such a small and insignificant action, one may argue, and yet St. Paul would see it as acting in a "more excellent way." In our second reading today, Paul is saying, "In small things as in great ones, love makes all the difference!"

Of the several Greek words for love, Paul chose the word "agape," a term used in the New Testament to describe the bonds of love between people, as well as the bonds between God and all humanity. Agape love is the highest form of human love. It is defined more by its action rather than by its "mushy" feelings or by its romantic words.

Agape love reaches out to affirm, to embrace and to accept another person, whether that other person acknowledges or even accepts the love offered. It's a love that is purely unselfish, totally extravagant and uncommonly generous. That's why it best expresses the love and affection God extends to all of us, in and through the person of Jesus Christ.

One thing Paul knew about was the agape love of Jesus for him and for all humanity. He didn't just dream up his own, that beautiful description of love in today's second reading. No! He learned about that type of love from Jesus—the Jesus who was kind and forgiving, who was not rude or jealous or did not put on airs, who is not angry or self-seeking. He learned from Jesus that true love "bears all things, is full of trust and hope and has the power to endure all things.

Let me give you a few "real life" examples to help you better understand what agape love is.

Maximilian Kolbe, a Polish priest, trembling in his shoes, steps forward and offers to die in the place of another prisoner in a Nazi concentration camp in 1945. He does so because the other prisoner is much younger, is married, and has children. That's agape love. Jesus once said that a man has no greater love than this than to lay down one's life for a friend.

On one retreat I attended, the priest retreat master shared how he prays. Whenever he hears the news about a terrible, vicious crime, he prays for the victim or victims but he would also pray for the person who committed the crime. "I prayed for Saddam Hussein," he told us, "before, during his trial, and after his hanging. He was a wicked, depraved man that evoked nothing but feelings of revulsion. So why did I pray for him? Because Jesus told us to love your enemies and pray for those who persecute you. Jesus doesn't ask me how I feel about him. He simply tells me to love and pray for everyone, even for those who do evil. It's really hard to do because our feelings seem to get in the way but that's real agape love."

When William Stafford, the American poet and pacifist was a young boy, he came home from school one day and told his mother that 2 new students had been surrounded on the playground and taunted by the others because they were black. "And what did you do, Billy?" asked his mother. "I went and stood by them," Billy said. Although sick to his stomach at the thought that he too might be beat up, Billy decided to stand by them. Fear didn't interfere with his decision to love.

One more story about agape love. Karl Downs, the pastor of a church in Oakland, California, died at an early age of a heart attack. Several years before that, he was asked by Juvenile Court to take responsibility for a teenage boy who was always getting in trouble. With some misgiving, he accepted that responsibility and in a tough love kind of way, became a substitute father for the boy. No one remembers Pastor Karl Downs today, but we all remember the name of that boy. He was Jackie Robinson, the first black man to play Major League baseball—an outstanding young man. Agape love is the decision to love no matter what--the harder decision, the greater is the love. Jeremiah knew this, Jesus and Paul knew this. The question for us to answer is, do we know this?

5th Sunday "C" Luke 5: 1-11

Our Gospel reading for today tells a story about two kinds of failure. One failure was small and of little consequence. The other was much more serious. They both occurred in the life of our old friend, Simon Peter.

In the first instance, Peter had fished all night long and had nothing to show for his efforts. That was disappointing but not tragic. No doubt it had happened to Peter before, and if he kept on fishing, it would happen again. But this kind of failure is not terribly difficult to overcome. Usually all it takes is one more effort. That was the case with Peter, so at the word of Jesus, he pushed out into the deep water and tried again. He cast out his net one more time and the net was so loaded with fish, that it was on the verge of breaking.

This story is usually called, "The Miraculous Catch of Fish." The assumption is that Jesus used his divine power to bring about that unusual feat and that may be true. Or could it be that Jesus simply saw what was already there? He saw the possibilities—a large school of fish just a few yards from shore. Peter could not see it because he had already tried and had given up. Perhaps the real miracle here may have been that Jesus simply kept Peter from quitting too soon!

Peter's other failure was much deeper and much more serious. Peter took an honest look at himself and was overwhelmed by what he saw. Perhaps, for the first time in his life, he had faced the dark side of his own soul and he was ashamed of himself. So, falling down at the knees of Jesus, he said, "Leave me, Lord, for I am a sinful man." Peter knew he was in the presence of Holiness and he was overwhelmed by feelings of his own unworthiness. But Jesus told him not to be afraid and from now on he would be catching people. For Peter that was a new beginning, a true conversion, an invitation to a life of discipleship with Jesus. Our failures can become new beginnings

351

for us as well. It was a turning point in Peter's life. Jesus accepted him and loved him, despite his sins and failures.

Peter had good reason to feel unworthy. In a sense he was a failure in the great adventure of life. He was hot tempered, impetuous, bigoted, disloyal to Jesus, and proud. But Jesus accepted all of that. In effect Jesus was saying to Peter, "This is what and who you are. Now let's start with that and see what we, together, can do with it." We now know that the two of them, Christ and Simon Peter, did a remarkable thing with it. Simon is no longer called Simon. He is called Peter, the spiritual rock upon whom the Church is built. Who knows what the outcome will be when we accept ourselves as we are and go to work on them with Christ.

Is someone here today feeling unworthy or feeling like a failure? Well, I have some good news for you. Like Peter and the other disciples, Jesus calls you to follow him. He accepts you with all your faults, and promises you his forgiveness and holiness. Jesus believes in you. All you have to do is believe in Him and believe in yourself. Our failures need not be final because with Christ all things are possible.

So the moral of this gospel story is to never give up on yourself or never quit trying too soon. Jesus sees the school of fish just a few yards from shore. All we have to do is cast our nets just one more time.

6th Sunday "C" Luke 6: 17, 20-26

I recently came across an early American Indian story that reminded me of today's gospel. Once in the dead of winter, when it was bitter cold, a bird of prey was scouting the frozen land for food. The bird spotted the remains of a deer left behind by some hunters. It was left in a large ice flow, floating down the river.

The bird swooped down and began to feast, but the bird was so "consumed" by what it was "consuming," that the bird paid no attention to the sound of water thundering not far away, and the roar was becoming louder and louder each moment!

In a matter of seconds, the whole ice flow was just about to go crashing over the river's falls. The bird immediately began flapping its wings to escape—but it's claws were frozen solid in the icy remains of the deer. The bird was trapped and powerless to escape falling to its death.

What is the moral of the story? Like the doomed bird on the ice flow, we also can be consumed by what we go after. If we only go after the things that the world tells us will bring true happiness and success, then we may lose our lives in the process.

We can become so absorbed in pursuing the things of this world, that we begin to devalue the real riches of our lives: the love of family and friends, the special joy we experience in giving ourselves to others, and the peace of mind that comes from centering our lives on the things of God.

In today's gospel, Jesus challenges us to embrace a new attitude, a new vision as to what separates the "Have" and "Have Nots" the rich and the poor of this world.

Luke's version of the Beatitudes challenges everything our consumer-centered society holds dear. While wealth, power and being a celebrity are the sought-after prizes of the world, the treasures of God's Kingdom are love, humility, compassion and generosity. In freeing ourselves from the pursuit of the things of this world, we free ourselves to seek the "lasting things of God!

7th Sunday "C" Luke 6: 27-38

The one line that jumps out at me in today's gospel is, "Do to others as you would have them do to you." It's the Golden Rule--treat others the same way you want to be treated. Jesus is asking us to put ourselves "in the place" of others, to walk in their shoes, to ask ourselves, "What if it were me?"

Imagination is a wonderful thing. We all have it. For children, imagination is a kind of "magic toy." It enables them to go anywhere, to be anybody, and to do anything. With the passing of time, they will outgrow their childish games but hopefully they will not lose their magic toy because they will never outgrow the need for it.

Just look at Jesus. Have you ever noticed the role that imagination played in his life? He pictured himself in the place of others, so much so, that he could identify with them and feel their pain. "I was hungry and you gave me no food, thirsty, and you gave me nothing to drink." Yes, Jesus had a vivid imagination. In fact, Jesus pictured himself in the place of others so clearly, that their need became his need and what happened to them, happened to him.

The stories that Jesus told came from his imagination. For example, do you remember the story about the rich man and Lazarus, the poor man? One lived in luxury and the other begged for the crumbs that fell from his table. What was wrong with the rich man? As far as we know, he was an honest and decent person, but he had no imagination. He saw Lazarus begging at his doorway every day, but he walked right by him as though he were invisible. Why? Because he failed to put himself in the place of the poor beggar. It's called compassion or empathy, the ability to feel what someone else is feeling.

The same problem can happen to husbands and wives. Both are trying to carry their part of the load. He does his work and she does hers. But, in a sense, they live in two different worlds. Neither one ever looks at life through the eyes of the other. Their marriage would be so much better if, once in a while, they could imagine what the other one was really feeling.

When Jesus came into the world, one of the first things he taught people was to pray, "Our Father." These two little words, "Our Father", more than anything else have torn down the walls of prejudice and misunderstanding that so often divide us.

If I pray to God by saying "Our Father," and you also pray by saying "Our Father," that means we are brothers and sisters and we are also committed to one another. Calling God "Our Father" broadens our appreciation and respect for other people. For example, it allows us to imagine what it's like to be poor or hungry, to be handicapped, or to be a minority living in an all white society. We may never know the answers to these questions, but we know we cannot be followers of Christ unless we pray "Our Father," and really mean what we are saying.

Fr. Tony DeMell, S.J., tells the story about a soldier who was rushed back from the front line because his father was dying. The exception was made because he was the only child, and the only family member the dying man had left. When the soldier walked into the hospital room and saw the semi-conscious old man connected with all sorts of tubes and wires, he realized a terrible mistake had been made. This man was not his father. The Army had sent the wrong man home.

How much longer does he have to live?" asked the soldier. "A few hours at the most," the doctor said. "You just made it in time." The soldier thought of the dying man's son fighting a war thousands of miles away. He also thought of this dying father, waiting to be reunited with his son before death would arrive.

The soldier then saw his own father in this old man who was holding onto life, in the hope of being with his son one last time, so he could say "goodbye." The soldier leaned forward, held the old man's hand and said softly, "Dad, I'm here. I'm back."

The dying man clutched at the hand offered him. His failing eyes looked up, but the soldier's face was only a blur in the darkened room. A peaceful smile came over the man's face and remained there until he died an hour later, with the solider remaining at his side. In the blurred image of the compassionate soldier, the dying old man felt the love of his son. He also felt the love of God, granting him a happy death.

The love of God lies within each one of us as well. The challenge of the call to discipleship is to let that love emerge and transform our own lives and the lives of others. By breaking down the walls that divide us, we overcome the barriers of prejudice and misunderstanding in order to become father, mother, brother and sister to one another. Just imagine what good we can do!

8th Sunday "C" Luke 6: 39-45

In today's gospel, Jesus asks the question, "Why do you observe the splinter in your brother's eye and never notice the plank in your own? How can you say to your brother, Brother, let me take out the splinter that is in your eye when you cannot see the plank in your own? Hypocrite! Take the plank out of your own eye first and then you will see clearly enough to take out the splinter that is in your brothers eye." (Luke 6:41-42) That is good advice. Jesus is trying to tell us that we need to correct our own faults before we can correct others. The world is filled with all kinds of would-be reformers… husbands trying to reform their wives and wives their husbands. Parents are constantly trying to reform their children, no matter how old they are. Older children try to reform their parents. Is there any priest who does not seek to reform his parishioners, or any parish that would not like to reform its pastor?

This tendency to reform is not all bad. Heaven knows that human behavior needs reforming. But reformation, like charity, begins at home. If we want a better world, the place to start, said Jesus, is with ourselves. But that is hard to do…we would much more prefer to correct the faults and failures of those around us.

I guess the underlying quest is this, why is it that we are more inclined to reform others than we are to reform ourselves? Is it because we are brazen hypocrites? I don't think so. Bad as we sometimes are, we're not that bad. I think it's because we tend to be blind to our own faults. We simply do not see them. Perhaps we refuse to see them. However we explain it, the fact remains that it is very difficult for us to see ourselves as we really are. Most of us tend to judge our own behavior much more kindly than we judge the behavior of others.

When someone loses his temper, for example, we think that he is a spoiled brat and needs to grow up, but when we lose our temper, we explain it away by saying that we are tired or have a headache, and we have a right to get angry.

When someone expects to have things her own way, we reflect that she is selfish and uncaring. When we expect to have things our way, we are only protecting our rights. After all, if we failed to do that, people would always take advantage of us. Other people have obvious glaring faults, but we have minor little faults that matter very little. There is an old saying, "The man who points a finger of guilt at another, points 3 fingers of guilt back at himself."

A TV commercial for a mouthwash points out that it's possible to have offensive breath and not even know it. Unfortunately, that is true. But it's also true that we can have other faults and not be aware of them. For instance, we can be cranky and not know it. We can fall into the habit of nagging people (and resent being told about it). We can indulge in self pity and never suspect that we are feeling one bit sorry for ourselves. We can be conceited and honestly think we are humble. We can be stubborn and consider ourselves to be courageous. And whoever suspects that he is opinionated or narrow minded or prejudiced; whoever suspects that he is severe in his judgments of others but lenient in judgment of himself?

Yes, Jesus hit the nail right on the head. We have blind spots that keep us from seeing the planks in our own eyes.

Is there anything we can do about this tendency? We could start by listening, occasionally at least, to the kindly criticism of our friends, but this is difficult. Even if we have invited criticism, we don't like it. We usually are offended by it and immediately become defensive.

But this raises another question. Is it really possible for grown people to make any real changes in their lives? We have a folksy proverb that says, "You can't teach an old dog new tricks." That might be true of old dogs. I don't know; I've never tried it. But I have seen some older people learn a few new tricks. My brother-in-law, Vic Johnson, started playing golf when he was 70. He plays in our foursome on Tuesdays and plays a pretty good game. He even beats me once in a while with his handicap.

So, we concede that it is possible for grown people to develop new physical habits. Why then is it not possible to develop new spiritual habits? For example, if you're a grouch at 40 or 50 or 60, there's no law of nature that says you have to remain a grouch for the rest of your life. If you are aware of that trait and if you make up your mind to do something about it, you can. It's something to think about for Lent. Lent is a time to change, a time to grow, a time to develop some new spiritual habits, no matter how young or old we might be. I can say that with some confidence, because I have seen it happen many times. I have friends who are recovered and recovering alcoholics. I know of people who have gone back to school after their children were grown and got an education. I know of convicts who have turned their lives around and become useful and productive citizens. There are 3 ordained priests in the archdiocese who were married at one time, but after the death of their spouse, entered the seminary for the 4 years of preparation for priesthood. None of this is magic. It's a combination of desire, determination, hard work, faith in God, and the help of other people. In today's gospel, Jesus said the reformer should start with himself or herself. If we are willing to do that, we will find that Jesus is more than willing to help us.

10th Sunday "C" Luke 7: 11-17

It was not just by chance that Jesus and his friends found themselves walking on that cemetery road. Somehow it was God's will that life should meet death, and that on that day, Jesus, who is the Resurrection and the Life, would walk away victorious.

Today's gospel is another compassion story. Jesus really felt pity and empathy for the widow who lost her only son. So Jesus reaches out to heal her broken heart by raising her dead son back to life. The death of her only son meant she was facing a life of poverty and begging.

But this gospel story is not just about raising a physically dead man back to life (for that man would someday have to die again). It's rather a story about us. We are that widow, and we are that dead man being carried to the cemetery for burial. We are all walking on that road that leads to nowhere, and it's not just by chance we also are going to meet Christ along the way on that road. We can ask ourselves the question, what is it that brings death to us...not just physical death but spiritual death and unhappiness? Could it be some type of chemical dependency, perhaps alcohol, or drugs? Is it a destructive relationship? Are my friends leading me down a path that leads to nowhere? Is it a bad attitude that alienates me from the very people who love me, or is it my pride, which does not allow me to say, I'm sorry or I forgive you?

Perhaps I'm in pursuit of the Great American Dream called success... and I have brought into the whole value system of this world that promises me happiness but never brings in satisfaction. The world tells us the formula for success; Money + Power + Success, and that my value as a person depends on my possessions. But, as Billy Graham says, "I have never seen a U-Haul trailer behind a hearse."

This gospel is saying to me that Jesus also has compassion on us. He really wants to heal us and to mend our broken hearts. He wants to bring us to life, to show us how to live and enjoy that life. Jesus wants to interrupt our sad procession leading us to the cemetery.

How often in our lives does the Lord interrupt our journey toward death. I'm not thinking just of physical death, but spiritual death. We choose a path we believe will lead us to where we want to go. But somehow, in some way, that journey is interrupted, and in looking back on it, we discover that God was choosing a different path for us that would lead to more growth and spiritual fulfillment, the path to a better life.

St. Paul experienced this in his own life. He spent many years of study and prayer, so that he might be a good Pharisee. One day, he was given an important job, to go to Damascus and bring back Christians to trial. He was on a mission of death. But on that road to Damascus, he met the risen Lord Jesus; he met Life, and he would never be the same again.

Like Paul, and like the widow of Nain, we will all experience times when we encounter Christ. Let us remember it is never by chance, and Christ is always waiting for us, no matter which road in life we choose.

11ᵗʰ Sunday "C" Luke 7: 36 – 8:3

In today's gospel, Jesus asks Simon pointedly, "Do you see this woman?" Yes, as a matter of fact, Simon did, but Simon quite clearly sees her only as an inferior person, as a public sinner, as someone to be avoided. And what's more, he just as clearly sees Jesus as a fraud and a phony prophet, because if Jesus saw what Simon saw, he would have nothing to do with this woman. But Jesus did see her in a different way. He had no illusions. He saw that the woman was indeed a sinner, but he also saw something else, something beyond that. He saw her tears. He felt her kisses. He smelled the fragrance of the oil on his feet. He felt the softness of her hair she used as a towel to dry his feet. He sensed her genuine sorrow and repentance. And above it all, he recognized her love.

It's Simon's spiritual blindness that makes him see the woman only as a sinner and not who she can be. It is his blindness that prevents him from seeing who Jesus really is, a rabbi to be respected or even as a prophet sent by God. That's why Simon deliberately snubs Jesus when he arrives for dinner. There's no welcoming kiss, no water to bathe his sandaled feet, and no anointing the head with oil, which would be normal gestures of good manners and respect.

Simon, in short, is one of those people who puts other people in categories, in boxes, and identifies them only by race, by sex, age, economic status, reputation, or their past mistakes. Simon doesn't seem able to see beyond the woman's past sins, to see the great love she is capable of giving.

And what about the woman? How did she see herself? Did she see herself only as a sinner or possibly as a forgiven sinner when she boldly crashed Simon's private dinner party? When she approached Jesus, did she have in mind the story of King David recorded in our first reading, who sinned grievously but through the prophet Nathan, saw his evil ways and repented?

And how did she see Jesus? Could Jesus do for her what the prophet Nathan did for King David and bring her repentance and God's forgiveness? Simon saw Jesus as a Sabbath law-breaker, who ate and drank with sinners. But the woman sees Jesus as someone kind and merciful, because she heard the rumors and the many good things said about him.

In the second reading today, Paul, who was another forgiven sinner, reminds us that it is faith in Jesus alone that makes a person justified or holy, and not the works of the law. Paul writes, "By faith in Christ…I live; no longer I, but Christ lives in me."

I wonder if Paul heard both of these stories of conversion and forgiveness, the story of David and the story of this woman, and came to realize that his own past sinful ways need not define him forever. Paul came to realize that Jesus looked at him differently, that Jesus saw Paul not only as what he had been, but as what he was now and was able to see his potential for goodness in the future. That's how Jesus sets the stage of forgiveness for all who love him.

The point of the parable Jesus tells Simon is easy to understand. Great love flows from having been forgiven much. Simon seems to understand it, but we are left to wonder if he really got the point. After telling the parable to Simon, Jesus asks him, "Do you see this woman?" Jesus was asking him, what do you see? Simon doesn't answer.

So Jesus tells Simon what he himself saw in her, a great outpouring of love and gratitude to him for having been forgiven. He then contrasts her great capacity to love and to receive forgiveness to Simon's puny capacity, but then Jesus invites Simon's love also.

Did Simon accept Jesus' offer of love or did he join his table companions in murmuring about Jesus' ability to forgive sins? We don't know how Simon responded. Luke doesn't record it.

The story turns the question to us as well. How do we perceive or see other forgiven sinners? How do we respond to Jesus' offer of forgiveness and love? Are we willing to forgive those who have hurt us? If we have hurt someone, are we willing to ask for their forgiveness? Are we truly grateful for all that we have received from God? Only we can answer those questions.

12th Sunday "C" Luke 8: 26-39

Sometimes Jesus says things that take us by surprise, things that make it difficult for people to follow him. One of these sayings is found in today's gospel and that is that if we wish to come after Him we must deny ourselves and take up our cross daily so that we mighh follow.

Translated into a bumper sticker, it might read something like this, "Come joint the Christian faith and suffer." Not a very attractive invitation from Jesus, but when you think about it, what Jesus is saying is merely a common sense insight into life itself; namely, there are no free rides. No crosses, no growth. No pain, no gain, as they say. The mark of true discipleship involves taking up one's cross daily and following in the footsteps of Christ.

Crosses come in various forms and sizes. Some are big and heavy; others are small and light. The three most common crosses God sends us are the cross of inconvenience, the cross of witness, and the cross of martyrdom. Perhaps some examples can help.

The cross of inconvenience often shows up in our prayer life. For example, an elderly nun went to see her spiritual director. She shared the story of a young nun who had left the community. The elderly nun liked this young nun and appreciated the spark and vitality she brought to the community. For a whole year, she noticed the young nun was in distress, agonizing on whether or not to leave the convent and whether indeed the community even wanted her. So, the elderly nun prayed for her that she might stay; prayed that she might realize she was wanted and valued; prayed that God give her the strength to see beyond her doubts.

But she never once went and talked to the young nun or encouraged her to stay or told her how much the community appreciated the many gifts the young nun had to give them. And now she was upset that the young nun had left.

The spiritual director pointed out the older nun's mistake. She had prayed without taking up the cross of inconvenience. She never put herself out or tried to bring about what she was asking God to do. She never took up the cross. She left things entirely up to God. But how was God to let the young nun know that she was appreciated by the community when she or the community never told her?

Another form of the cross is the cross of witness. We are all familiar with this cross. Trying to be different in a world that demands conformity is difficult. Just ask any teenager about "peer pressure." Friends will say, "Don't be a prude; everybody's doing it; drugs and drinking won't hurt you. Lying and cheating are normal. Don't stand out from the crowd and be a nerd." And of course, not having the right designer clothes will consign you to the limbo of shame and disgrace. It seems the older we get, the heavier this cross of witness becomes. Keep up with the Joneses. The only sign of success is money.

The cross of martyrdom is the third type of cross I want to talk about. We're not talking about shedding your blood for your faith, but rather a "dry" martyrdom; no bloodshed, but a wounding of the spirit. It's the martyrdom of surrendering of your own security for Jesus and for doing what is right. It's the martyrdom of grace under pressure. Sometimes, this martyrdom is harder than dying for your faith.

Let me give you an example. The writer, Robert Coles, tells of interviewing a little black girl during the early years of the Civil Rights movement. Norman Rockwell did a painting of her being escorted by two burly policemen to a newly integrated school in the south. The little girl was exposed to a lot of harassment. Hate words were scrawled on walls and fences along her street. Threats were made to her family. On her way to school, she was subjected to racial slurs and name calling. At school, she was shunned by the white students.

During a visit to her modest home, Robert Coles asked the girl how she kept her composure. The little girl replied she knew all the Bible stories of holding fast to God no matter what people said or did to you. She knew what people did to Jesus and how he held fast. And so she just put everything in the hands of Jesus. She said Jesus was her rock. Still, that didn't make the pressure any less.

People of honor, like this little girl, or people like all "whistle-blowers" or like those who sacrifice jobs and livelihood to hold onto principles, all bear the heavy cross of martyrdom.

So here we are, left with the haunting words of today's gospel, whoever wishes to come after me must deny themselves, take up their cross of inconvenience, the cross of witness, or the cross of martyrdom, and follow me. But remember, there is a promise that follows; "whoever loses their life for my sake will find it." The Christian life is as complex and as simple as that.

13th Sunday "C" Luke 9: 51-62

In general, Jews and Samaritans disliked, distrusted, and disdained each other. It had been that way for centuries. No one knew for sure where or how or when the hatred had gotten started. That no longer mattered. Each generation (on each side), had their own reasons for bitterness and hatred toward the other side, and each side saw themselves as the offended ones, rather than as the offender, and each felt more than justified in their contempt of the other.

Today's gospel tells of a time when Jesus and his disciples were on the receiving end of that resentment. They were on their way from Galilee to Jerusalem, which carried them through Samaria. Their planned trip called for a stay in a particular Samaritan town. But the people of that town would not allow them to stay there simply because they were Jews on their way to Jerusalem.

James and John, whose nicknames were "sons of thunder," were furious and wanted Jesus to call down fire from heaven to destroy that town and all of its inhabitants. Talk about road rage! But Jesus, of course, would have no part of that. His only reaction was to reprimand his two hot-headed friends. Then he calmly and sadly walked away from that bigoted little community and went on to another town.

In the Sermon on the Mount, Jesus had once told the people that if someone had struck you on the right cheek, then you should turn and offer him the other. That day in Samaria when Jesus accepted insult without any retaliation, he showed his disciples the meaning of that teaching. Jesus knew that the only way to break the vicious cycle of hatred and resentment was for someone to refuse to strike back, and Jesus chose to be that person.

Many of us find it difficult to really believe in that teaching of Jesus. Perhaps we have not believed it strongly enough to put it into practice. Our ethic still bears a striking resemblance to the ancient code of "an eye for an eye and a tooth for a tooth." We tend to answer evil with evil, bitterness with bitterness, hatred with hatred, insult with insult.

This process seems to be at work everywhere we look today in the world; between nations, between races, and between religions. Of course, you and I can excuse ourselves by pointing out that there is little or nothing that we can do about international affairs. Our hands are not on the levers that control those giant events. Admittedly, this is true, but we dare not give up trying. If sanity ever prevails in the world, it will surely begin as a grass roots movement among people like us.

Here's one example of how one person can make a difference. Elsa Joseph was a Jewish woman who got cut off from her two daughters during the Second World War. Years later, she discovered that both of her daughters had been gassed at Auschwitz. As a former concert violinist, Elsa's response to this tragic news was to pick up her violin and go and play it in Germany. And there in the concert halls of the homeland of her children's murderers, she played her violin and told her story that cried out for vengeance. But she herself did not seek any vengeance. She spoke of the world's deep need for reconciliation and forgiveness, without which it is tearing itself apart.

"If I, a Jewish mother, can forgive what happened," she told her audiences, not only in Germany, but in Northern Ireland and in Lebanon and in Israel, "then why can't you forget your differences and be reconciled to one another?"

So in our personal lives, how do we respond when someone does us wrong? Do we operate on the basis of retaliation? If the store clerk is rude to you, will you be rude to her? If the driver of another car blasts his horn at you, will you blast your horn back at him? If a coworker is unfair with you, will you think and scheme how you're going to get even? It's the age-old law again of an eye for an eye and a tooth for a tooth all over again.

Jesus had the wisdom to see that resentment was an endless thing, until someone had the courage to break the cycle. He had the courage. When the people of that Samaritan village scornfully slammed their doors in his face, he refused to retaliate. Instead, he quietly walked away and went on to another town.

Jesus felt no need for revenge. Retaliation was the farthest thought from his mind. His only concern was to break the cycle of bitterness, hatred, and resentment by his nonviolent action.

Jesus told the story of the "Good Samaritan" to help tear down the walls of hatred and prejudice between the Jews and the Samaritans. Seeing the goodness in each other was the first step to acceptance, to respect, and to eventual reconciliation. So the question is, do we have the courage to break the cycle of resentment when we are wronged?

14th Sunday "C" Luke 10: 1-13, 17-20

In today's second reading, Paul proudly says, "I bear the marks of Christ on my body." We are all marked people, whether it's a wedding ring that marks you to the world, as someone who is completely committed for a lifetime to your spouse. Whether it's a cross you wear around your neck that indicates you are a Christian, or the uniform you wear that indicates your profession as a police office, a member of the military, a nurse, a firefighter, or a baseball player.

Many of us bear the marks of our life's journey, like a scar from a surgery that marks us as people who have endured pain and suffering, who perhaps can sympathize with those who lost or have experienced a threat to their health. Some people have been marked with a tattoo, which signifies something special or someone special to them. It tells the world something about their individual personality or character.

The apostle Paul considered himself a marked man as well. In today's second reading, he says, "I bear the marks of Jesus on my body." What are these marks of Jesus? They may refer to the suffering God allows in the lives of good, innocent people. I know some of us struggle with life issues, because we hold only a false world view that believes good things happen to good people, and bad things happen to bad people. That world view is not only wrong, it's also bad theology. God simply does not treat us that way, with a capricious reward/punishment scheme. It's true that God sometimes allows bad things to happen to good people, but why? Let's look at the life of St. Paul for the answer.

Paul was a good man who suffered a great deal in his life, but he was able to identify his suffering with the suffering of Jesus on the cross. "May I never boast," he wrote, "except in the cross of our Lord Jesus Christ, through which the world has been crucified to me and I to the world." He viewed his own suffering as bearing the marks of Jesus on his body.

Paul suffered rejection from his own people. He suffered the loss of his professional respect as a former Pharisee who turned Christian. He suffered misunderstanding, suspicion, shipwreck, imprisonment, and death threats. If God provided a protective shield around "good" people, then why did Paul suffer so much?

The centuries of Christian martyrs also give testimony to this truth. Suffering is not punishment for our sins. It's not God's way of getting back at us. Suffering is rather an opportunity for spiritual growth.

So where is God when good people suffer? God is right there beside them and right there within them. God knows suffering intimately. Jesus endured it on the cross. God does not abandon us when we or a loved one suffers. God draws especially close. God's promise is not that we will avoid suffering and pain in life. God's promise is that we will not endure it alone.

Paul found strength in his own suffering by realizing Jesus had suffered also. Paul did not resent his suffering, nor did he feel that God had abandoned him. No. Rather, he interpreted his own suffering as an extension of the suffering of Christ. Thus, Paul's suffering became redemptive, and therefore gave a sense of meaning and purpose to his suffering.

Paul considered his physical and emotional hardships as marks of his connection to Christ, and all of us who claim to follow Christ bear the same relationship to his suffering. Great love always exposes the lover to the risk of being hurt. The same is true for us. We, who are called to love a broken world, if you carry the wounded, you will get blood on your clothes. Nurture the poor, and you will carry the scent of their poverty for days. Keep company with sinners, as Jesus did, and you will endure the scorn of a polite society.

Legend has it that St. Francis of Assisi spent so much time contemplating the crucifixion of Christ that his hands and feet began to show the signs of the nails of his Lord, the stigmata of Christ's suffering. We don't have to show the actual physical prints of nails on our hands and feet to share in the sufferings of Christ. Simply love the world that he loved, and we will get scarred up enough to bear our own unique marks.

So, we Christians are indeed marked people, marked as God's adopted children with the indelible sign of our baptism, signed and sealed with the gift of the Holy Spirit in confirmation, and we are branded with the signs of suffering that identify us as truly belonging to a loving God. So wear your marks of Christ with joy. Yes, rejoice for we all have been spiritually branded as belong to Christ forever.

15th Sunday "C" The Good Samaritan – Luke 10: 25-37

Jesus told the story of the Good Samaritan almost 2000 years ago, and yet it's just as modern today as this morning's newspaper. Only the names and the places have changed. Instead of the road that connects Jerusalem and Jericho, it's the names of the streets of our own cities, but the events and problems are essentially the same. In the story Jesus told, there is the violence of thieves who turn their greed and anger on innocent victims, and there is the indifference of the priest and the Levite who look the other way and refuse to get involved. But fortunately, there is also the compassion of the Samaritan who does what he can to help.

Behind the story, are the same attitudes and conditions that help to encourage the violence and injustice today in our society. Take for example, the lawyer who raised the question, "Who is my neighbor?" Inherent in that question is a spirit of arrogant discrimination. He was not seeking information from Jesus but self justification. He wanted to divide people into two groups; to love and respect some, but to hate and ignore others. That is the very attitude, which produces the anger and frustration that so often erupts in violence today.

So the parable of the Good Samaritan is the story about the social attitudes and problems of our own day, but more specifically, it is a story about you and me. Like it or not, we are involved, because each of us is either a part of the problem or a part of the solution.

When it comes to doing something about the injustice in our society, there is a tendency to excuse and justify ourselves. We are somewhat like the lawyer in our reading. He knew the law of God well enough that he could quote it from memory, "Love God with all your heart and your neighbor as yourself." But rather than changing his life to follow the law, he tried to limit the law so that it would fit his definition of who is my neighbor. Luke says, "He wished to justify himself," so he could exclude certain people, like non-Jews or his enemies or people he didn't like, like Samaritans…to exclude them from the obligation of loving them.

We've all been tempted to do the same thing by picking and choosing who is deserving of our love and our forgiveness and who is not.

And you can be certain that the Priest and Levite also justified themselves. They saw a fellow human being in need and knew in their hearts that they ought to stop and help him, but all kinds of excuses came to mind; excuses like, maybe the robbers were still nearby waiting to attack them, or perhaps they thought of their busy schedules and heavy responsibilities waiting them at the end of their journey. Besides that, surely someone else would come along and help this poor fellow. With such reasoning, they excused themselves and went on their way.

I wonder if we can see a little bit of ourselves in their patterns of behavior. Probably no one here has ever seen a person beaten and robbed, but how many of us have seen something that was wrong, and we recognized it as an injustice but ignored it and excused ourselves and went on our way?

Yes, few if any of us have ever seen a person lying by the side of the road, and we went on our way and left him there. But what about other responsibilities we have that are less dramatic, like a father taking time to play with his children, or grown children writing a letter to a parent or making a phone call to say I'm sorry, or going to visit some elderly person? Or a young person befriending another young person who is lonely or in trouble? All of us are busy, and we can tell ourselves we haven't got time for such simple acts of kindness, but that's what the Priest and Levite did on the road to Jericho. Thus, they were just like the robbers. They became part of the problem rather than part of the solution.

There was, however, one other traveler on the road that day. Jesus called him simply, a "Samaritan." As far as most Jews were concerned, Samaritans were inferior and a despised race. But to the world, this man has become a symbol of kindness and compassion. History has named him as the "Good Samaritan."

What this man did was not especially earth shattering. He did not solve the crime problem. As we know, hundreds of muggings still take place every day. He did not eliminate racial and religious hatred. The road that leads from Jerusalem to Jericho is, to this very day, an armed camp where people still glare at each other with distrust and hatred.

All this man did was take a little time out of his day and a little money out of his pocket to help a fellow human being who was in need. The fact that he was in need made him his neighbor. In short, this Samaritan chose to be part of the answer instead of part of the problem. That same option is open to you and me. We are not spectators looking on from afar. Our lives are involved in this world with all it's social injustice needs. We are either adding to the problems or helping solve them. The choice is ours, either to be part of the problem or to be part of the solution. Our world needs more Good Samaritans.

16th Sunday "C" Luke 10: 38-42

As a young priest, I spent one summer as chaplain at a CYO camp, Camp Don Bosco. I still remember one little 9 year old camper who came to my cabin with tears in his eyes. I thought it was just another case of homesickness, but the problem was much more serious. "My parents don't love me," he sobbed. "They are too busy to talk to me. They are always going places without me, and they never seem to have time for me." He went on to say, "They give me everything I want. I have a room full of toys and nice clothes. They are always trying to buy things for me, but I don't want things... all I want is to be loved."

I wrote his parents but never heard back from them. That was some 40 years ago. That young boy would be in his 50s today. I sometimes wonder how he turned out and I wonder if he treated his own children any differently.

That true story illustrates the point of today's gospel, which is simply this: We get so involved in what we are doing that we forget why we are doing it. We get so involved in living that we forget the purpose of life. We get so involved in pursuing the things that money can buy, that we forget about the more important things money can't buy.

It's this kind of mistake that Martha makes in today's gospel. She got so involved in cleaning the house and cooking a meal for Jesus that she forgot why Jesus had come. He didn't come just for a free meal or to see a clean house. No, he came to be with friends, to enjoy their company, and to share his time, his life, and his faith.

During World War II, a young soldier was stationed on the island of Saipan in the South Pacific. He said that during his time off, he and his buddies would go swimming in a secluded spot. It was a beautiful place surrounded by rocks, and the water was so clear they could actually see fish 20 feet below the surface. After the soldiers had swum for an hour or so, however, the water became so clouded with sand churned up from the bottom that they couldn't see one foot below the surface. But the next day, when they returned for another swim, the sand had settled, and the water was crystal clear once again.

Our life is sometimes like that pool of water. It, too, can sometimes get so clouded and dirtied up from the turmoil of everyday living that it's hard for us to see clearly. We lose sight of the important things, our perspective gets clouded, our priorities get confused, and our balance gets thrown off. What we need to do when this happens is to pause and let the murky waters of life become clear once again. We need to do what Mary did in today's gospel. We need to simply sit at the feet of Jesus in quiet prayer and listen to Jesus. We need to let him teach us anew what is important and what is not.

So today's gospel is an invitation for us to sit and pause daily at the feet of Jesus in prayer, just as Mary did. She chose the better part. We need to choose the better part in our lives. For example, when you have the choice to hang onto a hurt or let it go and be reconciled, choose the better part. If you have the chance to say, "I'm sorry," or to hang onto your pride, choose the better part. If you have the choice to communicate with your family or hide behind the newspaper or TV set, choose the better part. When you have the chance to say something bad about a fellow worker or a chance to say something good, choose the better part.

Yes, Christ must be the center of our life, not our egos, not our pride or vanity, not our ambition or our anxieties, but Christ must be the center. That is the one and only thing required in order to clear these murky waters of our life.

17ᵗʰ Sunday "C" Luke 11: 1-13

When I was about 10, my dad asked me and my two brothers and two sisters to pray for Uncle Herman. We had never met Uncle Herman, because he lived on a farm in Iowa and never traveled to Tacoma. We had only seen pictures of him. He bore a striking resemblance to our dad. We asked why we should pray for him. Was he sick or dying or was he in some sort of trouble? "No, nothing like that", Dad said, "just remember him in your prayers every night before you go to sleep." And so we did.

About 5 years later, Dad said we could stop praying for Uncle Herman. Our prayers had been answered. Uncle Herman had come back to the church he had left so many years before. On his death bed, he asked to see a priest who came to anoint him, hear his confession, and give him communion. Uncle Herman had a happy death.

In today's gospel, Jesus talks about prayer. He tells the story of the man who keeps banging on a neighbor's door in the middle of the night asking for some food. The neighbor finally gives him all the food he wanted, not out of love or their friendship, but because of his persistence. Jesus uses this story to tell us how we should pray. Never give up asking God for what we need, even though God already knows what we need before we ask.

Jesus made some amazing promises about prayer. He tells us to ask and we will receive; look and we will find; knock and it shall be opened to us; and whatever we ask in His name He will give to us. But this often creates a difficulty for a lot of us. I know in my own personal prayer life, my prayers, even my persistent ones, don't always produce glowing results. Most of us have experienced asking God for something we think is very important and not getting it. We ask, but don't always receive. But why?

Some members of Luke's community felt the same way. Jesus describes how a loving father listens to the needs of his children, no matter what the request. Then how much more will your heavenly Father give you the Holy Spirit? For Luke, the Holy Spirit is the ultimate and greatest gift. It's a gift of peace of mind, acceptance, courage to face problems it bring us understanding, and joy. Prayers that appear to go unanswered are answered in surprising ways, but in God's own time. It's true, often we become what we pray for. For example, prayers for peace create people of peace, prayers for healing form hearts of compassion, the emptiness of seemingly unanswered prayers is filled by the gifts of God's Spirit. Yes, prayers are always answered in some way.

Our model in prayer is Jesus. We are to pray in Jesus' name. Praying in Jesus name means more than simply ending our prayers with the formula, "we ask this through Christ our Lord, amen." To pray in his name means to pray in his spirit, with his attitude, with his mind and heart, with his faith and confidence in his Father. In prayer, we should try to enter into God's will (God's plan for us) rather than trying to entice or convince God to enter into our will (our plan for ourselves). That's the way Jesus prayed. For example, just a few hours before his death, cringing in human fear as he faced pain, suffering, and death, Jesus prayed to the Father that if it is possible, to let this cup of suffering pass Him by. Then he also believed that it was Gods will and not his that would be done. To say to God, "your will be done" is the hardest prayer to say and really mean it. Notice how Jesus persisted in his prayer. It was not until after the third time he prayed that his prayer was heard. Jesus kept praying until he was the one who heard what his Father was asking him to do. A well-known theologian Kierkegaard, once said, "Prayer doesn't change God; rather, prayer changes the one who prays."

Charles de Foucauld spent the last 15 years of his life alone in the Sahara Desert surrounded completely by Muslims. A Muslim friend one day asked him, "Are you praying for my conversion?" Charles replied, "No, I'm not praying for your conversion. I'm praying that you do the will of God." Charles would later write, "I could hope for a change in my friend, which would make me happy, but would that change in him correspond to the will of God? That's the ultimate test of prayer.

I no longer pray to change God's mind. I now pray for God to change me and to change those things in my life that need changing, so I can be more aware of God's plan for me, not my plan for God. I think that's the secret of Christian prayer. It has taken me a long time to realize that.

And so today, we ask Jesus as his disciples did, "Lord, teach us how to pray. Jesus is teaching us to pray the same way that He did by believing it's Gods will and not ours that will be done. And never, ever give up trying to pray.

18th Sunday "C" Luke 12: 13-21

In today's gospel, Jesus doesn't let himself be drawn into a probate dispute between two brothers. Instead, he addresses both brothers by warning them to be on guard against all forms of greed. He tells them that a man's life should not be spent piling up as much abundance as is humanly possible, and that whatever abundance we do have should not be hoarded but should be shared with others and that the true value of a person is not measured by how much or how little that person has.

While the two brothers are trying to figure out what Jesus is trying to tell them, he tells them a parable. It's a story about a farmer who had a bumper crop one year. That year was a magical year, when the rains came just at the right time and in the right amounts, when the seeds didn't rot in the ground, when the sun was nice and warm and not too hot to bake the sprouts, when the frost and cold weather didn't come too early, and when the birds and beetles didn't eat the seeds. All these things, which were beyond the farmer's control, produced an abundant harvest that year. How easily we humans forget where our abundance comes from, but we have little or not trouble in taking undue credit for its success. In the story Jesus tells, the farmer asks himself the question that every recipient of abundance should ask, what should I do with all this abundance? We know his answer. The farmer plans to build larger barns to store all his crops; then he plans for a long and very comfortable retirement, so he can eat, drink, and be merry. But that very night, he died and never got to put his retirement plans into place. God said to him, "You fool; now who will get all that you have prepared for yourself?"

I think we have to be careful not to misunderstand this parable. The farmer was not a bad person. He was an honest, hard-working man, like all farmers. It is not a mortal sin to build larger barns, and it's not a sin to be rich or successful and to prepare for a comfortable retirement. Then why did God call him a fool?

It was because the farmer failed to recognize God's stewardship plan in the abundance he was given. He failed to understand that the bumper crop was a gift from God entrusted to him, and it did not totally and exclusively belong to him alone. God's generosity was meant to flow to him and through him to share it with others. The farmer was blinded to any possibility that God had given that abundance to his care so that he might join God in the joy of sharing part of that abundance with others.

The farmer was self centered in the sense that he was only concerned about himself; he had no concern for anyone else. He had an "everything is about me attitude." Just listen to the language he uses in the story… "crops, my barns, my grain, my goods, my soul". It was all about "me, and mine," and no one else. That was his fatal flaw. He died before he learned the lesson of generosity, a generosity that God wants for all of us. He was blinded to any possible needs of a neighbor, or the needs of the poor or the needs of a brother who might just be asking for a fair share of his inheritance.

It probably never occurred to this farmer that there was already plenty of room to store his bumper crop in the half empty barns of his neighbors upon whose land the rain did not happen to fall so freely.

Leo Tolstoy wrote a famous short story entitled, "How Much Land Does a Man Need?" The story is about a poor peasant who makes a deal. The deal is very enticing. For 1000 rubles, the peasant can have all the land he can circle in one day, but if he does not make it back to the starting point by sunset, he will lose his 1000 rubles and receive no land.

In a thrilling finish to the story, the peasant is racing against the sunset, but he was too greedy. He tried to cover too much land, and he drops dead from exhaustion just short of the finish line.

The peasant is then buried in a grave only six feet in length. Thus answering the question posed in the title of Tolstoy's short story, "How Much Land Does a Man Need?"

In today's gospel, Jesus tells the crowd and us to "take care to guard against all kinds of greed, for though one may be rich, one's life does not consist of possessions."

19th Sunday "C" Luke 12: 32-48 – Luke 12:32-40

A missionary in Africa was translating the gospel into a local dialect. When the missionary couldn't find a word to translate "to believe," he asked a native African how to translate it. The native thought a moment and said, "I think to believe should be translated, to hear with the heart." Hearing with our heart means responding with our heart too. Faith is a noun, but it's also a verb calling us, as Jesus says in today's gospel, to be dressed for action and our lamps lit. In our modern-day images, dressed for action and our lamps lit might make us think of first responders, fire fighters, or perhaps a search and rescue team prepared and ready to go into action. Or, it might also remind us of a mother of a sick child. The mother is half asleep in the dark but instantly hears and responds to the cry of her child. She is alert and ready for action, because she hears her child's cry with her heart.

In today's parable, Jesus' image is one of attitude as we await his return. Jesus expects us to be so alert in faith that we can see what is expected of us and once we see what Jesus wants, we will act. So, to be a follower of Jesus is to be one who is ready to put our faith into action, even if the need to serve arises inconveniently, at midnight or at dawn.

A teacher at a Catholic university begins each freshman class by asking students to write a short biography. One question he always asks is, "Have you ever been part of a service organization?" He is not trying to recruit the students, but he is preparing them to better understand the gospels. In his course on Christianity, they will discover that faith is not just a matter of believing in a set of dogmas or a bunch of laws and regulations, but it's a matter of doing works of service in response to hearing the Good News with their hearts.

The world we live in is a messy place, but this is where we are expected bring about the kingdom of God that Jesus speaks of in today's gospel. The kingdom of God doesn't just magically fall from heaven. No, the kingdom of God and the gospel values (such as love, goodness, peace, and justice) appear only when we have a faith that we listen to with our hearts.

Today's gospel stresses the fact that we are all gifted, and the more gifted we are, the more obligated we are to serve others as Jesus says, "From everyone to whom much has been given, much will be required."

Perhaps the one question this parable is asking us to answer is, how does Jesus expect us to live while we await his return? I suppose the first thing Jesus expects us to do is to do our work. If your job is putting fenders on cars, Jesus expects you to put fenders on cars. If your job is teaching school or going to school, he expects you to be a good teacher or a good student. Whatever work you do, he is saying to do it to the best of your ability.

Another thing Jesus expects; in fact, requires, is to be good to each other, to treat one another with love and respect, to help each other, to see the needs of others and respond, to help others in the ordinary events of daily living like helping someone pay a bill or perhaps babysitting so a mother can have the afternoon off, or visit a shut-in or offer to give someone a ride to the store or to the doctor. We aren't talking about doing big important things.

I'm talking about doing little, ordinary acts of kindness, simple things like these are what Jesus is talking about when he says, "Be on guard. The Son of Man will come when you least expect him." He comes to us in the simple needs of people.

An older woman was going through some difficult times, and she began to doubt God's existence. This both puzzled and troubled her, because it had never happened before. She went to her priest for help. She expected some convincing arguments that would prove beyond all doubt that God was alive and well, but to her surprise, the priest didn't do that.

His advice was very simple and at the time, didn't make much sense to her. He told her to go and do specific acts of love and kindness for the people in her life, and everything would be just fine, not to fear. She followed his advice and in time, all her doubts about God completely disappeared.

She found God alive in the people she reached out to in love. She discovered that faith is a verb and when she did, her faith came alive in her newfound service of love. For the first time in her life, she heard the gospel message of love with her heart.

20th Sunday "C" Luke 12: 49-56

It's a fact, Jesus himself generated a lot of hostility and division in his day. It all began when, as a child, he remained lost in the temple for three days. Mary and Joseph had to search for him. They were upset and wondered why he did such a thing. Conflicts and divisions arose between himself, the scribes, the priests, and the Pharisees, over his teachings about the Sabbath, the Mosaic laws, and his acceptance of sinners and foreigners into the kingdom of God. The religious leaders accused him of blasphemy, and the words, "they were seeking to kill him," more than once appear in the gospels.

People were either for Jesus or against him. They either shouted, "Hosanna; blessed is he who comes in the name of the Lord," or they shouted, "Crucify him, Crucify him!"

The conflicts that marked the life of Jesus mark our lives as well as Christians. True believers in Jesus today can also expect hostility, hatred, and rejection, even by their family or friends. Faith in Jesus doesn't always bring peace and joy. Sometimes, it brings opposition, misunderstanding, and division.

Many of the prophets in the Old Testament, like Jeremiah in today's first reading, were persecuted or even killed. After all, no religious or political leader likes to hear the truth about their mistakes, and the times have not changed that much for modern-day prophets.

When Martin Luther King Jr. led the nonviolent civil rights movement, authorities turned police dogs and fire hoses on him and on the people who were marching peacefully. President Kennedy had to send federal marshalls to ensure the safety of an African American student entering a classroom at the University of Alabama. Worshippers in black churches were threatened and even killed. Martin Luther King himself was often jailed and finally died by an assassin's bullet.

Even today, prophetic voices who cry out for justice and religious tolerance are killed. The Lutheran pastor, Dietrich Bonhoeffer, who spoke out against Hitler and his hatred for Jews, was sent to a concentration camp and put to death. Archbishop Oscar Romero of El Salvador was shot to death while saying mass, because of his strong opposition against the political forces who exploited and murdered those who spoke out for the poor and powerless of their society. And, closer to home, we probably know people who were disowned by their family, because they converted to a certain faith community or entered into a mixed race marriage.

What Jesus is saying in today's gospel is that the decision to follow him can sometimes meets with harsh rejection. Often, a decision that is made based on faith is a commitment to walk a lonely road alone, a decision that leads to misunderstanding and unfair criticism.

Sister Helen Prejean, the prison chaplain who wrote the book, "Dead Man Walking," sought forgiveness and reconciliation between prisoners on death row and their victims' families. Her efforts were often met with harsh words and actions. Her motives and her sense of justice were questioned.

Sometimes, there's a high price to pay when you buy into discipleship, especially the discipleship of healing and forgiveness. But, as someone once said, "Christianity isn't a spectator sports where we just sit on the sidelines and watch." No! Remember what we heard in the letter to the Hebrews today? "We are surrounded by clouds of witnesses. We are to run the race with our eyes fixed on Jesus, who inspires and perfects our faith. Hence, do not grow despondent or abandon the struggle."

Jesus knew that the Christian message would arouse anger and division, because he knew that when it is preached and lived with conviction, people can't remain neutral. They have to react, either in a positive or negative way.

But adverse comments and negative press can be a good thing, because they can be signs of hope that what we say or do has not been met with indifference. Such negative comments tell us that our Christian lives and our faith have something important to say to the world we live in.

Following Jesus means to light a fire on the earth, the fire of Christian faith. Jesus wants our faith to burn brightly for all to see. He wants us to light up the darkness right here, in the places we live, in our homes, in our places of work, in our community, and in our churches.

Let's take the advice we have heard from the letter to the Hebrews, "Do not grow despondent; do not abandon the struggle."

21st Sunday "C" Luke 13: 24-30

To the question, "Lord, will only a few be saved?" Jesus replied, "Try your best to enter by the narrow door, because, I tell you, many will try to enter and will not succeed." (Luke 13:23-24) The narrow door is a strange figure of speech. What does it mean?

The adjective, narrow, doesn't refer to the door as such. The door is a perfectly normal-sized door. It's narrow only for those with too much baggage to get through.

I saw a Charlie Brown cartoon that showed him going skiing. He put on his bulky clothes; his fur hat, large shoes, and heavy gloves. He then strapped on his snowshoes across his front and crisscrossed his skis and poles across his back. Then he hung his camera and first-aid kit over his coat. Finally, he was all ready... the only problem was, with all that stuff on him, he couldn't get through the door. That's the meaning of the narrow door.

The obvious homily to preach about this gospel would be to point out the fact that we have too many possessions, too many toys, and too many sins—all of which can prevent us from entering heaven through the narrow door. So, we had better repent and get rid of all this stuff. That would make a great homily.

But today, I want to look at the narrow door from a different point of view. I want to preach about the many missed opportunities that prevent us from entering a richer, more fulfilling and more productive life, here and now, in this present life.

As we stand before the narrow door that leads to a happier life, what prevents us from getting through besides being loaded down with our sins? Is there something else? Could it be that we're loaded down with unfulfilled hopes and dreams, with missed opportunities for doing good, with broken promises and resolutions and all those could-haves and should-haves in life that we let slip by over the years.

We also stand before the narrow door with unwritten letters, unseen sunsets, unloved children, unspoken compliments, uncelebrated friendships, unwrapped joy, and unresolved hurts—all these accumulated gifts of life, all being saved for some other day. Like Charlie Brown's ski equipment, they make it difficult, if not impossible, to enter a richer, happier life.

That's why Jesus is telling us that many will try to enter and will not be able. We are guilty of letting our chances for good pass us by. Every one of us lets some of these golden opportunities of life slip by unclaimed. All of us could learn more, love more, feel more, give more, and live more. The possibilities of life are almost unlimited.

How is that we miss so many opportunities? Where did they all go? I think most of the time, we miss them through neglect. That's what happened to the people in today's gospel. They waited until the door of opportunity was already closed and when they tried to enter, it was too late. The door was already locked.

That can happen to us and often does. The opportunities of life come and go. They don't wait around forever. That's why we should live each day to the fullest. Don't let the possibilities of today go unclaimed. They are much too valuable to throw away.

At the end of life, it's those little things left undone that will make us angry…angry because we put off seeing good friends with whom we were going to get in touch with, soon…some day. Angry, because we hadn't written those certain letters that we intended to write, one of these days. Angry and sorry that we didn't tell our husband or wife, or children often enough how much we truly loved them.

Well, I think you get the point. It's really Jesus' point in today's gospel, "Try to come in through the narrow door. Many, I tell you, will try to enter and will be unable."

And we will ask, "Why Lord? Is it because of their wicked sins?" The Lord will shake his head sadly and reply, "No, it's because of their lost opportunities and their unused acts of goodness."

———

22nd Sunday "C" Luke 14: 7-14

Back in Chicago in 1953, city officials and reporters waited for the arrival of that year's Nobel Peace Prize winner. When he stepped off the train, they were impressed by this 6'4" man with bushy hair and a large moustache. As you can imagine, there was much fanfare and flashing of bulbs as they welcomed him. But after he arrived, he thanked them and then asked to be excused for a few minutes.

He walked quickly to the side of an elderly woman struggling with 2 big suitcases. Smiling at the woman, he picked up her luggage and walked her to her bus. There, he helped her aboard and wished her a safe trip. Then he returned to the officials and others following him and apologized for keeping them waiting.

This man was Albert Schweitzer, the famous doctor/missionary, who for many years, worked with the poorest of the poor in Africa. One of the reporters turned to one of the city officials and said, "That's the first time I ever saw a sermon walking."

I tell this story because today's readings are about humility. Humility is a hard concept to explain, especially in our world, when the temptation is to be bigger and better, richer and better-known than the person sitting next to us.

Being humble doesn't mean debasing yourself or thinking you are the worst person in the world. We are all made in God's image and likeness. We're all children of God, redeemed by the life, death, and resurrection of Jesus. In the eyes of God, we are all equally important.

Being humble means being honest with ourselves, and with our gifts and talents. It's realizing that everything we have and everything we are is a pure gift from God.

When Jesus comes to dine at the home of a high-ranking Pharisee, he is being closely watched by everyone. He had healed a sick person on that

Sabbath morning, and everyone knows that's a sin against the Mosaic law. Any work done on the Sabbath, including healing the sick, was strictly forbidden. So now he is being watched closely, but so is Jesus watching them.

Jesus notices how some people are finding themselves the best places at the table, and he tells them that's not a good thing. It's better to be honored by being invited to the best place of honor rather than simply taking the best places themselves. Be humble we are being told and you won't be embarrassed.

And Jesus also notices that the host invited only the beautiful people to his dinner, the money people, the powerful, those of equal social or religious status, people who think and act like himself.

Jesus tells the host that if we are to live by God's standards, we are to bear witness to God's kingdom by welcoming all people as God's beloved, where the poor, the crippled, the lame, and the blind are accepted as equals. The host and his guests didn't want to hear this. Such "outcasts" were not equal to them, and they would never be invited to their tables. So, Jesus is turning things upside down. He cures the sick on the Sabbath and welcomes the unwelcomed to God's kingdom. What next?

Jesus went after the religious establishment with a vengeance, because of their pride, their arrogance, their complacency, and self righteousness. But like it or not, we are part of today's religious establishment. We are part of a church that has its liabilities.

For example, we seem to lack the freshness and energy that characterized the early days of Christianity. The early Christians challenged and upset their society. We seem to have tamed the gospel and the liturgy and drained the faith of its excitement. This may be our greatest sin.

Oh, we love our conversion moments when we sense God's presence. We know God loves us, and we're filled with the wonder of our faith, but then there are other times, like what Mother Teresa wrote about in her journal, when we feel nothing, we are plagued with doubts of faith, prayer is difficult, and God seems so distant.

Today's gospel isn't about where we should sit in church. Have you noticed, the front seats are the last to be taken? Rather, it's about humbly knowing our need for God. We come to church with an awareness of our brokenness, our blindness, and our pride. We never know what God has in store for us.

We must always assume we have enormous room for spiritual growth and that God will help us find it. So, notice the good others do; then go and do likewise without telling anyone else. Quietly, be a walking sermon like Albert Schweitzer. This is how we can grow in humility and in grace in the eyes of God.

It's the needy and humble, not the proud and the complacent, to whom the Divine Host at the banquet of heaven will surely say, "Friend, move up higher."

23rd Sunday "C" Luke 14: 25-33

It's rather shocking to hear Jesus seemingly preaching hate in today's gospel. He announces to the crowd following him that, unless they hate their parents and family and even hate themselves, they can't be counted as his disciples. What kind of talk is that?

Well, it's part of the ancient Semitic way of speaking in Jesus' day. It's called hyperbole, an exaggeration used to make an important point, something said for its dramatic effect, for its shock value, to help people see some deeper meaning or hidden truth. Jesus often used hyperbole to make an important point, like when he once said, "If your eye is an occasion of sin, pluck it out, or if your hand is an occasion of sin, cut it off." People understood what he said was hyperbole and not to be taken in a literal way.

So, what precisely is the important point Jesus is making in today's gospel, when he uses the word hate? It's a point Jesus often makes throughout the gospels. Like the time Jesus told the crowd to leave father and mother and all your possessions behind and come follow him. Another time, when his own mother and some of his relatives wanted to see him, he turned to the crowd and asked, If anyone knew if they were his mother, or brother, or sister? He answered his own question by explaining to them that it was anyone who hears the word of God and acts on it. Each time a question was shouted out to Jesus He always came back to the fact that anyone who hears the word of God and keeps it would be blessed.In these quotes from Jesus, he is saying that it's not blood ties that bind a person to Jesus; rather, it's the obedient response to his words that binds people to him. That's the important message Jesus is giving us in today's gospel, with its hyperbole (exaggerated talk) about hating ones' family and renouncing one's possessions.

His message to us today is really about our commitment to him, our own dedication to his gospel values, and our allegiance to Christ over everyone and everything else in our lives. His bottom line challenge is to ask us the question, is there any personal cost to you for being a Christian, for being my disciple, for trying to live the gospel? For example, has it cost you your time, your talent, your money or property, your reputation, or the possibility of a promotion, or your family peace and harmony to follow him?

Whenever Jesus tells us that we cannot be His disciples until we hate our father and mother, wife, and children, brothers, and sisters, and even our own lives, a more precise translation of the word hate is the word prefer. Jesus is saying whoever prefers the love of family or love of self, or love of possessions, to the love of Christ, cannot be his disciple.

So, today's gospel message is about our personal cost, the cost of being a Christian, the cost of being ridiculed, being laughed at, of being ignored or rejected, the cost of being foolish. Does being a Christian ever cost me anything? Just look over the past few weeks, months, or years and examine your life. Was there any time you felt you had to pay a price, even a small one, for being a Christian? Think about it.

Robert Mansfield was a white man in South Africa and the headmaster of an all white school. He used to take his teams to play soccer against the black schools. That is, until the Department of Education forbade him to do it any more. It was forbidden by law. So, he resigned as headmaster in protest.

Shortly after, Emmanuel Nene, a leader of the black community, came to meet with him. He said, "I have come to see a man who resigns his job because he wants to see white and black children playing games together."

Mansfield replied, "Do I look like a knight in shining armor?" "Yes," replied Nene, "but do you know you're going to get wounded?" "Yes, I expect that may happen," Mansfield replied. "Well," Nene said, "I'm thinking of joining you in the battle, and I'm sure I'm going to get wounded too, not only by the government, but also by my own people as well."

"Aren't you worried about the wounds?" asked Mansfield. "No," replied Nene. "When I get to heaven, I'm sure Jesus will ask me, where are your wounds, and if I say I haven't got any, he will say to me, was there nothing to fight for, and I just couldn't face answering that question!"

Is there nothing in my life worth fighting for is a question all of us can ask ourselves. Or, as today's gospel would put it, is there nothing in my life worth being "hated for?

393

24th Sunday "C" Luke 15: 1-32

Jesus lived in a society where caste lines were sharply drawn. It was clearly understood that people stayed with their own kind. Good people did not mix with bad people. The rich had little to do with the poor, except to drop an occasional coin into their cups. Righteousness was a matter of exclusion. The better you were, the more you kept to yourself, apart from sinners and, God forbid that your high and holy life should be defined by contact with any lower, lesser people.

Jesus refused to play that game. His righteousness was a matter of inclusion, not exclusion. To him, people were simply people, and he had room and time for all of them. He was an inclusive man, living in an exclusive society, and that created conflict. It rocked the boat and upset the status quo. Other religious leaders were trying to get him to act like a holy man ought to act, but he would not comply, and that caused problems.

Today's gospel is an example of this ongoing conflict. The Scribes and Pharisees observed, with scornful eyes, the crowd that was gathered around Jesus. Almost all of them were people of doubtful reputation. But in the presence of Jesus, they found acceptance and respect. How can a man like this call himself a prophet? He can't even tell the difference between good people and bad people. So, they murmured against him saying, "This man welcomes sinners and eat with them." And Jesus did not deny doing that. But he did explain it by telling three stories. These stories tell us two things about the inclusiveness of Jesus.

First, it is based on his understanding of people. Jesus saw all people as lost and in need of being found. They were like coins that had fallen to the floor and rolled under the furniture. They were like sheep that had wandered away from the flock. They were like a reckless son who had rebelled and run away from home. They were like the older son who had lived in anger and lonely isolation, separated from the great festival of life. For Jesus, people were lost in different ways and different places, but all of them were lost, and his desire was to help them find their way.

That's why he could move with such ease across all the dividing lines. To him, those lines were not real, so he crossed over them as easily as we step over lines in a sidewalk. One day, he could have dinner in the home of a respected Pharisee named Simon. Another day, he could visit the home of a despised tax collector named Zacchaeus. Both were the same to him, just two of God's lost children. The only difference was that one of them knew it, and the other did not.

The people with whom Jesus lived had built all kinds of barriers designed to shut themselves in and to shut others out. Some of them were based on gender; men were superior to women. Some were based on race; Jews were superior to Gentiles. And some of them were based on religion; those who carefully kept the law and traditions were superior to those who did not.

But Jesus rejected those barriers and would not acknowledge a single one of them. To him, all people were the same, just sinners in need of grace. And that is how Jesus sees us. When we are honest, really honest with ourselves, that is how we see ourselves. No one here has the right to sit in judgment on anyone else, because we are all sinners in need of God's grace.

The second thing we know about Jesus' inclusion is that it is based on his understanding of God. Some people thought of God as an angry judge, handing out severe punishments, but not Jesus. In his mind, God was a woman with broom in hand searching for a lost coin. God was a shepherd with a lost sheep on his shoulders, carrying it back to the fold. God was a forgiving father welcoming a wayward son back home and pleading with another son to come to the party. That is what Jesus was saying to the Scribes and Pharisees. He was inviting them to the party of divine grace.

Sometimes, we make the parable of the Prodigal Son an either/or story. We make the younger son the good guy and the older son the bad guy. But that is not how Jesus told the story. He pictured the father as reaching out to both of his sons. He cared for the one who came home smelling of cheap wine, and he cared for the one who came from the field with honest sweat on his brow.

Perhaps this is the real surprise of the gospel. It does not leave us anyone to scorn or condemn. Jesus has revealed to use the both/and God. God's grace embraces both Jew and Gentile, male and female, saint and sinner, friend and enemy.

The hardest thing about being a Christian is not joining the church. In church, we find people who think, pray, and live like we do. It's far more difficult to leave the comfort of the worship service behind and take our faith into a violent and indifferent world. There, we test the mettle of our faith and see the power of the love of an inclusive God.

25th Sunday "C" Luke 16: 1-13

Today, Jesus tells his disciples a story about a dishonest manager who is about to be fired by his employer for cooking the books. And Jesus holds up the dishonest manager to them as an example to follow; not the manger's dishonesty, but for his creative thinking, for knowing how to use his head. He thinks, he plans, and then he schemes to get personal advantage out of a sticky situation.

His plan is a simple one, to reduce the amount of the debts owed to his employer. He did it by giving up his own commission, which rightfully belonged to him in the first place. It was a stroke-of-genius idea that made everyone happy.

The employer got paid all that was owed to him. The debtors got a very generous discount that delighted them, and even though the manager lost his commission, he was happy, because in exchange for it, he felt he was buying the good will of the debtors. He was making friends with his customers, so that when he loses his job, he'll have some friends in business. And then perhaps someday, he could go back to them and say, "Hey, remember you owe me one."

In today's parable, Jesus doesn't admire the manager's dishonesty but his decisiveness and ingenuity in taking care of himself. He commends the shrewd manager for his ability to get things done. And, just as the manager goes to such lengths to secure a place in this world, so we should seek to secure a place in the world to come. The parable asks the question, do we use the same amount of planning and effort in our spiritual lives as we do in our worldly lives?

For example, we consider ourselves as shrewd business people. We know when to smile and when to say the right things, especially if it means a possible sale or perhaps a promotion at work. Or, we watch for the ads in the paper or on TV for the best buys in food or clothing and pride ourselves on saving all that money. We know how to plan for the future. We look for the best doctors we can find, to take care of our medical needs. We shop around for the best insurance policies to protect our home, car, and our family in case of a serious accident. We try to save enough money to plan for the best possible education for our children.

In short, we spend a lot of time, effort, and money just to survive in this world, and that's a good and necessary thing to do. But, Jesus is saying we have to be just as concerned and just as enterprising in our spiritual lives as we are in our physical well-being.

For example, when was the last time you made a retreat? Do you take the time to read the scriptures, to pray, to share your faith with your family or others? Have you signed up your children for religious education classes, youth ministry, or confirmation classes. Have you ever made a Marriage Encounter weekend? Have you ever invited a friend or family member to the RCIA program? Or have you offered to be a sponsor for someone interested in becoming a Catholic?

These are some of the opportunities of growing in your own faith or helping others to grow in theirs. These are some opportunities we can find close by, at home, at work, at school, within your extended family, in your community, or in your parish. They are there waiting to be found if we only take the time to look.

In this parable, Jesus is telling us to be spiritually clever and to live by the surprises of the gospel, where people forgive 70 x 7 times, go 2 miles when asked to go 1 mile, return good for evil, pray for enemies, choose the last place, wash the feet of others like a slave, and throw banquets for those who can never repay you. Living like that will turn things upside down and unnerve everyone around you.

Why? Because to their amazement, you have chosen to walk the road less traveled. And you have chosen to live the paradoxes of the gospel and to that degree, you have acted prudently, like the dishonest manager in today's gospel. It's true what Jesus says, "The children of this world are more prudent in dealing with their own generation than are the children of light."

———

26th Sunday "C" Luke 16: 19-31

Robert Frost, the well-known New England poet, has written a poem called, "Mending Wall." In it, Frost describes the annual task of mending the stone wall fence that separates his property from his neighbor's land.

While each works together on his own side, replacing the stones that have fallen during the winter, Frost wonders why they even have a fence. His neighbor keeps on working and then replies, "Good fences make good neighbors."

Yes, but why do fences make good neighbors, Frost continues to ask. Isn't it because people have cows? But here, there are no cows. Then he makes the observation, "Before I build a wall, I'd ask to know, what I was walling in, or walling out."

The poem ends by Frost saying, "There's something that doesn't love a wall,that wants it down."

According to an ancient proverb, "Two people in friendship are stronger than any walls of stone." That may be true; yet many people find comfort and a sense of security in walls. They prefer having fences that protect them and keep out those who are different; those people whom they don't understand, those who seem to challenge their own belief systems, those who are the Lazarus of their own time and place.

And so we tend to continue to build barriers that will keep "them" far away from us, as if we could catch their poverty or as if their pain and want would contaminate our own safe little worlds.

But in the gospels, Jesus comes to tear down the walls that divide us, the walls between rich and poor, between black and white, between man and woman, between young and old. Jesus comes to transform a world divided by race and nationality, divided by religion and politics, divided by fears and hatreds as old as the mountains and as deep as the oceans.

In today's gospel, Jesus tells the story about a very rich man and a very poor man names Lazarus. The dividing wall between them is symbolized by the rich man's gate, behind which Lazarus lies, daily begging for the crumbs that fall from his table.

The rich man is not really a bad person, but a self-centered complacent one. It was not his wealth that kept him from Abraham's side, but his faithless stewardship of what he had. He could have done a great deal for the poor around him; yet he was uncaring and unresponsive to the plight of one poor beggar at his gate. Lazarus was simply invisible to him. Why? Because the rich man lives in his own little, narrow, social cocoon. He lives in a gated community. He socializes only with his wealthy friends. He only talks to his equals and dines with his close companions. He lives life with a sense of entitlement. He deserves everything he has; after all, he worked hard for it. And Lazarus, he thinks to himself, deserves his poverty. It's his state in life. Some people are lucky and many others are not. That's life, and nothing can change it.

What is the lesson for us in today's parable? I think Jesus is asking us two basic questions. (1) Are there any gates (walls, fences, or barriers) in your life keeping you away from the poor, the homeless, the needy, the abandoned, the forgotten? (2) Are there any Lazaruses who may be lying at the door of your home begging for help? If so, what can you do about it?

Long, long ago, God the Father had a conversation with God the Son and God the Holy Spirit. It was decided that God the Son would come in human flesh and walk among us. This Jesus would one day proclaim in John's gospel that He is the gate and whoever comes and goes through Him would have everlasting life.

Only when we are willing to replace our gates of division with Jesus, the gate of life, can we become a safe place, a home, where all are welcome.

Perhaps this prayer could help us learn the lesson of today's parable: "O God, open our eyes to see the poor, the needy, the forgotten at our own gates, and open our hearts to welcome them into our lives with compassion and respect. In welcoming the Lazarus' to our tables, may we welcome you. In giving to them, may we give you thanks for the privilege of giving and sharing what you, in your goodness, have entrusted to us. Amen!

———

27th Sunday "C" Luke 17: 5-10

It wasn't easy being a disciple of Jesus. At times, the apostles were frustrated. They felt they were in over their heads, not up to what Jesus expected them to be.

At times, they were confused, uncertain, even afraid to accept what Jesus was teaching them to do. For example, in the verse just before today's gospel reading begins, Jesus was teaching them to forgive their brother even if he has wronged you seven times a day and has asked for forgiveness seven times. Jesus was telling them to do something very difficult, if not impossible to do. They weren't sure they could do that, and they weren't even sure it should be done. So, in the very next verse is when they ask Jesus, "Lord, increase our faith." Jesus' response to their request surprised them. He tells them they don't need an increase of faith. The little bit of faith they already have, even though it be the size of a tiny mustard seed (the smallest of all seeds), is sufficient for them to do what seems to be impossible.

Speaking of doing something impossible, reminds me of the two nuns who ran out of gas on their way home after work in a Catholic hospital. They looked around the car for a container to get some gas, but all they could find was a bedpan. They took it to a nearby gas station and filled it up with gas.

As they were pouring the gasoline from the bedpan into the gas tank, the local rabbi and his wife were driving by. When the rabbi saw what they were doing, he said to his wife, "Now that's real faith!"

The real faith Jesus is talking about in today's gospel is the gift God has given to all of us. We already have it. Faith is not a thing or a commodity; it's not a magical power. It's not something that is measurable. No, faith is our human response to God's loving power and God's presence already within us. It's not a question of how much faith we have or don't have. Rather, it's

401

a question of us finding ways to use our faith to do difficult or seemingly impossible things.

A few years ago, I had the experience of ministering to a young woman dying of cancer. I often think how I would react if I only had a few weeks or months to live. What an example of faith she was for me.

She told me how difficult it was for her at first to accept her sickness and her dying, to accept what was happening to her, to let go and let God take over, as she put it. "But," she said, "if Jesus did it, so can I." As he faced his own death, Jesus prayed to his father, "Not my will but your will be done."

"At first," she admitted, "I was looking for and praying for a miracle to be cured. I wanted to live to see my grandchildren. But in the process of my sickness and dying, I have seen many little miracles. I have had the chance to meet, talk to, and help some people, like my caregivers, my husband, my children, and visitors. Somehow, I feel God is working through me and my illness to help others face their own sickness and in the process, to somehow find God in all of that. Sometimes I wonder what people without faith do when they have to face suffering."

She shared with me her view of suffering. "Suffering is a mystery to me," she said. "I don't understand it now, but I'll fully understand it after I die and see God." She compared her suffering to looking at the back of a tapestry. When you look at it with all its loose ends, it doesn't make any sense. But once you go to heaven, you'll see the front side of the tapestry, and it will be a clear, beautiful picture of the wisdom of God who truly loves you and has allowed the suffering to happen in your life for a reason.

"My only sadness is for my husband and children, my parents and relatives and friends that they have to suffer too. I'm not angry at God. I know that God is not punishing me. My dying is just part of life."

She also described what her death would be like. She pictured it as Jesus, the Good Shepherd, appearing to her, taking her by the hand, and leading her back to heaven, her true home, where she will be happy for eternity. "So why should I be afraid of dying?" she asked.

What a beautiful example of faith for all of us. Sometimes, like the apostles, we find it difficult to do what Jesus is asking of us. Then is the time to pray, "Lord, increase our faith," and to know that with mustard seed faith, we can bring the presence of God, already within us, into the most ordinary dimensions of our lives and the lives of those we love. Now that's real faith!

28th Sunday "C" Luke 17: 11-19

Today's gospel about the ten lepers has something profound to say to us, and it does so in three ways. (1) It's a gospel that speaks about loss, (2) it speaks of time, (3) and it speaks of gratitude. First, it speaks of loss. I don't know how these lepers contracted it, but leprosy was very common in those days. Whatever the cause, the disease represented a terrible loss in their lives; the loss of health, loss of mobility, livelihood, and perhaps worst of all, the loss of community. For they were now totally cut off from the rest of society, even from their own family and friends and from the synagogue.

These lepers represent any one of us suffering with loss in our lives; the loss of health, loss of a job, loss of a marriage, loss of trust, loss of dignity, loss of self esteem, loss of a loved one and since 9/11, loss of security from a possible terrorist attack.

Secondly, the gospel today speaks of time. This is an important part of the story. Recall the gospel text, "Jesus, Master, have pity on us." And when Jesus saw them, he said, "Go, show yourselves to the priests," and as they were going on their journey, they were cleansed. Did you notice? As they were going, they were healed. They weren't healed instantly on the spot. They were healed later on their way.

I wonder when they first began to notice their healing? How far had they gotten? Did they simply, at one point, notice that their skin had cleared up and the spots disappeared? Was it sudden or was it gradual? We don't know. All we do know is that they were cured, not right away, but on their way, on their life's journey. And all I know is that in fact, this is how it happens for most of us.

Some people suffer with the leprosy of depression or the loss of a loved one, the loss of faith, the slavery of addiction to drugs, alcohol, or sex, or we are at our wits' end over a sick or wayward child, and we cry out, "Jesus,

Master, have pity on us," and Jesus does for some right away, but not for most of us. Most of us continue to plod on with our lives like the 10 lepers. We walk our life's journey deeply wounded, crying out again and again, "Jesus, Master, have pity on us," until we're tired of it, until we wonder if anyone is listening, until we wonder if we'll ever find peace.

But, encouraged by this gospel, I want to offer this hope, the promise the gospel holds out to you and me that almost unconsciously, on our life journey, healing does happen and will happen, but sometimes in strange and different ways.

During this past year, I have been corresponding with a man serving 20 years in prison. He is paralyzed in his lower body from a shoot-out with the police. Tom made some serious mistakes in his life, but while in prison, he has experienced an amazing conversion. His letters are filled with a sense of hope, gratitude, and even joy in his newly found life. The letters truly are inspirational! I asked Tom if I could use some of his letters in a homily. He wrote back," I would be honored if you did. That way, I might be able to help others find God when things aren't going so good."

He recently wrote, "You know, it's really ironic that I had to be shot, paralyzed, and sent to prison before I finally realized and truly accepted and believed that Jesus Christ should have been the number one priority in my life. I'm eternally grateful to him that he gave me the chance to realize it before I die and every chance I get, I tell my fellow prisoners and the jailers what God has done in my life."

Tom has risen above his painful losses to make a success of his life. But one thing is sure, it didn't happen overnight or all at once. It took a long time for it to happen, to be healed. He was healed "on the way," on his life journey, like most of us.

Finally, this gospel presents us with the opportunity for gratitude. Only one of the ten lepers returned to give thanks to Jesus for his healing, and he was a Samaritan. "Where are the other nine," Jesus asks. "Has none but this foreigner returned to give thanks to God?" Then he said, "Stand up and go; your faith has saved you."

Here is a lesson for us. If all goes well on your spiritual journey, we will return often to give thanks to God for the acceptance, the forgiveness, the patience, and the growth we have experienced as a result of our losses and failures. The one thing to learn from this gospel is that there are new and different opportunities ahead, new joys beyond the tears, new hope beyond the losses, and new spiritual growth beyond the despair. And when we find these opportunities then, like the one leper who returned to give thanks, we too shall often return to give thanks and praise to a loving God.

29th Sunday "C" Luke 18: 1-8

In today's gospel, Jesus talks about never giving up, especially when we pray. He told a story about a poor widow who was being treated unfairly by a crooked judge.

Probably she was the innocent victim of some kind of financial fraud. So here she is, all alone in the world, facing certain poverty and destitution, having lost everything. The widow sought justice by going to court, but the presiding judge was a crook. He didn't care that the widow was being cheated and since she was either unable or unwilling to pay him the expected bribe to hear her case, he kept putting her case off. But the widow never gave up. She kept coming back to court and every time the judge looked up, there she was pleading with him to hear her case. So finally, he settled in her favor just to get rid of her, because she was driving him crazy.

Jesus told this story to his disciples to remind them about the necessity for them to pray always without becoming weary. Keep praying and trust in God. Hang in there and refuse to give up. Never lose heart. After all, if a corrupt judge could finally be persuaded to grant a request, they can count on God to do the same and much more.

Jesus taught us by his own example that there are only two ways of praying. The first way is to let your heart cry out with childlike simplicity, asking God for everything you want, for yourself or others, but always end your prayer in these words, "Not my will, but your will be done." This was his prayer in the Garden of Gethsemane. The other way to pray is to leave out the first part of the prayer and simply say the ending, "My Father, may your will be done in this and whatever it may be, I accept it." This prayer He taught in the "Our Father."

So, if you beg for the healing of a loved one, if you cry out in pain, or if you pray for world peace, or if you ask for light on the road to follow, you should do it with childlike simplicity and trust, but also with an open acceptance of doing God's will. So, the focus of prayer is not what I want but what God wants.

Sometimes, when we pray, we treat God like a giant vending machine of grace. We pump the coins of our prayers into God, and we push the appropriate buttons for what we want, and we expect instant results for what we prayed for. And, if we don't get exactly what we prayed for, we bang on the machine with our fists and kick it out of frustration. That's when we get discouraged and give up praying.

But God is not a "means" put at my disposal reduced to my human level for the purpose of granting my personal needs. God is infinitely good and all powerful, unlike the corrupt judge. God will grant what we ask for, either by giving us the very thing we requested or by giving something better. If God makes us wait or if we receive it later or not at all, be sure the "wait" is best for us. I know this from experience.

Just after ordination, I got a phone call at 2 a.m. from the nursing home. The nurse said the man in room 211 was not expected to make it through the night, and he asked to see a priest. I was there in 20 minutes. I was surprised that his room was dark, and he was sound asleep. When I turned on the light, he woke up with a start. He didn't seem that ill and seemed surprised to see me.

I introduced myself and said I would pray for him and give him the last rites as it was called in those days. His eyes filled with tears, and he began praying in French. When I finished the prayers, I annointed him and gave him communion. Then he asked who had called me, because he had not asked to see a priest. About that time, I noticed the room number above his bed; it was room 212, not 211. I had gone to the wrong room and annointed the wrong person.

Then he told me his story. He was born in France. He attended a French convent school where he finished the 5th grade. When he was 14, he ran away from home and joined the Merchant Marine. He traveled all over the world. He was now 82 and had not attended church for over 70 years.

While he was in the 5th grade, one of the nuns made him promise to say a "Hail Mary" every night before he went to sleep, to pray for a happy death. If he did, she said, he would receive the last rites and the blessing of the church before he died. And he told me he never missed a day praying the Hail Mary.

I blessed him and went to room 211. He wondered what took me so long to get there. The next day, I dropped by to see the Frenchman. The nurse told me he had died about 3 a.m., soon after I had anointed him.

That experience made me a believer in the power of prayer and the necessity of praying always without becoming weary and never giving up, praying that God's will be done "on earth as it is in heaven."

When I die and go to heaven, one of the first people I want to see is the Frenchman. I want to thank him for teaching me such a powerful lesson about prayer and God's mercy.

30th Sunday "C" Luke 18: 9-14

Hidden within each parable Jesus told was a surprise. In today's parable, those who listened to Jesus would have looked up to the Pharisee as a model of religious life and assumed that his prayer was the one that found favor with God. They also would have looked down on the tax collector with scorn. The crowd was totally shocked when Jesus commended not the "saint," but the "sinner" by saying the tax collector went home from the temple justified but the other did not. Surprise, surprise!

In the story, Jesus made it clear that this devout and pious Pharisee was a good man. He not only followed the law but even went far beyond it. Jews were required by law to fast only one day in the entire year, on the Feast of Atonement. But this Pharisee honestly boasted about himself in his prayer, "I fast twice a week," not just once a year, but 104 times a year. Also, according to Jewish law, Jews were required to tithe (give 10% of their produce back to God), but he tithed on his entire net worth, on all he possessed. And yet in his prayer, he confessed no sin or fault before God, simply because he was blind to any personal sins. He only saw the sins of others, like this tax collector praying right next to him. Instead of praising God, he was praising himself. I would describe his prayer as a "Jack Horner" prayer, the bottom line being "What a good boy am I."

Humility is the recognition of the truth of who we are in relationship to God. It's the ability to clearly see that God is our creator and savior, the source of all life and goodness. Without God, we are nothing, and we have nothing. The tax collector had no illusions about himself. He could see that he failed God by his own actions and that he was in need of God's mercy and forgiveness. That's what Pope Francis said, "I am a sinner in need of God's forgiveness."

The Pharisee in today's gospel, however, was living under two illusions; one, that he had no sin and two, that his religious acts alone and his keeping of the law earned him God's favor. His greatest sin was his pride, the opposite of humility. He trusted in himself rather than trusting in God. He really had no need for God. He controlled his own salvation.

When we fail to recognize our need for God, we also fail to recognize our need for prayer. Whatever the tax collector's sins were, it was his humility, his recognition of the truth of who he was, that he was a sinner, and his desire to ask for forgiveness, that justified him. He received God's mercy, not because he deserved it or earned it, but because he humbly asked for it in prayer.

In trying to understand the parables, we should always note to whom the parables are addressed. Today, Jesus is talking directly to those who were convinced of their own righteousness and despised everyone else. His message was not just for some of the Pharisees of his days, but his message is for us as well.

As we look into the mirror of God's word and reflect on it, may we have the humility to see ourselves as we really are and have the grace to see God as God really is. For our God is merciful and compassionate, always willing and eager to justify each one of us when we come to God with repentant hearts.

This parable reminds me of the story of the old man on his death bed, who was asked by a priest if he was afraid of dying. His answer was a little surprising. "No, Father," he said with a smile, "I'm not afraid of dying, because frankly, I've never done anything really great or outstanding my entire life, something that would make me proud and arrogant, so I was never tempted to be judgmental of others or self righteous or compare myself to anyone else." That's why he was so sure of going straight to heaven when he died.

I'm sure we can find something of ourselves in today's parable. Jesus is telling us to get in touch with both the Pharisee and the tax collector, because there's a little bit of the "saint" and the "sinner" roaming around within each one of us.

This parable is inviting us to stand before God in all humility and honesty, to see ourselves as we are and to see others as God sees them. God doesn't condemn us for those things that make us proud, nor does God condemn us for those sins that hurt others and leave us broken.

No, God sees beyond our sins and failings and sees our potential for good. God sees beyond our excuses, beyond our cover-ups, and beyond the games that we play. In fact, God knows us truly as we are, with all our warts and imperfections. But here's the amazing thing, the surprise. God still loves us anyway, and that's the way God wants us to treat others.

31st Sunday "C" Luke 19: 1-10

Today's gospel tells the story of a most unlikely saint. He is obviously flawed. In fact, his sins and failures are so obvious, that his acceptance by Jesus is somewhat of a scandal to the folks in Jericho. But in the end, he becomes an example of God's gracious work and his inclusion in the circle of God; gives ordinary people like us great hope.

His name is Zacchaeus. His is the story of a lonely, sinful man who has an encounter with Jesus while Zacchaeus was perched high in a tree. Quite a strange place for a grown man, don't you think? But that encounter with Jesus changed his life big time. What lessons can this curious story teach us today?

First, if Zacchaeus can be a saint, anyone can. Zacchaeus was a tax collector. Even worse, he was a chief tax collector. Don't think IRS agent here…think more like a Mafia or drug dealer. In the time of Jesus, tax collectors were local Jews who purchased their tax collection jobs from the hated Romans and then collected taxes from their own neighbors plus whatever they could squeeze on top for themselves. Tax collectors had to be greedy enough to sell their own soul for a shekel and be willing to turn against their own family and friends to turn a profit. As you might imagine, tax collectors were very, very wealthy and very, very alone and friendless. They were outcasts from the synagogue and from all social gatherings in the town. So despised were tax collectors that the words "tax collector" and "sinner" were considered synonymous.

And yet, Jesus sought out Zacchaeus! As Jesus passed by, he looked up and spoke to Zacchaeus, "Zacchaeus, come down. Hurry, because I must stay at your house today." (Luke 19:5-6) And when Jesus offered a kind word of acceptance instead of a "fire and brimstone" sermon, Zacchaeus hurried down with wide-eyed amazement. How long had it been since someone from the "good part of town" wanted to come to his home and even have dinner with him and his family?

The point of this story for us is clear…Jesus has come to seek out and to save those who are lost. Even before sinners begin seeking God, God is seeking them, and sinners don't have to clean up their act before God will love them. Rather, it is God's love offered first that causes a sinner to want to clean up his or her act. It's true, every saint has a past, and every sinner has a future. That is the hope that keeps all of us humble and gives us the chance to be acceptable to God.

The second lesson we can learn from this story is this, God uses people like Zacchaeus to show the world glimpses of what the Kingdom of God is like. What is it that makes Zacchaeus a saint? It's his admitting he is a sinner in need of God's mercy and forgiveness. It's his telling God he is sorry for the ways he has mistreated and exploited people, and he wanted to make restitution, to make amends. He wanted to make things right, to change his way of living. In other words, he wanted to repent!

The story of Zacchaeus and his conversion is constantly being relived in the Kingdom of God today. Zacchaeus gives all of us hope, precisely because he is so lost and so unworthy. And so are we at times. But Jesus is constantly inviting us to the Kingdom, sinners that we are, in order to welcome us and transform us.

"Dear Abby," (wrote a woman asking for advice), "I'm 44 years old and would like to meet a man my age with no bad habits," to which Abby replied, "So would I." Of course, neither Abby, nor the woman who sought her advice will ever meet a "man with no bad habits." Mr. Perfect simply does not exist, nor does Miss Perfect or Mrs. Perfect. We're all flawed human beings. No exceptions. We're all sinners.

God does not only use lives that are pure and clean, like unbroken, shiny stained glass windows. Certainly, the light of the gospel shines through such people, but God can also use broken, stained lives, like odd-shaped pieces of broken and stained glass. God can assemble these into a beautiful picture of the gospel as well. The Church, the Kingdom of God, is a mosaic of stained glass lives put together in a way that only God could devise.

Zacchaeus became a new man after he invited Jesus to his home and had that meal with him. He lost his Midas touch, his goldmine, when he gave away half of his money to the poor and when in restitution, he paid back every person he had cheated four-fold, which was just about every person in town. He gave away his wealth but gained a loving community of faith and friendships, and what is more, he foreshadowed the cross that would come only one week later for Jesus, when Jesus would once again be in the presence of two thieves hanging on a tree. And again, with his last breath, Jesus would be welcoming every sinner in the future who would accept, a chance to sit at the banquet table of Paradise. Why? Because, he had come to seek and to save all those who were lost. People like you and like me.

When you approach the table of the Lord today in communion, think about Zacchaeus. Come humbly, come gratefully, and leave walking a bit taller than before, like Zacchaeus did after his encounter with Jesus.

32nd Sunday "C" Luke 20: 27-38

A priest was visiting a very old parishioner in her home. After giving her communion, he asked her if she ever thinks about the "hereafter." She answered, Oh yes, Father, I often think about the hereafter; in fact, every time I walk into another room, I ask myself, Now, what did I come here after?"

In today's gospel, the Sadducees did not believe in any hereafter. There was no heaven or hell. There was no resurrection, no life after death. And if, in fact, there was a heaven, they asked Jesus a crafty riddle to show that it would be an absurd concept anyway, but in bringing up that silly case about the woman with the seven husbands, they were unknowingly asking some of the questions we might have about heaven.

For example, we wonder whether babies who die as babies will still be babies in heaven, whether those who die at a very old age will be old in heaven also and if not, what age will they be? And for that matter, what age will we be or anyone else be? In the 4th century, St. Augustine suggested that everyone in heaven would be 33, because that was Jesus' age when he died and rose from death.

We also wonder whether we will recognize one another and whether we will even want to recognize one another or whether we want to be recognized by everyone. After all, there are people we didn't especially like here on earth, and we certainly don't want to "pal around" with them in heaven for all eternity.

Will our pets be in heaven? Is there ice cream in heaven? Will we be surprised at who's there or who's not there? Will our scars and wrinkles be gone? What will we do all day? Will we ever get bored? Will heaven be air conditioned? In short, what will heaven really be like?

Listen to what Jesus tells the Sadducees when they ask him what will happen to the woman with the seven husbands when they all die? He says that in heaven, the woman is not going to be anybody's wife. So their question is not relevant. Why? Because in the resurrection, all life will be radically changed and different. People will be different, heaven will be different. All will be totally beyond our wildest imaginations.

Just as a few hundred years ago, our ancestors could not even imagine an artificial heart or the wonders of a computer or travel to outer space or landing on the moon, so we cannot imagine what heaven will be like.

Jesus is saying, forget all your categories, all your paradigms, all your preconceived ideas. Heaven is beyond time and space, beyond all our human experiences. Heaven (eternal life with God) is so wonderful, so full and rich, that no questions are adequate, and no answers would be fully understood.

We are given no details about heaven, no final answers. We have no picture-postcards from heaven. Instead, we are told to hold all our questions and to just have faith and trust that God will handle things better than we could ever hope for or imagine.

In short, we are to remember that when we die, and when those we love die, that God's love does not die, that's God's love will continue to grow for us and that for all eternity, we will possess God, who is the source of all perfect truth and beauty and goodness. That's the definition of happiness. That's all we need to know about heaven, and that's enough for us.

When we think about the hereafter, I think we have to go back to St. Paul's description of heaven in 1st Cor. 2:9, where he writes, "No eye has seen nor ear heard, nor has it ever entered into our hearts what God has prepared for those who love God."

Paul is telling us, be prepared when you die to be totally surprised at the answers you will get, answers you never even had the questions for.

33rd Sunday "C" Luke 21: 5-19

Today's gospel doesn't sound like Good News; in fact, it's kind of scary and seems to be filled with gloom and doom. The only encouraging words are found at the very end of the gospel when Jesus says, "By your perseverance, you will secure your lives."

Jesus is warning us that in our lifetimes, we will be living in some troubled and difficult times. The evils that will come upon the world are of two kinds. The first evil is linked to nature, such as earthquakes, tornadoes, hurricanes, plagues, or tropical storms. A second evil comes from the sinful designs of people such as leaders of countries seeking more power through war or who trample on the human rights of people. When these things happen, Jesus tells us not to lose faith because God is still there with us to help and sustain us.

Jesus is also warning us that there will also be persecutions of people for political reasons and also for religious beliefs. In some countries, as is the case today, people are forbidden to worship God publicly together or even to possess a Bible. Missionaries are forbidden to instruct or baptize anyone. If caught doing so, missionaries will be put in prison or even be put to death. It's a fact, there are more martyrs in the 20th century than there have been in the 1st century. But in all of this, Jesus is saying to us, "Stand firm by patient endurance. You will save your souls."

The bad news you see televised on the evening news can often be devastating...the violence, the injustice, terrible crimes, wars and threats of terrorist attacks. But we have to put them in the right perspective. These also will pass away. We have to ask ourselves the question, what is it in this world that is truly enduring, truly worthwhile and important and will last forever?

In today's gospel, the disciples thought that the magnificent temple in Jerusalem would last forever. It was one of the great wonders of the world, "adorned with costly stones and votive offerings dedicated to God." So the disciples are shocked to hear Jesus say to them, "All that you see here, the days will come when there will not be left one stone upon another stone that will not be thrown down." That prediction came true some 40 years later when this magnificent temple was totally destroyed by the Roman Empire and some 200 years oater, the Roman Empire itself no longer existed!

Early in the 20ᵗʰ century, a spectacular ship, name the "Titanic" was built. It's builders claimed it to be unsinkable. But on its first voyage, it was hit by an iceberg—and it sank.

The temple in Jerusalem and the Titanic were destroyed. Why? Because they are material things, and all material things in this world will eventually be destroyed. They cannot endure.

What will endure in this life are the spiritual realities of love, compassion, concern, forgiveness, understanding, and friendship. We could also add to this list…laughter, joy, playfulness, and the sparkle in the eyes of a child.

We humans can build a magnificent temple, a spectacular ship a business, or a fortune, knowing it can be lost or destroyed some day. But instead, we need to build love, friendships, a happy home, and a peaceful world, knowing that these are the fruits that will endure and last forever.

Christopher Reeve, popularly known for playing the part of Superman in the movies, was severely injured while riding his horse. He was paralyzed for life. In his book entitled, "Still Me," he writes about his wife, Dana, coming to the hospital to visit him for the first time. She told him, "Chris, I will be with you for the long haul…no matter what." Then she added, "You are still you, and I love you!"

So when we hear about tragedies or experience tragedies in our own lives or when we read about the end times (the destruction of the world, the second coming of Christ, and the final judgment), it's comforting to know that God's unconditional love is saying to us, "Don't be afraid and don't worry. I will be with you over the long haul, no matter what!" Then God will also say to us, "You are still you, and I will always love you." That's the good news of today's gospel!

Solemnity of Christ the King "C" Luke 23: 35-43

When Jesus was crucified, an inscription was nailed to the cross above his head. It read, "This is the King of the Jews." Some say this inscription was Pilate's idea; in fact, he may have written it with his own hand. It was aimed not so much at Jesus as it was aimed at the religious leaders. They had forced Pilate's hand to condemn Jesus to death, and he hated them for that. So he decided to ridicule them by calling this weak, helpless man their king. To the soldiers who crucified him, it was all quite amusing. They knew of only one kind of king, and that was Caesar. He had the biggest and most powerful army in the world. No one dared to defy him, and anyone who stood in his way would be ground to powder. That is what the word "king" meant to them, and it must have made them laugh to think about a king hanging on a cross, so they ridiculed Jesus saying, "If you are the King of the Jews, save yourself."

To them, Jesus appeared to be nothing more than a helpless victim. He was just one more man who had run afoul of the system and gotten himself in deep trouble. They didn't know he was a king, because his kingdom was not of this world. His kingdom was not built on brute force but on justice, peace, forgiveness, and love. Brute force was futile. Only Christian love would destroy the power of evil in the world. The drama of the cross was as simple and as complex as that. Perhaps we have more in common with those Roman soldiers than we like to admit. Oh, we would not crucify a man and then make fun of him while he died. That kind of cruelty is unthinkable. But we still sometimes rely on force to accomplish our purposes. The best way to solve the crime problem is to put more police officers on the streets and build more prisons and bring back the chain gangs. The best way to succeed in business is to eliminate the competition. The best way to get elected is the character assassination of your opponent. The best way to resolve a disagreement with a neighbor is to sue them and bring them to court. The point is to win and to win so convincingly that that person would not dare cross us again.

Jesus had a better idea. He was of a different mind, because his kingdom was not of this world. He was a teacher, not a soldier. His purpose was not to crush his enemies, but to change the thoughts and feelings of his students. He wanted to break down the barriers of prejudice and to build in their place, bridges of understanding. He wanted people to stop thinking of one another as adversaries and to start seeing themselves as brothers and sisters. So, in pursuing that purpose, force was absolutely futile. For Jesus, it would do no good at all.

We all know that force can work for awhile. It cannot change the way people think or feel, and it can only temporarily change the way they act. Nelson Mandela, as a young man, was put in a South African jail because of his resistance to the Apartheid system. He stayed there for 27 years and then emerged to be elected president of his country. All the force that an unjust system could muster did not change his mind about justice.

Even love cannot be enforced. It can only be inspired. I think Jesus understood this better than anyone. It was the reason he chose to die on a cross rather than save himself by force, and that is why we call him not only "King of the Jews," but "King of all Nations."

We cannot compel or force anyone to be our friend. Nor can we demand a happy and harmonious home. All the force in the world will not cause your spouse and children to love and trust you. Just try it sometime. Point your finger at your wife and demand her love. You might as well try growing roses on concrete. But, be there when she needs you, stay true to her in good times and in bad. Tell her that you love her, that you would marry her all over again, and watch the roses bloom!

The same is true of your children. Take the time to be with them. Listen to what they have to say. Respect their thoughts and ideas. Let them know you love them no matter what. Only love can make a happy home.

The soldiers at Calvary thought Jesus was powerless. He had saved others, but he could not save himself. What they did not understand was that he would not save himself, at least not by force. That would have been totally ineffective. Not a single mind or heart would have been changed. Not a single convert would have been won. Force could not do what Jesus wanted done. But by not saving himself, the entire world was convinced of his love.

Today, at our mass, we have had the rite of acceptance and welcoming our catechumens. During the service, they were presented with a wooden cross to wear, and their ears, eyes, lips, hearts, and hands were signed with the sign of the cross. In doing so, they are asked to embrace the cross as Jesus did, that they might learn to know and follow him. Jesus once said, "If you would be my disciple, take up your cross daily and follow me." Taking up your cross daily means making choices as Jesus did, like choosing love over force, acceptance over prejudice, reconciliation over fighting, and goodness over evil. Yes, Jesus is our King, and he wants all of us to establish his eternal and universal Kingdom, a kingdom of truth and life, a kingdom of holiness and grace, and a kingdom of justice, love, and peace.

Made in the USA
Las Vegas, NV
18 February 2022

44142473R00240